PENGUIN BOOKS

SIR VIDIA'S SHADOW

'A fascinating, hilarious, disturbing and perplexing book'
Jeremy Gavron, *Financial Times*

'A gripping book . . . It fascinates the reader, and has a memorable
analytical force' Philip Hensher, *Mail on Sunday*

'Paul Theroux has given a wonderfully readable account of his
friendship with V. S. Naipaul and its bitter end' David Sexton,
Evening Standard Best Books of the Year

'Vigorous and evocative . . . The kind of story you force yourself to
savour slowly though you're dying to find out what happens next'
Washington Post Book World

'Exhilarating . . . A complex fabric, a tapestry . . . depicting the rich
companionship of two difficult men' *Los Angeles Times Book Review*

Paul Theroux was born and educated in the United States. After graduating from university in 1963, he travelled to Italy and then Africa, where he worked as a teacher in Malawi and as a lecturer at Makerere University in Uganda. In 1968 he joined the University of Singapore and taught in the Department of English for three years. Throughout this time he was publishing short stories and journalism, and wrote a number of novels, including *Fong and the Indians, Girls at Play* and *Jungle Lovers*. In the early 1970s he moved with his wife and two children to Dorset, where he wrote *Saint Jack*, and then on to London. A resident of Britain for a total of seventeen years, he wrote a dozen volumes of highly praised fiction and a number of successful travel books during this time. Paul Theroux has now returned to the United States, but he continues to travel widely.

Paul Theroux's many books include *Waldo*; *Saint Jack*; *The Black House*; *The Family Arsenal*; *Picture Palace*, winner of the 1978 Whitbread Literary Award; *The Mosquito Coast*, which was the 1981 *Yorkshire Post* Novel of the Year and joint winner of the James Tait Black Memorial Prize, and was also made into a feature film; *O-Zone*; *My Secret History*; *Millroy the Magician*; *On the Edge of the Great Rift*, containing *Fong and the Indians, Girls at Play* and *Jungle Lovers*; *My Other Life: A Novel*; *Kowloon Tong*; *The Collected Short Novels*; *The Collected Stories*; *The Great Railway Bazaar*; *The Old Patagonian Express*; *The Kingdom by the Sea*; *Sunrise With Seamonsters*; *Riding the Iron Rooster*, which won the 1988 Thomas Cook Travel Book Award: *The Happy Isles of Oceania*; *Travelling the World*; *The Pillars of Hercules*, which was shortlisted for the 1996 Thomas Cook Travel Book Award; and *Sir Vidia's Shadow*. Most of his books are published in Penguin.

PAUL THEROUX

SIR VIDIA'S SHADOW

A FRIENDSHIP
ACROSS FIVE CONTINENTS

PENGUIN BOOKS

PENGUIN BOOKS

Published by the Penguin Group
Penguin Books Ltd, 27 Wrights Lane, London W8 5TZ, England
Penguin Putnam Inc., 375 Hudson Street, New York, New York 10014, USA
Penguin Books Australia Ltd, Ringwood, Victoria, Australia
Penguin Books Canada Ltd, 10 Alcorn Avenue, Toronto, Ontario, Canada M4V 3B2
Penguin Books (NZ) Ltd, Private Bag 102902, NSMC, Auckland, New Zealand

Penguin Books Ltd, Registered Offices: Harmondsworth, Middlesex, England

First published in the United States of America by Houghton Mifflin 1998
Published in Great Britain by Hamish Hamilton 1998
Published in Penguin Books 1999
1 3 5 7 9 10 8 6 4 2

Portions of this book have appeared in the *New Yorker*

The Afterword originally appeared, in different form, in
The New York Times Book Review and the *Observer* in 1998

Grateful acknowledgement is made to Faber and Faber for permission to reproduce
extracts from 'The Whitsun Weddings' from *Collected Poems* by Philip Larkin and 'As
John to Patmos' from *Collected Poems 1948–1984* by Derek Walcott. The quotation from
'Poetry of Departures' by Philip Larkin is reprinted from 'The Less Deceived' by
permission of The Marvell Press, England & Australia.

Every attempt has been made to contact copyright holders. The publisher will be happy
to make good any error or omission in subsequent printings.

Set in Monotype Sabon
Typeset by Rowland Phototypesetting Ltd, Bury St Edmunds, Suffolk
Printed in Great Britain by Clays Ltd, St Ives plc

. You must give me the pleasure of seeing what I look like.
It would be like hearing one's voice, seeing oneself
walk down the street. You must feel free. I know, for instance,
that I was once young; and that I have changed; lost and gained
and sometimes strayed, as I have grown older. Show me!

– *V. S. Naipaul, in a letter to Paul Theroux,*
April 17, 1970

That one person should wish to arouse in another
memories relating to a third person is an obvious paradox.
To pursue this paradox freely is the harmless intention of all biography.
The fact of my having known Carriego does not, I contend – not in
this particular case – modify the difficulty of the undertaking.

– Jorge Luis Borges, *Evaristo Carriego*

Contents

Part One

Africa

I

Famous in Kampala

It is a good thing that time is a light, because so much of life is mumbling shadows and the future is just silence and darkness. But time passes, time's torch illuminates, it finds connections, it makes sense of confusion, it reveals the truth. And you hardly know the oddness of life until you have lived a little. Then you get it. You are older, looking back. For a period you understand and can say, *I see it all clearly. I remember everything.*

It can be a brief passage, for a revelation. Only a few days after Julian first met him, he realized that what he had taken to be a smile on the face of U. V. Pradesh was really a look of exquisite, almost martyrlike suffering. The man's whole name, Urvash Vishnu Pradesh, was the slushiest Julian had ever heard, a saliva-making name like a cough drop that forced you to suck your cheeks and rinse your tongue with sudsy syllables.

The fact that many people in Kampala had never heard of U. V. Pradesh made him more important in Julian's eyes. He was said to be brilliant and difficult. He was smaller, more frenetic than any local Indian – the local Indians could be satirical, but they were sly. U. V. Pradesh's face, tight with disapproval, gleamed in the Uganda heat. His hair was slick from his wearing a hat. Ugandan Indians didn't wear hats, probably because Ugandan Africans sometimes did.

U. V. Pradesh seldom smiled – he suffered a great deal, or at least he said he did. Life was torture, writing was hell, and he said he hated Africa. He was afraid. Much later he explained to Julian that he felt intimidated by 'bush people.' He had 'a fear of being swallowed by the bush, a fear of people of the bush.' New to Uganda, U. V. Pradesh looked at the place with his mouth turned down in disgust. From some things he said about African passions and his own restraint, Julian had a sense in him of smothered fires.

Actually, U. V. Pradesh had reason to be afraid. The Kabaka of Buganda, Sir Edward Frederick Mutesa, whom Ugandans called King Freddy, was being threatened with overthrow and death by soldiers from the northern tribes. The mess came later, and was in turn buried by greater calamities that were much sadder and more violent even than U. V. Pradesh had predicted.

'Listen to me, Julian.'

Julian did nothing but listen, and he wanted U. V. Pradesh to call him Jules, as his family and friends did.

'Julian, this will go back to bush,' U. V. Pradesh said, sometimes in a scolding way, sometimes as a curse. And that suffering grimace again. He walked in the slanting sun of Kampala, his shadow like a snare. 'All of it, back to bush.'

Sure of something, or pleased by the sound, he repeated the phrase, a verbal tic called *bis*. He was always sure, so his repetitions were frequent, a little chant and echo in his speech, still with the faintest singsong of the West Indies – U. V. Pradesh's birthplace, the setting of many of his novels – lingering in the intonation.

Julian started out knowing nothing, not any of this, not even what the initials *U. V.* stood for, and it was only long after that he understood. He was too young to look back, and knew only the terror of always having to look ahead at the looming darkness, and instead of reassurance seeing uncertainty and awful choices, or no choices, and risk, and doubt, feeling afraid.

When Julian was young and he squinted at the big unreadable map of his life, even the magnificent light of Africa was no help. Yet he was hopeful. He felt he had what he wanted, and especially he had *baraka*, as they said in Swahili – good fortune, blessings. He was a teacher, but he spent most of his time writing. It did not matter to him that he was unknown in America. He was famous in Kampala.

'Be grateful for what you have, Jules,' his father had told him before he left home. 'No one owes you a thing.'

It was wise advice for someone going to an African country. Julian felt lucky every time something good came his way, and luckiest of all his first full year in Uganda – his third in Africa. He had a good job, a reliable car, and a well-shaded house. Uganda was the greenest place he had ever seen. He was in love with an

African girl. She was nineteen and he was twenty-four. He was at work on a novel. His life had at last begun.

The African girl, Yomo Adebajo, was Julian's own height, nearly six feet, and slender, from a tall, stately tribe in Nigeria's Western Region. Julian had been traveling there the year before. He invited her to East Africa and, just like that, she crossed Africa to join him. In Uganda, which was a hothouse of steamy gossip and expatriate scandals, their liaison was singled out – their not being married, their living together, their aloofness from others in Kampala, and the way she dressed. West Africans, rare in Uganda, were much more exotic than whites or Indians. Ugandan women wore skirts and dresses – 'frocks' was their word – and Mother Hubbards, all drapes and frilly leg-of-mutton sleeves, oldfangled words for outdated fashions, designed by turn-of-the-century missionaries for the sake of modesty. Yomo stood out like a princess in a fable in her yellow and purple robes, her stiff brocade turban, and her sash that was woven with gilt thread.

This young woman had the dark, drugged eyes and sculpted face you see in certain bewitching bronzes from her region of Nigeria. In poor provincial Uganda she was taken to be an Ethiopian or an Egyptian – 'Nilotic,' people said, believing her to be a visitor from the upper Nile, someone who, from her looks, might have arrived sitting upright, cross-legged, on a flying carpet.

Ugandans goggled at Yomo – they were smaller and had to look up – as though she were from some nation of the master race of blacks that lived beyond the Mountains of the Moon.

She just laughed at them and said, 'These people in Uganda are so primitive.'

Yomo was even more sensual than she looked. When she and Julian made love, which was often and always by the light of candles, she howled eagerly in the ecstasy of sex like an addict injected, and her eyes rolled up in her skull and she stared, still howling, with big white eyes like a blind zombie that sees everything. Her howls and her thrashing body made the candle flames do a smoky dance. Afterwards, limp and sleepy, stupefied by sex, she draped over Julian like a snake and pleaded for a child.

'Jules, give me a baby!'

'Why do you want one?'

'Because you are clever.'

'Who says?'

'Everyone says.'

He was well known in Bundibugyo; people said hello to him in Gulu and West Nile; he was famous in Kampala. Part of the reason was that he wrote recklessly opinionated pieces in the local magazine *Transition*. He defended the Indians, he mocked the politicians, he insulted the tea planters and the sugar barons. A white planter wrote to the magazine and said he would hit this man Julian Lavalle if he saw him in the street.

But the deeper reason for his fame in Kampala had nothing to do with his writing. It was the fact that he had been named in court, in a prominent divorce case, as the Corespondent, the delicate legal term for the outside party who fornicated in an adultery. He had been promised that nothing would be revealed, but the day after the case was heard, his name was published in the *Uganda Argus*. Everyone read it, and he was put down as a sneak and a rogue because the cuckold (called the Petitioner) was his best friend.

Julian had not laid a hand on this man's wife (called the Respondent), though the friend swore Julian had done so repeatedly, as detailed in paragraph 5 – 'That on or about the 23rd day of August 1965 the said Respondent committed adultery with JULIAN HENRI LAVALLE (hereinafter called Corespondent) at Kampala' – and paragraph 6: 'That from the 23rd day of August 1965 the said Respondent has frequently committed adultery with the said Corespondent on dates and at addresses unknown to the Petitioner save that some were in Kampala, Uganda, as aforesaid.'

There were more lies: 'That the Petitioner has not in any way condoned the said adultery.' No, his best friend had said that if Julian wanted to make it true, and if this woman agreed, Julian could sleep with her all he wanted. And: 'The Petitioner has not in any way been accessory to or connived at the said adultery.' No, he had urged it, he had set it up, he had begged Julian to connive with him. And: 'That this Petition is not presented or prosecuted in collusion with the Respondent or the said Corespondent.' No, it was all collusion.

A disturbing knock on Julian's door one day was that of an Indian solicitor's clerk, who handed over a prettily made-up document. It was signed and sealed. The official seal of Uganda showed a native shield with wavy and dancetté divisions between the gules tincture, full sun argent above a native drum argent, crossed spears behind the shield, with two creatures shown, the dexter supporter a gazelle rampant and the sinister supporter a crested crane rampant. The compartment ground beneath the full achievement was strewn with native flora, and below that, Uganda's motto on a scroll: 'For God and My Country.'

The document was a Summons to Enter Appearance at the High Court of Uganda, signed by E. A. Oteng, the Acting Deputy Chief Registrar. It contained a warning. If Julian failed to enter an appearance by a specified date, the plaintiff – the Petitioner, his conniving friend – could proceed with the suit, and the judgment would be rendered in his absence.

'I wouldn't ask just anyone to do this,' his friend had said. 'I asked you because I respect you more than anyone else I know.'

Then the friend promised that nothing about the divorce case would appear in the newspaper. The ruse would remain a secret. So Julian agreed, and the two friends concocted the story of an adulterous relationship in order to speed the divorce. The man wanted to remarry. The woman wanted to enter an ashram in southern India. Fornication was unlawful, but Julian was much more a lawbreaker for his lies – in Uganda, connivance in such a case was a greater crime than adultery.

'Isn't this Mr Lavalle a friend of yours?' the magistrate had asked.

'Yes, my lord.'

'Some friend!'

The following morning, Julian's name was published in the *Argus*. The tiny print in the 'Court Proceedings' might as well have been a headline.

'These *shenzi* Africans let you down every time!' the friend said. *Shenzi* meant worthless. 'I was a fool to trust those idiot typesetters on that *shenzi* paper!'

So Julian became notorious. This wickedness fit the image he had of the writer. Writers then were not the frequent and genial faces they are now in this age of promotion, when they are involved in the selling and distribution of their books – reading before a small, solemn throng of people you might mistake for early Christians at your corner bookshop; chatting to the bland man with fish eyes and lacquered hair on morning television; bantering on the radio or late at night with an interviewer, who is the authentic celebrity and the real reason for the vulgar and overfamiliar encounter.

Before this age of intense peddling, which is the selling of the author rather than the book, the writer was an obscure and some-what mythical figure, inevitably a loner, the subject of whispers – an outlaw, an enigma, an exile. Writers were the more powerful for their remoteness and their silences; the name alone was the aura. In many cases, the author had no public face and all you knew was the work. Today the face is first, the book comes last. A writer then was gnomic, priestlike, a magician, not merely writing a book but making a world and creating a new language. This was when Julian was growing up, the fifties and early sixties. A writer was a hero.

In Kampala Julian was an upstart, known for his American brashness in this African town. He had an inkling of his impudence and considered it and thought: I am alone. I am making my own life. He had the freedom to do anything he wanted, but he had limited means. He saw himself staying in Africa, going deeper into the bush as the years passed, and finally setting up house somewhere beyond the Mountains of the Moon with Yomo, his Nigerian. He knew just the place, at a clearing near the village of Bundibugyo, in the shadow of the steep Ruwenzoris, in the damp mossy shade and vitreous greenness of the Ituri Forest, among the Mbuti Pygmies and the Bwaamba people, a small settlement on the Congo border in the heart of Africa.

He had made many visits there and loved it for its being unknown. The Verona Fathers at the Bundi mission just chuckled at the wilderness. They had long ago given up hope of a widespread conversion, and one priest in his mid-eighties working on a diction-ary complained to Julian, reader confiding to reader, that the local Africans, Mbuti and Bwaamba alike, often contradicted each other on the definition or the precise pronunciation of a word. The language was uncertain. *Ndongola* was Creator – no, it was *Gongora* – wait a minute, it was *Gangara*. The old priest knew he would never finish his translation of the Gospels. But it hardly mattered. The priests had been there so long they had fallen under the spell of the Bwaamba and gone bush in many of their habits. They even chattered and procrastinated like the Bwaamba and the Pygmies. At least one priest had produced some of the coffee-colored children who played near the rectory and who filled Julian with the desire to see his own dark children playing on that frontier.

'These people are so primitive,' Yomo said, with her deep Nigerian laugh and haughty heavy-lidded eyes that made her beautiful. But she said she would go with him. She imagined that she and Julian would be the only true humans there. She also said that she would go anywhere with him, and he loved her for that. This small wet valley behind the mountains, hemmed in by the vastness of the eastern Congo, was an ideal place in which to vanish. It was not on any map, and so it was for Julian to draw the map. As a writer he wanted that most of all, a world of his own, and he could make it himself, basing it on this almost blank and inaccessible place. It was not Bundibugyo, it was near Bundibugyo, and where was Bundibugyo?

It suited Julian, trying to write, that he lived in a mostly illiterate republic. It did not matter that so few people could read. His secret was safe, the very act of writing was improbable, and he spoke to no one about it, because he had accomplished so little. He knew the worth of being famous in Kampala. Anyway, he was much better known for being a named adulterer than a published author. And Yomo, who knew the true story of the court case, found it a hilarious deception, of a Nigerian sort, and the better for there being no victim, except the law.

Yomo slept late, her black nakedness starkly mummified in white sheets, calling out 'Julian!' and demanding a kiss, and kissing him, howling into his mouth, demanding a baby. Then he left to teach. After a few classes, he walked up to the Senior Common Room in the main building and had coffee and read the papers. He had lunch at home with Yomo, and then a nap, and she plucked off his clothes and they made love: 'Give me a baby!' In the late afternoon he picked up his mail, went to the Staff Club, and drank until Yomo came by to have a drink and tell him dinner was ready. The Ugandan men flirted with Yomo, but when they got too explicit she said, 'Fock you,' and they faded away.

The country was thickly forested, full of browsing elephants and loping giraffes, with soft green hills and yellowing savannah scattered with flat-topped thorn trees. The lakes were large. Lake Victoria was an inland sea. Even Uganda's crops were pretty, for there was nothing lusher than a hillside of tea bushes, jade-colored with fresh leaves. Coffee plants looked brilliant and festive when the berries were ripe. The cane fields were dense, and for a reason no one could explain, the road past them, on the way to Jinja, was always carpeted with white butterflies, so thick at times that cars had been known to skid when their wheels crossed them. There were hippos wherever there was water, and there were crocs in the White Nile. At Mubende a witch tree was particularly malevolent, but an offering of a snakeskin or feathers served as counter-magic. An old smoky-brown skull mounted in the roots of a banyan tree at Mityana was so ominous no one dared remove it. The nail driven into the skull was not an after-thought but rather the cause of death. A prince had carried out the execution, but a king had ordered it. Uganda was a country of kings with extravagant titles – the Kabaka of Buganda, the Omukama of Toro, the Omugabe of Ankole, the Kyabazinga of Busoga – and all of them lived in fragile and tumbledown palaces surrounded by stockade fences of sharpened bamboo stakes.

Down the dusty roads Julian drove with Yomo, stopping in villages to talk to rural teachers. He was in the Extra-Mural Department, which required him to travel in remote parts of the country: in the north at Gulu, Lira, and Rhino Camp; in West Nile, where Yomo was taken to be a Sudanese; at Trans-Nzoia near Mount Elgon, a perfect volcano's cone; to the border of Rwanda, where in the purple mist they saw a whole range of green-blue volcanoes.

Uganda had been a protectorate, not a colony, and had known such insignificant white settlement that there was no resentment against whites, and none had been hoofed out of the country as they had elsewhere in Africa. *Muzungus* were a curiosity, not a threat. Ugandans were proud of their kings, who were superior to any European – they had been more than a match for explorers as ingenious as Burton and for all foreign politicians. The lesson for missionaries was Uganda's notoriety in having produced many of

Africa's first Christian martyrs, when King Freddy's grandfather, Mutesa I, burned thirty of them alive. But these deaths only excited religious activity, and Uganda's martyrology served as an inspiration to the missionaries who stalked the bush.

Indians were a separate category – *muhindis*, 'Asians.' People muttered about them, but perhaps no more than Indians muttered about themselves, for they were divided between Muslims and Hindus, and they made jokes about each other, revealing some sense of insecurity. Many Indians seemed genuinely liberated from caste consciousness. Africans envied and disliked them for their supposed wealth and cliquishness. Indians regarded Africans as weak, unreliable, and backward 'Hubshees,' which meant Ethiopians. Yet Indians also felt that Africans were unfairly privileged for their political independence, to which some Indians had contributed but from which they were excluded. Indians thought it was laughable that Westerners paid so much attention to Africans. Money given to Africans was money wasted. Indians and Africans were in constant contact, for Indians were shopkeepers and Africans were their customers. There were no marriages between the two groups. Each said the other smelled.

They were all colonials, Indian and African alike. Just a few years earlier they had all been singing 'God Save the Queen.' Before each movie at the Odeon, on Kampala Road, there was a full minute's footage of the Union Jack flapping in a stiff wind and a trooping-the-colors close-up of Queen Elizabeth on horseback, in a crimson tunic and black military beret. Now that was gone, though the memory was fresh. Some butcher shops labeled the poorer cuts 'boys' meat' – the stuff bought for servants to eat – and the 'cook boy' might be a gray-haired man of sixty or more, and the 'garden boy' another grandfather.

'The housegirl is hopeless,' Yomo said.

Yomo had the African monomania regarding diet. A country where pounded yam and palm wine were unobtainable was a Nigerian's nightmare. She nagged on this subject effortlessly but with such passion that Julian was moved by how much she cared, how singleminded she could be on the subject of survival. She would be a good mother.

'The girl never heard of kola nuts!' Yomo said.

This housegirl was a married woman, thirty or so, with three kids whom Julian had allowed to play in the kitchen. Yomo exiled them to the back verandah.

'You said you liked kids,' Julian said.

'I want one of my own,' said Yomo. 'Give me one.'

Two months of trying, at least twice a day, yet there was apparently no progress. Julian remained complacent. His luck so far had been wonderful. It seemed right to him to leave the matter of children to chance, as that priest on the Congo border had done. If Julian meddled or fretted, it would surely go wrong. Whatever happened would be right. He suggested that Yomo go to his Indian doctor, but she procrastinated. From her various oblique remarks, always referring to bush clinics in Yorubaland, Julian suspected that she was afraid of doctors.

Yomo did not know what to make of his Indian friends, could not understand a word they said; nor could they understand the way she talked. But she was patient. She sat and smiled and afterwards she always said, 'They are so oggly!' She also said that Indian men smelled of Indian food, and Indian women of coconut oil.

The Indians in Uganda, despairing of India, loved living in East Africa – loved the weather, the mangoes, the empty roads, the greenery, and especially loved the parks where they promenaded every Sunday, airing their women and letting their children run. They put walls around their houses. The walls worked; the walls kept them private. There was profit everywhere, there was space. In many ways Uganda the republic resembled Uganda the British protectorate. Institutions worked well – the post office, the telegraph, the police, the railway trains, the ferries on Lake Victoria.

One day when Julian was talking with Indians about India, one of them mentioned U. V. Pradesh. It was the first time Julian had heard the name.

'You want to know the difference between East African Indians and the babus in India?' this man, Desai, said. 'Read *Mother India* by U. V. Pradesh.'

No one knew what the initials stood for. The initials gave the name a blunt, impersonal sound, like a weighty name you might see lettered on the door – a large door that was closed – of someone in authority you were anxiously waiting to see: a dentist, a headmaster, an inspector, someone unfriendly, possibly intimidating. That was how the name seemed to Julian, unconsoling, and so far the name was everything.

Whenever a book was recommended to Julian by someone whose intelligence he respected, he read it. *Mother India* was a book he took to immediately. He skipped to the portrait of the East African Indian, in the chapter 'Degrees.' This man was a liberated soul, a free spirit in Africa, but on a visit back to India he was lost, encumbered and bewildered by caste prejudice. Julian recognized the man, he trusted the book, and then he read the whole thing from the beginning. It was skeptical, tender, comic, complex, and the narrative voice was never raised, never hectoring, always finding the connection and the paradox. The dialogue was beautifully chosen and always telling. Yet U. V. Pradesh was only a name. At one point he made a reference to 'my companion,' but that only confused the issue. 'Companion' could not have been more ambiguous, and it also looked like deliberate concealment.

'You are still reading that book, Jules!' Yomo made his name sound like 'Jewels.' She was stretched out on the couch, an odalisque, knees apart, touching herself, deliberately trying to shock him.

'I like it, so I'm reading it slowly.'

'Come over here and bring your friend and give me a baby.'

She said no more than that, but the way she said it and stroked herself did shock him, and tempted him. He loved her for being able to speak directly to his body, and she seldom failed to get a hook into his guts.

So life went on. Yomo waited for him to finish work and they were together the rest of the time. She laughed at the Ugandans for being primitive. They stared at her with bloodshot eyes. Julian wrote poems and worked on his novel and took George Orwell's and U. V. Pradesh's essays as his models for nonfiction. On weekends he gathered up Yomo and they headed into the bush.

'Always the bush,' she said.

'I like the bush.'

Every morning he was in Kampala, he had coffee in the Senior Common Room. All the lecturers and staff sat there in shorts and

knee socks, like a lot of big boys, yakking. He read the *Argus* –
now he was a peruser and student of the Court Proceedings. He
drank coffee. He read his mail. In a country where telephones were
rare and unreliable and no one phoned overseas, the arrival of the
mail was an important event.

One day, a man named Haji Hallsmith sat heavily on the sofa
next to Julian in the Senior Common Room. The exertion was
intended to call attention to himself. His proper name was Alan,
but he had converted to Islam in order to marry a Punjabi. The
young woman's brothers had objected, given Hallsmith a severe
beating, and spirited the woman away, and all that remained of
the adventure was the religion and his nickname, though he had
not gone on the haj.

His face fattening with mockery, his eyes glassy, Hallsmith
leaned towards Julian, who could see that he was drunk, could
smell it too, the tang of *waragi*, banana gin.

'What's in that cup?' Julian said.

Hallsmith laughed. He had probably been on a bender and was
still drunk from the previous night, drinking coffee now to prepare
himself for a class. He was a lecturer in the English Department.

'Just coffee.'

'You've been drinking more than coffee,' Julian said. 'I think
waragi, mingi sana.'

'So what?' Hallsmith said with a drunkard's truculence.

'Isn't that against your religion?'

'Drinking is sanctioned, except during prayers!' Hallsmith
shouted.

Perhaps from the effort of summoning the strength to speak, he
belched and brought up a mouthful of air, more banana stink.

'Do you know about U. V. Pradesh coming?' he asked.

Julian said that he didn't but that he was pleased. He was more
excited than he let on, not merely because he had just read *Mother
India*, but because he had never met such an esteemed writer, one of
the powerful priestly figures whom he thought about all the time.

The larger world was elsewhere, and the little town and university
were seldom visited. Occasionally experts flew in – the Pygmy
specialist, the cautious economist, the elderly architect, the agitated
musicologist; never a poet, never a novelist.

People from beyond Africa were welcome. The expatriates needed company, for they had no society. They needed visitors and witnesses to bring them news of the outer world, to listen to their stories – because the expatriates were sick of listening to each other, irritated more by the sameness of the stories than the lies and liberties in them – and most of all they needed strangers to measure themselves against.

'I've ordered Pradesh's books,' Haji said. 'They're in the bookshop. I'm planning a drinks party for him next week at my flat. He's staying with me for a bit. Come and meet him.'

So Haji Hallsmith had appropriated U. V. Pradesh as his listener and witness. Haji also did some writing: confessional poems that embarrassed his friends. Yet they read them, always looking for clues to that brief, bewildering Muslim marriage.

'What about my *malaika*?' Julian asked.

It meant angel, and Hallsmith knew who he was talking about.

'Your splendid *malaika* is always welcome, Jules.'

That same afternoon, Julian went to the bookshop and bought all the U. V. Pradesh titles it had in stock – *The Part-Time Pundit, Calypso Road*, and several others. While he read *The Part-Time Pundit*, Yomo read *Calypso Road*.

She said, 'These Trinidad people talk like Nigerians.'

'What do you mean?'

She read, ' "If you vex with she, give she a dose of licks, and by and by she come quick-quick when you bawl." '

'That's Nigerian?'

'For sure.'

The character Pundit Ganesh Ramsumair, in *The Part-Time Pundit*, was unlike anyone Julian had ever met in fiction. The narrative, sometimes in the first person, sometimes in the third, was simple and strong, unusual, funny, oblique, very sure of itself. It described a world Julian knew nothing about. Every name, every character, every setting was new, and yet it was familiar in its humanity. Among other things, it was about transformation.

He read three more U. V. Pradesh books. They were also fantastical, assured narratives of transformation. He saw no literary influences, no antecedents. They were original and powerful, too plain to be brilliant, with a pitiless humor that gave them pathos.

The voice of the narrator he recognized from *Mother India:* impartial, remorseless, almost cold. In his essay on Charles Dickens, Orwell had said you could see a human face behind all third-person narration, yet there was no face that Julian could discern here. About U. V. Pradesh personally Julian knew nothing beyond the fact that he had been born in the West Indies, was educated in England, resided in London, had won a number of prizes, was about forty – nearly elderly, so Julian thought. The biographical note in the back of Pradesh's books was short and unrevealing.

Pradesh took no sides in these works of fiction. One, about an election, was plotty and sprawled improbably. Another, set in London, could have been written by an old, wise Englishman, and its observations about age and frailty gave it a morbid power. *Calypso Road* was slight but charming, full of curious characters. They were all confident, fresh, spoke with the concision of poetry and with an originality that was like news to Julian.

'So what you tink?' Yomo said. Reading made her impatient, lust corroded her English. She was tugging at his sleeve, pulling his hand between her legs.

'I like this book.'

The extraordinary ending of *The Part-Time Pundit*, so unexpected and yet so logical a transformation, overwhelmed him. Why had he not seen it coming? It made him wish he had written it himself. The best of it was this: after all his changes of direction, the Trinidadian pundit Ganesh vanishes, only to reappear in London years later.

The nameless narrator, now a grown man in London, looks 'for a nigrescent face,' sees the pundit from his island approaching him.

'Ganesh?' he says in disbelief.

The pundit seems utterly changed, wearing a tweed jacket and soft hat and corduroy trousers and sturdy shoes. He carries a walking stick and is marching through a railway terminal.

'Pundit Ganesh?' the narrator repeats, seeing Ganesh Ramsumair.

' "G. Ramsay Muir," ' he said, coldly, and the brown man scuttles away.

'Why are you smiling?' Yomo asked.

Julian was thinking, I'm going to meet the real man.

2

'I'm Not Everyone'

His smile was not a smile but his laugh was more than a laugh, especially when he –

Wait, wait, wait. You know I'm lying, don't you? This is not a novel, it is a memory.

The man is not 'U. V. Pradesh.' It is V. S. Naipaul, and the book I mentioned in the previous chapter is *The Mystic Masseur*, and the hero is Ganesh Ramsumair of Trinidad, who turned into G. Ramsay Muir in London. Yomo is Yomo, and Hallsmith is Hallsmith, but the young man is not Julian Lavalle. It's me, Paul Theroux, and I am shining my light upon the past. I cannot improve on this story, because Naipaul always said, *Don't prettify it*, and *The greatest writing is a disturbing vision offered from a position of strength – aspire to that*, and *Tell the truth*.

It is a morning in June on Cape Cod, bright and dry – hasn't rained for more than a month – and I have set myself the task of putting down everything that happened thirty years ago in Africa, when I first met him, because it all matters. I cannot change any of this. I am writing with a ballpoint on a pad at my desk. How can this be a novel? This narrative is not something that would be improved by the masks of fiction. It needs only to be put in order. I am free of the constraint of alteration and fictionalizing.

You would say 'Isn't that V. S. Naipaul?' in any case.

There is so much of it. This was going to be a short memoir, but now I see it will be a book, because I remember everything. Where was I? Yes. He was laughing.

– especially when Naipaul was laughing at one of his own pointed remarks. It was a surprised bellow of appreciation, deepened and made resonant by tobacco smoke and asthma. It made you wonder whether he saw something you didn't see. I learned all this within seconds of our first meeting, at Hallsmith's party. With a disgusted and fastidious face, Naipaul had commented on how dirty Kampala was. Having just read *The Mystic Masseur* – a better title than *The Part-Time Pundit*; I will stick to the facts – I said, quoting his shopkeeper in the book, 'It only looks dirty.'

With his deep, fruity smoker's laugh booming in his lungs, he showed me his delight and then gave me the next line, and the next. He recited most of that page. He could have given me the whole book verbatim. I was thinking how he knew his work well. He told me later that he knew each of his books by heart, storing them during the slow process of writing and rewriting them in longhand.

After he was introduced to more people, his martyred smile returned. He was soon in distress. When Yomo said, 'Your characters in your books talk like Nigerians,' he merely stared at her and frowned.

'Really.'

To someone with no sense of irony, his tone was one of shimmering fascination. He was thrown by Yomo's innocent statement, and perhaps by Yomo herself, who was very dark with high cheekbones and those drowsy eyes; in her stiffly wound turban she towered over him. She had the effect of making shorter people seem always to be ducking her. Naipaul behaved that way, moved sideways, nearer to me, dodging her, as if he were unused to discussing his work with such a tall, self-assured black woman.

'Where are you staying?' I asked.

'Here, I'm afraid,' he said, clearly intending to say more when his wife interrupted him.

'Vidia,' she said in a cautioning voice. That was the first time I heard his name, a contraction of it, which was Vidiadhar.

'Patsy,' he said, acquiescing, smiling in misery.

His wife, Patricia, was a small pale woman with a sweet face, premature gray hair, lovely pale blue eyes, and full lips with the sort of contour and droop that even in repose suggests a lisp. She was pretty, about ten years older than me, and though she was assertive, she seemed frail.

'They've promised us a house,' he said. 'Mr Bwogo. Have I got it right? Mr Bwogo.' He nodded and seemed to recite it, giving it too many syllables: '*Bah-wo-go*.' 'It seems nothing can be done without Mr Bwogo.'

'He's the chief housing officer,' I said.

'Chief housing officer,' Naipaul said, and just saying it, reciting it again in his gloomy voice, he made the title ridiculous and grand and ill suited to describe Mr Bwogo.

'I'm sure he'll take care of you,' I said.

With sudden insistence, as if demanding a drink, he said, 'I want to meet people. Tell me whom I should meet.'

This baffled me, both the question and the urgent way he made me responsible for the answer. But I was flattered too, most of all because of the intense way he waited for a reply. Nerves of concentration tightened in his face, and even his muscles contrived to make his posture more than just receptive – imploring. On that first meeting I had an inkling of him as an intimidating listener.

'What is it you want to know?' I asked.

'I want to understand,' he said. 'I want to meet people who know what is happening here. People who read books. People who are still in the world. You can find them for me, can't you? I don't mean only at Makerere.'

He smiled, making a hash of the university's name, pronouncing it 'Maka-ray-ray.'

'Because I suspect a lot of fraudulence,' he said. 'One hears it. One has vibrations.'

Pat had winced at 'Maka-ray-ray' and said in an exasperated way, 'He has no trouble at all with the most difficult Indian names.'

'Do you know Rajagopalachari's translation of the *Mahabharata*?' Naipaul said, and laughed hard, the laughter in his lungs like a loud kind of hydraulics.

I introduced him to my head of department, an expatriate Englishman named Gerald Moore, who was an anthologizer as well as an evangelizer of African poetry. Having spent some time in Nigeria, Gerald occasionally attempted a Yoruba salutation upon Yomo, whose way of replying was to mock his mispronunciation by repeating it in a shriek, opening her mouth very wide in Gerald's pink face. But he was a friendly fellow, and he had hired me. He mentioned his African anthology to Naipaul.

'Really,' Naipaul said, mocking in his profoundly fascinated way, and now I understood his tone as utter disbelief and dismissal.

The irony was not lost on Gerald, who fidgeted and said, 'Some quite good poems.'

'Really.'

'Leopold Senghor.'

'Isn't he the president of something?'

'Senegal,' Gerald said. 'And Rabearivelo.'

'Is he a president too?'

'Dead, actually. Madagascan.'

'These names just trip off your tongue.'

'I could give you a copy,' Gerald said. 'It's a Penguin.'

'A Penguin, yes,' Naipaul said. 'You are so kind.'

'I also do some writing. I'd like to show you. See what you think.'

Naipaul smiled a wolfish smile and said, 'Are you sure you want me to read your poems? I warn you that I will tell you exactly what I think.'

'That's all right.'

'But I'm brutal, you know.'

Gerald winced, and later on the verandah he said to me, 'He's different from what I expected.'

'In what way?'

'Rather patrician.'

But I thought: I want to show him my work. I want to know exactly what he thinks. I had never shown anyone my novel. I wanted him to be brutal.

I saw Naipaul talking to Professor Dudney, an authority on the pastoral Karamojong people of Karamoja, one of the northern provinces of Uganda. The Karamojong went mother-naked, and the men were often photographed posing unashamed, letting their penises hang as impressively as prize aubergines. Dudney had married a Karamojong woman, who was just as attracted to Kampala cocktail parties as Dudney was to Karamojong rituals during which the blood of cattle was guzzled.

At about five o'clock, Haji Hallsmith started turning the knobs of a large wooden radio. He urged the guests to be seated, to listen to the program, one he had made himself with his African students. I knew the producer, Miles Lee, an authentic Gypsy whose training for Radio Uganda consisted of working for many years as a fortune-teller at the Goose Fair in Nottingham. He too had become a Muslim, changing his middle name, Allday, to Ahmed, and could be found drinking with Haji Hallsmith. He was another one who said, 'Of course Muslims can drink. But not during prayers.'

The radio program was called *In Black and White*, and its subject was African writing. After some music, the pluckings of a seven-stringed instrument called a *nanga*, Hallsmith, suffering mike fright, began to introduce the poets in a shrill old-auntie voice.

Naipaul settled into his chair, his face darkening as the program continued. It was a look of intense concentration, or perhaps of desperate boredom. Poems were being read on the crackly radio, Africans reciting African poems, muffled by the cloth on the grille of the big speaker. Naipaul might not have realized that the hour for this welcoming party had been chosen because it was also the hour for the weekly *In Black and White*.

— *And now Winston Wabamba is going to read his poem 'Groundnut Stew.'*

Naipaul's face hardened into an expression of extreme impatience. I could see it was also a martyr's death mask. When Hallsmith smiled at him, Naipaul's eyes went out of focus, for it was a hot afternoon, the sun blazing through the windows over the tops of palms and tulip trees. There were jeers and curses from the low brick warren of huts where the servants lived.

Everyone else in the room was attentive, gathered around the radio, our heads cocked to one side or bowed in a meditative way. Gerald Moore massaged his eyes with his fingertips in concentration. We were mocked by the parrot squawks and cockcrows out the window, and as the sun dropped there was another sound, almost unearthly, like a riot of radio waves in a Martian invasion, a squealing and a mad ripping of the air.

Naipaul was startled.

'Bats,' I said.

He looked wildly at the bats streaking past the window and slumped again.

I had never before heard the whole radio program. It was broadcast at the time of day when I was usually headed to the Staff

Club. Now that I was compelled to listen to the entire thirty minutes, I was reminded of how sentimental and inept the poetry was. It did not look so bad on the pages of the university's literary magazine, but when declaimed on Radio Uganda, under the supervision of Miles Ahmed Lee, it sounded hollow and clumsy, and the clichés were the feebler for being spoken aloud with an attempt at feeling.

Was I also hearing it with Naipaul's ears? He was a newcomer. He had never heard it before. The poems sounded awful to me. The room was hot with the exhausted air of the day, the last blaze of the low sun, the dust and humidity and bird complaints, the servants' curses and bus horns.

When the program was over Naipaul got to his feet and, staggering slightly because of his mood, said, 'Splendid, splendid.'

'Can we go home now?' Yomo said, reaching into my front trouser pocket.

Naipaul was surrounded by party guests, but by the time we got to the door he had broken away from them, and he called out, 'Find me some people – I want to meet people.'

'It was a pleasure to meet you,' I said.

He followed us through the door to the verandah.

'I read *Miguel Street* last night,' Yomo said. 'The whole thing.'

Naipaul stared at her pityingly, shaking his head. He said, 'You must sip it like good wine.'

'Ha! I don't sip wine!' Yomo was laughing. 'I drink up the palm wine! I'm from Nigeria.'

'Really.' Naipaul looked indifferent. 'Uganda must fascinate you.'

'These Uganda people are primitive.'

Naipaul's mask slipped and he laughed. Then, sizing me up, he asked me what I thought of the radio program.

At first I hesitated to tell him I really had not liked it, because it seemed too unkind to Hallsmith, the host. And when he'd been seated in his armchair, Naipaul had looked enigmatic, if not disapproving, and afterwards hadn't he said 'Splendid'?

But I liked him, I liked his writing, I wanted to take a risk, I wanted to be truthful.

'I thought it was awful,' I said.

'Yes!' he said, and he laughed his deep, appreciative laugh. 'Dreadful! Dreadful!'

He looked happier saying that, less lonely and less tormented than he had appeared in the room. With conviction and a solemn friendliness, he touched my arm.

'We'll meet soon. We'll talk.' It meant everything to me. Then he said, 'Do you have a motorcar?'

'He doesn't talk like the people in his book,' Yomo said on the way home.

That was true, but I was thinking how I wanted him for a friend. I mentioned this, but Yomo said he was just an ugly little Indian man, and what was the point in talking so much about him?

'He's a wonderful writer,' I said.

'You are a wonderful writer,' she said. We were home now, and she was saying 'I want a baby. Give me a baby!' as she pulled off my clothes.

Within a few days I knew him much better. I showed him some of my poems, one of which began 'Mirrored images of bitches' murderous beauty,' and another, 'The girl who came with doves to sell will die.'

He said, 'Lots of libido.'

That made me smile.

He said, 'But I have given up sex, you see.'

We were alone, driving to the market.

'What about your wife?'

'I give her a chaste kiss at night.'

That was not my question, but I left it, because my car was now surrounded by market traders showing us baskets of fruit.

'I hate food that is uncovered,' he said. 'I have a horror of dirt.'

The Kampala Central Market was the wrong place for someone with a horror of dirt.

'The Italians make cheese out of dirt,' he said. 'But you knew that, didn't you?'

Flayed, stringy goat and sheep carcasses hung from iron hooks among buzzing flies, and some hacked-apart chunks of meat and cracked bones were stacked on plates under the sign *Boys' Meat*.

He liked that sign. He lingered, murmuring the expression. He said he was a vegetarian. I asked him why.

'The sinew. I could never chew through it.'

He would go without eating rather than touch meat, he said. He had had arguments in restaurants after being served vegetable soup made with meat stock. He gave me a running commentary on his health and digestion.

'Meat is *nyama*,' I said, instructing him.

'Yes.'

'The word for animals is *nyama*.'

'Yes.'

'Prostitutes – the slang. Same word. *Nyama*.'

'Really.'

We passed the locust stalls, where behind bulging sacks of locusts fried in hot *mafuta* fat, men and women sat measuring out single portions of the greasy insects on squares of newspaper. The wood-colored locusts gleamed, looking freshly varnished, and the locust sellers called out, '*Nzige!*'

It was the season, I said. They gathered the locusts under street-lamps all night.

'*Nzige, nzige.*' Naipaul said '*Nah-zeegay*' and chuckled and greeted a locust seller who was making up a large package for a man. 'Chap's absolutely mad about them, I imagine.'

He frowned at the baskets stacked around the basket sellers. He found the fish flyblown. He said that some vegetables, plantains especially, reminded him of his childhood.

'What sort of a family did you have?'

'I couldn't even begin to tell you.' He smiled helplessly, appealing to me, raising his hands to indicate that this was not a fruitful line of inquiry.

'I come from a large family,' I said, hoping to interest him.

'We've done the market,' he said. He had not heard what I said. He wanted to leave. And later: *We've done the bus station.* And: *We've done the park.* And: *We've done the museum.* And: *Churches depress me, man.* He was able to size a place up fairly quickly, and then he was ready to go. He had an inspector's gait, hands clasped behind his back, moving fast yet looking at everything. He was inquisitive, he was brisk. *I think we've done this.*

He seemed eager for me to know him. He said he slept badly, he was abstemious about alcohol, he got headaches, he had asthma. He claimed to have an explosive temper. He liked playing cricket and wanted me to help him find a pitch where he could practice bowling. He asked me about Gerald Moore, and when I said that Gerald had found him patrician, he seemed pleased.

'Jerry said that, did he?'

We never called the department head 'Jerry.'

'What about Dudney?' he said. 'His wife is incredibly ugly, which of course is why he married her. Unbelievably ugly.'

I said that in most parts of Uganda she was considered a beauty – plump and loud and fertile and maternal, and probably circumcised, with big lips and quarter-inch gaps between her teeth.

'That's precisely what I mean.'

The whites he had met in Uganda so far were most of them degenerate, he said. They drank too much. They were intellectually dead. They were low class. Sometimes he used that expression, but more often he said, 'They are common.' They were inferior.

'Infies' was his usual name for them. 'Listen to the infy,' he would say while one of the expatriates held forth in the Senior Common Room. 'Most of them are buggers, too.'

He found Swahili unpronounceable and was especially lost in nasalizing sounds, as when a consonant, following the rule of all Bantu languages, was softened or rubbed down by an initial *m* or *n*. He could not nasalize words such as *mbuli* (folly) or its opposite, *mwambo*, and while the meanings of more complex words, such as *mkhwikhwiziri* (b.o., the smell of an unwashed body), interested him as much as they did me, he found them impossible to say. Yet he sometimes made attempts, and it was difficult to know whether in garbling the words he was mocking them or simply making mistakes. 'Mahboya' he said for the name Mboya. 'Mah-zee' he said for *mzee*. An expatriate noted for his effeminacy and for patronizing African boys he called 'Mah-bugga' and sometimes succeeded with 'Mbugga.'

Looking for clues to his writing, I asked him what he read.

'One is reading the Bible. It's frightfully good, you know. And Martial – delicious. You read Latin, of course you do.'

He quoted salacious epigrams and poems, many of which were about buggery. He said they were lyrical. 'And so concise.'

He said frankly that coming to Uganda had been a great mistake, which he regretted. Although his trip had been financed by the American Farfield Foundation, he said he was losing money. But he had a book to finish.

Sure of himself and very direct, he commanded attention. He strode through Kampala, assessing it all, 'being brutal,' as he said, like a man sent from headquarters to inspect a lagging field office. His conclusions: Mass sackings were called for. Eliminate all funding. Shut it down. Seal it off. Say goodbye.

And that was after only two weeks or so. I had never met anyone so certain, so intense, so observant, so hungry, so impatient, so intelligent. He was stimulating and tiring to be with, like a brilliant demanding child – needy, exhausting, funny, often making a po-faced joke just to please me, and who was I? But he seemed to like me. He asked to see more of my writing. Watching him evaluate it, I could hear the crackle of the circuits in his brain, a succession of satisfying clicks, and the fastening of synapses, like buckles being fixed, as he processed information. 'Keep it up' was all he said. He had no small talk, and he pounced on incidental remarks.

'This is a pretty prosperous country,' I said casually.

'What do you mean by that?'

'I mean a successful agricultural economy. The tea, the coffee, the sugar –'

'Define the difference between success and achievement,' he demanded.

And he listened closely to all answers. It was hard to drive a car and hold this sort of conversation, but I did my best.

'We see the institutions that exist here,' he said. 'What matters most is how they are maintained. Maintenance of a civilization is the proof that it has meaning and is coherent. Here in Uganda, other people are doing it for them. Outsiders are the key. Take them away and Uganda will go back to bush. All this will be jungle.'

On one of those early days in my car he plucked at the plastic seat cover and said, 'American writers always know the names of these.'

'That's a grommet,' I said.

'And these.'

'That's a gusset.'

'And this.' He ran his thumb and forefinger along a seam.

'That's called piping.'

A laugh had been building in his throat from the moment I had said 'grommet,' and now he was laughing hard. No sound, except that of a lifelong smoker, was more satisfying than the dense laughter of an asthmatic, forcibly compressed, struggling and echoing through thickets in his lungs.

'You see? But they are silly words. They are purely technical. There is no picture. They say nothing. Don't be that kind of writer. Promise me you won't use those words.'

He was sure of everything he said, like a leader or a teacher, a man with no obvious doubts. So I listened, and I promised.

'Tell me what to read. I want to read something about this place.'

I recommended *The White Nile*.

'If only Alan Moorehead knew how to write.'

I told him I liked George Orwell.

'I have been compared with Orwell. Imagine. In a review. It was meant to be a compliment.' And he laughed again. 'It was lost on me. I have a very low opinion of Orwell's writing.'

I was reading Camus, I said.

'His collected fiction is a very slender book. I wonder about the achievement.'

He knew his own mind. He knew what he wanted. It was clear that he would not find what he was looking for in Uganda – anyway, he had already given up on us. He had impossibly high standards. He said there was no point in having standards unless they were high. He did not compromise. He expected the best, in writing, in speaking, in behavior, in reading. Martial? The Bible? Surely there were other books and writers he admired.

'It would be easier for me to tell you who I don't like,' he said, and then listed, with a sour-taste-in-the-mouth expression, like the visible memory of a bad meal, the giants of literature: Jane Austen, Hardy, Henry James. 'People tell me I should read James. I tried. I couldn't see the point. There's not much there.' He had not read widely in American literature. I was reading Emily Dickinson. He borrowed my book. The next day he said, 'I'm afraid I don't share your enthusiasm. Not much there for me.'

'What about African literature?'

'Does it exist?'

'Wole Soyinka. Chinua Achebe.'

'Did they write anything?'

'Novels,' I said.

'Mimicry,' he said. 'You can't beat a novel out on a drum.'

Naipaul was thirty-four but seemed much older, almost aged. He was opinionated and dissatisfied and restless, hard to please but still searching. This was a bad place for the search, however. For one thing, the whites were seriously unhealthy.

'Don't be an infy, Paul,' he said. 'I know I don't want to be an infy.'

Africans were not infies. Most whites were. Some Indians in town he liked. Others he despaired of. He interrogated them, demanded to know their backup plans. He predicted that they would be thrown out and their businesses taken over. Some of them were infies.

To battle inferiority in the equatorial heat, he came with me to the sports field. He would practice bowling the cricket ball while I ran around the track, six times usually, sometimes more. He tried to do the same but his lungs gave out, and he ended up panting and sweating. 'Must not be an infy!' The exercise gave me an appetite and a sweet tooth, and after each session we went into town and had tea and cakes. Stuffing myself, wolfing them down, I apologized, yet kept at it.

'The body knows,' he said. He was truster of instinct and hunches and cravings. 'Keep it up. Your body needs it. Let's get some more off the trolley. Waiter!'

To vary my craving for sugar, he introduced me to Indian sweets: *laddu, kachowri, rasgullah, gulabjam.*

'These *gulabjam* are made from broken milk.' He repeated it. He liked saying 'broken milk.'

In time he adopted, article by article, a mode of dress – first the bush shirt, then the bush trousers, the walking stick, and finally the bush hat. It was a floppy hat, the brim pulled down all around. Indians in Uganda never dressed that way, though tourists did. We saw them at the hotel entrances, climbing into zebra-striped safari vans or Land Rovers, heading west into the bush.

'Those African drivers tell me that the women tourists are always after them,' I said.

'That must make them frightfully happy.'

In his safari outfit, perspiring heavily, he walked in a district of Kampala called Wandegeya, where, following several steps behind him, I called out directions. I wanted to show him the colony of ten thousand bats.

He was not impressed by the bats. Instead, he said, 'Notice how there are footpaths everywhere – across every lawn, crisscrossing the campus, up and down. There are paths, but Africans don't keep to them. They make their own. Have you noticed that? They ignore the proper paths.'

I had not noticed, but it was true: a town of obvious shortcuts and trampled footpaths. I wondered why.

'Because,' Naipaul said, 'the Africans did not make the proper paths in the first place. This society was imposed on them.'

A six-foot circular medallion in bronze, at the top of the arched gateway in front of the Uganda Parliament building, depicted the prime minister, Milton Obote, his toothy frown, his bushy hair, a likeness of his disapproving face and gappy teeth. The medallion was crude enough to seem satirical. It had been put there after Uganda's first election, and the idea was that it would remain there forever, though no one ever questioned why. It was customary for African politicians to put up statues of themselves and give their names to colleges and main roads. We were, in fact, standing on Obote Avenue when Naipaul saw the Obote medallion.

'That is what is wrong with the country,' he said. 'That is the reason Uganda will go back to bush.'

Until Naipaul arrived I had not paid much attention to these details. I was grateful to be here teaching rather than in Vietnam fighting. Kampala was a small, friendly town with no society to speak of. The Kabaka kept to himself, in a regal way, inside the stockade that surrounded his palace on Kabuli Hill, one of Kampala's seven hills. Naipaul asked what I knew of the king and whether I had met him. It seemed an odd question, for the Kabaka of Buganda was much more remote than any American president, and in a place where each hilltop was occupied by an important structure – the main mosque on one, the cathedral, the university, the broadcasting service, the barracks, and so forth on others – the Kabaka's was just another bushy and inscrutable hilltop.

Obote was the Kabaka's main antagonist, but no one cared much about that. No one cared that Obote named streets after himself. No one paid much attention to politics. What was the use? In spite of Naipaul's misgivings, Kampala was a prosperous place, busy on weekdays, full of picnickers on weekends, strolling Africans, promenading Indians. The villages were sleepy, the townships were drunk. The city's bars and cafés were meeting places, and when I was not with Yomo at the Staff Club, I was with her at City Bar on Kampala Road. It was not a town of dinner parties or social functions, except among politicians and diplomats. It was movie theaters and nightclubs, restaurants and brothels. But I was happy with Yomo and she liked Kampala, although she always enjoyed pointing out how backward it was.

Into the green town of tall trees and friendly faces and natural wonders – the road carpeted with white butterflies, the tree branches full of bats, the marabou storks standing watch on the road to the dump, hungry for garbage, the crested cranes in the parks, and in many of the low-lying watery places masses of papyrus that had somehow crept on sodden roots up the White Nile from Egypt – into this drowsy place, where the locusts' whines were as loud as machinery, came the forbidding figure of V. S. Naipaul, with his hands behind his back, doing calculations. He could be severe. He could also be funny. But his style of conversation was mainly interrogatory. He had many questions. He demanded answers.

'What is the name of that valley?'

We had gone for a drive. He had liked the view. He had got out of the car and stopped a passing African.

'I am not knowing the name, sah.'

'But what do you call it?'

'We are calling it just "the valley," sah.'

'How long have you lived here?'

'I am born here, sah.'

'What do you do?'

'I am wucking, sah.'

'Where do you work?'

'Wucking in *shamba*, sah.'

'He has a garden,' I said.

'*Matoke*, sah.'

'Bananas,' I said.

'*Bwana. Mumpa cigara.*'

'He wants a cigarette.'

And when the man had moved on, Naipaul waved his walking stick in a generalizing way over the lovely landscape and said, 'Nothing has a name. They don't name things.'

'They name some things.'

'Tell me.'

'The hills in Kampala.'

'That's very much a colonial thing. The Africans were told those names – wait. What's that noise?' He lifted his hat brim and winced. 'You see? Even here. Bongo drums!'

'Bongo drums' was an all-encompassing term for the sound of a radio, for people singing or dancing, or for drums, which were never bongo drums but usually hollow logs that were beaten with sticks or tall upright cylinders that were thumped at sundown.

What he was hearing was Congolese music, trumpets and drums and marimbas, blaring from a radio in a hut.

'Music,' I said.

'I hate music,' he said as we walked on. 'All music. Not just that shit.'

'Really.'

He looked sideways at me, and when I glanced over at him I saw he was still peering at me, intensely but obliquely, as though watching to see what I would do next.

He said, 'You didn't react. Good. I once told someone that and he burst into tears.'

It was not a pose. He really did hate music. He hated most sound, whether it was music or the human voice; he regarded all of it as noise. Loud laughter appalled him too, although he himself laughed a good deal. He had come to the wrong place.

Out of the blue, on one of those early days he said, 'May I see your hand, Paul?'

He studied my palm, holding it to the light, squeezing it gently to make the lines more emphatic. He pressed his lips together and blew out his cheeks. He nodded, said nothing, but I had the feeling he liked what he had seen.

I was his interpreter, his guide, his companion. I was, most of all, his student. After a month or so he bought a car, a tan Peugeot, but at the beginning, when he had no car, I was his driver, and we went out every day. He had a sort of visiting professorship, courtesy of that dubious American foundation which was rumored to have links with the Central Intelligence Agency. He hated the foundation. He disliked his duties. He refused an office. He gave no classes. He ignored the other lecturers, though when they asked him his opinion of the university, he said, 'It's pretty crummy, but you know that, don't you?'

It was largely a waste, he said; it was a farce. Here were these overpaid expatriates patronizing Africans and giving the impression of imparting an education. But it was theater. They were going through the motions, flattering themselves with notions of their own importance. The worst of it was the tameness of it all, the absence of criticism, the complacency, the extravagant way African effort was praised.

'Did I hear someone say "parliament"? "democracy"? "social-ism"?' Naipaul made his disgusted face and repeated a bit of literary criticism he had just read. 'The words are all wrong. These fraudulent people are trying to prettify this situation. It's a huge whitewash, man. No –' The laughter began to tumble in his lungs. 'It's blackwash, that's what it is. Blackwash.'

He avoided the Senior Common Room. He made one visit to the Staff Club, and mainly for his benefit, one of the jollier members told jokes that all of us had heard before. Naipaul sat stony-faced. Afterwards he said he hated jokes. He hated the English when they tried to be colorful characters.

'Your infies,' he called them. And he was remembered in the Staff Club for having referred to Britain as 'that socialist paradise.'

'I've been a socialist all my life,' Haji Hallsmith said.

Hallsmith's apartment revolted Naipaul. 'It smells,' he said. 'And have you noticed the way Hallsmith dresses? Those African shirts he wears are ridiculous. I had always thought of a university lecturer as someone rather grand. Why, he's just a common infy.'

In an almost constant state of niggling annoyance, incessantly judgmental, but also playful, he liked to tease the other expatriates with the notion that they were all homosexual, living out a fantasy of sexual license in Uganda. He believed that their political views were insincere and mocking, merely a transparent justification for chasing boys. He laughed at the thought that they regarded themselves as liberals and intellectuals.

We were driving when he told me this. He was holding a cigarette – he tamped them and played with them as though fine-tuning them, packing the tobacco, smoothing the paper with his thumb, before he smoked them.

I said, 'So I guess you would agree with George Wallace in thinking of them as "pointy-headed intellectuals."'

He loved that. He repeated it twice, saying it was true.

'This place is absolutely full of buggers.'

'Please, Vidia,' Pat said from the back seat.

'And pointy-headed intellectuals.' He was smiling grimly out the window. He lit the cigarette and smoked it awhile, tapping the Sportsman pack on the back of his hand.

'How do you stand it, Paul?'

I was about to say how happy I was, living in Uganda with Yomo. It seemed a dream at times, to be in such a beautiful place with someone I loved. She was brave; she mocked the men who leered at her or who made remarks because she was holding hands with a white man. She didn't mind the long dusty drives or the spiders or the snakes or the little crawling *dudus*. Even the thought of living in the bush behind Bundibugyo did not faze her. I liked my job. I found my students vague but teachable.

But before I could say any of this, Naipaul piped up, 'Your writing, of course. If you didn't write, you'd go out of your mind.'

He had read only a small amount of what I had written, but he seemed to see that it stood for more. I had written many poems and published some in American and British literary magazines. 'Little magazines,' Naipaul called them, making a face. 'Lots of libido,' he always said of my poems, but it was not a criticism. He liked one I had published in the *Central African Examiner* about an old car I had seen rotting in the bush. He quoted it word for word to me a few days afterwards. It was a trenchant comment about colonialism, he said; it was about Africans letting things go to ruin. I reread it and thought: Maybe.

My writing project at the time was an essay on cowardice, inspired by Orwell's clear-sighted and confessional essays. I had been writing it for the American magazine *Commentary*. Naipaul had approved; it was not a little magazine, but the essay needed work. 'I warned you, I'm brutal,' he said. 'Forget Orwell for the moment.' I was on my fifth or sixth revision with him. It was like whittling a stick, but I was learning.

'It's true, Patsy. You know that. He'd go out of his mind.'

I kept driving, heading back to town, wondering whether it was true. I had been content for two years at a bush school in Malawi. I had been writing the whole time. Had the writing kept me sane?

'More bongo drums,' Naipaul said as we passed a roadside market.

There was noise, for sure, but no bongo drums. I said, 'The only bongo in Uganda is an animal that looks like a kudu. They're hunted with dogs by wealthy tourists who go on safaris here. When the bongo turns to battle the dogs with his horns, the hunters shoot him. They're mostly in the Ruwenzoris. In the *bundu*.'

'I want to see the bush,' Naipaul said. 'The bush is the future.'

We were on the outskirts of Kampala, passing a row of Indian shops, where on the verandahs some African men sat at Singer sewing machines, working the treadles with their bare feet, running up missionary-style dresses. Another African was squatting at a box, looking serious and intent, writing a letter in clear copper-plate script for a customer, a woman who knelt, wringing her hands.

'And the president of Gabon is called Bongo,' I said. 'Omar Bongo.'

'Omar Bongo! Did you hear that, Patsy? Omar Bongo. Oh, how I don't want to go to Gabon.'

He brooded for a moment, then asked me to slow down at the next row of Indian shops.

'It is hopeless for them,' he said. 'They should leave. You know that Indian boy, Raju? I told him to go away, to save himself. Of course I didn't say it so simply. I asked him, "What is the message of the *Gita*?" The *Bhagavad-Gita*. You've read it, Paul, of course you have.'

From the back seat, Pat said, 'You were too hard on Raju.'

'"The message of the *Gita*," I said to him, "is action."'

'It's just as bad for him to go as to stay here,' Pat said.

'Action. He's got to take action. These people' – Naipaul was gesturing at the little shops and the people on the verandah, who were baffled by the gesticulating Hindi in the bush hat in my car – 'will be dead unless they read the *Gita* and take action.'

'No, no!' Pat Naipaul cried out from the back seat. 'How can you say that?'

A growling in my guts told me that a quarrel was starting. I had never been in the presence of a husband and wife having an unselfconscious quarrel. I felt fearful and helpless.

'They should forget England. The bitches will lie to them. India is the answer. It is a real country. A big country. They make things in India. Steel. Paper. Cloth. They publish books. What do they make here? Nothing, or some rubbish that no one wants, while the infies tell them how wonderful it all is.'

'It would be worse for them in India. You've seen it,' Pat said with passion, and she seemed to be sobbing. 'They'd be licking the shoes of those horrible people.'

Coolly facing forward, Naipaul said, 'You always take that simple senseless path.'

'India would destroy them,' Pat said, and I could see in the rearview mirror that she was wiping tears from her eyes and trying to speak.

'I was offering him a real solution,' Naipaul said.

Pat replied, but her weeping made it difficult for her to speak, and while she faltered, saying how unfair he was, Naipaul became calm, rational, colder, and did not give an inch.

'Stop chuntering, Patsy. You're just chuntering, and you have no idea of what you're talking about.'

The tears kept rolling down Pat's cheeks, and though she dabbed at her face she could not stanch the flow. There were tears on her pretty protruding lips. I was shocked, but there was something in her tear-stained face and her posture that aroused me.

'I think we've done this,' Naipaul said, tapping the cigarette pack.

After I took them home, I told Yomo about the Naipauls' argument. She said, 'Did he smack her?'

'No. Just talked, very coldly.'

Yomo laughed. 'Just talked!' She was not shocked in the least. She shrugged, pulled me to the sofa, and said, 'I want to give you a bath.'

The next afternoon, in the blazing sun, Naipaul and I were on the sports field again, being watched by urchins from the mud huts in the grove of trees beyond the field's perimeter. They jeered at the perspiring runners – it was so odd for them to see white people run or sweat or suffer. They mimicked the movements of the cricketers. I ran around the track while Naipaul flung cricket balls at a batsman. Naipaul seemed to know what he was doing. He knew cricket lore. He had told me it was a fair game – that it was more than a game, it was a whole way of thinking. 'There is no sadder sound of collapse than hearing a wicket fall,' he said. 'The best aspect of cricket is that no one really wins.'

He did not say anything about the argument with his wife until we were on our way into town afterwards for tea and cakes. He lit a cigarette and faced away from me, looking out the window – the same posture as the day before, the same time of day, the sun at the same angle, him smoking, me driving.

'I hate rowing in public,' he said, and nothing more.

At the teashop I had chocolate cake, he had cucumber sandwiches.

'These are cooling, but you need your cake. The body knows.'

He clutched the empty teacup.

'They warm the cups at the Lake Victoria in Entebbe. That's nice. But not here.' He poured the milk, he poured the tea, he added sugar, he stirred, he sipped. 'We're moving into our house tomorrow. Do you know those houses?'

'Behind the Art Department, yes.'

'They're pretty crummy.'

He was more restless than usual. When he had gone without sleep his eyes became hooded and Asiatic. He looked that way today. He began talking about the Kabaka again, asking questions.

36

People in Uganda, even expatriates, seldom mentioned him. He was an institution, a fixture, a symbol. No one ever saw him.

I said, 'He is fairly invisible, but people say that he knows what's going on. He has his own prime minister, the Katikiro, and even his own parliament, the Lukiko. He takes an interest in things.'

'He has taken no interest in me,' Naipaul said.

I smiled to show my incomprehension. Why should the Kabaka, the king of Buganda, even be aware of Naipaul's existence? The Kabaka was forty-two, handsome, androgynous, aloof, a drinker, the ruler of almost two million people. He had been a thorn in the flesh of the British. He was a thorn in Obote's flesh. The Kingdom of Buganda belonged to him.

'I sent a little note to the palace. I had a letter of introduction. He hasn't replied. Not a word.'

What a good thing it was that we were alone. Any local person overhearing him go on about not receiving an invitation from this king would have found the complaint absurd. And a more delicate aspect was that the Kabaka was never discussed in public; his name was not spoken. It was bad form to do so if you happened to be in the presence of one of his subjects, and politically unwise if you were in the presence of one of his enemies.

'He has other things on his mind,' I said.

Naipaul chewed his cucumber sandwich and faced me, as though challenging me to give him one good reason why the Kabaka could not reply to the note informing him that V. S. Naipaul had arrived in Kampala.

'They want to kill him,' I said, lowering my voice in this crowded Kampala teashop. 'Obote wants to overthrow him.'

This was news to Naipaul, who I felt had mistakenly lumped the king together with the clapped-out maharajahs and sultans he had come across in India – men down on their luck, feeling wronged and dispossessed, grateful for a sympathetic hearing. The Kabaka was strange but he was vital, and he had a palace guard and a whole armory of weapons.

'It's not a good idea to talk about him,' I said.

'Excellent. I have no intention of doing so. I have lost all interest in him.'

Leaving the teashop, we bumped into Pippa Broadhurst, a lecturer in history, who had been at Hallsmith's party. A feminist, hating the prison of marriage, the jailer husband, the life sentence, clucking 'I am a human being too,' Pippa had found in the smoky bowl of the Ngorongoro crater in Tanzania a hospitable *manyatta* (village) and had had a brief affair with a spear-carrying *moran* (warrior) of the Masai people – another blood drinker, like Dudney's Karamojong missus. The upshot was Flora, a brown long-legged daughter, with whom Pippa went everywhere. The warrior was still in his thornbush kraal in Masailand.

'Hello, Vidia,' said Pippa. 'And congratulations. I understand Mr Bwogo's found you a house.'

'The house is pretty crummy.'

'Everyone gets those houses,' Pippa said, snatching at Flora.

'I'm not everyone,' Vidia said.

The house, one of a dozen just like it, was newly built and raw-looking, set on a hot, rubbly slope of baked earth above a brick warren of ruinous servants' quarters. The afternoon sun struck the house and heated it and made it stink of risen dust. The small brick buildings down the slope, too close together, were jammed with squatters and relatives, and I could hear music and chatter coming from the area of woodsmoke. Cooking fires and laughter: it was life lived outdoors, people eating and cooking and washing themselves. The clank of buckets and basins and the plop of slopping water reached me as I tapped on the front door.

'Come in,' Naipaul called in an irritated voice.

I could see what he disliked about the house. It was new and ugly, it smelled of fresh concrete and dust, it had no curtains.

'Paul,' he said in an imploring way, 'do sit down.'

Pat said, 'Go on, Vidia, please.'

'Listen to the bitches!'

'Vidia,' she said, trying to soothing him.

He continued to do what he had been doing when I entered, which was to read aloud from closely typed pages a scene about a farewell Christmas party in London, a meal at which presents were being given and toasts proposed. It was something from his novel, I supposed, the one he had brought to Uganda to finish. He went on reading, speaking of the tearful meal and the emotion, of people weeping.

Pat pressed her lips together when he finished, pausing before she spoke. The last time I had seen her was in the back seat of my car, when she had been sobbing openly and trying to speak ('Stop chuntering, Patsy'), her face contorted, her hair a mess, her cheeks and lips wet, her large breasts tremulous with her grief.

But today she was cool and very calm. In the most schoolmistressy way she said, 'Too many tears.'

I was seated by a small table on which there lay a carefully corrected paragraph of small type, which I glanced at. The first words, in boldface, read *Naipaul, Vidiadhar Surajprasad*. It was his *Who's Who* entry, with meticulous proofreader's marks in the margin in black ink, Vidia's precise handwriting, deleting a semicolon, adding a literary prize and a recent date.

He had only briefly interrupted the reading of his novel when I entered. I felt he wanted me to hear it, to mystify and impress me. I was impressed. He was admitting me to this ritual of reading; he trusted me.

He turned to me and said, 'Do you hear those bitches and their bongos?'

No bongos, but I knew what he meant.

'Do you suppose we could flog them?' He knew it was an outrageous suggestion, but he wanted to gauge my reaction. He took a harmless pleasure in seeing people wince.

We went to the window and looked downhill at the roofs of corrugated asbestos, moldy from the damp, at the woodsmoke and the banana trees, at barking dogs, crying children, all the elements of urban poverty in Uganda.

'That's what they need, a good flogging.'

'Vidia, that's quite enough of that,' Pat said, strong again, no sign of the tears and sobs of the other day.

His reading from the typescript and his unembarrassed candor in allowing me to hear it encouraged me to ask him again about writers he liked. So far, all I knew was that he disliked Orwell and that for pleasure he read the Bible and Martial. I had Nabokov's *Pale Fire* with me and told him how much I liked it.

'I read *Pnin*. It was silly. There was nothing in it. What do people see in him?'

'Style, maybe?'

'What is his style? It's bogus, calling attention to itself. Americans do that. All those beautiful sentences. What are they for?'

His interest, his passion, was located solely in his own writing. He saw it as new. Nothing like it had ever been written before. It was an error to look for any influences, for there were none; it was wrong to compare it with any other work; nothing came close to resembling it. It took me a little while to understand his utter faith in this conceit, but the day I did, and acknowledged that his writing was unique, and that he was a new man, was the day our friendship began.

Some people mistook the apparent spareness of his sentences for a faltering imagination, or a lack of stylistic ambition, or sheer monotony. But he said he was deliberate in everything he wrote, calculating each effect, and the simplicity was contrived. In his view, he was like someone making a model of an entire city out of the simplest material, a Rome made of matchsticks, say, a Rome whose bridges a full-sized human could stand on and run carts over. He detested falsity in style, he loathed manner in writing. He said he never prettified anything he saw or felt, and 'prettified,' a new word to me, like 'chuntering,' was added to my vocabulary.

'The truth is messy. It is not pretty. Writing must reflect that. Art must tell the truth.'

But early on, I had kept after him for the names of writers he admired. He shrugged. 'Shakey, of course,' he said. 'Jimmy Joyce. Tommy Mann.'

What books, I wondered, and why?

'Forget Nabokov. Read *Death in Venice*. Pay close attention to the accumulation of thought. Notice how each sentence builds and adds.'

What about American writers? Surely there was someone he liked.

'Do you know the first sentence of the short story "The Blue Hotel" by Stephen Crane? About the color blue?' he asked. 'I like that.'

His own work served as a better example of how complex and

yet transparent prose fiction could be. It was original, freshly imagined in both form and content. Its brilliance was not obvious – he did not use the word 'brilliance,' but he was wholly satisfied with the work, had no misgivings, saw nothing false or forced in it.

'*Miguel Street* is deceptive,' he said. 'Look at it again and you'll see how I used my material. Look at those sentences. They seem simple. But that book nearly killed me, man.'

Marlon Brando had read *Miguel Street* with pleasure, he had been told by a mutual friend, the novelist Edna O'Brien, who had also reported that Brando was attracted to women with dark nipples. It pleased Naipaul to know that Brando admired the book, and that knowledge made Naipaul feel friendly towards the actor. *The Teahouse of the August Moon* was a film he had liked, he said. He had not gone to many films lately, but he had seen every film that had come to Trinidad between the years 1942 and 1950, when he left for Oxford.

'You know what Brando says about actors?'

I said I did not know.

'An actor is a guy who, if you ain't talking about him, ain't listening.' Naipaul laughed his deep appreciative laugh and repeated the sentence.

Yomo was in bed when I got back home.

'*Bibi gonjwa*,' the housegirl said in a low voice, sounding as though she had been scolded. 'Your woman's sick.'

Yomo said in a feeble voice that she was feeling awful and wished she had some kola nuts. I made a cup of tea for her and then rooted through my bookshelf and found an anthology of American short stories, which included 'The Blue Hotel.'

This was how the story began: 'The Palace Hotel at Fort Romper was painted a light blue, a shade that is on the legs of a kind of heron, causing the bird to declare its position against any background. The Palace Hotel, then, was always screaming and howling in a way that made the dazzling winter landscape of Nebraska seem only a gray swampish hush.'

Then Yomo was at the door, wearing the bed sheet like a toga, blinking in the lights and saying, 'Please read to me.'

*

Naipaul complained so heartily about his house that I told him about my upstairs neighbors – newly married, a middle-aged man and a much younger woman – who giggled and chased each other around the house. They splashed in the bathtub and clattered plates and silver when they ate and called out constantly from room to room, 'I can't hear you!' But we could hear everything they said. It seemed at times they were carrying on for our benefit, using us as witnesses, proving something. They made love noisily – she was a screecher in her orgasms; it was a noise that built in volume and frequency, like someone working hard, pumping a tire, sawing a log. Their bed rocked and squeaked. At times it sounded like a muffled inquisition, the ordeal of someone whose confession was being painfully extracted.

'Who are they?' Naipaul asked.

'New people. From Canada.'

'Infies,' he said. 'Doesn't it make you hate all Canadians?'

I said no, and Pat laughed.

'Well, it would make me hate them,' Naipaul said. 'Do you speak to them?'

'Sometimes.'

'You should cut them.'

'You mean not speak to them?'

'I mean not see them. You walk past them. You cut them. They don't exist. Nothing at all.'

Not even the G. Ramsay Muir treatment – you just walked on.

The point about the rocking, squeaking hobbyhorse of a bed was that when I heard it, its first murmurs and jerks and hiccups, hesitating, just foreplay, nothing rhythmic yet, I prepared myself, and soon it was swaying and calling like a corncrake, and the woman was urging this late-night plowing. Then, almost against my will, I became aroused and woke Yomo and we made love.

One of those nights Yomo turned me away, hugged herself, and said she was really ill.

'You might be pregnant,' I said. 'You have to see the doctor.'

'I don't want the doctor. I don't need him.'

'He's good. He'll need to examine you.'

'Indian doctor,' she said. 'Bloody shit.'

Dr Barot was a Gujarati, Uganda born, trained in the Indian

city of Broach, who in the past had treated me for gonorrhea and for malaria. I asked him if he would see Yomo. He said of course, that he was also an obstetrician, and that it was important that he see Yomo soon.

Sleepy-eyed, reluctant, slightly sulky, Yomo finally agreed. She always took pains to dress up before leaving the house, but this was a greater occasion than most. She put on her brocade sash, her expensive cloak, her best turban. I loved seeing her dress up, and she became haughty and offhand when she wore her elegant clothes.

The February heat was oppressive. In the car Yomo said, 'You don't know. Black people get hotter than white people. It's our skin.' I wondered whether this was true.

Dr Barot greeted her and took her into his examining room. I heard the scraping sound of her disrobing, stiff colorful clothes sliding away, of her folding them. If she was going to have a baby, I would be happy. It was not what I had planned, but really I had no plans. There was something wrong with the very idea of a plan, and anyway I half believed that my life was prefigured – perhaps, as people said, like the lines on my palm. My random life was pleasant enough, and everything good that had happened to me had come accidentally. I just launched myself and trusted to luck. *Mektoub* – it is written.

I sat waiting, thinking of nothing in particular. When the examining room door opened I smiled, having just been reminded of why I was there.

'What's the verdict?'

'Four months pregnant,' Dr Barot said.

Yomo looked shyly at me and slipped next to me as we watched Dr Barot write his bill on a pad. While he wrote, he said that Yomo was healthy and that she should see him regularly from now on so he could monitor her blood pressure.

In the car, sitting on the hot upholstery, I said, 'How can you be four months pregnant? You've only been here three months.'

I felt innumerate and confused and was not blaming her but rather trying to explain my bewilderment.

Yomo said, 'I had a friend in Nigeria before I came here to see you.'

Now it became harder for me to drive. The road was full of obstacles, and it was much hotter in the car.

'What are we going to do?' I said.

She was silent, but I could see she was sad, and her sadness seemed worse because she was dressed so beautifully.

'Do you think you should see your friend?' I asked.

She said nothing. She did not cry until that night, when her clothes were neatly folded on the chair, all that stiff cloth in a deep stack. She was in bed, hiding her face, sobbing.

I did not know what to say. I did not have the words. I loved her, but I had just discovered that I did not know her. Who was this friend, and what was this deception? It must have been obvious to her that she was at least one month pregnant soon after she arrived in Uganda.

'I want to go home,' she said in a voice that broke my heart, and it was awful to hear the Canadians upstairs fooling around and calling out.

'This is your home.'

'No,' she said, and went on weeping.

Yomo was one of only three passengers on the plane from Entebbe to Lagos a week later. Her posture was different, her sadness making her slower and giving her a halting way of walking, and she sighed as we moved toward the barrier, where I kissed her goodbye. It seemed a kind of death, because it was as though we were losing everything.

'I liked it when you read that story to me,' she said. She began to weep again.

The road from Entebbe to Kampala was known for its frequent fatal car accidents. I drove it that day feeling fearless and stupid, not caring if it was my turn to die on this road, because hadn't everything else come to an end? I was numb, but when I got to my house I knew that I had lost my love and would have to begin again, and all that helped was my knowing that for Yomo it would be worse. So I helped myself by sorrowing for her.

Naipaul asked me where I had been. He had not seen me in the painful week that had just passed.

'Oh, God,' he said. 'Oh, God.' His voice cracked, his face was tormented. 'Are you all right? Of course you're not. Paul, Paul, Paul.'

He was truly upset. He was sharing the burden. That was the act of a friend.

He took my hand and turned it over and studied it again, this time tracing it with his finger, and this time he spoke.

'You must not worry. You're going to be all right.'

'Thanks, Vidia.' It was the first time I used the name.

'That is a good hand.'

3

The Kaptagat Arms

It was the month of bush fires, smoky skies, black hills, fleeing animals; the season of haze and hawks.

With all my love lost, I lay in the bedroom alone where we had slept together, staring at the long-nosed stains on the ceiling, goblins with the voices of the yelling Canadians upstairs. I was sorrowful without Yomo and her laughter. Naipaul – Vidia, as I now called him – was kind, but kindness was not enough. I needed a more intimate friend or else no one at all, just the consolation of the African landscape, which was a reminder to me that life goes on.

It was the season when Africans set fire to the bush, believing the blaze to be helpful to next year's crops. I set off for the north, drove almost to the Sudan, and walked among the elephant palms to the shriek and twang of the same insects the people ate there; then I drove on to Arua, in West Nile province, on the Congo border, with its scowling purplish Kakwa people, of whom the chief of staff of the Uganda Army, Idi Amin, was the stereotype.

Hawks hovered above the grass fires and swooped down on the mice and snakes and other small creatures that were roused and panicked by the flames. There were hawks all over the smoky sky. Something about the wildfires and the hovering birds and the scuttling mice spoke to me of sex and its consequences.

At Kitgum, in the far north, I hiked in a hot wind, sinking in sand to my ankles, kicking at dead leaves to scatter the snakes. Each night in the village where I stayed a toothless old woman squatted on the dirt floor of a hut and sang a lewd song in an ululating voice. 'She is beautiful and has a neck like a swan, but she has stroked the spear of every man in the district' was the way her song was translated for me. It was coarse and upsetting, but this hidden corner of Africa was peaceful for being hot and remote. Black water tumbled over Karuma Falls. To justify my trip to my department head, I traveled southwest and slipped between the Mountains of the Moon and visited schools at Bundibugyo, where Yomo and I had planned to lose ourselves in the bush. One night after rain I went outside and found thirsty children licking raindrops off my car.

Hawks, bush fires, heat, envious songs, and desperate children: so far, not much consolation on this safari.

A sign reading *Very Big Lion* was nailed to a tree near Mityana, where I stopped on my way back to Kampala. Another sign said *Good News – To See A Very Big Lion – It eats 50 lbs of Meat Daily.* A coastal Swahili man with gray eyes in a grubby skullcap asked me for a shilling and then showed me the lion.

'*Simba! Simba!*'

Covered with flies, the lion lay in a pen made of corrugated iron, thrown up in a clearing near the road. The man in the skullcap made the beast growl by poking it with the skinned and bloody leg of a dead animal, a gazelle's perhaps. The lion thrashed but could not seize the meat in its yellow stumps of teeth. I looked into the lion's eyes and saw the sort of lonely torment that I felt.

'*Bwana. Mumpa cigara.*'

Within a week the lion had escaped and killed six villagers and was finally shot by the Mityana district game warden. All that violence for the lion's being in a pen. I saw a link between that hunger and the animal's captivity – that appetite, that denial. I tried to write a story about it, but there was no story, only the incident.

'Someday you will use it,' Vidia said, though he said he disliked animal stories. He told me that when he was my age, working on his first book, a man had told him to read Hemingway's story 'Hills Like White Elephants.'

I said, 'For anyone who lives in Africa – for me, at any rate – Hemingway is unreadable.'

'Nevertheless, I read the story immediately it was recommended to me.'

Vidia was still helping me with my essay on cowardice, frowning over it, the tenth version. He said that it was improving but that it would be better if I cut it by half. I nodded but doubted that I would.

He said, 'I know when I make comments on it you listen and get very tired.'

That was exactly how I felt.

'It's normal. But this is an important statement – how you feel about Vietnam, how you feel about your life. You must get it right.'

The problem was language, he said. He was passionate on the subject of misapplied words and meaningless mystification. I had lived too long in a place where the wrong words were used. Africans called Kampala a city. But it was not a city. '"University" is a misleading word for this crummy place, and is this a government?' The teaching was not teaching, these were not real academics, the daily newspaper, the *Uganda Argus*, contained no news. 'This is all fraudulent!' The writing by credulous well-wishers about African literature had corrupted the language. He emphasized that I must pay close attention to the words I used and evaluate how they worked. Putting his fastidious finger on the page, Vidia made me justify each word in the essay. 'Why "fat"?' 'Why "hapless"?' 'Don't use words for effect,' he said. 'Tell the truth.'

'I have said before that writing is like sleight of hand. You simply mention a chair and it's shadowy. You say it's stained with wedding saffron and suddenly the chair is there, visible.'

This was spoken at his house, which smelled of fresh cement and red floor wax and new paint; the sun streaming through the windows that had no curtains; the house he hated, within earshot of the noise from the brick-and-thatch servants' quarters.

'And that is not music. Listen to the bitches!'

Sometimes students brought him their work. He did not encourage them, but he allowed them. He saw the occasional lecturer. Sometimes he was asked a question about literature or the world.

I was present when he told a man with a serious inquiry, 'I can't answer that. I would need written notice of that question.'

After the man left, Vidia said, 'That's what he wanted to hear, you know. He didn't really want me to answer his question.'

A female student brought him an essay. She had come to his house because he refused to hold classes.

'Your essay is hopeless,' he said. He chose a few examples to illustrate how bad it was, and then he said, 'But you have lovely handwriting. Where did you learn to write like that?'

Another student, celebrated as a rising Ugandan poet by Hall-smith, sent Vidia a poem, entitled 'A New Nation Reborn,' and showed up some days later at Vidia's house wearing his crimson student's gown. These gowns, introduced by the same English vice-chancellors who had contrived Makerere's Latin motto – *Pro Futuro Aedificamus*, We Build for the Future – mimicked those worn by Oxford students. The young poet gathered his gown like an older woman taking a seat at a doctor's office. He said, 'Have you read my poem?'

'Yes, I've read it.' Vidia paused, tapped a cigarette, and said nothing for a long while. 'I have been wondering about it.'

'It is about tubbulence.'

'Really.' Vidia found the boy's eyes and fixed them with his weary stare. He said, 'Don't write any more poems. I really don't think you should. Your gifts lie in some other direction. A story, perhaps. Now, promise me you won't write any more poems.'

The boy shook his head and made the promise in a halting voice. He went away baffled and dejected.

'Did you see how relieved he was?' Vidia said. 'He was glad I told him that.'

Vidia rubbed his hands and disposed of other students in the same fashion. I was surprised when he agreed to be the judge of a university literary competition, but he carried out his duties his own way. He insisted that there be only one prize, called Third Prize, because the entries were so bad there could be no first and second prizes.

'Make it absolutely clear that this is Third Prize,' he told the people in the English Department.

Some of the members objected to this.

Vidia said, 'You are trying to give the African an importance he does not deserve. Your expectations are misguided. Turn away and nothing will happen. It's the language again. Obote is just another chief. You call these politicians? They are just witch doctors.'

When the term 'Third Prize' was converted to 'The Prize,' Vidia smiled and said, 'Blackwash.'

'The Africans who carry books around are the ones who scare me, man,' he said around that time.

He was dimly aware of, but not impressed by, some of the distinguished men and women who were living in Kampala or doing research at the university. An anthropologist, Victor Turner, was then at Makerere. You would not have known that this small, soft-spoken man with the diffidence of a librarian had spent years in mud huts on the upper Zambezi and on the Mongu floodplain and written pioneering studies of the Lozi people of Barotseland. Colin Turnbull had studied the Mbuti Pygmies. In the course of illustrating his encyclopedic studies of the mammals and birds of East Africa, Jonathan Kingdon, a painter and naturalist, had discovered at least two new species of mammal and several birds that had never been described. Michael Adams, a friend and contemporary of David Hockney's, was our Gauguin. Colin Leakey, son of Louis Leakey, was our botanist. Rajat Neogy, the editor and founder of *Transition*, published Wole Soyinka, Chinua Achebe, and Nadine Gordimer.

'What should I think about Africa?' Vidia demanded of an anthropology professor one day.

'Mr Naipaul, I don't think it's a good idea to have too many opinions about Africa,' the man said. 'If you do, you miss too much that's really important.'

'Really.'

Later, walking back to his house, Vidia said, 'Foolish man. He refuses to see the corruption. He accepts the lies.'

But he blamed himself, saying he should never have come, should not have accepted money from the Farfield Foundation. 'Don't ever accept money from a foundation,' he said. 'It will ruin you. There are strings attached to all money you don't earn yourself.'

This mistake in coming to Uganda inspired him, he said, to write an essay about all the rules he had made for himself and how disastrous it had been when he had broken one.

'Every time I've broken one of my own rules I have regretted it. Like this . . . Maka-ray-ray. Or the weak and oppressed. They're terrible, man. They've got to be kicked.' He kicked a stone. 'Like that.'

His own behavior alarmed him.

'This is turning me into a racialist, for God's sake. What a dreary, boring thing to be.'

Until I met Vidia, I had never known a person who recognized no one as his equal. He's a Brahmin, the local Indians said: all Brahmins are fussy like that. Early on, seeing me solicit directions from a villager, he stood silently by, listening to the flow of Swahili, and then said, 'You talk to these people so easily.'

I told him I had made a point of learning the language. People told the truth in their own language. They were nervous or inaccurate or more easily mendacious in a second language.

'I don't mean that,' he said.

What did he mean? Perhaps that I spoke to them at all, and that I listened. His manner made him an impossible colleague but a natural *bwana* and employer of servants. He said I was too easy on my staff. 'Your housegirl is an idler.' My cook, he said, was dirty. My gardener was a drunk.

'Your gardener is a drunk too,' I said, unwittingly indulging in the asinine debate between *bwanas:* my Africans are better than your Africans.

'Only on Sundays. A servant has a right to get drunk on Sundays. You have no right to criticize him for that, Paul.'

One of his pleasures was in taking his houseboy, Andrew, to the market and buying him half a pound of fried locusts and watching the man devour them, the dark *mafuta* grease smearing his cheeks.

'Good, eh, Andrew? Delicious, eh? *Mazoori*, eh?'

'*Ndio, bwana. Mzuri sana.*'

'You see, Paul. The occasional treat. The occasional reprimand. Works wonders. He's frightfully happy now.'

He complained that we were out of touch in Uganda. I said that we got the London newspapers on Sundays.

'Bring me the English papers this Sunday,' he said. 'We will read them and then go for a walk.'

But he was in a foul mood when I arrived. I knew the reason: Sunday was the day when African families congregated outdoors. There was music, laughter, singing, fooling. 'Bongos.' I thought the London papers might help.

'If there's nothing about me in those papers, I am not interested in reading them,' he said in a sharp voice.

'Vidia,' Pat said, chastising him with his name.

'All right, let's go for that fucking walk.'

His fluctuating temperament fascinated me, because it was so unusual, even self-destructive. Expatriates in Africa were generally even-tempered, and the farther into the bush you found them, the more serene they were. In Africa, nitpickers were those people by the side of the road plucking at someone's louse-ridden head. The expression described no one else. So it was strange to find someone losing his temper, almost constantly on the boil. Such people never lasted. Vidia was especially fanatical in the matter of timekeeping.

'Come at seven,' he said to me one day, inviting me to dinner.

I took this to mean drinks at seven and then dinner. I showed up casually at seven-fifteen and found him at the table with Pat. Pat looked embarrassed; Vidia said nothing. He ignored me. He was eating quickly, like someone who was himself late. He was gobbling prawns.

'We've finished the first course,' he finally said. His mouth was full, to put me in the wrong and make a point. 'You're late.'

His obsession with punctuality governed his relationships. I was lucky in having merely been reprimanded for my lateness; the usual penalty was rejection: 'He was late. I wouldn't see him.' An African painter I knew ran out of gas on his way to an appointment with Vidia and, having to walk the rest of the way, arrived half an hour late. Vidia sent him away.

'The oldest excuse in the book, man. "I ran out of petrol." All the lies!'

He began to rant more often, which was now most of the time. He stopped working. He grew morose.

One day, all he wrote was the word 'The' on a piece of paper, nothing more. He showed it to me. It was large and very dark. 'It took me seven hours to write that.' He smiled insanely at it, a grin of satisfaction, as if to say, See what they made me do! He looked crazy, but he said he was sad. The problem was his house. The noise was also an assault. 'Those bitches!' He hated the smells – cooking fires, rotting vegetation, human odors. 'No one washes. Is soap expensive here?'

There had always been a note of humor in his rage, but today he was not joking. He looked older, angrier, insulted, trapped. He was miserable.

'I had to take to my bed,' he said.

In her gentle, trembly, imploring voice, Pat said, 'We've heard of a hotel . . .'

The hotel was outside the town of Eldoret, in the highlands – the White Highlands, as they were still known then – of western Kenya: a wooded refuge in the middle of the plateau. It was called the Kaptagat Arms and was run by a man known as the Major, who was noted for his rudeness. He was an Englishman, a retired army officer, Sandhurst trained, who had spent his military career in India. He was in his late sixties and very gruff. Stories about him circulated in Uganda, emphasizing that the Kaptagat Arms was a place to avoid. The most recent story, one I told Vidia, concerned a woman faculty member who had asked the Major for a Pimm's Cup in the hotel bar. The Major had said, 'We don't serve that muck. Now get out,' and showed the woman the door. Woman-hating was a recurring theme in the Major's rudeness.

Vidia had told me he loathed colorful characters. He hated clowns, comedians, yakkers, virtuosos, village explainers, and hollow jokesters, vapidly Pickwickian, who spent their lives monologuing in country pubs. He felt insulted by their insincerity and foolishness. Buffoonery caused in him a deepening depression. Yet he liked my story about the Major for its rough justice. The woman in question he had singled out as an infy. Pimm's No. 1 Cup was an infy drink.

'One of these suburban drinks,' Vidia said.

I was apprehensive. It seemed to me that the Major was the sort of colorful character who would either antagonize Vidia or lower his spirits. He had told me of a fistfight he'd had in a London restaurant once with just such a presumptuous person. It was hard to imagine this tiny man provoked to physical violence. But he never lied, so I believed him.

The three of us, Vidia, Pat, and I, went to the Kaptagat together. It was a long drive. First the Jinja Road out of Kampala, with its sugar estates and clouds of butterflies that settled on the road and posed a skidding hazard at the curve near Iganga. Then Jinja itself, the cotton mills, and Owen Falls – the headwaters of the Nile – and the conical hill outside Tororo where a dangerous leopard was said to live. Near the Kenyan frontier and the customs post, we came to the end of the paved road. Eighty miles of dusty, stony road had to be traversed, and on it, outside Bungoma, which was just some Indian shops and a bicycle mender, we saw six or seven naked boys with white-powdered bodies running along the road, having just 'danced,' as Africans said, meaning they were initiates in a circumcision ceremony. Their white faces were ghostlike. Farther on, seeing the sign *Beware of Fallen Rocks*, Vidia muttered the words to himself, liking the sign for its precise language.

After we left Eldoret and its single gas station, we traveled north down narrow red clay roads, past corn fields, following wooden arrow-shaped signs saying *To the Kaptagat Arms*. We found the place in the early afternoon. It was utterly silent and abandoned-looking: no guests, no cars, only flitting birds and a few Kikuyu gardeners working in the flower beds. The hotel had one story, a converted farmhouse with an added wing of single rooms that looked out on the flower garden.

'Hello?' I said. '*Jambo.*'

No one answered. Inside in the reception area there were Indian artifacts on shelves – Benares brassware, carved ivory, wall hangings, some baskets – as well as the sort of paraphernalia found in English country pubs: horse brasses, pewter tankards, tarnished trophies, old blurred photographs of anglers struggling to hold prize fish upright, hunting horns, ribbons, and the sort of fluted glass that offered a yard of ale. There were mounted racks of gazelles and oryx and kudu. There was a shoulder mount of a zebra on one wall and a zebra skin on the floor. The most ominously impressive object was a large, dusty tiger skin nailed to one whole wall, where it sprawled disemboweled in an arrested growl.

I rang a tinkly bell that was propped on the gold-stamped leather of the reception book and blotter, whereupon a tall craggy figure marched out from the back office. His posture was crooked and peevish. He had white hair and a deeply lined chain smoker's face and a burning butt between his fingers. Undeniably the Major, he looked cross, with an English scowl that meant 'nothing impresses me.' Staring with puzzled, just-interrupted eyes, he stuck his chin out and said, 'Yes, what is it?'

'We've just driven from Uganda,' Vidia said.

'Shocking road. But we do get quite a few people from that side.'

'We are inquiring about your hotel,' Vidia went on. 'We'd like to have lunch and look around.'

'Give me a moment to get sorted out,' the Major said. 'Have a *shufti* at the garden. I'll give you a shout when we're ready to seat you. What was the name?'

'Naipaul.'

'Are you the writer?'

It was an inspired response. The heavens opened. A trumpet sounded, flocks of doves soared, and all the *malaikas*, the choirs of black angels, in the skies of western Kenya burst into song.

'Yes,' Vidia said, stammering with satisfaction. 'Yes. Yes. Yes. Yes.'

He was home, welcomed, at ease, in his own element, in the presence of a reader, happier than I had ever seen him.

'And what can I do for you?'

The Major had to repeat the question. He was speaking to me. I was lurking near the tiger skin, feeling awkward, but also wondering how you managed to kill one of these enormous creatures without making a mark or leaving scars.

'I am with them,' I said. 'And I am looking for the bullet hole in this thing.'

'You won't find it,' the Major said. 'I shot him in the eye.'

The big glass eyes of the tiger stared like a martyr's into the room with its ridiculous curios.

'How did you find us?' the Major asked.

'I had a vibration,' Vidia said.

Over lunch in the dining room, where we were the only diners, the Major was attentive. He said that business was terrible and that he planned to sell the place. He was breezy and somewhat stoical, as though fighting a rear-guard action and about to announce his surrender. He pulled the cork from a bottle of wine. 'This is an Australian hock.'

'But this is awfully good,' Vidia said, examining the label as he worked his lips together.

'Try some of that sherry sauce in your soup. Joshua will be right back with your entrées,' the Major said, marching away.

Pat had begun to cry. She sobbed miserably and said she could not eat. It was the thought of the hotel's closing, she said. All the flowers, all the order and neatness, all the hope. And they were shutting up shop.

'Oh my, Vidia, look,' she said, and gestured towards a waiter. 'His poor shoes.'

There was something pathetic in the shoes. They were broken, without laces, the counters crushed, the tongues missing, the heels worn. They seemed to represent battered, tortured feet. The sight of the shoes reduced Pat to tears once again. Each time she saw the man wearing them, she began to sob. I did not tell her that Africans got such shoes second- and third-hand. Used to being barefoot, the Africans who owned them rarely found that they conformed to their misshapen feet; the shoes, like the torn shirts and torn shorts they wore, were often merely symbolic.

'Don't be sad, Patsy,' Vidia said. 'He'll be all right. He'll go back to his village. He'll have his bananas and his bongos. He'll be frightfully happy.'

Later, the Major said that after India's independence, he had followed some other Anglo-Indians in coming to East Africa. Kenya, for its good climate, had been a choice destination. Tanzania was regarded as a rough place, difficult to farm, full of Bolshie Africans in Mao suits. Uganda was black, an agglomeration of incoherent kingdoms with bad roads. In any case, the Major had come reluctantly. He had liked India. Africa was all right, but Africans infuriated him. His Swahili was just a stern litany of orders and commands, and I saw something rather strict, even domineering about him, a coldness, and a defiant cynicism. He embodied the worst of the settler severity and the woman-hating mateship of the officers' mess.

Ignoring her tears, the Major took a dislike to Pat from the first, and afterwards he sometimes mimicked her to me – clumsy, overstated mimicry that betrayed a kind of rancor. To him she was the *bibi*, the *memsahib*, the whiner, but for Vidia's sake he was polite to her. Vidia used the old-fashioned-sounding word 'pathic' to describe the Major. I had never heard the word before.

Vidia said English prostitutes used it, which seemed a curious attribution and an even more questionable authority. *Oh, tarts said it, did they?* I took it to mean that the Major was bent. Vidia's more particular word 'bugger' was never uttered here at the Kaptagat Arms.

They talked of India: the beauty of Punjabi Muslims, the ferocity of Sikhs, the plains of Uttar Pradesh, the Englishness of hill stations, polo at the Poona Club. The Major had been posted all over. He said to Vidia, 'I could tell you some smashing stories. I am sure you'd be able to use them.'

'No, not me,' Vidia said. 'You must write them yourself.'

Over the years, I heard him give that same advice to everyone who offered him a story to write. He could not write their stories; it was for them to do. When they protested that they could not write, Vidia said, 'If your story is as good as you say, you'll write it.'

The Major was also a reader and had admired Vidia's book *An Area of Darkness*. Soon after we arrived, I saw him reading Graham Greene's *The Comedians*, which had just been published in Britain.

'What do you think of it?' I asked.

'Characters called Smith and Jones and Brown. That's no bloody good. What should I think of it?'

He did not like Americans, he said. He made no secret of his contempt for me. I had a sissy way with the sherry sauce. 'Yanks!' he cried, and then told long, implausible stories. Once, the Major said, while in the United States on a military errand, he had ordered a slice of ham in an officers' club. Unbidden, an American officer at the table had spooned a dollop of marmalade on the ham and said, 'That'll make it taste a whole lot better' – spoken in one of the Major's cruelly inaccurate accents.

'Bloody Yanks,' the Major said. 'I couldn't eat it.'

With minor variations, he told me the same story four times. I did not mind. I felt that this casual abuse would give Vidia a perspective on an American's life among these English settlers in Africa.

Vidia found a room in the hotel he liked. He negotiated a weekly rate, and soon he and Pat moved in. The idea was that Vidia would finish writing his novel there, and it was at the Kaptagat Arms that he told me its title, *The Mimic Men*. Pat did some writing too. She kept a diary. She also had literary ambitions – she wanted to write a play – but she seldom discussed her plans, always deferring to Vidia. From time to time she broke into helpless blubbing, either as the result of a disagreement or simply because of some sorrowful sight – broken shoes, a snotty-nosed child, a woman bereft, a gardener laboring on his knees. Often her tears roused me. I did not know why, but her weeping made me want to hold her and fondle her breasts.

There were no other guests at the Kaptagat Arms. The Major had several mild-mannered Labrador retrievers, which nuzzled our legs, their tongues lolling, hoping to be scratched. Some British teachers from a nearby prep school came to the bar most nights and got drunk.

'That silly Jewess,' a male teacher shrieked one night.

Vidia said to avoid them. 'Infies.'

He understood the Major, he said. The Major's Indian Army nickname had been 'Bunny.' The poor man was tormented by passion and frustration. Clearly, he was a very sensitive soul, Vidia said. 'Look at those eyes.' (To me, the Major's blue eyes seemed cold and depthless.) The Major had a feeling for India, which was a mark of his sensibilities. He had heart. He was a good soldier and respected his men. He understood the culture. He was intelligent. He had brought this sense of order to Africa, where, imparting skills, building an institution, he was in a way running a miniature colony of his own.

Vidia, suspecting that the Major found him to be a puzzle, seemed to look for ways to make himself more puzzling. Yet Vidia had such simple, inflexible rules that, if they were strictly followed, he was happy. For example, Vidia's vegetarianism caused a dilemma in the kitchen. Omelets were a frequent solution. 'I have had to buy more cookery books,' the Major told me.

I visited Vidia whenever I could, at first for weekends and then for weeks at a time. The Kaptagat routine was quite different from my life in Kampala, and I grew to like playing bar billiards and eating steamed chocolate pudding, putting sherry in my soup and walking the Major's dogs.

What occupied me – though I never spoke of it – was my own novel. It was understood that my writing consultations with Vidia were just about over. My cowardice essay was nearly done. 'I think it's an important statement,' Vidia said, 'though you might have revealed too much of yourself.' I had moved on. I did not say what I was doing. Anyway, no one asked. I was the Sorcerer's Apprentice.

'My narrator has something to say about that,' Vidia would say in the middle of a conversation, and it was often as simple as a reference to the fluctuating price of land. He was close to all his characters – he quoted them, and he often quoted the narrator, who was a wise, if world-weary, forty-year-old with opinions on politics and oppression, friendship and money. Vidia was happy with his novel's progress now that he was the resident of this comfortable hotel. All his needs were seen to. He had rusticated himself and was looked after by the Major and his Kikuyu servants, whom in Kenyan fashion he had begun to call 'Cukes.'

Pat said, 'Amin asked, "What work does the *bwana* do in his room all day?" I told him that your work is like praying. So he has to be very quiet.'

'"The *bwana* is praying,"' Vidia said. 'Yes. It's true. I'm glad you put it that way.'

He had started the novel in a hotel in the southeast London district of Blackheath, having deliberately checked in to find atmosphere and enter the mood of his narrator, who was a temporary hotel resident writing a novel-memoir. It was appropriate that he was finishing the book in another hotel. He said many times, 'My narrator likes hotels. I like hotels.' He enjoyed the attention he received, the tidy rooms, the staff toiling away, the illusion that this was a manor and he was the lord. And such conditions were perfect for the writing of a book.

'This is an important book,' he said of his novel. 'These things have never been said.'

It's just a book, I thought. It amazed me that he could talk about his work so admiringly and with such fondness. But I also thought: I want to feel that respect about something I have written. I want to value it. I want to have that confidence. I want to invest all my intellect and my effort in it. I want to be rewarded.

'Patsy objects to something I wrote,' Vidia said over dinner one night. 'Patsy doesn't want me to say "wise old coon."'

'Oh, Vidia,' Pat said, and her eyes became moist.

'Patsy wants me to say "wise old negro."'

They both seemed awful to me, but I could tell from Pat's anger and the argument that ensued – more tears at the dinner table – that she would prevail.

He worked on an Olivetti portable, one of those lightweight flat machines that seemed modern to me and that went *chick-chick-chick*. I used an old black Remington that clacked loudly when I typed, going *fika-fika-fika*.

'I love to sit in the garden and hear you both typing,' Pat said.

In the bar one night Vidia said, 'How do you spell "areola"?'

I thought he was saying 'aureole' and began to spell it, but he said no. He asked the Major for a dictionary and found the word.

'Isn't it a nipple?' asked the Major.

'It's the portion that surrounds the nipple,' answered Vidia.

While they talked, I looked up the word 'pathic,' but it was not in the Major's small student dictionary, which must have belonged to one of the Kikuyu staff.

'Is that for your book?' the Major was asking Vidia.

'My narrator mentions it, yes.'

'I must read this book.'

Pat smiled at this but said nothing. She had a smooth pale face, a slightly jutting jaw, and a pendulous lower lip that made her seem thoughtful, on the point of speaking. She was shy, she spoke sweetly, she was modest and always polite. I was careful never to swear in her presence. I had seen how the word 'fuck' upset her when spoken by a man in the Kaptagat bar. I did not want to ask myself why her reaction stirred me.

In the garden, beyond the hedge of purplish bougainvillea, she read, she wrote in her diary, always looking lonely and somewhat embarrassed, as though she were obviously waiting, keeping an appointment with someone who would never show up. She was small and demure and shapely. *I give her a chaste kiss at night.*

'Keep Pat company,' Vidia would say. He was wholly occupied with his book.

I wondered what his words meant and wanted them to be less

ambiguous, or for her to take the initiative. I was twenty-four and still missed Yomo badly, although in Kampala I sometimes took women home from the Gardenia bar.

Pat and I drove to nearby villages or to Eldoret, where there was a post office. We went for walks. It was not unusual to stumble across an African couple rutting, or a boy chasing a girl through a field, or to hear, as we did one day, shrieks of pleasure from a corn field. This sort of thing roused me. Pat appeared not to notice, as a well-bred woman will avert her eyes from two dogs copulating in the road. She was friendly and receptive but always polite. Was her politeness her way of keeping her distance?

Wooing was unknown to me. I did not know anything about the rituals of English courtship. I had so far, in the four years I had lived in Africa, made love only to African women. That sex had liberated me and given me a habit of straightforwardness. Once I asked an American woman in Kampala if she was interested in having sex. She said, 'You'll have to be a little subtler than that,' and when I attempted subtlety – though I knew it was too late – she confessed that she was a virgin. I was so shocked at her innocence I lectured her, warning her to be more careful. We were all dogs here, I said.

'Come home with me. I want to make love to you,' I would say, but the statement was even blunter and without euphemism in Chichewa or Swahili. It was as unambiguous as describing the insertion of a cork in a bottle, but wasn't that better?

'*Mimi nyama, wewe kisu*' usually worked when I said it with a smile. I am the meat, you are the knife.

'No,' one woman laughed. '*You* are the knife, *I* am the meat.'

'*Sisi nyama mbili*,' I said. We're both meat.

Sometimes no words were necessary. Just being alone with a woman in Africa meant that you had complete freedom. She might not say 'Let's do it,' she might make no sound at all. Her silence or her smile meant yes. I had lived what I felt was a repressed life in the United States. It was a relief that no negotiation was necessary. If I met a woman I liked, I soon mentioned sex. It seemed to me, and nearly always to the woman, that what was being proposed was no more serious, or lengthy, than a game of cards.

'I have given up sex,' Vidia had said to me. The statement

strangely teased me. I regarded Pat in light of that disclosure and saw both timidity and hunger and a hint of frail susceptibility that only made her more desirable.

We went for walks and were often together, yet I could not find the words to broach this subject. I had no technique and I knew straightforwardness would not work. She was simply too polite and circumspect for me to speak bluntly to her. I wished that she would help me, either by frankly putting me off or encouraging me. Her politeness was like the reaction of a coquette, and perversely that attracted me as much as her delicate face and pale damp eyes and lovely hair – only thirty-three, and yet her hair was silver-gray, another provocation.

She caught me staring at her one day and she became self-conscious. 'My clothes have shrunk so,' she explained, and tugged with her tiny fingers. Tight slacks, tight blouse, and her pretty lips. This never went further than my lingering gaze, but my feelings of desire for his wife made me guiltily hearty towards Vidia whenever Pat and I returned to the hotel from a walk or a ride. I would not know until much later that in the novel he was writing, Vidia's Indian narrator-hero's English wife, who somewhat resembled Pat (a whole page was devoted to the pleasures of her breasts), has an affair with a young American. The narrator looks on; the American who cuckolds him is 'slightly too hearty towards me, who felt nothing but paternally towards him.'

Eldoret had a noisy bar on a back street called the Highlands. In spite of the music there were not many people inside, and most of them were women from that area, very dark, from the lakeshore town of Kisumu. I went to the Highlands one night after dropping Pat at the hotel. I took a seat at a table and saw an African woman nearby smiling at me. Her face gleamed like iron in the badly lighted bar.

'*Mumpa cigara.*'

I gave her one and asked in Swahili, 'Do you want a drink?'

'Yes. If you buy it, I want a *pombe*,' the woman said, and joined me.

'So what are you doing?' I asked.

'I have been waiting for you,' she said.

This is how it should always be, I thought, because I knew that it would not be a question of if or when, but merely of finding a quiet place afterwards where we would not be disturbed.

The car the Naipauls had acquired before leaving Kampala, the tan Peugeot, was a popular model in East Africa; it was used as a bush taxi because of its solid suspension and reliable engine. Their driver's name was Aggrey. His English was poor. He often told me in Swahili what he wished to communicate to the *bwana*. When, as frequently happened, Vidia was annoyed with him, he pleaded with me to explain why the *bwana* was angry. I was never privy to Vidia's petulance, and it could last for days at a time, like the master—servant fury in a Russian novel. While it was in progress, Vidia drove the car himself and made Aggrey sit in the back seat. It was a cruel reversal of roles, and as Vidia was an erratic driver – he had never before owned a car – it was a peculiarly humiliating punishment for the driver to be turned into a passenger, stuck in the traditional *bwana*'s seat while the *bwana* blunderingly chauffeured him.

To Vidia, all of East Africa was a single maddening place, but anyone who lived there knew it was three distinct countries. Uganda Protectorate had had a peaceful transition to independence. Tanzania, perversely ideological, was a Maoist experiment throughout the sixties: the leaders wore Mao suits and parroted Chinese slogans, and in return for this flattery (the Cultural Revolution had just begun) the Chinese began building a railway that would connect Dar es Salaam with Zambia. Kenya was a cranky tribalistic place with polarized political parties and deep regional and ethnic resentments. The Mau Mau conflict, still fresh in people's memories, had been violent and divisive, full of rumors of ritual murder and blood ceremonies and cannibalism. Kenya had been a battleground and was now presided over by the sly and sententious old warrior Jomo Kenyatta, who regularly extorted money from foreign governments and Indian businessmen. The governments played along, but sometimes businessmen jibbed and refused to pay up.

Six Indian businessmen who refused to pay were deported from Kenya while Vidia was at the Kaptagat Arms. Vidia inquired and discovered what we had known all along, that Indians in Nairobi had helped lead the Kenyan struggle for independence. They had been discriminated against by the British, barred from living in certain areas, forbidden to grow cash crops, and kept out of clubs. After *uhuru* (independence) they were treated shabbily by Kenyatta's government. Now some were being thrown out.

Vidia was visibly a *muhindi*, an Indian. Even he said that he had gone several shades darker in the equatorial sun. His bush hat and walking stick were a poor disguise. He was now living in a country where a *muhindi* was unwelcome. 'Bloody Asian' was one of the less offensive ways Africans in Kenya referred to Indians, and *muhindi* was what the Kaptagat's servants called Vidia when they spoke among themselves.

Tough-minded, Vidia reacted in much the same way as he had in Uganda. Whenever he met Indians in Kenya, he challenged them, demanding to know their backup plans in case of trouble. He called it 'crunch time.' 'Very well then,' he would say after the first pleasantries, 'what are you going to do when crunch time comes?' He urged them to leave for India or Britain and to take their money with them – to teach the Africans a lesson. He quoted the *Gita*. He said, 'You must act.' But they smiled uneasily and said that he did not understand. He decided that Pat and I should go with him to Nairobi to discuss this matter with the Indian high commissioner and the US ambassador.

'Do you remember what I told you?' he said to me as we drove through the Rift Valley (*Beware of Fallen Rocks*) toward Nairobi. 'Hate the oppressor, but always fear the oppressed.'

I recognized the tone of voice from the main character in his novel in progress. It was also often Vidia's own tone of voice. Vidia and his hero agreed on most things, it seemed. They even used the same expressions, or 'locutions,' as they called them: 'latterly,' 'crunch time,' 'some little time.'

'I have been contemplating this visit to Nairobi for some little time,' Vidia said. 'Yes. Some little time.'

Nearer the Rift Valley escarpment we saw a sign saying *Hussain Co. Ltd. Sheepskin Coats for Sale*. Vidia said he wanted to see them, though I suspected he merely wished to lecture Mr Hussain. The coats were cheap. They were thick and bulky. Mr Hussain took our measurements and said he would make the coats to order. He would send them in a month or so.

'And what are you going to do when the crunch comes?' Vidia said to Mr Hussain after we paid our money.

'I have plan,' Mr Hussain said, wagging his head ambiguously.

When we were back on the road Vidia said, 'He was lying, of course,' and then, 'I wonder if I can bring it off?'

He was speaking of the sheepskin coat.

'Of course you can,' Pat said from the back seat, always the encouraging spouse.

'Perhaps in Scotland,' Vidia said.

There were giraffes in the distance, crossing the valley, and a herd of grazing zebra and clusters of gazelles.

'Frosty weather. Snow. I can see that coat being useful. But I don't know whether I can bring it off. I don't think I'm big enough in the shoulders.' After a moment he said, 'Paul, you must come to London. Meet real people. Bring your sheepskin.'

Nairobi was a small town with wide streets and a colonial air. 'Mimicry,' Vidia said, but he liked the Norfolk Hotel, its cleanness, its comfort. He quoted his narrator on the subject of hotels. After we checked in, he said he had the address of a Nigerian man here in Nairobi who had access to the Kenyans. At first Vidia wondered if it might be too much trouble – Pat had already decided to stay behind in the hotel room – but then he grew curious. It was always this curiosity that overcame his reluctance. The Nigerian at the very least would have a West African point of view. His name was Muhammed, and he was a Hausa, from the north of his country. He met us at the door of his apartment wearing a blue pinstriped double-breasted suit. Vidia introduced himself.

'Jolly good,' Muhammed said. He led us to a room with a large bookcase and offered us tea.

'That would be very nice,' Vidia said.

'What about some music?'

There were stacks of record albums on one shelf.

'No music. No music.'

'Jolly good.'

While we drank tea, Muhammed spoke with Vidia about the persecution of Indians in Nairobi, but instead of interrogating him, Vidia grew laconic and impatient. I just looked at the books. I saw *Tropic of Cancer, Tropic of Capricorn, The Kama Sutra, Naked*

Lunch, Lolita, Lollipop Lady, A Manual for Lovers, and others – variations on a theme.

Vidia was rising. 'We must go.'

Muhammed, stopped in midsentence, said, 'Jolly good.'

In the car, Vidia said he was disgusted.

'What's wrong?'

He made a nauseated face at Muhammed's building and said, 'Masturbator!'

It took him a while to calm down, but when his mood eased I said, 'I have to see Tom Hopkinson.'

'Hopkinson? The chap who was editor of *Picture Post*? He's in Bongo-Wongo?'

'Yes. Want to come?'

'One has no interest.'

I dropped Vidia at the hotel and spent the afternoon with Tom Hopkinson. He was a well-known editor and journalist, and his highly successful *Picture Post* had been Britain's answer to *Life* magazine. Hopkinson, in vigorous semi-retirement, ran the Institute of Journalism in Nairobi. It was my hope that he would come to Kampala and speak about freedom of the press at a conference I was trying to organize. A tall, thin, white-haired man, he was friendly and straightforward and clearly a Londoner: wearing a tie and long trousers and black shoes, he was overdressed for Kenya. We talked about novels – he had published two. He said he was too busy to give the lecture, but I suspected the rumors of violence in Uganda put him off. Most people in Kenya regarded Uganda as the bush.

'Tell me, tell me, tell me,' Vidia said that evening in the Norfolk's bar. He said nothing else, but I knew it was his way of asking about Hopkinson.

'He's writing a novel,' I said.

'Oh, God.'

'It's his third.'

'Oh, God.'

'He spoiled the first two, he said. He rushed them. He said he was not going to rush this one.'

Vidia gagged on his tea and released great lungfuls of laughter, his smoker's laugh that was so fruity and echoey.

'He's just playing with art.'

'He was a friend of George Orwell,' I said.

'One has been compared to Orwell,' Vidia said. 'It is not much of a compliment, is it?'

The Indian high commissioner in Nairobi, Prem Bhatia, gave a dinner party for Vidia. Now, as at the Kaptagat, I saw a contented Vidia: a respected visitor in the house of a man who admired his work. This role of guest of honor calmed Vidia and made him portentous and unfunny and overformal, and at the table he became orotund.

'One has been contemplating for some little time . . .'

Bhatia had been a distinguished journalist in India. He had lively talkative teenage children and the sort of ambassadorial household that was like a real family. It was not a stuffy party. Two dining tables had been set up in the courtyard of the residence for the Kenyan, Indian, and English guests. Vidia and his host sat at a head table.

As an elderly Sikh servant in a red turban poured wine, Bhatia followed him and said, 'Now do enjoy your wine, but be very careful of the glasses. They cost five guineas each. I had them sent from London.'

Hearing this, one of the Englishmen picked up his wine, drank it down, and flung the glass over his shoulder at the courtyard wall. The glass made a soft watery smash as it hit the flagstones.

There was a sudden hush. Bhatia kept smiling and said nothing. The Englishman laughed crazily – he might have been drunk. His wife, her head down, was whispering.

'Infy.' It was spoken loudly from the head table.

After the party, when all the guests had gone and the servants had withdrawn, Vidia talked in his pompous visiting-elder-statesman manner, which was also the tone of his narrator, whom he had told me was a politician. The subject was the Indians who had been deported.

'This is disgraceful,' Vidia said. 'How are you planning to respond?'

'We've lodged a very strong protest,' Bhatia said.

'You must do more than that,' Vidia said. 'India is a big, powerful country. It is a major power.'

'Of course –'

'Remind the Africans of that. Latterly, the Africans have behaved as though they were dealing with just another shabby little country. Latterly –'

'I've sent a letter.'

'Send a gunboat.'

'A gunboat?'

'A punitive mission.'

'I don't think so.'

'Shell Mombasa.'

'Who would do this?'

'The Indian Navy,' Vidia said. 'One has thought about this extensively. Send the Indian Navy on maneuvers off the Kenyan coast. Anchor off Mombasa – a fleet of ships. Remind them that India is a formidable country. Shell Mombasa.'

The high commissioner was frowning.

'Punish them,' Vidia said. 'When Mombasa is in flames they will think twice about persecuting Indians here. Aren't there fuel depots in Mombasa? Yes, they will leave the Indians alone for some little time.'

The following noon we were having drinks by the pool at the residence of the American ambassador, William Attwood. Vidia was in the midst of his punitive-mission speech when, without prelude, a large, smiling, familiar-looking African appeared. He said he wished to consult with the ambassador. They went into the house.

'He's asking for money, of course,' Vidia said. 'What else would he want? And did you see how fat he is? He's just another thug.'

After ten minutes the ambassador returned. He said the man was Tom Mboya, a leading politician and government minister.

'Mah-boya,' Vidia said.

'Very impressive man,' Attwood said. 'Mboya's going to be the next president of Kenya.'

Vidia simply stared. He was thinking, Fat thug.

Mboya never became president. Within a few years he was murdered by his political enemies.

The ambassador's wife joined us for lunch while Vidia continued describing the maneuvers in a possible punitive mission. The rant may have made the ambassador nervous, for, passing the sugar tongs to his wife, he bobbled them and dropped them. They skittered toward the edge of the pool and fell in.

'Never mind,' Attwood said.

We stared as the silver thing swayed downward and settled into the deep end of the pool.

Vidia said, 'Do you have a bathing costume that would fit me?'

'Lots in the changing room there,' said Attwood. 'We keep them for visitors.'

Vidia excused himself and was back in a few minutes wearing a blue bathing suit. Without a word he dived neatly in and propelled himself to the bottom – eight feet or so – and brought up the dripping sugar tongs, which he handed over. While the ambassador was still marveling at his athleticism, Vidia changed his clothes, and lunch resumed.

It was a reminder of his island childhood. He had been brought up near water and was clearly a wonderful swimmer – I could see it in the way he had launched himself off the edge of the pool, diving with hardly a splash, going deep without apparent effort. At that moment I saw him as a skinny child, diving off a splintery pier in Trinidad, in view of the anchored cruise ships. All his pomposity had fallen away and he had become graceful, a child of the islands.

The ambassador thanked us for coming.

'I think he needed to hear that,' Vidia said of his proposal to shell Mombasa and set it aflame. 'Did you notice how attentive he was? He at least realizes there is a problem. I know your people can do something.'

Over the next few days, in Nairobi's Indian restaurants and shops, Vidia demanded to know what the Indians would do when they were expelled. They had no future in Africa, he said. They had to make plans for crunch time now.

'Yet one has a vibration that the Indians won't rise to the occasion,' he said to me.

Passing Khannum's Fancy Goods shop on Queen's Road, Pat said she wanted to buy a few yards of printed cloth to use as a dust cover for a table in the room at the Kaptagat. Vidia and I waited on the verandah, where a small Indian girl of about seven or eight was sitting on a wooden bench being fanned by her African ayah. The girl wore a pink sari and long Punjabi bloomers and had the prim look of a child on her way to a party.

'*Jina lako nani?*' I said to the girl, asking her name in Swahili.

The ayah smiled and nudged her gently, a tender gesture that made the girl recoil and scowl at the servant in a bratty way. Vidia sighed – perhaps because I was speaking Swahili, perhaps because of the little-princess look of the skinny girl in her partygoing sari.

'*Wewe najua Kiswahili?*' I asked. Did she speak Swahili?

The ayah made the soft tooth-sucking cluck with pursed lips that meant yes in East Africa, but no sooner had she sounded this cluck – answering for the girl – than her mistress, silly little *toto*, scowled again and folded her arms.

'I am knowing wery vell how to speak Inglis!' she said.

'What a horrible child,' Vidia said, looking away. 'People are always writing magazine pieces about children – parents and children. They are foolish. I have no children. My publisher, André Deutsch, has no children. My editor has no children. It has been a conscious decision. People say, "You'd have lovely children" – the Indian-English thing. I do not want children. I do not want to read about children. I do not want to see them.'

Watching Vidia, the little girl seemed to understand that she was being insulted. Her large eyes had darkened with anger, and as she looked up at the man maligning her, Pat came out of the shop and said, 'Hello. What a sweet little girl. What's your name?'

'Nadira.'

I might have misheard. She spoke just as we were stepping off the verandah into the sunshine, but at the sound of her sharp voice, like the squawk of a mechanical toy, the three of us glanced back – Pat smiling, Vidia frowning in contempt. I was shaking my head, thinking, *Wahindi!*

Time is so strange in its logic and revelation. The little girl would go to Pakistan, and after thirty years passed (and Pat lay dying in a spruced-up cottage that was at that Nairobi moment tumbledown and lived in by a pair of elderly Wiltshire peasants) Vidia would meet the girl again, now grown up and divorced, never guessing where he had first seen her – nor would she – and fall in love.

How were we to know that little girl being fanned on the Nairobi verandah by her African ayah would be the future Lady Naipaul?

Back at the Kaptagat Arms, Vidia resumed his novel. He was also reading a Victorian account of travels in West Africa in which he came across the expression 'our sable brethren.' He began using the expression, building sentences with his other favorite phrases: 'For some little time, our sable brethren . . .'

Before I left for Uganda he asked me, 'So what are our sable brethren up to in Kampy, eh?'

There were rumors of trouble in Uganda, though nothing to do with Indians. I said, 'People say there's going to be a showdown between Obote and the Kabaka.'

'One will watch from here,' he said. 'Eh, Patsy? Latterly, one has begun to think that one's returning to Uganda would be completely foolish. Anyway, we were thinking of spending some little time in Tanganyika.'

The country had changed its name to Tanzania five years before, at independence, but Vidia went on using its colonial name, as he did Ghana's, always calling Ghana the Gold Coast. When he saw that using these names enraged Africans he did it even more, teasing them. He pretended not to know the new names, and when he was angrily corrected, he said 'Really' and expressed effusive thanks.

From Dar es Salaam he reported 'extensive buggery' and asked for news.

The news was bad in Uganda. This was in late May 1966, during the confrontation between the prime minister and the Kabaka – King Freddy. One Sunday four of the king's important chiefs were arrested on charges of sedition. Because they were so closely linked to the king, the chiefs' subjects, their villagers, became a mob and stoned the police. Early the next morning the Uganda Special Forces, commanded by Idi Amin, launched an attack on the Kabaka's palace at Lubiri.

All day there was fighting – the sound of cannon fire and automatic rifles firing in stuttering enfilade, raking the bamboo pickets of the stockade. From my office desk at Makerere I could see smoke rising from Lubiri. The shooting was continuous. In late afternoon there were still gunshots, and much darker smoke – the fires had taken hold.

'The Kabaka is holding them off with a machine gun,' my colleague Kwesiga said.

No one knew what was happening, though.

'Whose side are you on?' I asked him.

Kwesiga was of the Chiga tribe from the Rwanda border, a despised people who practiced wife inheritance – passing the widow on to the dead husband's brother – which was based on a curious marriage ceremony that involved the bride's urinating on the clasped hands of the groom and all his brothers. One of the wedding-night rituals required the bride to fight the husband, and should he prove weak – for she was expected to struggle hard – his elder brother was allowed to take charge, and subdue and ravish the woman while the groom looked on. Kwesiga was being summoned to take his recently widowed sister-in-law as one of his wives.

'I am an emotional socialist,' he said. 'But Freddy is a good king.'

In the evening the explosions were louder – mortars, perhaps. And flames were visible where during the day there had been smoke. At last the palace was captured, but when Amin and his men rushed inside, the Kabaka was not there. The clumsy siege of this wood and bamboo palace had taken an entire day and had not accomplished its objective. The Kabaka had escaped to Búrundi – dressed as a bar girl, one rumor went.

That was the first night of a curfew. It was illegal to be out of the house from seven in the evening until six in the morning. It was still light at seven, so confinement in bright daylight seemed strange. The enforced captivity and severe censorship also produced many rumors, often conflicting and violent-sounding: stories of arson and beatings and killings, the murder of Indians, cannibal tales and incidents of vandalism, humiliation of expatriates at roadblocks. The Uganda Army was said to be wild – furious that they had failed to capture the king. When darkness came, the gunfire started. I collected rumors in my specially begun curfew notebook.

Besides King Freddy, Kabaka of Buganda, there were three other kings. Sir William Wilberforce Nadiope, a fat little man noted for his bizarre robes and blustery speech, was Kyabazinga of Busoga. The Omukama of Toro was a twenty-year-old Mutoro named Patrick, whose sister Princess Elizabeth was a *Vogue* model. The Omugabe of Ankole was a cattle owner. When the Kabaka fell, the other kings caved in and went quietly, and the government commandeered their palaces – though 'palace' was a misnomer for what were actually comically lopsided houses.

The curfew was a period of intense confusion and fear. There was widespread drunkenness too, which added to the atmosphere of insanity. People boasted of their boozing. No one worked. The urgency about drinking was marked, because the bars closed at six P.M. in order to allow people time to get home. Food was scarce because the trucks from the coast were held up at the Ugandan frontier. Matches became unobtainable, no one knew why. There was much petty crime: robberies, looting, a settling of scores. People traveled in convoys if they were headed upcountry. Mail was suspended for a week. The distant gunfire continued, *pok-pok-pok*, until dawn.

The curfew was for me an extraordinary event; it was also the perfect excuse. I did no teaching. I got on with my novel. I spent the day collecting rumors – always violent, always of massacres. Indians often figured in them. My curfew notebook thickened and I considered writing a book like Camus's *The Plague*, describing the deterioration of a city during a siege and curfew.

I realized that in time of war or anarchy people lived out their fantasies. There were many fights, but just as many love affairs. Scores were settled because the police were not a presence – the army was in charge, but its roadblocks were used for intimidation and robbery and, if the rumors were true, killings. Roadblocks were always manned by the most thuggish and rapacious soldiers. Most were from the far north, from a minority tribe noted for its ferocity.

I carried my curfew notebook to the Staff Club. Each rumor had a date, a time, a place.

'What is the point of that?' one colleague asked.

I said, 'I want to calculate how many miles an hour a rumor travels.'

The breakdown of order had its excitements. People became reckless and slightly crazed. A Muganda man committed suicide after an atrocity in his village. His friends and family were summoned over the radio.

'He has hanged himself,' the announcer said.

My own fantasies took the form of being a real writer and writing all day. I had two books on the burner: my novel and this detailed curfew journal. In the late afternoon I hurried into town and got drunk as quickly as I could. I was energized by the tumult and the noise, which would, I knew, stop dead at seven, when we had to be indoors.

'Can you come home with me?' I asked when I saw a woman I liked.

Sometimes, without my asking, a woman would say, 'Take me home with you,' because it was more pleasant to be stuck in a large house than in a small hut in a turbulent township.

Boredom was the cause of all sorts of unruly behavior, and the streets were always littered with broken glass. I enjoyed the drama, the release from the routine, and found it a period of stimulating turmoil.

One day, hurrying home with a woman in my car, worrying about beating the curfew, I took a side road and a bat crashed against my windshield. It was a large fruit bat, and my thought was that it could have broken the windshield. I stopped the car, and before I knew what I was doing I began stomping on the bat, killing the injured creature. The woman in the car was screaming, 'Let's go!' The curfew was changing me, too.

Vidia was shocked by it. The curfew seemed to confirm his fears of African anarchy – casual violence and a climate of fear. From a distance it must have looked awful. He wrote from the Kaptagat Arms saying that he was just about through with his novel and that as soon as the curfew was over, and law and order was restored, he would return to Kampala.

And, 'May I use your spare room?'

I was just a young man in Africa, trying to make my life. He was one of the strangest men I had ever met, and absolutely the most difficult. He was almost unlovable. He was contradictory, he quizzed me incessantly, he challenged everything I said, he demanded attention, he could be petty, he uttered heresies about Africa, he fussed, he mocked, he made his innocent wife cry, he had impossible standards, he was self-important, he was obsessive on the subject of his health. He hated children, music, and dogs. But he was also brilliant, and passionate in his convictions, and to be with him, as a friend or fellow writer, I had always to be at my best.

I said, 'Of course.'

4

On Safari in Rwanda

The evening before we left for Rwanda, Vidia asked, 'What would you normally be doing tonight?'

I said, 'Going to the Gardenia.'

It was what I usually did before I left for the bush. I explained that it was a bar where strangers were welcome, and there were always women around.

He said, 'I want to see it.'

To tell him the Gardenia was a brothel would have made it seem more efficient, more of a business than it was; to describe it as a pickup joint would have misrepresented it as sleazy. It was an African bar, outwardly a hangout but in its complexity and character a sorority of rebellious women. Far from having the sexual ambiguity and low self-esteem of cringing, pimp-bullied Western prostitutes, these African women were as liberated as men. They were not castrators. The Gardenia was a sisterhood of laughing adventuresses and cat-eyed princesses.

Young and old, they had left their villages, because African villages were full of restrictions on women. Fleeing bad marriages, ditching boyfriends and family quarrels, escaping blood feuds and hoeing and child rearing and agonizing circumcisions in mud huts, they had come to Kampala for its freedom. Most came from upcountry districts, but some were from the coast and from as far away as Somalia and the Congo. At the Gardenia every woman's face was different. These women were not coquettes; there was no wooing involved – they wanted to dance – and as for sex, they were more direct than most men. If they wanted it, they said so, and if not, they did not waste your time. I went there to be happy; always I left in a good mood. If I happened to be going on safari, it was the best farewell.

I knew I was a dog, but so what? Such a lively place made me

hate polite company and loathe the tedium of dinner parties –
parties generally, all chitchat and ambassadorial bottom-sniffing.
Most of the expatriates lived at a great remove from the real
life of Kampala, and the diplomats were even more remote, and
consequently paranoid. From the embassy residences on Kololo
Hill this would have seemed like lowlife, yet African women fascinated me. Their common language was Swahili. Many spoke better
English than my students. They lived by their wits. They fluttered
like moths around the lights of these bars.

On the way to the Gardenia, Vidia said that Pat had gone to
London to put their house in order and prepare for his arrival in
about a month. She awaited his return. I thought fondly of her. I
said I hoped that, in time, I would be married to a woman who
would treat me this way.

'Marry a woman who can earn a few pence,' Vidia said. 'Then
you can get on with your writing.'

He smiled at the Gardenia. It was a friendly-looking place, a
three-story building on a side road at the edge of town, beyond
Bat Valley. It was brightly lit, with strings of light bulbs on its two
verandahs and more bulbs in the mango trees next to them. Several
women who stood on the upper verandah called out softly, welcoming us.

It was early, so there were many more women than men. The
miniskirt, popular that year in London, had arrived in Kampala,
but some of the women wore wraparounds and robes, and the
Somalis were dressed in white gowns. We were the object of their
attention. The women stared and smiled, but they would not sit
with us until they were beckoned.

Seeing us on the upstairs verandah talking, the women were
more teasing towards Vidia, because he apparently was not interested. They saw him as a challenge. Vidia debated what to drink.
He disliked beer and cheap wine. He asked for sherry. There was
none. He decided on a glass of *waragi*, banana gin – the word was
a corruption of 'arrack.' I drank pale ale and called to a woman I
knew, Grace.

'What is your *muhindi* friend's name?' Grace asked me in Swahili.

'Bwana Naipaul,' I said. 'But my friend is not a *muhindi*. He is
British.'

She laughed at the notion of this Indian's being British. Vidia looked content. He had picked up the word *rafiki*, friend. And this was clearly an abode of good humor and ease. The Gardenia had private rooms where people could lounge and canoodle without disturbance, but I never used them. I usually stayed awhile in the bar, talking, and then asked a woman if she wanted to go home with me, or go dancing. She nearly always said yes. Afterwards I drove her back to the Gardenia. A present was expected, but there was no set fee, never a specific sum. Often no money was asked for, and the woman feigned surprise when I handed over some twenty-shilling notes.

'*Muhindis* have lots of shillings,' Grace was saying.

'He is a writer. He has small-small shillings.'

Vidia frowned at the mention of *shillingi*. Money was on Vidia's mind, and therefore on mine. He constantly talked about the money he had lost in coming to Uganda.

The front door opened, a woman muttered *muzungu*, and I saw two burnt-nosed planters heave themselves into armchairs and yell for beer. The best-dressed drinkers were Africans, wearing suits and ties, and they mingled with Indians – the hard-drinking Sikhs, the more abstemious Gujaratis, the teetotal Muslims.

'I see perfect integration here,' Vidia said, and he laughed, repeating it in his usual way. I suspected that such a pronouncement was like a rehearsal for something he intended to repeat in another place (*And I sat back in the brothel and said, 'I see perfect integration . . .'*).

At just that detached and observing moment, as he was being so objective, I realized that, pleasant as he was, I did not want to be with him. How could I take a woman home with me? I was too self-conscious. And yet I wanted to, because we were leaving for Rwanda in the morning and I needed some sort of farewell.

As I brooded, Vidia said, 'When you come to London I want you to tell my brother that you sleep with African girls. I want you to shock him.'

'I don't get it. Why should he be shocked?'

'Because he's always talking this liberal nonsense. And he was brought up in Trinidad. Yet it would not occur to him to make love to a black woman.'

'That's too bad. He doesn't know what he's missing.'

And I also thought: This brother of his is a fool. I knew that he was at Oxford, studying Chinese, and that Vidia thought he was lazy. His name was Shiva.

'I think we've done this,' Vidia said.

'So you are leaving, then?' Grace said, seeing us stand up to go.

'Safari tomorrow,' I said.

'I want to dance,' she said. She raised her arms and took a few dance steps, African dance steps, swaying her hips. A whole message, an unmistakable promise, moved through her body.

'I am coming back for you,' I said, and I meant it.

At home, Vidia noticed my kitchen was dirty – dishes in the sink, food left uncovered, some scuttling cockroaches on the floor.

'Sack Veronica,' he said fiercely. 'Sack her!'

I said I would speak to her. I hated anyone criticizing my servants, especially Vidia, who didn't know her.

'At least have a row with her. It will keep her on her toes.'

A safari was not a hunting trip but any long journey upcountry. 'He's on safari,' people said when someone was out of town. But for our safari Vidia was kitted out like a hunter or a soldier: bush hat, bush shirt, thorn-proof khakis, and a stout walking stick that doubled as a club, should he wish to disable or brain an attacker. He wore heavy, thick-soled shoes that he called *veldshoen*, an Afrikaans word meaning skin shoes. Though he had a purposeful, marching way of walking, what wrecked this attempt to seem soldierly was his small size, his delicate hands, his tiny wrists. He had bought an expensive camera at a discount from an Indian shopkeeper in town. He wore it as an accessory, a big thing thumping on his chest or smacking his hip as he strode along. With his downturned hat brim and his downturned mouth and the way he sweated in these heavy clothes in the Ugandan hot season, Vidia appeared conspicuous and comic.

In those days of roadblocks and sneering soldiers, it was not a good idea to dress in a military way. Casual clothes were best, the less serious the better, to advertise nothing but innocence or naïveté. Any ostentation was seized upon. If you wore an expensive watch it would be taken. I worried that the simple brutes who manned the roadblocks outside Kampala would wonder about this *muhindi* in bush clothes with the severe expression. Soldiers wore hats identical to Vidia's khaki one. Indian shopkeepers never dressed this way, and being an Indian, Vidia would be seen as a shopkeeper. But I hadn't the heart to tell him any of this.

We set off through early morning Kampala just before dawn, when the roads were still clear. Africans got up with the sun and mobbed the roads in daylight; their bicycles and animals made it slow going. Even in the murky light we could see the effects of what was now known as the Emergency. The fall of the Kabaka meant that his kingdom was no longer the dominant province, and as if to prove it the soldiers had become an army of occupation. The whole city looked vandalized and neglected, there was garbage in the road, cars had been tipped over and burned – another rumor confirmed – and some houses and shops looted and torched.

'Good God,' Vidia said. 'But you see? I told you. It is going back to bush.'

We were stopped at a succession of military roadblocks and asked where we were going. At one of them the soldiers took an interest in Vidia's bush hat and sunglasses, but Vidia scowled back. One soldier said, 'Nice goggles,' and I thought he would demand them, but he just smiled in admiration.

Soldiers made Vidia nervous. These men had a fearsome reputation for incompetence and bad temper. They had recently been engaged in a messy full-scale siege and many of them had been involved in killing. I told Vidia how, during the Emergency, a Ugandan soldier had stopped an Indian friend of mine. The soldier's friends had called 'Hurry up!' to him from their Land Rover.

'What should I do with this *muhindi*?'

'Kill him and let's go,' one of the soldiers yelled.

'Please don't kill me,' my Indian friend said.

'Hurry up! Kill him and let's go!'

The soldier waved his rifle back and forth and was so flustered by the nagging of his comrades and the pleading of the Indian that he left the man standing, gibbering in fear, beside his car. There wasn't enough time to kill him. Many of the murders had happened in that casually violent way. *Kill him and let's go!*

'That scares the hell out of me, man,' Vidia said.

But soon there were no more roadblocks and we were on the open road, in sunshine, heading southwest in a swampy area near a stream called the Katonga, which drained into Lake Victoria a few miles south. The Katonga was famous for the density of its reeds – masses of papyrus, a lovely pale green plant with a feathery crown on its stalk that always reminded me of Uganda's connection to the Nile. Papyrus was Egyptian in its beauty; its image had been carved into ancient tombs along with hieroglyphics; it had been prized for its many uses – not just to make paper and cloth, but its pith was eaten and its root used for fuel. Yet in Uganda it was just another plant that choked the waterways and was good for nothing.

'Do you find those African girls frightfully beautiful?' Vidia asked. 'The ones at that bar?'

'Some of them, yes. Very beautiful. A few remind me of Yomo.'

'What do you hear from her?'

'She had an abortion and is planning to go back to college.' I had recently had a sorrowful note from her and a letter from her brother. 'The father of the child wouldn't marry her.'

'Oh, God.'

I could not say anything more. I missed her badly and my life had been empty since she left. We traveled ten miles before I spoke again.

'Do you find them beautiful?'

He thought awhile. 'No,' he said. Then 'No' again. And 'No' after another pause. 'But Derek Walcott is married to a woman of mixed race who is very beautiful.' He considered this. 'I could just imagine myself with her. Do you know Walcott's poetry?' He recited:

This island is heaven – away from the dustblown blood of cities;
See the curve of bay, watch the straggling flower, pretty is
The wing'd sound of trees, the sparse-powdered sky, when lit is
The night. For beauty has surrounded
Its black children, and freed them from homeless ditties.

'That word "ditties" sounds precious, but it is right somehow,' he said. And then he made his disgusted face and said, 'The narrator of my novel goes to prostitutes.'

He had a way of letting his narrator stand for him, and so I knew what he was driving at and we discussed the narrator.

'Frequents prostitutes,' he said, trying out the literary phrase. His expression was still sour. 'Afterwards, you hate yourself for being a man.'

That shocked me. Making love to a woman did not have that effect on me at all. Afterwards I was calm, happy, tired, at rest, the opposite of disgusted. I felt rewarded and fulfilled. Sex was magic, mind-expanding, enacted in energetic postures that I recalled later, seeing myself kneeling, standing, knotted, on all fours. It was knowledge, too – not blind lust, though wild monkey-lust was part of it, helping to illuminate the act, which was for me a source of serenity.

I enjoyed every aspect of it, from its first intimation, which was the woman's returned glance, to the quiver of anticipation, sensing my scalp tighten at the prospect, the warmth on my skin and my fingers becoming tremulous, the sense of blood beginning to pound behind my eyes and my breath coming in gasps, my chest tightening, my mouth dry, as though I were on a narrow path, working my way slowly into a jungle, following a bird with brilliant plumage and a flicking tail.

To touch a woman who wanted to be touched was for me the height of pleasure; to kiss her and be kissed with the same desire, to feel the great excitement of being touched by her, the pressure in every fingertip a wordless promise. I changed by degrees from a reflective smiling soul sifting through my dreams to an engine of desire, and my whole body burned. However casual the act may have seemed – for I had a tendency to mask my desire when I mentioned it – it was passionate and serious. It was the slap of bodies, the crack of bone on bone, and it left me breathless. There were groans of pleasure, but it was a profound raking of the nerves and a wrenching of muscles: no laughter, no jokes. In this descent into the deepest part of my body, I felt an inarticulate animal fury, like a drone in pursuit of the queen, frantic to mate. It exhausted me and helped me understand the single-mindedness of desire, the urgent monomania of the libido.

I said this in a simple form to Vidia, not wishing to reveal too much: that I loved being with a woman; that I was alone the rest of the time because there was no one in my life; that I hoped to meet someone and fall in love.

'But prostitutes can be so depressing,' he said.

'Maybe in Europe, but not here. This is Masaka, by the way.'

Mid-morning in Masaka, which was a stretch of Indian shops on either side of the road: fruit vendors and hawkers crouched near verandahs, the open-air businesses of bicycle mending and cobbling shoes, the bright clothing of the rural African women. Vidia fingered his camera but took no pictures.

'In Britain, I suppose they hate their customers,' I said. 'They're famous for hating men, aren't they? Here the women are eager, they're hungry. They take pleasure in it. Half of them are looking for husbands. They're not prostitutes in the classic sense. A lot of times they don't mention money. They just want to go dancing afterwards.'

'I was a big prostitute man at one time,' Vidia said. 'I was with a prostitute in London one day. It was in the afternoon. When we got to her room she said, "I saw you on the telly last night." It was one of those panel games.' He laughed at the incongruity of it, then murmured the woman's words again.

'Then what happened?'

'We talked about the television program!'

That I could understand. The African bar girls were full of opinions, about other tribes, about politics, about neighboring countries, about Indians. The women were sometimes religious and always superstitious. Many had children, some had husbands, but they were on their own. I knew that Vidia saw a vast cultural difference, and of course there was, but living in Uganda there was also common ground and like-mindedness. I saw aspects of my own temperament in them.

'I have often gone to Amsterdam and made myself sick, eating and drinking,' Vidia said. 'And then getting a woman, one of those Dutch prostitutes.' He made his disgusted face, frowning miserably, looking poisoned. 'You hate yourself.'

'I've never felt that, actually.'

'It's so dreadful,' he said. He was still talking and watching the road ahead but probably seeing the red-light district of Amsterdam or a whore's tiny room with its meretricious décor, the clock and the calendar and the horrible little dog.

'I've never been to Amsterdam.'

'You're a man and you're sick with it,' Vidia was saying.

'I hate it when they say "Hurry up." But that's not an African thing.'

'Or "Are you done yet?"'

'That's more your clock-watching Western hooker.'

Vidia laughed and said, 'Graham Greene goes to prostitutes all the time. He's absolutely addicted, so I'm told. Greene will be walking down a street at night. He will see one, catch her eye, then move on. Ten minutes later, still thinking about her, he will go back. You see, he becomes obsessed.'

'That has happened to me – a lot.'

Vidia had made it sound like a distraction, but it was deeper than that. When my work was done and I was alone, I looked for a woman and always hoped to find one who was looking for me.

'You're young. And I've seen your poems, Paul. All that libido!'

'Lord Rochester, that's me,' I said. 'But I sometimes get jealous if I see a bar girl I know with another man. Odd, isn't it?'

'Paul, Paul,' he said in an uncle-like way.

We jogged along the dusty road past thorn trees.

'I'd like to find a woman to marry,' I said.

'I met Patsy at Oxford. We got married in 1954. The ceremony was a small affair. She has always worked. That's good, you know. And it's rather grand being the history mistress at an English girls' school. She earns a few pence.'

'It would be great to be married to a woman with money.'

'I don't know,' Vidia said. 'But I was at university with a chap who was studying Malory. He had no money. His fiancée was very well off, though – had a sort of stipend. I used to say, "It will work beautifully. You have your Malory and she has her salary."'

Smiling beneath his sunglasses, he said he loved the expression 'lots of money.' Someone saying 'I have lots of money' tickled him. As we drove along he tried out the words, saying them in different ways: 'Lots of money . . . Lots of money . . .'

The road was dustier now, and in this rural district where passing cars were rare, Africans walked in the middle of the road, always barefoot, sometimes with their cattle. The women carried heavy-looking burdens on their heads, baskets of fruit or stacks of firewood.

We were traveling along the dry savannah to Mbarara and could see gazelles and antelopes and African buffalo and herd boys tending goats. I refueled at a new Agip station in Mbarara. We bought some fruit and ate it. Vidia would not eat anything he could not peel – a healthy rule in Africa. There would be no more fuel or food until Kabale, several hours down a winding road that climbed through the hills. The road slowed our progress, but there was hardly any traffic except the enormous trailer trucks that came at us down the center of the road from Rwanda and the Congo.

Vidia was alert the whole time, and talkative. At one point, speaking of discipline, he quoted a calypso song with approval.

'I thought you hated music,' I said.

'I do. But the calypso is something else.'

'Harry Belafonte.'

'A complete fraud.'

I sang, 'Ma-til-da, she take me money –'

'No, no.'

Vidia cleared his throat with the sudden scouring and hoicking of an asthmatic clearing his pipes, and after a moment a reedy sound vibrated in his throat – his voice, of course, but the words were fragile, rustling scraps of dusty tissue paper being slowly torn. I recognized at once the rattly sound of a wind-up phonograph, the needle on a revolving black disk, a quavering dirgelike song coming out of a huge scallop-edged horn: 'It was loooove, love alone, cause King Edward to leave his throne.'

'That sounds like an old record,' I said.

'I heard it on an old record.'

It was also the title of a story in *Miguel Street*, a book in which ten calypsos were quoted. So what was all this business about hating music? I didn't ask.

He had perfectly imitated the sound, as when my parrot, Hamid, mimicked the agony of the hinges of my door squeaking. I thought, Now I've heard everything.

On the subject of the calypso singers of Trinidad he was both knowledgeable and enthusiastic. The culture they sang about was tough, breezy, unsentimental. Vidia had written, in *The Middle Passage*, 'It is only in the calypso that the Trinidadian touches reality. The calypso is a purely local form.' It was important and peculiar, dealing with local life in the local language. *Tell your sister to come down, boy. I have something here for she.* That was Mighty Sparrow, whom Vidia called Sparrow. Lord Invader, another calypso singer, he called, familiarly, Invader.

One of Lord Invader's songs was 'That Old-Time Cat-o'-Nine,' which Vidia sang in his scratchy needle-on-record voice:

The only thing to stop these hooligans from causing panic in the
    island;
Well, I go by the government,
Say they need another kind of punishment,
I say one thing to cool on this crime
Is bring back that old-time cat-o'-nine –

He took a breath and, in the same tone-deaf voice that oddly affected me, sang the chorus:

That old-time cat-o'-nine
Bring it back!
That old-time cat-o'-nine
Hit them harder!
Send them to Carrera where it licks like fire
And they bound to surrender!

'Words to live by,' I said.

'Where are we?'

We had left the Kingdom of Ankole, ruled by the now emasculated and chastened Omugabe, and filled with wild game – antelopes (specifically, the Uganda kob) and elephants and zebras. We were approaching the Kigezi district, in the southwest corner of the country, where Uganda, Rwanda, and the Congo met. But the borders were obscure because they lay at a high altitude, among the volcanic Virunga Mountains, which were forested and thick with browsing gorilla families. The people here were called the Bachiga, who were sneered at for their diminutive size and their unusual customs. In addition to the urine ceremony, there was something called the fire dance, which encouraged sexual precocity in young boys. And, unlike the cow-tending, beef-eating Banyankole, the Bachiga ate monkeys.

Vidia wanted to know this. He wanted to know much more. He was the most wide-awake person I had ever traveled with. He needed to know the name of that river, that large tree, that flower, that mountain range, and when he saw a peak on the horizon, he had to know what it was called. It was called Mount Muhavura, 13,500 feet and beautifully shaped, like all these mountains, which were symmetrical cones, the very emblem of vulcanism, some of them still smoking.

He asked about my name. What was my reaction when people spelled it wrong?

'Everyone spells it wrong.'

'That's an insult,' Vidia said. He said he had once received a letter from Penguin Books addressed to 'V. S. Naipull.' It was from a man named Anthony Mott. Vidia replied, typing on the envelope, 'To A Mutt,' and began his letter, 'Dear Mr Mutt . . .'

It was a long journey. We talked about everything. After circling through the terraced gardens and stepped fields of the Virunga foothills, we came to Kabale, which lay in a steep green gorge. I stopped at the White Horse Inn, which was known for its hospitality. It was mid-afternoon, and we had hardly stopped since leaving Kampala in the early morning.

'I'm hungry,' I said.

Vidia did not move. 'You go ahead.' He smiled. 'I'll wait here.'

'Aren't you hungry?'

He yanked his bush hat lower on his head and said, 'Please go on. Don't worry about me.'

'Vidia,' I said. 'This might be a good place to stop for the night.'

'Oh, no. Not that. Not that.'

I could not understand his reluctance. I said, 'The only places between here and Kigali are two really tiny towns, Kisoro and Ruhengeri. The border might be closed by the time we get there.'

'We'll stop at Kisoro then, at the Traveler's Rest.'

'What's wrong with this hotel?'

At first he hesitated. Then he said, 'I couldn't possibly stay here. I've quarreled with the manager.'

'You were here before?'

'With Patsy.'

This was news to me.

'Quite a while ago. You were in the north. We stopped for lunch. I was quite taken with the place. It's Oldie Worldie, isn't it? But' – he made his disgusted face, his sour mouth – 'it was a mistake. I said I wanted to talk to the manager. When he came to our table, I said, "You have very strange rules here."

'"Strange rules? What do you mean?"

'"Rules governing the condition of your staff uniforms," I said.

'"We have no such rules. Only that they wear them."

'"Don't you have a rule saying that all staff uniforms must be dirty?"

'"No," he said.

'"Oh," I said, "I thought that, because they were all dirty, your staff must be obeying a rule.

'The manager glared at me. But I was not through. "The other rule I noticed was the one about serving. Whenever a plate or bowl is brought to the table, the waiter has his thumb stuck in the food. That's surely a rule, because they all do it."

'The manager fumed and said that if we did not like it, we could leave. I said, "With pleasure." But you see, he wanted to have a row. I'm afraid I obliged him. So it's better that I stay here. Take your time. Enjoy your lunch.'

But lunch had ended, so an African waiter told me. The manager confirmed this. He was a thin, irritable-looking man in a crumpled white shirt and club tie and black trousers.

'I'll have tea, then.'

'You'll have to take it in the lounge. We require a jacket and tie in the dining room.'

Over two hundred miles from Kampala, in the Virunga forest of wild Kigezi, among the pissing, monkey-eating Bachiga, where gorillas were commonplace and bird squawks filled the air, where everyone went barefoot and many women bare-breasted, I could not enter the dining room of the White Horse Inn without a tie knotted around my neck.

Sniffing defiantly at me, the manager shuffled papers and was gone. I had tea in the lounge: cookies, sandwiches with the crusts cut off, and fruitcake. An elderly African hovered next to me, pouring tea through a silver strainer, adding hot water to the teapot, smoothing the napkins.

'Did you see him?' Vidia said when we were under way again.

'Yes. He was rude to me. He said I needed a necktie to eat in the dining room. He stuck me in the lounge.'

'Infy.'

Before Kisoro, misreading a sign, I took a wrong turn. We traveled down a narrowing road that seemed to be going nowhere except into deeper forest, one that had only thickened and risen and never been cut, where there were no huts, no straying chickens. Such a place, like the Ituri and the woods near Lake Edward and some others, was distinctive for its darkness, the green-black shadows of dense ferns under a tall canopy of foliage.

After twenty minutes in that dark forest we came to a border post with a wooden shed, a barrier, and a few men wearing colorful shirts. They were drinking beer and smoking cigarettes. I saw the pack in one man's shirt pocket with the name Belga. It was Primus beer. Congolese brands. We were on the wrong road.

'*Bienvenue à la frontière congolaise,*' one man said, swigging beer and welcoming us.

Vidia was delighted. The Congo! He spoke to the man in beautifully accented French. '*Incroyable! Nous n'avions aucune idée que nous nous dirigions vers le Congo!*' he said. We had no idea we were headed for the Congo!

'*Monsieur, vous êtes au Congo,*' said the beer-drinking man with the loudest shirt, its pattern of big red poppies like a mark of his authority. The Congo is here, sir. His foot was propped on the barrier, a rusty horizontal pipe.

They bantered for a while and Vidia finally said, '*C'est dommage que nous allons à Rwanda.*' It's a shame that we're going to Rwanda.

'*Rwanda est par là,*' the man said. Rwanda is that way. '*Mais retournez un jour et visitez le Congo.*' Come back sometime and visit our country.

I reversed the car and drove away from the shed, heading back the way we had come. This was the easternmost border of the Congo, as distant as it was possible to be from Leopoldville. I kept thinking of that Congolese frontier post, the little shed, the tiny postern to a great and enigmatic castle of a country.

'They seem far less foolish when they're speaking French,' Vidia said. 'It doesn't sound like rubbish in French.'

At the Rwanda frontier the formalities were cursory, and Vidia muttered the French words the soldiers used as they examined our papers, repeating their mispronunciations.

As we left the border post I said, 'I forgot to ask them what side of the road to drive on.'

'Oh, God.'

Just then a large trailer truck approached, throwing up dust, traveling down the middle of the road. In Uganda we drove according to British custom, on the left, but Rwanda-Burundi had been a Belgian colony, and surely they drove on the right.

'The moment of truth,' I said, and swerved and began driving on the right.

The truck, a beer truck, carrying a load of loudly jingling empty bottles in wooden crates, passed us in a fury of noise and gravel, and a dust cloud obscured the road for the next two hundred yards.

The dust settled like a view in a telescope twisting sharply into focus, and the looming scene was that of a mob, the road filled with people moving like a ghost army through the sifting-down dust particles in a distortion that was splashed with light. They were tall and thin, the women carried bundles, there were many children and some animals – dogs and goats. It was the sort of exaggeration for effect that could have been a stock scene in a Tarzan movie – a crowd of toothy implacable natives, and a terrifying sight because the whole road was claimed by them. There was no space for us to proceed.

'What is this?' Vidia was nervous.

The mob parted slowly, reluctantly, as my car penetrated it like a dinghy nosing through an ocean of breaking chop. Passing the car, the people peered in, screwing up their faces and pressing against the windows.

'Probably the market just closed and they're heading home,' I said, trying not to sound as alarmed as I felt.

'They're blocking the road, man.'

He was very jittery, whispering wildly – a whole crowd of Rwandans compressed into a narrow road and no other traffic, just my little car inching along against the chop of gaping people.

'I don't like mobs at all,' he said.

But even after I got past them and the road cleared – although there were always crowds of people on Rwanda's roads – it was still slow going. The road was a deeply rutted track lined with elephant grass. Further on, we went higher and could see Mount Muhavura close up: the intensively cultivated slopes, the masses of mud huts. I told Vidia that Rwanda was the most densely populated country on earth.

'What are these people like?' he asked, returning the stares of the people passing.

'Pretty violent,' I said, and told him how, four years before, at independence, there had been a gruesome uprising, the Hutus against the Tutsis. The Hutu people had been a despised underclass, and their tremendous resentment erupted into a massacre. A journalist friend of mine had actually witnessed Hutus torturing Tutsis. They hacked the Tutsis' feet off and forced them to stand up. Then they cut their legs off at the knees and laughed as the Tutsis were propped on their bleeding stumps. More mutilation followed: the cutting off of ears, of noses, eye gouging, castration, all of it while the victims were alive. Hundreds of thousands of Tutsis had been butchered in this way, and so the country had been partitioned, the Tutsis taking Burundi, the Hutus Rwanda.

Vidia listened, horrified, grimacing. The car filled with dust that whirled into the open windows. To close the windows would have suffocated us. Now Vidia had started humming a tune.

'Toot-toot-Tutsi, goodbye,' he sang in an Al Jolson voice. 'Toot-toot-Tutsi, don't cry.'

We came to the crossroads of Ruhengeri. To the left was the road climbing to Kigali, to the right was the way to Kisenyi and Goma. We sat and pondered this in the slanting sun. Vidia ate a cheese sandwich and drank a cup of coffee from a thermos. Even in this remote place, where food was scarce, he kept to his strict dietary rules.

'There's a better chance of finding a place to stay in Kigali,' I said, and he agreed: it was, after all, the capital. We had no reservations, no prearranged route; we were simply on safari, winging it in the bush.

Dusk like ground fog obscured the road as we entered Kigali, but even so, we could see that the town, though crowded, was very small. That was the Rwanda problem: so many people, so little space. There were three or four hotels, none of them good. We stopped at each one. Vidia expressed first amazement that we were stopping at all – 'Such low places' – and then, inevitably, discouragement. There was no room for us.

'They're filthy,' he said.

'Maybe they just look dirty.'

He did not laugh. 'What are we going to do?'

'Let's try the US embassy.'

It was now past seven in the evening, and after more than thirteen hours on the road it now seemed that we had no place to stay. The embassy was closed, but we found an American woman on the premises – the duty officer, she said, dealing with a consular problem.

'We are totally stuck,' I said, and explained that I was an American, a lecturer at Makerere University. 'We have no place to stay in Kigali. Is there anything you can suggest?'

'We have a guesthouse,' she said. 'You can use that.'

I then introduced my distinguished friend, the visiting lecturer and writer V. S. Naipaul. The duty officer had not heard of him, but never mind, there would be no problem. She drew me a map to the place, which was near the center of town. So we were saved, and we each had a room. She even suggested a restaurant where we might eat. Vidia relaxed – I could sense it from a few feet away, what he would have called a vibration. Cleanliness and order were everything to Vidia. He was relieved and consoled by this sudden intervention.

'This is perfect,' he said at the embassy guesthouse, yet he sounded sad, and I guessed that he was tired.

On a back street in Kigali we found the restaurant, which had a pompous French name, something like La Coupole. Vidia still looked melancholy, perhaps because we had been so lucky here. He had once told me how he had a cynical Hindu nature and that he was suspicious of good luck, believing that it attracted bad luck.

The restaurant was small, and warm with aromas of good food, herbs, and fresh bread. It was full of people, Africans and whites, all of them talking. The manager was a thin Belgian woman in late middle age. She was clearly harassed yet gentle and helpful, entirely at our service, apologizing for being so busy. She brought us a bottle of wine. Vidia tasted it and said it was first rate and grew even sadder as he spoke of how amazing it was to find a great wine in such a crummy town. The woman, flattered by Vidia's praise, became even more solicitous. She chatted with him, complimenting him on his fluent French. I had a glimpse of Vidia's sympathy and compassion. He was moved by the good nature of the woman, who was struggling to run a decent restaurant in this remote place. He admired her the way he admired the Major at the Kaptagat, seeing someone fighting to overcome the odds, bringing order to chaos, a sort of colonizer. The woman moved among the tables, setting out dishes, filling glasses, advising waiters, folding napkins, rearranging forks. Where was this fish from? Vidia wanted to know. Lake Kivu, she said.

He praised the woman with feeling. He watched her work. Then he looked around and said, 'In a few years, this will be jungle too.'

He had not ceased to be melancholy. He ate his fish. I tried to draw him out on the subject of vegetarianism, but he was monosyllabic and unwilling. He drank most of the wine. It was a good bottle, he repeated. Why was he unhappy?

'You Americans are so lucky,' he said at last. 'You come from a big, strong country. You are looked after. If there was trouble here or in Uganda, serious trouble, your government would send a plane for you. You would be airlifted out.'

'They were promising that during the Emergency and the curfew,' I said. 'But I was having a good time.'

'You're a writer. That's why you don't go insane. You can define and order your vision. That is so important. If you didn't, your life in Kampy would be insupportable.'

It vitalized me to hear him say this. What had I written? Poetry, some essays, part of a novel. What had I published? Hardly anything. Yet to V. S. Naipaul, a writer I admired, I was a writer. He had seen it as much by reading my essay as by reading my palm.

'What's all this about being airlifted out?'

'The embassy here, man. Your embassy. We had no place to stay. They provided it. Don't take it for granted.'

'What would have happened if we'd gone to the British embassy?'

'Nothing, man. Nothing.'

'I'm sure your country would help you if you were stuck.'

'I don't have a country,' Vidia said.

Now I knew why he was sad.

Kigali, not anything like a capital, was pitiful even by African standards. There were few streets and no buildings of any size. It had no breadth, it had no wealth, and it was dirty. The paved road ended at the edge of town. Yet Kigali swelled with people, who had flocked to find work and food, to feel safe in a crowd. The Hutus thronging the place had the watchful covetous gaze of hungry people, and when they set their eyes on me they seemed to be looking for something they could eat, or else swap for food. They lingered near the market, along the main street, and at the church that was called a cathedral. Easily seen from the main street were slums and shantytowns on the nearby slopes.

'I think we've done this,' Vidia said.

He said he did not want to see the cathedral. Churches filled him with gloom. He wanted to avoid the market. Mobs, he said. The crush of people. The danger, the stink. The colonial architecture, the shop fronts, the high walls of yellow stucco with glass shards planted on the top, the tile-roofed houses, all these Belgian artifacts, he said, were already looking neglected and would soon be ruins.

He saw the roots of a banyan forcing their way into the paved sidewalk and pushing at a wall, the knees and knuckles of the roots visible in broken masonry and paving stones.

'The jungle is moving in.'

We left Kigali in the heat and traveled back the way we had come, on the winding rutted road, to the crossroads at Ruhengeri. Again the road was almost impassable because of all the pedestrians.

'This road is black with people,' Vidia said.

At the same café, Vidia sat under a beer sign and ordered another cheese sandwich. I thought, Vegetarians eat an awful lot of cheese. I ate an enamel plate of stringy chicken and rice. We were watched by kneeling Hutus as we ate. When we left, we took the road that led west, to the border town of Kisenyi, on Lake Kivu. The place was famous for its smugglers' dens. Like most of the Congo's border towns, it was said to have an air of intrigue because it was also the haunt of white mercenaries, who had names like Black Jack and Mad Mike and Captain Bob. There was often trouble in the Congo's large eastern province of Kivu and in the southeastern province of Shaba. When fighting broke out, refugees fled across the border. From time to time, angry expatriates or white mercenaries would take over a Congolese town, causing a panic flight of people into Rwanda.

The people on this road could well have been refugees, for there had been fighting near Goma in the past month. But after a while there were no people at all. The empty road cut through yellow woods that gave way to greener, denser forest, and the car labored on stony inclines that were the foothills of more assertive volcanoes. On one of the bends of this road stood a man in a white shirt and dark pants, holding a basket. He waved as we approached him.

'Don't pick him up,' Vidia said.

But I had already begun to slow the car.

'Why are you stopping?'

'Maybe he has a problem.'

The man leaned at the window. '*Pouvez-vous m'emmener à Kavuma? J'ai raté le bus*,' he asked. Can you take me to Kavuma? I missed the bus.

'Get in,' I said, in English and then in Swahili.

Sliding into the back seat, the man apologized for not speaking English.

Vidia said, '*Mon français n'est pas particulièrement bon, mais bien sûr c'est comme ça. J'ai peur que vous ne soyez contraint à supporter cet accent brisé.*' My French is not particularly good, but of course that is the way it is. I am afraid you will have to endure this corrosive accent.

'*Vous parlez beaucoup mieux que moi*,' the African said. You speak much better than I do.

Vidia protested this, even a bit crossly, and then he fell silent, and so did the African. Vidia was angry. He had not wanted me to pick up the hitchhiker. He believed that Africans often took advantage of expatriates.

Ten miles down the road, the African said, '*Mon village est près d'ici.*' My village is near here. Getting out, he once again complimented Vidia on his French, and he vanished into the trees.

Before Vidia could say anything, I said, 'I spent two years in Africa without a car. I hitchhiked everywhere. People picked me up. That's why I picked him up.'

Vidia said, 'Let the idlers walk.'

He sniffed and made a sour face, twisting his lips. The man's pungent earthen odor lingered in the car. I said nothing for a few miles.

'This is the bush. People depend on each other.' I could see that he was not impressed. 'Anyway, it's my car.'

What was his problem? Years later Vidia said to an interviewer, 'I do not have the tenderness more secure people can have towards bush people,' and he admitted that he felt threatened by them. But who were 'bush people'? Anyone – African, Indian, *muzungu* – seeing the dusky distinguished author V. S. Naipaul standing beside any road in East Africa would have grunted, '*Dukawallah.*' Shopkeeper.

We got to Kisenyi in the late afternoon, having had to go very slowly on the hilly road. Kisenyi was a lakeside town of villas and boarding houses and several hotels. We chose one at random, the Miramar, which was run by an elderly Belgian woman. She had untidy hair and wore a stained apron, but she seemed a kindly soul. You knew what such people were like from the way they talked to their African servants. She spoke to her staff in a polite and patient way that was clearly masking her exasperation.

Belgians – just one family, but a large one – filled the dining room, and, being related, they were uninhibited: they shouted, they worked their elbows, they reached across the table for more food. We ate at the same table, family style. Vidia winced and seemed to lose his appetite as he watched the display of boisterous manners, the chewing, the squawking women, the shouting, growling men.

The Miramar was more a boarding house than a hotel, with an intimacy, a disorderly domesticity, the shared facilities meaning intrusions on privacy – the bathmat was wet most of the time, bedroom doors were usually left ajar. Vidia, intensely private, hating proximity and confidences, disliked the place from the first and found the dining table, this common board, unbearable for its quarreling, gnawing Belgians. He hated their appetites. He said the Miramar smelled. He loathed the Belgians for their being big, pale, overweight, loud, ravenous, unapologetic. 'Potato eaters,' he called them.

By contrast, the Africans here were tall, dark, skinny, whispering, and whipped-looking. I mentioned to Vidia that I thought they were Watutsi.

'Toot-toot-Tutsi, goodbye,' he said. 'But you wonder how they stand these Belgians.'

He had hardly touched his food. He had eaten the fish. He disliked salad. 'What kind of a vegetarian hates salad?' the Major had muttered to me. The Belgian food was heavy and meaty.

'I think we've done this,' Vidia said.

We left the dining room early, before dessert was served.

'I don't think I could stand watching these Belgians having their pudding.'

It was his first experience of the true bush settler in Africa. I had seen such people in Malawi and Zambia and Kenya, but these Belgians were the apotheosis of the type. You knew their days were numbered. They were farmers and mechanics and operators of heavy equipment – tractors and road graders. They were clever at fixing cars. They mended machines with the simplest tools. They drove the largest trucks. They had maintained the colony but, newly independent, the black republic would find them too expensive and ornery and would send them away. Without these simple capable folk keeping it maintained, the country would begin to fall apart. Although I always doubted it, I often heard that there was idealism in colonizing; but really, whenever the word 'colony' was mentioned, especially in Africa, I thought of these simple-minded mechanics. And I suspected that when Africans talked about whites, it was the mechanics and their attitudes they were usually denouncing.

'Let's get out of here.'

We went for a walk in the darkness, keeping to a path near the lakeshore. At the far end of the road, the Congolese town of Goma was visible. Goma was better lighted than Kisenyi.

'This deteriorating road. These crummy houses,' Vidia said.

I told him my thoughts about colonials as mechanics.

'My narrator mentions how a society needs to be maintained,' he said.

'Your novel,' I said, 'is it based on a sort of political memoir?'

'Not exactly. I had to find a form for it. It was terribly difficult.'

We had walked through the center of town, past a bandstand, an abandoned fun fair, and some banners and lights strung across the main street. We came to a part of the road that was severely potholed and with villas that were shuttered and rundown.

'I suffered over it,' he said. 'I wasn't sure how to tell the story. One day it came to me, the structure. I was so pleased. I called Patsy at her school. I said, "I've got it."'

It was easy to imagine Vidia doing this, but I could not see myself on the phone, calling my wife and telling her about my unwritten book. Anyway, I had a book, but where was my wife? The whole business seemed enviable, someone caring that much about my writing. I had been working in the dark, just groping, until I had met Vidia.

'When I started out, I found it so hard to write I got sick,' he said. 'I couldn't do it. I couldn't perform the physical labor of it. It exhausted me.'

I knew better than to tell him that I did not find the process of writing difficult. I sat, I wrote, the words came. I did not suffer. But he distrusted writing that was so fluent. 'When it comes easily, throw it away. It can't be any good,' he said. There had to be an element of struggle in all writing, which reflected a struggle in life. It was also why he hated hitchhikers.

Writing was a relief to me. Everything else was a struggle. I knew that I was nowhere – just a teacher living alone in the middle of Africa. It had been my luck to meet Vidia, but now he spoke all the time about leaving. He made it sound as though he were going to the center of things, back to his house, his friends, parties, his publisher, his wife, his life. I did not envy him his fame, or the glamour, but I admired the life he had made for himself.

'This is already starting to go back to bush,' he said. 'Look, the jungle.'

As in Kigali, the sidewalks were erupting. The glass-spiked walls around the lakeside villas were cracking. Some walls had been vandalized, others had been painted with slogans or had political posters stuck to them. It was tropical Belgium, suburban Brussels gone jungly, penetrated by rubber trees and fungoid growths. Colonial decrepitude depressed Vidia, but it fascinated me – the crumbling houses, the chipped cornices, the remnants of the dead past, the Africans squatting against the high walls that were scorched and blackened by their cooking fires.

I told him this.

'Horror interest,' he said.

We walked on.

'I am going to see André when I go back,' he said.

André Deutsch was his publisher. He was still thinking about his novel, thoughts I had provoked with my questions about writing.

'I am going to say, "André, I want a thousand pounds for this book."'

It seemed a great deal of money to me, yet it was less than I earned in a year on my Uganda government contract.

'I think he'll understand,' Vidia said. 'I think he'll give it to me.'

We were still walking in the empty rubbly road, the fallen leaves and blown papers unswept, in the middle of Kisenyi, among the darkened villas, hearing the lap of lake water where the night was blackest.

The dogs did not warn us – perhaps they were watching, waiting for us to walk closer. At first there was no barking at all. But it was soon clear that we had gone too far into the residential part of the town, for we were at once beset by a pack of dogs, panting in fear and effort, and only when we were surrounded did they begin to bark. They barked horribly, all their teeth bared, their neck fur bristling. They made odd choking noises. They slavered near my ankles and sounded crazy, as though they were going to kill us and eat us – that hunger and cruelty and strength were in their barking.

'They've been trained to attack Africans,' Vidia said.

He was calmer than I expected. I retained a childhood fear of aggressive dogs. 'They know you're afraid,' people had said. 'That's why they're barking.' That was crap. Most dogs were wolfish and reactive and pack-minded, which is why they barked. Their owners were the alpha males, encouraging this behavior in the dog, their weapon, their slave.

'*Kwenda! Kwenda!*' I yelled – Go away! – believing they might know Swahili. This only maddened them more.

Vidia was careful not to turn his back to the dogs, which were perhaps both guard dogs and strays. He lunged at them and made as if to punt them.

'What they need is a kick.'

The dogs scattered, moving back but still barking fiercely.

'If they felt this *veldshoen* on their hide, they'd know it.'

He was wearing his heavy shoes and swinging his walking stick. His bush hat was crammed on his head. Seeing the dogs react, he went after them again, driving them further back. I was impressed by this small man in the dark street of a remote African town, taking on the dogs.

They did not stop barking. In fact they barked louder, protesting, after Vidia intimidated them. But now we were able to move along. I was grateful to him. He had not been fazed in this showdown. He was frowning.

'Another one-whore town,' he said.

The Belgian family were still quarreling when we got back to the Miramar. They were in the lounge, drinking coffee and shouting amid the glaring table lamps. There were armchairs and doilies and footstools and little porcelain shepherdesses on shelves and framed lithographs of Liège and Ghent and Antwerp. An African servant stood in the hallway, doing sentry duty, holding a tin tray, waiting to be summoned.

'It's all so crummy.'

Yes, I saw that, but I also felt it was a glimpse of the colonial past, a curious antique that was now worn out and broken. I did not really think that the jungle was moving in, as Vidia had said. I felt that this Belgian culture would be displaced by Rwandan culture and that we had no way of anticipating what it might be.

'Is your business always this bad?' Vidia asked the Belgian proprietress of the Miramar, in his challenging way.

The big woman shrugged and matched his directness, saying, 'Business is good whenever there is a revolution in the Congo.'

The next day we drove across to Goma and had lunch at a café on Lake Kivu. Cheese sandwiches again: Africa was an unrewarding place for a vegetarian.

'I will meet you at "the coffee," they say in France and Italy and Spain. Even quite educated people make that simple mistake.' He saw that I was only half listening. He said, 'You are thinking about your writing.'

'No,' I said. But I had been – the simple problem. How did I get from where I was to where he was?

'Are you sure you want to be a writer?' he asked. 'It's a terrible profession. Yes, you have your freedom. But it can kill you if you're not up to it.'

I said I was up to it.

'Come to London. I will introduce you to some people.'

I said I would try to visit, perhaps at Christmas.

'These people are infies. They know nothing. Their leaders – Ian Smith, for example –'

Ian Smith had recently issued a unilateral declaration of independence in Rhodesia, and a minority of whites were governing the country.

'– Ian Smith is an infy. He is qualified to mend bicycles in Surrey. Nothing more than that.'

Vidia had been looking into the distance as he had been talking. After we finished lunch, he suggested we walk down the adjacent road. When we were on it I realized he had been looking at a sign that said *R. J. Patel*, and that evangelism was on his mind.

'Hello,' the Indian shopkeeper said, smiling at the Indian in the bush hat who had just entered his shop. 'You are not Congo people. I am knowing.'

'We're from Uganda,' I said.

Vidia got to the point. 'How is business?'

'So-so. Not bad. People are needing. I am exclusive stockist for a large variety of goods.'

'Do you have a family?'

'That is my daughter,' Mr Patel said, gesturing at a young woman near the shelves whose back was turned. Mr Patel was standing before a large basin heaped with salt. 'She is running shop. I am attending to so many other businesses.'

'What sort of businesses?'

'Too many to tell you,' Mr Patel said. He opened his mouth wide and the approximation of a laugh came out of it. 'This is just a simple shop. My other businesses occupy my time. Properties also.'

'But the money here is worthless,' Vidia said. 'How do you manage?'

'I am managing. I have many ways.'

'So you're not worried?'

'Ha! I am doing very well.' *Wery vell* was what he said.

He began filling a paper bag with scoopfuls of salt, murmuring with each scoop.

'What will you do when the crunch comes? The crunch is coming, you know.'

'I have my ways,' Mr Patel said. He had grown solemn under Vidia's questioning. He was still scooping, murmuring, crinkling the brown paper bag. 'I will be okay.'

'And your daughter?'

'She will be all right.' He then went silent. He said, 'Excuse me,' and turned his back on Vidia.

'So what do you think?' I asked.

We were out of the shop, swinging along the empty Goma road, Vidia marching like a soldier.

'He's lying.'

He had not believed a single word the man had said.

'He can't move his pence. The Africans will take his shop and all his goods. He's lying about those other businesses. And look what he's doing to his daughter, forcing her to work there.'

Lake Kivu was dull silver under a gray equatorial sky that sagged with humidity. The grayness gave the trees along the lakeshore a dark, impenetrable look. People on the street stared at us, though the soldiers in their faded uniforms did not glance our way but walked heavily past, stirring up the dust in big clomping boots. Their boots and their rifles were old-fashioned and indestructible-looking. Music played, the Congolese songs that sounded Brazilian, with marimbas and blaring trumpets. Soldiers, waifs, dogs, chickens, and broken signs in this distant corner of the Congo.

'He's a dead man,' Vidia said of R. J. Patel. 'They're all dead men.'

I had heard him say that before, in Kampala and Nairobi. But I had believed Patel when he said he would be all right. And I had been excited at being in the heart of Africa. It seemed to me that if you put your finger on the middle of a map of the continent it would be on this place, Goma, this muddy lakeshore. I tried to see it with Vidia's eyes, but I could not. I had neither lived his life nor written his books. He made up his mind quickly: observation for him was about drawing conclusions. I knew that whatever I wrote would be different from his view. It was probably a good thing that he did not ask me what I thought.

'I'm glad I saw this,' he said. 'Now I think it's time to go.'

Another night at the Miramar, among the squabbling Belgians and the food-strewn dining table and the overbright lamps, and then we were off to Ruhengeri again and the Uganda border. We stopped only to snap pictures at a dramatic curve, dangerous for its being unprotected, over an abyss called the Karnaba Gap. I was wearing my tweed jacket and my horn-rimmed glasses that gave me a scowling expression.

'I think you will do well,' Vidia said. He was upbeat, cheerier now that we were heading home.

I had turned twenty-five in April. I had not published anything outside Africa. I ached to have a publisher for my novel. In a halting way, I told him so.

'Don't worry,' he said. 'The most important thing is to avoid making an enormous amount of money before you're forty. Promise me you won't do that.'

I made this promise, that I would not make my fortune in the next fifteen years.

'Concentrate on your writing. After you're forty, fine – make all the money you like.'

Vidia was well under forty, yet he seemed older than my father.

We drove on, up and down the Kigezi hills, squeezing the car around corners, into the savannah again, past the big game and the long-legged herons and the marsh of papyrus, under the vast African sky. It was all familiar now.

Back in Kampala, at my house, where he was still a guest, I was full of his talk and of ideas I wanted to write down. Even before I had a bath or washed off the dust of the safari, I hurried to my study and sat and began to write.

Passing the room, Vidia looked in and exclaimed, 'Yes!' He was delighted. 'I used to do that. Sometimes at night, after we got home from a party I would go to my room and write, just like that, without even taking my coat off.'

He stepped into the room and glanced at the pages. He was looking at them upside down. I was about to turn them so that he could see, but he said, 'No, I'm not reading. I'm looking at your handwriting.'

He looked closely.

'Yes. Yes. Yes.' He nodded. 'It's not American. It's distinct. Hasty. Intelligent. It's you.' This was more of his approval.

For weeks he had been speaking eagerly of leaving Uganda, of going back to London. Before he left, he gave me a necktie he had brought from England. 'I knew I would meet someone to give this to. I want you to have it.' It was new and very narrow – that was the style – and orange. It was still in its shallow box. I never wore ties, but I was grateful for the gift. He gave me another gift the day he left. He told me in detail a dream he had had, which concerned his brother and a murder he had committed. I listened closely, and when he was gone I wrote the dream down in my notebook.

I was sorry to see him go. I was losing my teacher, and he had also become my friend. It mattered to me that he took me seriously, that he treated me like a fellow writer. No one else did, but that did not matter, because I had him.

Then an unexpected thing happened. I had never been homesick in Africa, nor had I despaired at what I saw. I was there to work and was grateful for the job. I liked my life. I was self-sufficient. Some days I was Albert Camus, a schoolteacher in remote Algeria. Some days I was George Orwell, preparing to shoot an elephant. There were days when I was myself, writing something that I believed had never been written before, that would surprise the world. But when Vidia left on the plane from Entebbe, I drove back to town feeling lonely, and my loneliness stayed with me. From then on, I liked the place less. I had begun to see it with his eyes and to speak about it using his words.

He had believed in me. He had talked about how in writing you served an apprenticeship. He said we were freer than any writers had been in the past. 'We are free from dogma, religious and political dogma. Use that freedom.' I remembered the many times that he had peered into my face ('a man's life is in his face') or traced my palm and said, 'You're going to be all right, Paul.' What did he see?

A note of comedy crept into my writing. It was an effect of my loneliness, and it startled me, but it gave me vitality. And it seemed more authentic than the solemnity it had displaced. I began to understand that the truest expression of life was humor, especially at its most disturbing. Much of what happened in Africa was not tragedy but farce. It was the influence of Vidia.

Friendship is plainer but deeper than love. A friend knows your faults and forgives them, but more than that, a friend is a witness. I needed Vidia as a friend, because he saw something in me I did not see. He said I was a writer. He spoke about it with his customary directness. That meant everything to me, because I had no idea what I was going to do next.

And I certainly had no idea that my meeting with Vidia would loom so large in my life, or his. But long after this, in an introduction to one of Vidia's books, the English critic Karl Miller wrote, 'The novelist Paul Theroux was with Naipaul in a disrupted Uganda, rather as one might once have been said to have been with Kitchener at Khartoum.'

Part Two

The Writer's Writer

5

Christmas Pudding

Just before he left Kampala, Vidia released me. He looked one last time at my much-slashed and -amended essay on cowardice, which was already scheduled to be published. He said that it was finished, though I guessed that it still did not seem quite right to him.

Move on to something new, he said; the new thing would be better for what I had learned from him. I was sorry to see him go. I had come to depend on his reading and his friendly advice. Needing him to put his whole philosophy into a sentence, I mocked myself by thinking of the man who asked Christ, 'Good Master, what good thing shall I do that I may have eternal life?' Christ gives him a quick summary of the essentials, beginning with 'Do not kill' and ending with 'Sell everything you have.'

I found a way of framing the question and managed to stammer it to Vidia.

Vidia's answer was 'Tell the truth.'

And there was his dream, the one I had written down. It went this way.

Vidia and his brother, Shiva, were staying with a family in which there were two other children, a boy and a girl. Shiva hated the boy, and one day when Vidia, his brother, and the boy were on an outing, an argument started. Shiva set upon the boy and killed him.

'Look what you've done – you've killed him!' Vidia said.

Vidia and Shiva dug a hole and hid the corpse of the boy in it.

Now it so happened that the boy was to have been away for several days; there were no questions or suspicions when Vidia and Shiva returned to the family. They were feeling horribly guilty for the murder, however; they could not screw up their courage sufficiently to tell the truth. They knew that the body would be found and that they would be blamed.

A few days later the newspapers were full of the story of the disappearance, and the body was soon found. During this time the child's father underwent a severe change – he remembered various petty cruelties he had inflicted on the boy, and he began blaming himself for the crime. He said, 'I know what happened . . . I made him cut his throat.' Naipaul and his brother remained silent – guilty but so far not blamed. They did not speak of the crime, and yet they were not off the hook. End of dream: night sweats, terror, anxiety, guilt.

I was impressed because it revealed so much. It amazed me that a dream that reflected no credit upon him, that showed him as guilty and sneaky, depicting his brother as a killer, was one he told me coldly and in detail.

Vidia was in London, and I was alone in a land that now seemed dustier and flimsier and fictitious. I had grown used to being alone in Africa: the solitude had sharpened my concentration, and this intensity served my writing. But for the first time I was lonely and felt listless with disappointment. Africa had once seemed limitless and powerful and liberating. Vidia had left me with doubts. He had belittled the politicians, ridiculed the currency, sneered at the newspapers, and Africa now seemed tiny, self-destructive, and confining. It was full of crooked opportunists and it was dangerous. It was ruinous and random. *Do you notice how they make their own paths everywhere?*

In the Senior Common Room and the Staff Club and the Kampala Film Society, the word 'infies' rang in my ears. On Sundays I went for long bird-watching walks up the Bombo Road and in the bush. *Nothing has a name here – it is always 'hill,' 'tree,' 'river,' 'bird.' They don't differentiate. There is no drama. They don't see.*

My habits were the same: work in the morning in my office, do some teaching, eat lunch at home or at the Hindoo Lodge. After a nap, writing in the afternoon, then into town through the big iron gates under the Makerere motto, *Pro Futuro Aedificamus.* At the gates and in the road and in Bat Valley and in town I heard: *This will go back to bush. The jungle will move in. Look, already it has started.*

At the Staff Club people inquired insincerely about Vidia.

'What do you hear from your friend Naipaul?'

Their insincerity was tinged with sarcasm, because for the whole period of Vidia's stay in Kampala I had been his shadow. He had been my friend, not theirs. They saw it as my abandonment of them – I had rejected them and become Naipaul's friend. It was true: I *had* rejected them, but I thought it was my secret. In being Naipaul's shadow I had revealed myself, revealed my literary ambitions most of all. Until then I had been seen as a village explainer, indulging myself. I knew, even then, that a writer lives in his writing. I suspected I had given myself away, perhaps had shown my ambition, certainly had exposed my wound. That was all right with the Staff Club. It was okay to be a local writer, but in befriending Naipaul it appeared that I was getting above myself, looking to London for approval. Expatriates both hated and hankered for London. I had ignored them. Naipaul had ignored them. They knew his contempt, his indifference; they knew his insulting word for them.

To most of them he was a bird of passage, the most undesirable expatriate: an enigma, a mocker, a complainer, someone who would bolt when things got bad. Some had bolted when the Kabaka fell. People flew in and said all sorts of things about Uganda, and like Vidia even mocked it. When they left, we mocked them. What did they know? This was our home, our place of work, our risk. We lived here because we liked it. It was regarded as bad form to jeer at Africans or to speak slightingly of the students. It was dangerous to laugh at the government. Vidia had broken most of the unspoken rules. No one had openly disagreed with him – indeed, in our hearts many of us agreed – but he was resented for trying to demoralize us. Africans said he was typically English. The English expatriates called him typically Trinidadian. The Indians in Kampala called him a typical Brahmin. A number of people said he was a settler type, which was the worst you could say about anyone.

Naipaul also gave the appearance of being a snob. He ridiculed our beer drinking and our bad wine and the power that our servants had over us. He had no faith in the students. The news had circulated that he had awarded only one prize, Third Prize, to Winston Wabamba, and no one found it funny. Some of his scorning observations were repeated. People said, 'I feel sorry for his wife.' 'Patrician' was the kindest word I heard used for him. The Staff Club was noted for its foul language, and Vidia was described in the crudest anatomical terms. The local Indians generally felt he had been browbeating them when he had talked about their days being numbered and nagged them about their exit strategy.

Dust devils, those furious little whirlwinds, were common on our roads and in the dry fields. Vidia had appeared like a dust devil, had sternly questioned every received opinion and demanded answers, and then, like a dust devil, he had whirled away – shivered into the distance, leaving a small scoured trail in the earth.

After Naipaul left I had to explain him, and, exposed as someone aspiring to be like him, I was regarded with suspicion, as unreliable, a secret mocker, like him. I would never again be a Staff Club hearty, taking turns as barman.

'I used to like you,' an expatriate woman said to me one night in the club's bar. Her name was Maureen. She was drunk and truthful. 'I don't like you anymore. I think you're a shit. So does Brian.'

Brian was her husband, a mathematician who taught Boolean algebra. He also did the Staff Club accounts. Hearing Maureen denounce me, he said, 'Fucking Yank.'

He seemed to lose his footing as he spoke, but instead of regaining his balance he kept falling. He was drunk too, and he brought down one of the bar stools with him as he fell. Maureen had not moved; she still glared at me.

'Aren't you going to help him?' I asked.

'He can't fall any further,' Maureen said, and raised her glass to her lips.

It was just the three of us in the bar on this hot night, with the cicadas chattering outside. On the bar were the *India Pale Ale* and *Tusker Beer* mats, on the wall the clock that said *Watney's*, the *Guinness for Power* sign, the stylish African couple – man in brown suit, woman in frilly dress – on the sign that said *Waragi – Uganda's National Drink!*, and stacked to the side were year-old copies of *Private Eye*.

Maureen pressed her lips together, sloshed the *waragi* in her mouth, and swallowed it, blinking and smiling. It was terrible stuff, banana gin.

'What the fuck are you doing here?' she said.

The things they said to me were the things they had wanted to say to Vidia.

To console myself, I went to the Gardenia more often. I nearly always took a girl home. It was so simple, always the direct question: 'Do you want to come back to my house?' And the greatest satisfaction of the question for me was that the word for house, *nyumba*, was the same as for mud hut. Usually the answer was yes, or else 'Let's go dancing first.'

'I'm the meat, you're the knife.' That was my life again.

The expatriates at the Staff Club went on complaining about Vidia long after he had gone. How little they knew of him. 'The mob,' Vidia had called them. He had urged me to leave, saying it was dangerous to the intellect to live in such a place. I did not have time to waste, he said. I knew he was thinking of himself.

'I am old and slow,' he had said, and talked about the past in the regretful yearning voice of an elderly man. Things had been different years ago; so much had changed for the worse.

Old-crock expressions were the ones he liked best: 'latterly,' 'a few pence,' and 'some little time.' He called all magazines 'papers,' which was perhaps not as quaint as old Duffield, who called them 'shinies.' Still, Vidia lamented the age, its scruffiness, its whining low-class people, and its crooked aristocrats. 'What is a title?' he would shout. It was just something to impress the Americans. It was meaningless. Literary agents were 'idlers' and many publishers were 'crummy.'

He was often unwell. His asthma had come back to him in Africa and gagged him. He had insomnia or else bad dreams. He was often low or depressed. Perhaps these afflictions were to be expected in someone so old. He was thirty-four.

As colonials, he had said, he and I had a great deal in common. Was I a colonial? I had never thought so. Never mind. He was my friend. Nor did I question his feeling of being elderly. Perhaps, I thought, when I am in my thirties I will feel that way too. Thirties seemed like middle age, forty was old, fifty was past it, sixty cadaverous.

I was ten years younger than Vidia, which seemed a long time, long enough for someone like me to be transformed into an old man. I had finished my novel and started another. I was confident. What mattered most was that Vidia, a brilliant writer, believed in me.

No one else I had ever known had looked into my face and seen a writer. Vidia did that and more: he said I was a writer of promise, and he marveled at how quickly I worked. I could call him my friend. He paid me the compliment of writing to me regularly after he got to London, and each letter was a lesson.

In his swift, decisive way, in an early letter he analyzed my keeping a journal and rejected the idea. I must abandon it, he said. It was just a way of anthologizing experience. A writer was not a writer because things happened around him. A writer did other things. A diary, more detailed, was worse – I should not even think about it. I ditched my journal, I abandoned my diary for good.

I should consider writing for *The New Statesman*, he said. I ought to avoid 'little magazines': literary journals, university quarterlies, the small-circulation nonpayers.

If I wrote a story, I had to know why my story happened. I had to know why I was writing my novel. He mentioned *Miss Lonelyhearts*. I had urged him to read it. He disliked it and could not understand my enthusiasm for it. He did not see its point. I did not argue with any of this, though secretly I went on admiring the book for its wicked and wayward satire.

Vidia advised me, also by mail, to settle down with an agent and a publisher in England. American publishers were interested only in a single book; English publishers were interested in a writer – all the work. He would help me find an agent, and I should then look for a good publisher.

If I insisted on staying in Africa, I ought to consider, he said, writing a monthly 'Letter from East Africa' for an Indian paper. He would arrange everything. I might get as much as £20 for each piece.

'Aim high,' he said. 'Tell the truth.'

The worst thing a writer could say was 'I am just a storyteller.' He suggested that it was a form of boasting. Vidia despised the description and disliked the very word 'story.' It was a misleading and perhaps meaningless word. He had once told me that many stories did not have an ending. He used the word 'narrative' instead. It was vaguer but more helpful. Structure and form were of utmost importance. The notion of style irritated him: it was showing off, a display of ego and inexperience, pretentious and pointless. He said that art was not pretty.

About two months after arriving back in London, he wrote to say that he was reviewing a life of Ian Fleming, the author of the James Bond books. The biography was not important, the review was not long, yet he said the writing was torture. In the piece that was published in *The New Statesman*, he mentioned in a jeering way that Milton Obote, the Ugandan prime minister, had attended a special screening of a Bond film. Obote's Rolls-Royce had been parked outside the Rainbow Cinema with *Thunderball* on the marquee.

In the Staff Club some expatriates who had heard of the review said Naipaul was sneering again, and they trashed him. What was wrong with the P M's seeing a ruddy film? Better than reading one of Naipaul's *shenzi* books! But Obote had been the nemesis of the Kabaka, and he had recently overthrown him, in James Bond style, by attacking the Lubiri palace with commandos firing machine guns. The Kabaka had fired back with a machine gun before fleeing to Rwanda disguised as a woman. It was all Bond.

Vidia mentioned the Kabaka in his letters. He knew the people who were taking care of him in London – wealthy people, some aristocrats and royalists. Although he had no money, the Kabaka lived stylishly in Paddington and had opened an account at the Ritz.

London life flowed through the letters: the lunches with editors, the dinner parties, the weather, the traffic. Vidia even mentioned the objectionable sound of planes going by overhead. He informed me that the best parts of London were on the flight path to Heathrow. Buckingham Palace, for example, was constantly strafed. He complained of taxes. He was busy judging a literary prize. He reported his friends' reactions to Africa – they took a dim view. He mentioned walking through the rain.

In Africa we never walked through the rain. We sheltered, waiting until the deluge stopped, as it always did after a few minutes.

He urged me to visit London. It would be good for me, he said.

I thought about it, and kept in touch, but I went on living my life. I had students in Kampala, I had responsibilities upcountry. My routine: work, the girls at the Gardenia, my writing.

One night a girl from the coast named Jamila slipped out of my bed to look for the bathroom. She hesitated at the doorway – the lovely scissorlike silhouette of her legs – and took a wrong turn in the hall. I heard the clatter of plopping papers and 'Sorry!'

I switched on the light and found her standing naked among the mass of scattered sheets that was a typescript.

'What is it?' Jamila asked, tweaking the sheets of paper with her toes.

'*Kitabu*,' I said.

A book! She opened her pink mouth and howled with laughter. How could this mess of scrambled papers be a book?

Within a week I bought a ticket to London. I left Uganda just before Christmas.

From the descending plane, London was a blackness overlaid by a map of yellow lights. I had flown from the simple blind night of Africa to the yellow glow of a predawn city picked out in twinkling sulfurous streetlamps. The plane banked, tipping the map upright.

Outside it was cold. The drafty passageway at the plane's door shocked me, the airport itself, the stinky bus. Early morning in London was still pretty dark, and with the bad big-city smell.

The telephone fooled me. To operate it I prepared my coin, placing a threepenny bit on a slot, and found button A and button B. When the call went through and I heard 'Hello, hello,' there was an urgent noise in the receiver – the repeated pips, loudly and awkwardly announcing that I was struggling at a pay phone, becoming rattled. While they sounded I pressed the coin past a resisting barrier in order to complete the call. It took two tries. You had to be quick.

'Vidia?'

'Yes, yes, yes, yes, yes.' It was Vidia's habitual chant of anticipation when he was impatiently pleased. 'I am so sorry I couldn't meet your plane.'

'That's all right.'

'We don't have a monkey wagon, you see.'

It was his name for the cheap little cars that crowded the roads.

'I'll take a taxi. I have some English pounds.'

He gave me directions, assuring me that a taxi driver would know how to get to his house, but if the driver drew a blank, I should mention the South Lambeth Road.

'And how are our infies?'

'I didn't tell them I was coming.'

Because it was so extravagant, I had kept my London trip a secret from my colleagues at the Staff Club. Visiting Naipaul was also further proof that I was abandoning them. London was a destination for an expatriate on leave, not on holiday. 'Going to the coast,' they usually said at Christmas. That meant Mombasa, Malindi, or Zanzibar, Tanga or Bagamoyo, where you could swim without risking bilharzia. London was for the three home-leave months every two years, not a fortnight's holiday. Were my Christmas visit to become known, the expatriates would say I was getting above myself.

In the taxi, heading through London, I understood Vidia's idea of order. It was this, the solid buildings and well-swept roads gleaming under the streetlamps. The shops, spiked iron railings, brick terraces, and clusters of chimney pots; the symmetrical spans of the great bridge we were taking over the Thames. London was reliable, built to last, and the whole city looked sealed in black glaze. No wonder Vidia had thought of Kampala as thrown together and ruinous and chaotic, and that it would fall down and return to bush.

But the London dampness and the London cold intimidated me. Even wearing the sheepskin coat that I had bought in Kenya, I was shivering, tired from the flight, feeling fragile in the vast glazed city that was still dark at eight o'clock on this December morning.

The taxi swung left and right and then shot up a side street. I saw some black faces and was reassured. Another corner and the taxi rattled to a halt and kept rattling.

'Number Three Stockwell Park Crescent.'

It was a small gray-brick Georgian house, set back behind a low wall, with a similar but larger house to the right, a poorer one to the left. Number 3 had a newly planted sapling in the front yard.

Vidia had heard the taxi. With a pipe in his mouth he greeted me from the doorway, and before we entered he pointed to the house on the right. 'That frightfully grand house belongs to communists, of course. And that one' – the scruffy one on the left – 'well, they are home all the time. They don't work, you see. I thought, Goodness, they are all unemployed. But no, they are being "redeployed." All this time I thought they were a pack of idlers, but no – "redeployed"!'

I had almost forgotten that work, or the lack of it, could be material for a joke. In Africa there was no point to such a remark, and certainly no humor in it, because there was hardly any paid work in the usual sense; there was subsistence farming. If that work wasn't done, you starved. It wasn't funny or sad, it was taken for granted.

Pat kissed me as Vidia shut the door. It was warm in here. Had I not just come from East Africa, I would have said the house was too hot, but I found it perfect. Double glazing, Vidia's remedy for his hatred of noise, kept the house silent.

While Pat protested his impulsiveness, Vidia showed me around the house, sourly gloating over the blunders the workmen had made – the badly cut corners, the poorly drilled holes, the asymmetrical beading, the slapped-on paint.

His study was off the parlor. A chaise that was a folding chair – like a beach chair – was set up in the middle of the floor. The chair grunted and squawked when he sat down on it and stuck his feet out.

'So this is where you work?'

'This is where I worry, man. This is where I smoke. My work is done. That novel wrecked me. I have the proofs. Will you help me read them?'

I said I would. 'Did you get your thousand pounds?' I asked.

He made a face, set his mouth in an expression that meant 'almost.' He said he was mentally exhausted, but with his work done he was free.

It was a quiet, tidy house, like a kind of padded box with a tight lid. Vidia said he seldom went out. Pat, who taught history at a girls' school three days a week, did all the shopping, all the cooking, made all the beds, even did some of Vidia's research. Most of the cleaning and the laundry was done by a charlady, Mrs Brown, whom Vidia called Brown.

'Brown will do your laundry. When you leave, you might give her a few pence.'

'Five pounds?'

'Too much. No, no. That would spoil Brown.'

That was my first day. He spent most of the next morning in his pajamas, reading the proofs of *The Mimic Men*. We had lunch. Vidia was still in his pajamas.

'I dress for dinner,' he said, and laughed – a more bronchial laugh than his East African laugh.

In the next few days he gave me a lightning tour of London, starting from his nearest tube station, Stockwell, on the Northern Line, and heading for Tottenham Court Road. A gasping dusty wind coursed through the station and up the wooden escalator: it was a city of cold dead smells, of rust and damp brick and oil – smells of prosperity and traffic. Being here was an adventure, but I thought: I could never live here, ever. Another thought that stayed in my mind was that we were on an island, a cold island in winter.

From Tottenham Court Road we crossed Oxford Street and walked to the British Museum. Now I understood why Vidia felt there was such ignorance and poverty in Uganda's place names: London ones were so grand, much grander than the streets and squares they described. Vidia seemed to be following a route he had taken many times before. At the British Museum, as though programmed, he showed me the glass cases containing manuscripts of Byron, Keats, Browning; then onward and downstairs, through the Roman and Greek rooms to the Egyptian artifacts, the mummies and the sarcophagi, some like water troughs, some like cupboards.

'Notice the decadence in this period. They become rubbishy and repetitive with the Roman occupation. This isn't art. This is just mimicry, man.'

Down the road to Holborn, through an alley, a gateway, into a parklike square: Sir John Soane's Museum. Without looking left or right, Vidia led me to the Indian miniatures and the Daniell aquatints and Hogarth's series of four paintings titled *The Election*. Nearby, at Gaston's in Chancery Lane, he sold the armful of books he had been carrying – his review books, half price for clean copies.

He bought a tin of Player's Navy Cut pipe tobacco with some of the proceeds. Then we had lunch at Wheeler's, on Old Compton Street. He had prawns, I had 'Sole Walewska.'

Vidia ordered an expensive bottle of wine. He said, 'You university lecturers have lots of money, don't you?'

I didn't. I had spent all my spare cash on the airline ticket, but I was so grateful for his hospitality I paid for the lunch.

In that restaurant with close-together tables and smoky air we talked about Africa. Vidia was not a mocker anymore. East Africa had affected him. The food was real there, he said – fresh vegetables, lettuce and broad beans, and fish from Lake Victoria, Nile perch from upcountry, the first plantains he had eaten since he was a child. And the light was wonderful. And that sky, all those stars. He worried about the Major at the Kaptagat Arms and the other people whom he had met, whom he liked, some expatriates, some Indians.

'They're not all infies,' I said.

'Of course not. But they will all be destroyed by Africa.'

'You belong here, I guess.'

'I belong nowhere,' he said. 'I have no home.'

He had that disconcerting way of turning chitchat into metaphysics about the human condition.

'Who do you see here?'

He did not answer this. He looked aside and said, 'I don't want to meet new people.'

He looked at his watch and pinched it, the way people do when they are making a point, impatient to go. But no. He said, 'My father gave me this watch,' and he looked as though he were stifling tears.

I did not think I could bear his weeping. I said, 'Shall we go?'

He was silent on the way to the National Gallery, and then among the paintings he brightened. The specific circuit he made in the galleries – bypassing some rooms, lingering in others, selecting one painting in certain rooms – told me that he had unshakable habits and preferences. He moved so quickly I could hardly keep up with him. He hurried past twenty pictures to get close to one, to put his face against particular details on that canvas. One was a Matisse with a daub of red, like the simplest Chinese character stroke, splashed near the center of the landscape.

'Look. Come close. It's nothing. It is utterly meaningless.'

He poked his finger at the eyebrow-shaped splosh of a brush stroke. Then he dragged me back like an agitated teacher provoking a response and urged me to look again.

'See? Now it's a person. It has life. It has shape and meaning. It even has emotion – all that from a brush stroke. Matisse knew exactly what he was doing when he touched his brush here.'

It was conversation in the form of a lesson, but I did not mind this teacher–student relationship with him because I was learning so much. His attention to me made me surer of myself. He was right: the random-looking swipe of paint was a daring experiment in form.

We went to the Victoria and Albert Museum. In the taxi, going through Parliament Square, he saw me looking at the statue of Abraham Lincoln standing before a chair.

'That's called "The Hot Seat,"' Vidia said.

There was another statue just past it, of Jan Smuts, also standing but canted forward like a skater.

'And he's skating,' I said.

'On thin ice,' Vidia said.

At the V and A, again he followed his own route, ignoring most of the rooms, concentrating on the Indian pictures, the Mogul paintings, the miniatures, the bronzes. I was following; he saw my concentration flag.

'What do you want to see?' he asked.

'Henry Fuseli. Salvador Dalí.'

'They're at the Tate.'

He stood aside at the Tate Gallery while I looked at Fuseli's nightmares and Dalí's *Autumn Cannibalism*, and then he introduced me to the Turners – another lecture on the subtle technique of brushwork – and the Blakes and the Whistlers.

Back at home in Stockwell, he put on his pajamas and read the proofs of *The Mimic Men*. And he asked what I had been writing. I told him my book was about the dusk-to-dawn curfew in Uganda, the strangest and most telling episode I had known in Africa. I had the typescript with me.

'I think you should offer it to André.'

We went the next morning to André Deutsch Ltd. Vidia

instructed me to leave the typescript with his editor, Diana Athill. Vidia stayed outside, puffing his pipe under an awning in Great Russell Street, while I asked for Miss Athill. Hearing my name, she invited me into her office and we talked awhile. She said she was eager to read the book. I was hopeful when I left, but when I saw Vidia he lunged at me and began shouting.

'Where have you been!' he said. He made stabbing gestures with his pipe. He looked furious. He looked betrayed. He had been standing all this time under the awning. 'What have you done?'

I could not understand his anger. He knew where I had been, talking with Miss Athill.

'You said –'

'The man must never precede the work!' he shouted. In the fifteen minutes I had been absent, he had gone from being the soul of kindness to the embodiment of pure rage. 'Do you hear me? The man must never precede the work.'

He said that he had to go home, that he had work to do and no time to waste, but that I should stay out and enjoy myself. He descended the steps to the Northern Line, biting the stem of his pipe. I walked the streets, feeling wronged. When I returned to Stockwell, Vidia was in his study, sitting in the chaise, smoking in the dark.

Each night we read the *Mimic Men* proofs. He had one copy, I had another. I skipped ahead and looked for Africa in it, for any indication that the last part of it had been written at the Kaptagat Arms in western Kenya. It was an elliptical story of a West Indian politician, his rise and fall, his love affairs, his flight to England, his exile in a London hotel. It was, subtly, about power, money, friendship, and failure, about a small fragile country, a Third World island. Perhaps he had been influenced by Africa after all. I looked for, and found, 'wise old negro' in the sentence 'he had created for himself the character of the wise old negro who knew the ways of the white world.' So Pat had prevailed.

In the Stockwell house there was a television set in the lounge, but it was seldom on. Having heard that British television was inventive and entertaining, I turned it on, just to see. Vidia entered the room, standing behind me. A commercial with a jingle was on the screen.

'I thought there were no commercials on the BBC,' I said.

'That's not the BBC, that's the Monkey.' It was his word for the independent station.

I changed the channel. I found a fashion show. Vidia uttered an awful groan. I changed the channel again. A man I took to be a politician was giving a speech about Rhodesia.

Still standing, Vidia said, 'You think he's smiling? He's not smiling. That's not a smile. He's a politician.'

A heckler in the audience cried out, 'Good old Smithy!'

'Hear the infy yelp?'

I turned off the television.

After I went to my room, I took out my new novel. It was about a Chinese grocer I knew, Francis Yung Hok, in Kampala's Bat Valley. He was the only Chinese citizen of Uganda – the smallest ethnic group in the country, a persecuted minority of one. I called him Sam Fong and titled the book *Fong and the Indians*. The novel, inspired by Vidia's urgings to look hard at the absurdities in Uganda, was also my way of testing Vidia's maxims in narrative technique. I wanted Vidia to see it as a kind of homage to him and his friendship.

When Vidia was out of earshot, Pat asked me about the servants they had left behind. Visitors, part-time residents, and embassy people always talked about servants in a patronizing and possessive way, like little girls monologuing about their dolls. Vidia had felt victimized by the servants and their connections – they were all plotters, looking for work. But Pat regarded them with uncomplicated affection and had seen them as helpers and allies, which they were. She had been kind to them. She said she missed them. She whispered to me that she wanted to be remembered to them.

Pat attended to Vidia in a maternal way, maternal most of all for her sleeping in an adjoining room, in a single bed. Seeing her piteous little bed, I remembered how I had thought of making love to her in Africa. My wild impulse would perhaps be allowable in such a disorderly place as Uganda, but not here. This was different. This was her tidy home; here was her convent-style room; that was her narrow bed, and beside it her nightstand: glass of water, two books, bottle of pills, none of it very tempting, much less an aphrodisiac. I knew that any wooing by me would be an abuse of hospitality, yet I wished for a woman friend.

I soon found someone receptive to my ardor. My one solitary excursion that first week in London was to a publisher that would soon be bringing out a textbook I had coauthored with a British linguist. I had devised this English textbook in Malawi, where all books were in short supply. This one was designed for speakers of Chichewa, which I had learned as a teacher in a bush school. I had been deported from Malawi on a trumped-up political charge, and because I was in bad odor there, my name could not appear on the book. Vidia had just laughed. He said, 'Someday you'll be glad your name isn't on that book.'

Half the advance on royalties was mine. I had asked that it be paid to me in London, so that I could cash the check and have spending money in sterling. The publisher's office was in Mayfair, near Grosvenor Square. The day I picked up my check I was introduced to the editor of the textbook division who had commissioned the book. He introduced me to his staff. One of them was a young woman about my own age, named Heather.

While the editor's attention was drawn by someone needing a decision on a dust jacket, I said to Heather, 'Would you like to have a drink later?'

'I'd love to,' she said, and suggested a pub nearby. She would meet me there after work.

Entering the pub in her winter coat, her face framed by the high collar, she seemed even prettier than she had in the office. We talked for a while and drank wine and at last I said, 'I'm staying with a friend in Stockwell, so I can't ask you back there.'

'That's all right,' she said.

'No. It's inconvenient,' I said, and solemnly translating from Swahili to English, I added, 'Because I want to take you back there and sleep with you.'

What lovely teeth she had – she had thrown her head back and was laughing, and I thought, Oh, well, at least she heard me in the din of this crowded pub. She said nothing more about it. Another hour passed. I told her African stories, about the Pygmies, about the butterflies that gathered and made a white fluttery carpet on the Jinja Road, about the man-eating lion that escaped from its cage at Mityana. I taught her to say *Mimi nyama, wewe kisu* – I am the meat, you are the knife. I talked so that I could study her pale eyes and pretty face, the way she listened with her lips. Afterwards, in the taxi to Victoria, where she lived, she kissed me, and the kiss meant yes.

It was late when I arrived back in Stockwell. I tiptoed to my room. Vidia was already up reading his proofs when I went downstairs the next morning. He said, 'I think you've made a friend.'

Pat and I went shopping in Brixton Market for a dinner party she was giving that night. It was a street market, mostly black vegetable sellers and stall holders I took to be West Indians. I saw a woman spanking a child very hard and scolding loudly as the child wailed. I told Pat that I found it upsetting. Children were seldom spanked in Africa. There was little necessity for it; anyway, young children were raised by patient older sisters, practicing to be mommies, and took the place of dolls. Mother was always working in the garden, while Father sat under a tree with his friends, drinking some sort of sour, porridgelike beer. Such was life in a village, a far cry from this flogging.

Pat was smiling. She said, 'Vidia would like that. He says that children aren't spanked enough.'

The dinner-party preparations were a strain for Pat. Vidia played no role at all other than supervising the wine. Pat did all the cooking, she worried about the food, she fretted over the seating arrangements. Vidia was serene. He said he was planning to change out of his pajamas and robe.

'I can offer sherry to start off,' he said. 'I had a bottle of whiskey, but one of the neighbors came over a month ago and punished it.'

The purpose of the party was for Vidia to introduce me to his friends. They were old friends, he said. He repeated that he did not want to meet new people. The guests were Hugh Thomas, who had published a book on the Spanish Civil War (he had just returned from Cuba); his wife, Vanessa, who was 'grand,' Vidia said; Lady Antonia Fraser and her husband, another Hugh, a Member of Parliament; and Tristram Powell, who was my age. When they arrived, they were all on such intimate terms that I felt excluded. Their talk startled me; I said very little.

'Paul's just come from Africa,' Vidia explained.

'I thought he looked a bit stunned,' Hugh Thomas said. 'That explains it.'

Instead of replying to that, I complimented him on his book about the Spanish Civil War. A few days before I had found a copy of it in Vidia's library and had read the first chapter.

Over dinner, Tristram Powell said he was making a film for the BBC. Lady Antonia was writing a book. Her husband, the MP, said that Vidia should visit him at the House of Commons one day when he was free.

Vidia said, 'I don't want to meet new people.'

When it came time for them to leave, Hugh Thomas said to me, 'We're giving a party the day after tomorrow. Come to the dinner beforehand.'

Vidia was pleased for me. He said the invitation was significant. I would meet new people. I would get on. London was not socially static, he said. London was interested in new people.

'But I am not interested in meeting any more new people,' he said.

Heather had invited me to dinner the night of the Hugh Thomas party and was annoyed when I called her to say that I had to go out with my friend and his wife.

'Who is this friend?'

'Do you know the writer V. S. Naipaul?'

'He's a friend of yours? He's famous,' she said. 'Okay, what about tonight?'

'There's a publisher's party. Jonathan Cape.'

'You're doing all right for an African,' Heather said.

'Maybe I can meet you afterwards.'

'You know where to find me.'

I loved hearing that. I loved her address – Ashley Gardens, Victoria – and it excited me to know that after the party I would find her waiting for me in her warm room.

It was a Christmas party at the Cape offices and also a book launch for a young novelist, Paul Bailey, whose book, *At the Jerusalem*, was already being praised. Bailey was a slim, sweet-faced boy with blush patches on his smooth cheeks. He looked shy, even fearful, but he was poised. When Vidia asked him whether he earned a living with his pen – a Vidia expression – Bailey said no, he worked at Harrods. 'Tell me, tell me, tell me,' Vidia said. In which department did Bailey work? How did he answer the telephone? How were staff instructed to address the customers? He asked Bailey to verify every rumor he had ever heard about the rituals at Harrods. Bailey obliged him with answers, his face reddening, yet he spoke with extreme politeness, as though this were Harrods and he a clerk and Vidia a customer. Vidia did not mention Bailey's novel.

In the middle of the questions, a stout, hearty man loomed over Vidia and said in a mocking tone, 'If it isn't old V. S.!'

'Hello, Kingsley,' Vidia said, biting his pipe stem, and watched the man sway through the room. It was Kingsley Amis, he said. 'He's drunk. He's sad. I wonder at the achievement.'

A hollow-cheeked man with deep, close-set eyes spoke earnestly to Vidia. He was not old but he had that gaunt, imprisoned look of someone who was overworked.

'Paul, this is Alan Sillitoe.'

I began to understand how a London party might be full of familiar names, while the faces were unfamiliar and even grotesque. Talking inconsequentially to Sillitoe, I kept thinking how, just a few years before, I first read *The Loneliness of the Long-Distance Runner* and *Saturday Night and Sunday Morning*. For their power and directness I regarded them as better than Lawrence, the clearest glimpse I'd had into English life and work – lives and households I had never seen before. But we talked about the rain and Rhodesia.

After Sillitoe drifted away, Vidia said, 'He brings news. That is what he does. Brings news from Nottingham, from working-class people. It's not writing, really. It's news. Don't be that sort of writer, bringing news.'

I promised I would not be that sort of writer.

Vidia attracted the notice of other party guests, and he introduced me to them: John Bayley, John and Miriam Gross, and Tom Maschler. Maschler was Paul Bailey's editor. Vidia told him I was working on a book.

'Send your book to me,' Maschler said.

Vidia was saying to the others, 'I don't want to meet new people.'

It had become another of his old man's maxims, like the sentences that started 'Latterly, one has begun to wonder . . .'

When we left the Cape party we saw Kingsley Amis again, and again he said, 'Good old V. S.!' Vidia simply walked on. He would have said he was 'cutting' Amis. He did not see or hear him. For Vidia's sake I did not refer to Amis, so as not to call attention to his existence.

In the lights of Bedford Square, the falling rain seemed stiffened by brightness and the black street glistened and the puddles were full of plainer light. Vidia was hurrying, looking for a taxi. He hated the expense of taxis, but after a certain hour he felt that London became menacing and unpredictable, and he feared taking the Underground because of the louts, the racists, the disorder; there were irritable tramps who rode the Circle Line continuously, for the warmth, going round and round. The tube was much dirtier at night, too, the cars having grown filthier throughout the day.

In the taxi back to Stockwell, I saw a sign to Victoria and said, 'I promised to meet someone. I'll get out around here.'

'Your friend,' Vidia said.

'Would you like to meet her?'

'No, no. But don't be offended. It's just that I don't want to meet any new people.'

He rapped on the window that separated the driver's seat from us and told the driver to let me out at Victoria Street. Soon after that I was lying in bed with Heather. As the days had passed there were fewer and fewer preliminaries. That night she opened the door wearing a silk dressing gown, and when she kissed me, I touched her and found she was naked underneath it, and her skin was also like silk.

We hardly spoke until we had made love once, and then, calmed by it, I lay on my back feeling buoyant. She rested her arms against my chest and put her forehead against mine, letting her long hair sweep over my face.

'Tell me about the Pygmies again.'

'Let me tell you about the "men whose heads do grow beneath their shoulders."'

'I don't want to be your Desdemona,' she said.

I kissed her and said, 'I like you because you're lovely and because you know how to read.'

'I know how to do lots of things.'

She kissed me and filled my mouth with her tongue. She ran her hands over my body. Her fingers were cool and my skin was tender, still raw and damp from sex. I tipped her over and parted her legs and breathed in her body's smell like fresh meat. When we made love a second time it was as if our nerves were exposed and we were peeling the skin from our flesh. The act heated me – more than that, it scorched me, and at her most passionate Heather howled like a cat that I was holding down and stabbing to death, except that they were howls of pleasure, and her only fear was that I would stop too soon. When we were done, we simply died for an hour and woke up still sweating.

'I have to go.' It was after one on the luminous dial of her bedroom clock.

'Stay until morning.'

'My friends expect me to be there at breakfast.'

This was not quite true – we seldom had breakfast – but it seemed rude not to go home.

'Naipaul is supposed to be very clever,' said Heather. 'But incredibly difficult.'

'He has been kind to me.'

'That's the one thing people never say about him.'

'I guess I know his secrets.'

'I guess you do,' she said, stressing 'guess' for its being American. 'Right. I'll let you go on one condition – that you come back to me.'

'Tomorrow,' I said.

In the street some minutes later I was amazed by the emptiness of London at night. It wasn't even two in the morning. As soon as the pubs closed at eleven, the streets were full. By midnight they were empty again. My taxi to Stockwell always traveled down deserted streets, over a solitary bridge, and south through a city that seemed imaginary and antique, without people or other vehicles, just black streets and yellow lamps.

My late nights fascinated Vidia, I could see, but they created distance too: I had another life, another friend, and that friend lived in a different London. Vidia asked oblique questions, but beyond that he did not inquire. I think he detected a greediness in me, something uncontrollable and animalistic – desire that he associated with shame. I remembered how he had said of his sexual urge, 'One is ashamed of being a man.'

I was not ashamed. I was delighted to have a girlfriend who was uninhibited and intelligent and as free as I was. But I could see the end was coming. No sooner had we met than she began saying, 'You're going to leave soon and go back to Africa, and I'm going to be miserable.'

This was too gloomy a thought for me to respond to.

She said, 'I want you to be miserable too.'

'I will be.'

'I don't believe you.'

Heather was more annoyed the night of Hugh Thomas's party. I went to her apartment afterwards and we made love and she begged me to stay. I said I couldn't.

'You're always running back and forth to your friend Naipaul.'

It was true. I never spent the whole night with her. But I was fond of her and I knew I would miss her. I even wondered what sort of wife she would be. Maybe she would visit Kampala. She said she might. As for Naipaul, this friendship I now realized was as strong as love. He was my friend, he had shown me what was good in my writing, he had drawn a line through anything that was false. I was inspired by his work and his conviction. I wanted always to be his friend.

'I had an Indian boyfriend at Oxford,' Heather said.

'I don't want to hear about him,' I said.

All this took a week: the dinner party, the Cape party, Hugh Thomas's party, the nights with Heather. Christmas was a few days away. Heather invited me to spend Christmas with her family in the country.

'I can't. The Naipauls have plans,' I said. They had not mentioned any plans, but I was sure they had them. All Vidia had said was that his brother, Shiva, was coming to stay but that he was unreliable – so Vidia had said – and had not confirmed it. 'I can't let them down.'

Heather said, 'I wanted to be your Christmas pudding.'

Why did that silly statement arouse me so much? Perhaps because it was silly and because it also meant something.

The day before Christmas, Vidia said we might go to an Indian restaurant, Veeraswami's, on a lane off Regent Street. But when we got there, he sulked. He said it was suburban. He could not eat his meal. He crunched a popadam into flakes on the tablecloth with his forefinger and grumbled about Shiva, whom he called Seewyn.

'He has long hair,' Vidia said, and indicated with his fingers how it fell on both sides of his face. He pursed his lips and spoke again, sourly. 'Like Veronica Lake.'

That night we were invited to dinner at Edna O'Brien's. She lived in Putney, some distance from Stockwell. Vidia said that her house backed onto the river.

'It sounds a nice place to live,' I said.

'Those suburbs fill me with gloom.'

'How are we getting there?'

'Edna is sending a car at seven.'

At just seven o'clock Vidia said, 'The car is not here.'

He was so punctilious that he grew agitated as an appointed time approached and regarded anything after the specified minute as late. He was sitting upright, stiff with annoyance, the hardback book on his lap open to its flyleaf. He had written, *To Edna O'Brien from V S Naipaul.* He seemed to be hesitating over the date.

'What is she like?' I asked, trying to distract him.

He thought a moment, then grimaced and clawed his hair. He said, 'She has drunk London to its dregs.'

The thought of this Irish woman guzzling London in this way excited me as much as *I want to be your Christmas pudding.*

Vidia snapped the book shut – it was his *Mr Stone and the Knights Companion* – and said, 'I knew the car wouldn't be here on time.'

'How did you know?'

'I had a vibration.'

Pat was becoming anxious, and she said without any confidence, 'I expect the car will be along any minute now.'

But at seven-thirty it still had not come. The three of us remained seated, listening, leaking energy. It was impossible to talk about anything except the car that had not arrived.

Without a word, but biting his pipe stem, Vidia leaned over and put the inscribed book back on the shelf, slotting it angrily and jamming it tight between two fatter books, as though finishing an obscure bit of masonry.

'I don't want to go anymore,' he said. In a frivolous woman's voice he said, 'Oh, don't worry, I'll send a car for you.' He chewed his pipe stem. 'But there is no car!'

Vidia's eyes went black. His anger resonated in the air like a high-frequency hum of such pitch and intensity that everything in the room seemed fragile, as though at any moment it could all shatter or explode.

'Ring her,' Pat said. 'I'm sure it's a mistake.'

More coaxing at last got Vidia on the phone, and he held the heavy receiver against the side of his head like a weapon.

'Edna.' Vidia's voice was stern. 'The car has not come.'

There was a pause, the twang of a hurried explanation, and 'sorry' repeated over and over. Her apology was as distinct as the call of a particular species of bird.

'I see.' Vidia listened some more, looking grim. 'In that case,' he said, 'I will see if Rogers will take us.'

Rogers was the minicab driver, although from the way Vidia spoke of him, he sounded like his personal chauffeur. All such flunkies were for Vidia just surnames, like Brown the charlady. It was after eight when Rogers arrived in his Rover.

'You sit next to the tiger,' Pat said to me.

Vidia was still angry. The angle of his pipe in his mouth told everything. And he had not brought his book. We traveled in silence along cold streets to Putney.

The house, on Deodar Road, was tall, and with a Christmas wreath on the door and all the lights burning it looked festive. Edna O'Brien greeted us with kisses and apologies. Several guests had already arrived, including an American named Coles and the writer Len Deighton. I did not know Deighton's writing, but Heather had a copy of *Horse Under Water* on her bedside table, and I associated this book with our sexual postures, another prop in the love nest, like the little lamp, the ashtray, and the clock face that glowed in the dark. Deighton was a rumpled, soft-spoken man. Coles looked overdressed and agitated.

Edna was pretty, Irish to her fingertips, slim, with a friendly girl's face and red piled-up hair and a lace blouse. She said, 'Vidia's told me all about you. Now do sit down – what will you drink? I should warn you, we've just been discussing the American expression "credibility gap." I can't understand it for the life of me.'

Coles said, 'It means just what it says. It's the difference between how much you believe and how much you don't.'

'I must be stupid,' Edna said. 'I don't get it.'

What made Coles unpersuasive was his beard, which he had just begun to grow, making him look unshaven more than bearded. His bristly face was a distraction and gave him a dubious appearance. He said he was a publisher in New York and was hoping that Edna would write something for him.

'You live in London?' he asked me.

'No. Just visiting. I live in Uganda. I'm at the university.'

'So what are you studying?'

'I'm a teacher.'

'Pretty dangerous down there, isn't it?'

'No. It's wonderful. New York is dangerous.'

'That's bullshit,' Coles said.

Pat Naipaul winced as he said this. She did not understand that when I was with Americans I tried to provoke them, or even be offensive. I would not have dared do this with an English person, but I resented Coles's complacency. This sort of older man would expect me to join the US Army and be sent to Vietnam so that he could sit and grow his ridiculous beard in New York City.

'Dad, I broke my watch strap.'

A small boy was tapping Coles on the shoulder. He wore a school uniform and had a whining English accent. *Dad?* It could only have been Coles's son. Coles did not introduce him. In fact he seemed slightly embarrassed by the boy, who was making a whiffling complaint in his prissy English accent to his gruff New Yorker father who took little notice of him.

Another boy entered the room, one of Edna's sons, dressed in sneakers and jeans and a sweatshirt. Like the other boy, he was about ten. He said, 'I'm going to do a magic trick. Does anyone have a pound note?'

I gave him one. He inserted it between the rollers of a little machine and it disappeared. Everyone groaned, to encourage him.

Then, just as I had abandoned any thought of getting it back, he made the pound note reappear.

'I need help carving the turkey,' Edna said.

'Vidia's no use,' Pat said, glancing at Vidia, who looked horror-struck, as though he had just remembered something.

'I have some salmon for Vidia,' Edna said, and Vidia relaxed. 'Come help me in the kitchen, Paul.'

She handed me the carving knife and a long fork and the platter for the meat. The turkey gleamed in its wrapper of roasted skin. Edna seemed so pleasant and hospitable that it struck me as unfair that Vidia had left the dedicated book behind.

She said, 'Have you been to the Congo?'

'Twice,' I said. 'It's an amazing place. It looks just the way you expect it to – green and colorful and violent, and that big muddy river.'

'I'd love to see it. It has Irish connections, you know. Roger Casement.'

'Oh, yes, that's right.' But it was a meaningless name to me. I said, 'I'll meet you in Leopoldville. We'll go up the river in a steamer. We'll penetrate the Congo and drink it to its dregs.'

Vidia's phrase for her had bewitched me.

'Oh, get on with you,' she said with affection, and she touched me tenderly. She put her face close to mine and made a fish mouth. 'Carve the turkey.'

I helped serve it. We ate in the dining room. Vidia's salmon was presented to him like a prize he had won.

Len Deighton said, 'The painter Sidney Nolan lives over the road.'

'I don't want to meet any new people,' Vidia said.

The American, Coles, was talking about Vietnam, what a mess it was, but what else could we do? It was the sort of line that made me recklessly offensive.

'I think Wallace is right,' Vidia said. 'The problem is with the pointy-headed intellectuals.'

Coles said, 'George Wallace?'

'That's the man. He has an awful lot of common sense.'

Deighton said, 'I am more interested in the case of that colored cricketer from South Africa. Did you see the write-up in today's paper?'

'The important thing to remember,' Vidia said, 'is that he is a slave.'

Coles was scratching at his half-grown beard. He said, 'I don't get any of this. Are you serious?'

Edna said, 'Now I have to make Irish coffee. If anyone watches me pouring the cream in over a spoon, I'll make a mess of it and it'll sink.'

Vidia was not listening. He was facing Coles. 'When you understand that he is a slave, you will be able to discuss him.'

Edna served the coffee with the cream floating on top, and we drank it in the lounge. Coles, bewildered by Vidia on the subject of slavery and South Africa, once again began to talk about the Vietnam War. He spoke in such a futile way, I remembered why I had decided to stay in Africa, and I longed to be back in Uganda.

It was snowing when we left. Edna kissed me and said that I could come back anytime. Putney was the first part of London I had seen that I felt I would be able to live in. I liked the wide black Thames behind her house, the way the river sucked and eddied at the end of her garden.

Rogers had been huddled in his minicab, waiting. In the car, Vidia said, 'That obnoxious American and his son. Did you notice the way the son spoke? So precise. Such an English schoolboy. The father was embarrassed.'

Pat challenged him, though it was what I had felt.

Vidia said, 'I had a vibration.'

Pat said to me, 'Are you going to see your friend?'

'No. She's spending Christmas with her folks in the country.'

'The English thing,' Vidia said. 'Did she invite you?'

'Yes.'

'The English thing,' Vidia said.

Pat said, 'Vidia's rather impatient with Christmas.'

'Christmas pudding,' Vidia said. He chewed his pipe stem. 'Christmas pudding.'

The next day was Christmas. London was cold and bright under a clear sky, as blue as an African sky, yet in this unforgiving light the city looked cracked and senile and the streets were bare. I went for a walk up Clapham Road towards the Clapham North tube station. The only other pedestrian was a woman ahead of me pushing a baby carriage, wearing a coat so long its ragged hem dragged on the sidewalk. The wheels of the carriage scraped and squeaked. When I overtook this person, I saw that it was really a shabby man wearing a filthy shawl over his head, and instead of a baby in the carriage there was a dog crouched in a knot of rags and some old shoes and bits of metal and glass bottles.

'Fuck off,' the man said, because I had come too close to him. His face was damaged, with crusts of dried blood on his cheek. 'Get away from me pram.'

His face had frightened me. An instant later I remembered how Vidia said that ugly people seemed dangerous. I stopped in a pub, and because of the encounter with the tramp, I was very careful to be polite. I drank a beer, telling myself it was Christmas.

Back in Stockwell, I sensed something was wrong. Vidia's moods filled the rooms like an odor. But I didn't ask. I gave Pat a snakeskin purse I had bought from an Indian at the arcade in Kampala. Pat remarked on how real it looked. I took it as a criticism. The crinkled scales were still flaking from it. She gave me a woolen scarf.

After lunch, which was solemn, Vidia went into his study and lay on his lounge chair and smoked in the dark.

Pat said softly to me, 'Shiva's not coming.'

6

Excursion to Oxford

When the knock came, the rap of the small hinged horseshoe on the brass plate on the door, Vidia remained silent. We were reading in the front room. He could give the impression of hearing nothing – like an unwelcome sound – as he could give the impression of seeing nothing – like an unwelcome face. The knock came again. Vidia did not hear, or pretended not to. I answered the door.

Shiva – it had to be him. I remembered about the hair and 'Veronica Lake.' He was twenty or so, he looked apologetic, though it might have been simply the sorrowful cast of his face, which was thin, or his eyes, which were hooded and Oriental, not Indian but Asiatic. Those features were appropriate to the only other thing I knew about him: he was studying Chinese.

Vidia never answered the door and he seldom answered the phone. I once asked him why.

'One doesn't like surprises,' he said.

Stepping through the doorway, Shiva said, 'You're Paul.'

In the parlor Vidia greeted him, saying, 'What did you do with the coat we sent you?'

'I like this one better.'

'Yes.' The way Vidia said it, the word stood for a whole pronouncement of contempt.

Shiva was scruffily dressed, in a student's way, with a ragged coat and fraying scarf and scuffed and trampled-looking shoes. Pat sighed over him, calling him Seewyn, as Vidia had, and kissed him in her unconfident old-auntie way. Then we had tea.

Shiva had long and delicate fingers, which made him seem polite when he was picking at the cookies on the plate Pat handed him, and which were expressive when he smoked cigarettes. There was also something in the movements of his hands that suggested languor and fatigue. This tiredness was especially apparent in the droopy way he sat and the way he walked, bent over in a sloping gait, kicking his shoes, dragging his feet. He was round-shouldered, and when he became thoughtful he arranged his long hair with those delicate, smoke-yellowed fingers.

'We were expecting you yesterday,' Vidia said.

He was stern with Shiva, much more an uncle than a brother. There was a marked difference in age, thirteen years, and in attitude – crabbed Vidia, college-punk Shiva. But Shiva wasn't bothered.

'It's a long story!' he said, and laughed. He had a delightful laugh that encouraged you to share the hopeless joke, the unconvincing excuse.

Vidia went to his armchair and sat down. He filled his pipe. He set it alight and puffed it. When Pat left, fussing with the tea things, Vidia said, 'Tell him, Paul.'

'Tell him what?'

'Tell Seewyn about your African girls.'

'What about the African girls?' Shiva said, smirking.

'Tell him, Paul.'

'That I sleep with them?' I said.

'See? He's shocked. Seewyn's shocked.'

'I am not shocked,' Shiva said.

But he was. I could see his discomfort, and I could not understand why he was so flustered. He was tapping at his face with his fingertips. He awkwardly lit a cigarette and blew smoke nervously.

'The big liberal,' Vidia said. 'All that Trinidad racial mumbo-jumbo. And he is shocked.'

The moment was tense, two brothers in a standoff. And I had been put on the spot. Trying to explain, I said, 'It's pretty simple. It would be odd if I didn't have African girlfriends. I live in Africa.'

'It would not occur to Seewyn to sleep with a black woman.'

Shiva laughed and said, 'There are no black women at Oxford.'

The conversation had started to embarrass me, and this argument was being made as much at my expense as at Shiva's.

I said, 'You don't know what you're missing, Shiva.'

Vidia had been reading a book with the red label *London Library* on its cover when Shiva had knocked. He put his finger between the pages, preparing to open it.

'Did you bring some work with you?' Vidia asked.

'Mencius,' Shiva said.

'Do you know Sun Tzu?' I asked him.

He squinted at the name and then verified it, giving it the proper Chinese pronunciation, and said, '*The Art of War.*'

'Is it studied? I was reading it in Kampala and want to know more about it.'

'It's pretty well known,' Shiva said. 'Sun Tzu was a general during the late Tang dynasty. The Chinese have revived the book because Mao praised him.' He turned to Vidia. 'Do you have anything to drink?'

'You've just had tea,' Vidia said.

'I mean a stronger potion,' Shiva said.

He laughed again. I saw that his laughter, especially the giggly sort, was prompted by embarrassment, his awkwardness in the presence of his brother.

Vidia scowled. 'What about your Chinky book?'

Shiva tapped his cigarette, flicked his long hair. He said, 'I think I'll go out to a pub. Want to come with me, Paul?'

I said okay, but I had the feeling that Vidia disapproved of my going.

The pub in Stockwell was so noisy and dirty I was glad Vidia had not come – anyway, he avoided all pubs. Shiva smoked and we drank pints of beer at a small table. I liked his sudden friendliness, and he had an air of idleness that was a relief from Vidia's demanding attention. Shiva seemed sad, almost desperate, but forgiving, and so he was easy company.

'My brother told me all about you,' he said. 'Your African adventures.'

He sounded mocking and envious, but he was just self-conscious, not the words themselves but the gauche way he said them.

'Everyone says that. Vidia's my champion.'

'He means it. He is your friend. He is really proud of you.' Then Shiva laughed sadly. 'I'm afraid he's not very proud of me.'

To avoid this subject I said, 'You should visit Africa sometime.'

'I don't think so,' Shiva said. 'Do you have any money on you? I need some cigarettes.'

I gave him a pound note.

'I'll pay you back,' he said, with such unnecessary force that I smiled, and when he bought the cigarettes and pocketed the change I knew I would never see the money again.

I said, 'Are you planning to be a writer?'

He laughed his giggly laugh, which meant he was mortified by my question. He said, 'I know better than to do that.'

'Vidia told me that you know his work well.'

'I memorized *The Mystic Masseur*. I can actually recite it.'

So it was true. This amazed me: the novel was two hundred pages long.

'When my brother came back to Trinidad after it was published, I recited parts of it to him. I was just a little schoolboy. It was my party piece.'

'What was his reaction?'

'Vidia didn't seem to notice. He was very tired all the time. I just remember him sleeping, lying in a bed in the house. He hardly spoke to me or to anyone. No' – Shiva stroked his hair – 'there was one thing. He took me out and we bought a dog. The dog was an awful nuisance, not housetrained or anything like that. Vidia said, "I think that's enough of this dog." We took him some distance from the house and let him go. "Just walk away," Vidia said. But the dog followed us. Then we took him really far, and walked away very fast, and hid. That did it. We never saw the dog again.'

I could see Vidia's frowning face and hear him saying *Just walk away*.

I said, 'You know, that business about sleeping with African girls . . . It's not a big deal. I had a Nigerian girlfriend when I met your brother.'

'He teases me,' Shiva said.

He said that he had hoped to go to Trinidad in a few days but that he didn't have the money and couldn't decide whether it was worth pressing Vidia for the airfare. It was a dilemma. He wanted to go – he had not seen his mother or sisters for a year.

'We should go back to the house,' I said.

'Do you mind buying me another drink?'

I agreed, though I feared that it was going to make us late for dinner, and it did. Back at the house, Vidia was at the table making a point about punctuality: he had started eating. Pat was flustered.

Shiva hardly noticed, but I could tell that I was out of favor, having contributed to Shiva's dereliction.

That night, after Pat and Vidia went to bed, Shiva and I talked about Mencius and Africa and his airfare dilemma. At ten or so, Pat appeared in her robe and slippers, looking sleepless and harassed. She said, 'Vidia wants you to please stop talking. You're keeping him awake.'

Apart from Vidia, the only other writer I knew in London was a young novelist named B. S. Johnson, who was notorious for being hot-tempered and unstable. He was a big boisterous man who lived with his wife, Ginny, in an apartment in Myddleton Square. His baby son he called Sausage. He was poetry editor of *The Transatlantic Review* and had printed some of my poems, the poems with 'lots of libido.' I had phoned Johnson before Christmas, on the day Vidia ditched me, cross that I had made him wait under an awning in Great Russell Street. I phoned Johnson again.

'Come to a preview of my film,' he said.

There were screenings all the time, he said. It was an experimental film, called *You're Human Just Like the Rest of Them*. He had written several novels, one about Gypsies, called *Traveling People*, and one about a teacher, *Albert Angelo*. His newest novel, *The Unfortunates*, was sold unbound, just loose pages in a box that could be read in any order.

I mentioned that I was staying with Vidia.

'Naipaul is a prick,' Johnson said.

'No, he's all right,' I said.

'You're a bloody Yank. What do you know about the fucking English class system?'

This was not a debating point – he sounded, if not paranoid and deranged, then aggressively energetic. His books had that crazy, selfish energy. *Albert Angelo* especially had an arresting narrative structure, beginning as a po-faced novel in the third person and becoming a first-person confession.

Fearing a confrontation between Vidia and Johnson, I invited Shiva to go with me to the screening. The theater was in Soho. Johnson was lingering in the doorway with a young Pakistani man. I introduced Shiva.

'Zulfikar Ghose,' the Pakistani said, and stuck out his hand.

The film was short and unfinished-looking, with abrupt, irrational cutaways and a stuttery soundtrack. The main character was a teacher. The action centered on a class of nasty-minded students. I had the feeling that Johnson approved of the way these unruly students baited their teacher. The film was inventive, but it went nowhere. Mostly it seemed outraged, but it did not present enough information for me to share the outrage, and anyway it was a mess.

'It's great,' I said to Johnson afterwards. 'It's fabulous.'

'Everyone will hate it,' Johnson said. He seemed pleased at the thought. 'They'll say it needs work.'

That was exactly what I would have said if I had had the nerve.

Shiva smiled and said, 'Yes, it's got something.'

We all went to Zulfikar Ghose's house for tea. Ghose's wife was Portuguese. When she greeted us, Zulfikar said, nodding to Shiva, 'Guess whose brother this is?'

'Leave it out,' Johnson said. 'Who the fuck cares?'

I was thinking that perhaps this was a lesson in the English class system, since, having met Vidia's upper-class admirers – Lady Antonia, Hugh Thomas, Sir Hugh Fraser – I was now meeting his proletarian detractors.

We talked some more about the film. Shiva said, 'I take it to be a comment on the comprehensive-school system.'

'Among other things,' Johnson said. With force he added, 'I'll never turn my back on the working class.'

'Everyone's saying good things about the film,' Zulfikar said.

'I want to show it to Samuel Beckett,' Johnson said.

Shiva said, 'Do you actually know Beckett?'

'I see him when I'm in Paris,' Johnson said, looking into the middle distance with his bulbous blue eyes. He had a puffy face and an adenoidal way of speaking. 'I've shown him quite a bit of my fiction. I acknowledge him as a major influence on my work. I told him, "I hear your rhythms in my head." Beckett understood. He said to me, "I hear Joyce's rhythms in my head."'

Vidia would have said, *What rubbish*. I listened with Vidia's ears and saw with his eyes. Johnson uttered this pretentiousness with such pompous defiance that he killed the conversation.

At last Zulfikar said to me, 'What are you writing?'

'A novel,' I said, thinking of my Chinese-grocer book.

'You should be writing poetry,' said Johnson. It was a stern instruction. 'Remember that you are first a poet.'

After we left, walking through Myddleton Square to the Angel tube station, Shiva said, 'Do you write poems?'

'Not anymore.'

I had abandoned poetry for the way it brought out affectation in my writing. It made me self-conscious, and the form limited me to saying so little. The fault was with me, of course, not with poetry. The sort of poetry I wrote forced me to be a miniaturist. Also, Vidia's remark 'lots of libido' had demoralized me.

Shiva was smiling, probably at the thought of the silliness of writing poetry.

At the Angel – London seemed full of ugly structures with beautiful names – I called Heather from a public phone to see whether she had returned from Christmas with her parents. She answered and, hearing my voice, said, 'Come right over. I want to show you my Christmas presents.'

I said to Shiva, 'I'll be back late.'

When Heather opened the door of her apartment she was wearing a white vinyl raincoat and high boots, also white and shiny, that were just becoming stylish. Her blonde hair was braided, two strands framing her face, and she was holding a tube of pink lipstick between newly painted purple fingernails – her lips gleamed. I sniffed her sweet perfume.

'Christmas presents,' she said, and opened one flap of the raincoat by putting one hand on her hip. She was naked underneath.

Nine hours later, I took a taxi back to Stockwell. I was scorched and chafed: sex for Heather was both suffering and pleasure, and she was an active scratcher with those purple nails. During sex, she howled like someone being punished, but when I stopped she demanded more. In the darkness afterwards she said, 'Next time I want you to spank me.'

It seemed to me that the taxi driver and I were the only people awake in the city. Creeping into Vidia's house and past Shiva's room, I felt that everyone except me was tucked in bed, sensible and virtuous. I felt like a dog again.

*

I woke late. Vidia was in his armchair, reading the bound proof of *The Mimic Men*. He read with such concentration that his face, dark and tight, looked completely shut. He did not appear to notice me enter the room. I sensed something wrong, that he was tensely trying to control his agitation.

I sat for a while smoking, saying nothing.

'Shiva left,' he said at last, looking up from the proof. 'I never saw him.'

I gathered there had been a crisis. Vidia often spoke about how he felt vibrations. I believed him, because he also gave off vibrations. I knew when something was on his mind long before he said anything about it.

'Shall we go to Oxford?' he asked, and answered himself, 'Yes, I think we should go to Oxford.'

I knew the Oxford train from my close reading of the *Mimic Men* proofs. The book's narrator was a womanizer. His ardor struck me because Vidia seemed uninterested and sometimes hostile towards women. 'There were always women to be picked up at the British Council,' the narrator said, speaking of his student days in London and not sounding at all like Vidia. But the next sentence was pure Vidia: 'Those halls could be disagreeable with acrid-scented Africans.'

The Oxford train figured in the narrator's womanizing, for after it drew out of Paddington and the conductor asked for tickets, he noted the young women who held excursion tickets to be punched. That meant they were foreign tourists on a day trip and thus easy prey. The narrator is watchful: 'When one is in vein, as the French say, when dedication and commitment are total, a mistake is rare.' Four weeks in a row he buttonholes a woman on the Oxford train and ends up in bed with her.

Vidia and I took the train late in the morning from Paddington. I did not mention *The Mimic Men*. Passing through Uxbridge I saw, clearly lettered on a brick embankment by a bridge, the sign *Keep Britain White*.

Vidia smiled at it. He said, 'Have I told you my joke? I would put a comma after "Britain."'

It was my first experience of British Rail. I was reassured in the big warm bosom of this friendly monster, sitting on a cushion in a corner seat, watching Berkshire go by, and the lovely fields, still green in an English winter, and the solid houses and the clumps of woods that bordered meadowland. I had not realized how disoriented I had been in black, labyrinthine London until I saw the open countryside. English people in Africa boasted of everything, but I had never heard any of them boast of the beauty of these green fields and pretty hills and indestructible-looking villages. They never spoke about such things.

I mentioned this to Vidia.

'Because they're infies,' he said.

A little later, I said, 'You must have done this many times, taken this train.'

'Oh, God.'

I was asking about *The Mimic Men* but without saying so. He gave nothing away, he seldom reminisced, but he set great store by faces – how much they told; and by expressions – what a grimace revealed. So I knew that his experiences on this London-to-Oxford line had been painful and possibly bitter. He often spoke of poverty, of the misery of having no money. His version of his past was one of turmoil and deprivation. He looked back all the time, as his writing showed, but he did not talk about it.

For lunch we both had cheese sandwiches in the buffet car. I knew that Vidia ate fish. But to me, at that time, a vegetarian was someone who ate nothing but cheese sandwiches.

Traveling on this train, reading newspapers, was so pleasant I would not have minded going further. My only other real experiences of trains were the overnighter to Nairobi and the Mombasa express and the gasping steam locomotives of Malawi and Rhodesia. The train soothed and comforted me and stimulated my imagination. It offered me a glimpse of the best of England and provided access to my past by activating my memory. I had made a discovery: I would gladly go anywhere on a train.

Oxford was soon outside the window, first a platform, then a sign, finally the place itself: gray stone buildings, devotional in their contours, a wilderness of churches and cloisters, a town of ecclesiastical stone. There were more walls than steeples and spires, and many narrow streets, every stone seemingly chiseled with a coded message which, when translated, read *No Trespassing*.

Before we left the station, Vidia went to the timetable on the wall and made a note of the times of the later trains to London. It seemed a wise thing to do. I never would have thought of the precaution – another lesson from Vidia in the importance of having an escape route. Once again I felt like a beginner, but I had Vidia to show me the way.

Leaving the station, I stuffed the newspapers I had read into a barrel.

'Why did you buy three newspapers?' Vidia asked.

'I don't know,' I said, because I sensed he disapproved. One had been the *Daily Mirror*.

'Most of the English press is such rubbish.'

But I had felt starved for news in Uganda. Although we got the English Sunday papers, always late, news in Uganda was by word of mouth, rumor and speculation, just whispers. The *Argus* was timid, and the government paper, *The People*, was a mouthpiece. I was stimulated by English papers, the freshness, the frankness, the humor. But what was new to me was stale to Vidia.

We walked up High Street.

'This dampness,' Vidia said. 'When I was here I had such terrible asthma that I lay on my bed and Patsy held me – held me in her arms – and warmed me so that I could breathe.'

University College – Shiva's college, and it had also been Vidia's – was in High Street, with a large gateway, like the entrance to a cloister. A small window, like that in a tollbooth, framed the ugly face of an older man dressed in black. He stepped into the walkway, scowling, looking cruel.

'Hello, Mr Naipaul. What brings you 'ere, then?'

It was a thick country accent, sure of itself, and its confidence and strength made the man seem more like a prison guard than a porter.

'Looking for my brother,' Vidia said.

Vidia seemed somewhat uneasy; it was the way the man faced him. Vidia needed servants and flunkies to be more humble and respectful than this.

''Aven't seen 'im at all. They've been told to sign the book, but

I don't suppose he takes a blind bit of notice of what the master says.'

'No. One imagines not. He's not in his room?'

'Your brother, Mr Naipaul? He left 'is key. Wasn't 'ere yesterday, neither.'

'Very well. We will leave a note for him.'

Vidia wrote the note while the porter stood with his arms folded.

'You can put it in my brother's mailbox.'

'If 'e fucking looks in 'is mailbox, which I doubt.' The porter handled the note as if it were something of no value. 'So, 'ow 'ave you been keeping?'

'Yes, quite well, um, latterly, one has been very busy, thank you.'

I had not imagined it: Vidia was uneasy in the presence of this domineering servant. It was as though they had no language in common, which was perhaps actually the case. It was one of the strangest conversations ever – the rough, unapologetic, cursing servant who was in charge, and the oblique, inquiring master at his mercy.

'I shall hand this to your brother personally.'

'Yes. So good of you.'

The telephone jangled in the tollbooth.

'You will excuse me, gentlemen.' The porter stepped inside and shouted into the phone.

Vidia showed me the quad, the buildings, the spire, and in one anteroom a bright white marble statue of Percy Bysshe Shelley, once a resident of University College. The porter was still on the telephone when we left.

Passing Blackwell's bookshop on Broad Street, I expressed an interest in browsing and we went in. Vidia waited and looked at books, all the while giving off a signal that indicated that I should hurry up. Vidia's impatience was a vibration that was almost audible, a distinct high-pitched whine. I saw some first editions of Hemingway and Orwell.

'How much is this?' I showed him the Orwell.

'Twelve shillings. You don't want that.'

We left the bookstore and soon passed a round tower.

'The Bodleian,' Vidia said.

After a short walk we entered the gateway of another college, with paler, taller spires set beside a wide meadow.

'Where are we?'

'Christ Church.'

Places like this reminded me that I was in many respects an African. I needed a simpler and less demanding world. I was at my happiest in the bush. And it was not merely that the orderly and ancient buildings overwhelmed me; the students also seemed aloof and proprietorial. They were much younger than me, and they looked right at home here. I knew I did not belong, that I would never belong.

Back on High Street, we walked as far as Magdalen Bridge and into Magdalen College itself – more cloisters, another quad, buildings like monasteries. Being a student here seemed to me like my being an actor in a pageant in which I did not know any of my lines, one of those terrible dreams.

I said, 'I wonder what happened to Shiva.'

Vidia said, 'Seewyn's problem is that he was raised by women, who adored him. So he takes no responsibility.'

We went to the Ashmolean Museum. As he had done at the National Gallery, the Tate, and the V and A, Vidia made a beeline for certain rooms, for specific paintings, for particular details in those paintings, none of them obvious. He darted to a Watteau, a Whistler, a Hilliard miniature, and always indicated the tiniest features. 'Look at this,' and 'See how he handles paint.'

I looked for anything of Africa – a mask, a spear, a landscape, anything of the bush. I realized how Ugandans must feel, stuck in Oxford or London after leaving the vast, deep savannah or the slopes of the Mountains of the Moon. And then I saw a painting that reassured me.

It might have been done in Fort Portal or Mubende, with big generous trees and tall elephant grass and flat-topped fever thorns in the distance. There were small figures at the side, some animals – gazelles, impalas, no big game – and rich colors and flowers in the foreground. I did not recognize the artist's name. I liked this wide green canvas and the accuracy of the view and the easily identifiable plants, the precise leaves, the blossoms, and the dome of sky. Even the scraps of cloud looked right.

I did not call Vidia's attention to it. I was afraid he might disapprove and spoil a moment that had cheered me. It was not his Africa. My reaction to this painting made me think I should leave England soon. Vidia walked quickly over to me and frowned at the picture.

To distract him I said, 'Maybe we should go past Shiva's college one more time, to see whether he's come back.'

'No, no.' Vidia turned away from the picture. 'He's on his own now.'

I noticed that he was wearing the heavy shoes he called *veldshoen*. He had been wearing them that night in Kisenyi, by the shore of Lake Kivu, when he had said, 'What that dog needs is a good kick.'

On the way back to London on the train, Vidia said, 'I wonder whether any of my books will last?'

I said that I thought *A House for Mr Biswas* was a masterpiece that would last as long as people read books.

'You're so kind,' he said. He seemed to consider the word 'masterpiece.' Then he said, 'One hopes so. It's a big book.'

We talked about the book. Vidia said that although he had never reread it, he had put everything into it – his family, his island, everything he knew. Even small things in the book pleased him. He smiled at a memory.

'There are three Negro workmen in the book – just simple fellows, with shovels. Do you remember them? They only have first names, Edgar, Sam, and George.'

'They work on Biswas's house.'

'Yes, yes.' But he was already laughing. 'Edgar Mittelholzer, Samuel Selvon, and George Lamming,' he said, naming three black novelists from Trinidad.

He almost gagged laughing at this private joke, but after a while, still talking about the novel, we discussed Mr Biswas's views on typefaces. Vidia became animated again. With his mouth close to the window of the train, he exhaled on the glass.

'This is Times.' He sketched a letter with his finger, then added embellishments and more letters. 'This is sans serif. And this' – he was still adding letters to the steam-clouded glass – 'is Bodoni. I like this.'

He was intent, still sketching with his finger, still describing.

I said, 'Sometimes they put that information on the last page of a book. I never know what to make of it.'

'I love it,' he said.

'And this,' he said, working his finger on the window, 'this is Caslon. Notice the difference?'

The letters seemed to fade. But no, they remained on the glass. As soon as we got near London they were lit again by the city's lights, all those different letters.

The day before I left, there were workmen in Vidia's house. They were hammering in his bedroom, fixing some shelves that Vidia considered badly built. It was a Saturday. I called Heather and asked if we could meet. She said yes but suggested a pub, not her apartment. She knew I was leaving. At the pub, she complained that I cared more about Vidia than about her.

'He's my friend,' I said.

'Thanks,' she said.

Seeing I had hurt her, I said, 'You're my friend too, of course you are.'

I could not explain how Vidia mattered, and how his friendship was different from anyone else's. I knew he loved Shiva, but he seemed to depend on me so much more than he did on his brother, and he knew more about my writing ambition than I had ever dared tell my own family.

Heather and I went on drinking. We did not make love that day. The omission made it more final a farewell.

Vidia looked grief-stricken when I got back that night. Pat was on the parlor sofa. He was sitting in his armchair, an expression of sorrow on his face, but when he began to speak to her, he sounded like a small child who had been wronged.

'I can't sleep in that bed,' he said. 'It's tainted. Why did he do it? The foolish, ignorant man!'

He was disgusted and near to tears.

'What happened?' I asked.

'One of the workmen in Vidia's bedroom was explaining something,' Pat began. But she seemed too frightened to continue.

His face twisted in nausea, Vidia said, 'And he sat on my bed, Patsy. He put his bottom on my bed.'

The next morning, Vidia was still seated in his armchair in the parlor. He looked grim. Fatigue made his skin grayish. He had not slept. It would be a long day, and I could not begin to comprehend how the bed that the workman had tainted by sitting on it would ever be purified.

He looked weary. He said he was sorry I was leaving, and he meant it – he looked as though he needed to be propped up. Pat was fretful and weepy, but I could not tell whether my departure was the cause.

As always, Vidia said, 'You're going to be all right.'

7

Air Letters: A Correspondence Course

Vidia claimed that handwriting spoke volumes. Even if you could not read the words, the way they were written, just the loops and slants and how a *t* was crossed, told you what you needed to know. He had taught me to read the moods in his handwriting, for which he always used a fountain pen and black ink. Large and loopy meant he was idle and calm, regular squiggles indicated concentration, small meant anxious, tiny meant fearful and overworked, and at its most minuscule he was at his wits' end. It was perhaps some consolation that, graphologically inclined, he knew what his own handwriting told him.

For the next five years, we conversed by airmail over long distances. I was in Africa and later in Singapore; Vidia was in and out of England. He usually wrote me on blue air-letter forms from the post office, the ones with preprinted stamps on the front. They unfolded to narrow lengths of paper that seemed Chinese to him, he said. He used them vertically, cramming them with his handwriting.

These letters were for me a source of wisdom and strength and amounted to a correspondence course in creative writing; from Vidia I learned the reality of being a writer. During this period I had no telephone, I had no other close friends, I did not leave the Equator. The mail was everything. Face to face, anyone can say he is your friend and can promise to write faithfully, but the test of friendship is the letters themselves, the fondest proof that you are remembered. I did not want to be forgotten, for once again I was buried in Africa.

It bewildered me when the first letter I received from him was cold. Worse than cold: somewhat offensive. That curfew book I had given to his editor Diana Athill, at André Deutsch, had been turned down. Her letter had discouraged me in what I had thought was a great idea: a book about Africa in the form of a chronicle about a violent curfew. I had complained to Vidia of her indifference.

In his letter, a Lebanese stamp on the envelope, written on the stationery of the Bristol Hotel in Beirut, Vidia stood by his editor. He said her judgment was sound. He would not give me any further advice about publishing. He suggested that I was patronizing him in the language of my letter, that I misread Africa, that I did not understand Martial's epigrams, and he wished me well in my journalism. This seemed belittling to the fiction I was trying to write. He closed with a mention of Francis Chichester, at that moment sailing his *Gipsy Moth IV* solo around the world. He wrote, 'I hope he drowns.'

It was a bad-tempered letter, written in one of his moods. I could have guessed that when I saw his handwriting. Though he was in Beirut, he did not refer to it, except by using the hotel's ornate letterhead – I suspected him of ostentation. He did not say where he was going, or why. It was a grand gesture, his letter from Lebanon, a romantic and cosmopolitan place that was on the itinerary of a successful writer.

In fact he was on his way to India, Pat wrote, in a letter I received a week later. She called his trip 'a journalistic assignment' and said he would be in India two months, for a long article. His dismissive mention of my journalism, which had rankled, perhaps also explained why he had not said he was going to be a journalist in India.

They were terrible letter writers, all of them, Pat said. Shiva did not even write home. I should not expect too much, and yet she said that it had pleased her to see that we were exchanging letters regularly – it was uncharacteristic of Vidia to write so often.

She reported Vidia's comings and goings like a doting mother. He had been living in the Kent town of Sandwich, in a loaned house, while Pat had commuted by train every few days from her teaching duties. Running on the beach – *running on the beach*? I had to read the sentence three times – Vidia had sprained his ankle, but he had looked so comic falling down and gesturing that Pat had not taken it seriously. A swollen ankle was the upshot, and, as a fellow athlete (the man had once water-skied to France), the doctor was sympathetic.

Pat Naipaul's affectionate letter lifted my spirits and explained Vidia's mood. He was much sweeter, his old encouraging self, when I heard from him again, on his return from India two months later. He praised me, he praised my letters – I was gifted; he complained that he was dull, he was slow, and that he often gave offense without meaning to.

The answer was to acknowledge one's limitations and as a letter writer to write the simplest, most businesslike notes, so that they could not be misconstrued.

I need not have feared that he would be businesslike with me. He described how, at the house of Anthony Powell, he had seen an advertisement for my novel – my first novel – in a New York magazine. He talked about the way Israel, a place he had been bored by, was being praised while the Arabs were being scorned. He recalled how noble the stereotype of the Arabs had once been: 'fine gentlemen, romantic desert folk, fair in battle, unconquerable in love' – no more!

After all his travels and all his work, he had insomnia again. His life was a monotony. He welcomed the morning. Sleeping pills made him asthmatic. He had lost weight – he was down to 120 pounds. This suffering was an omen: 'It is time I set up house in another country.'

He had started his Port of Spain book, a history, which he would eventually title *The Loss of El Dorado*. Doing research, reading everything on the subject, he stumbled across oddities of scholarship, such as the Spaniard who had devoted his life to proving that Columbus, Cervantes, and Saint Teresa were Jewish.

In an aside in one letter he mentioned that I seemed very happy. That was astute of him. I was happy. I had fallen in love. This was about three months after returning to Uganda. I told Vidia about it and that I planned to get married to this woman, a teacher in Kenya whom I had met in Kampala. She was from London. He congratulated me, said he was delighted. He was also pleased to hear that his magazine pieces about India – the journalism – had been reprinted in Nairobi. I admired his confidence in saying, 'It was a good piece of work, and I think one of the best things I have written.' He was putting India aside for good. He had no interest in writing about it ever again, he said.

To cheer himself up, he took a trip to Denmark. But the place depressed him – all the conformity, and the prison cells of houses, the high taxes. Vidia found Danes to be bored and lonely and solitary. To lighten their hearts they drank themselves silly on booze cruises, called 'spirit boats,' but ended up more depressed. The saddest expression of Danish solitude was their pornography, which was mere exhibitionism, without innovation: women with 'legs wide apart' or men sitting naked on steps 'so that the genitals hang visibly down.' He now hated the very word 'Scandinavian' as 'full of ice and death and sullen coitus.'

A brilliant phrase like 'sullen coitus' made me glad I knew him, and also glad to be in Africa, where coitus was never sullen. By the way, Vidia said, the Carib Indians worshiped a devil god called Mahboya, who probably resembled his namesake, the Kenyan politician Tom Mboya, whose name Vidia always mispronounced.

Still collecting gossip and hearsay for my study of rumors in Africa (their strangeness and their speed of travel), I reported to Vidia a story that involved Tom Mboya. A year before, Mboya's infant son had mysteriously died. The death was mentioned in the newspapers, but without giving any details. According to the rumor, Mboya had murdered his own son because he had discovered the baby to be half white, the love child of Mrs Mboya and the US ambassador, William Attwood. This rumor, totally false, was circulating in the British expatriate community in Nairobi.

Any day now, Vidia said, he was going to fly to the West Indies and the United States, to finish his book. But he did not go. His book continued slowly. The next time I heard from him, six weeks later, he was still in London. All his plans had changed.

I had to promise, he insisted, that I would say nothing about a scoop he had just been offered by a magazine that had assigned him to do a profile-interview, in utmost secrecy, with Jacques Soustelle, a French intellectual and political renegade. I had never heard of the man. I had finished my Chinese-grocer novel and had started another; I was now spending all my free time in Embu, in upcountry Kenya, with my fiancée, who taught in an African school. I knew no one who was interested in Vidia's secret.

I wondered what to make of the journalism he was doing. He had told me once that he did such work for the money. His assignments meant foreign travel. They meant breaking off work on his book – a hard thing to do. I was teaching every day and also working on a novel, so it consoled me to hear about his interruptions.

He asked in one letter whether he should call his West Indian history *The Quest and the Question*. The book was about two related stories separated by many years: the quest for El Dorado, the golden land, and the question of torture involving a notorious case in Trinidad. I timidly suggested that it seemed a weak and mechanical title and that El Dorado was such an evocative name, couldn't that be part of it? To ingratiate myself, I told him I was also having a title problem with my new novel.

He was scrapping his title, he said in reply, and was glad to hear about my novel. Returning to his role of teacher, he asked me whether my novel had arisen out of 'a still centre.'

He went on, 'Every good book suggests that the writer, however painful its subject, has arrived at some inward peace about it, some inner resolution, even of anger and despair, even though this peace and resolution is purely temporary. So that you know where a man stands.'

That perception had come from the magazine work he was doing. He was opinionated, he had a strong personality, and magazine editors liked this kind of writer. He was being given many assignments. He also wrote pieces for American magazines. One was entitled, 'What's Wrong with Being a Snob?' In it, he made a case for the snob, as though snobs were a victimized minority.

I had never met a snob who was not also a liar, and that was what was wrong about snobbery. But I did not say so to Vidia. His snobbery, like his article (which he never reprinted), seemed to be harmless posturing and pulling rank and, as I had seen, fueled mostly by fear.

I got married in Kampala at the end of 1967. Vidia wrote to congratulate me and mentioned that he himself had been married for thirteen years. In closing, he asked me to buy him an ivory cigarette holder (elephants were still being recycled into such items then). And how about a big yellow meerschaum pipe? Could he have one of those too?

Vidia was in the midst of change. He had decided to sell his house – the house he seemed so fond of. He was selling it for £12,000 to Tristram Powell, whom I had met at the dinner party at Vidia's. It was actually worth £14,000, but this way Vidia would not need to pay an agent's commission or have to deal with delays.

He wanted to go to the United States. He wondered whether my older brother, Eugene, could help him find a house to rent in order for him to finish his book. After his book was done, he would be a journalist for a while, just for the money. When he had some money he would start a new book. He suggested that he had an idea for one.

My writing about Africa stimulated him, he said. He too had been thinking of writing about Africa. He sent his love.

In the middle of 1968, in his tiniest handwriting, an effect of concentrated writing and worry, he reflected on the paradoxes of being a writer. He was in Scotland, a houseguest at a baronial mansion. He complimented me on my letters to him.* They reminded him of Scott Fitzgerald's, which he had been reading. Fitzgerald had written many letters to his daughter, Vidia said, all about writing. It was the sort of obsession that writers developed about their art. The origin of this was that we all started by wishing to be writers and by mimicking what we had read. Through work we eventually arrived at another level, doing a sort of writing we didn't really understand. We became lost and questioned the point of writing.

There was a strong, almost Buddhist element in writing, he said, in that good writing canceled out what had existed before. Even the second half of a book canceled out the first half, and each book canceled out the previous one and existed as a reincarnation of the earlier work.

In this meditation in the Scottish mansion, Vidia reflected on the vanity of fame and posterity, because all the books in the library there seemed so dated. They no longer mattered; fame was nothing.

---

* I did not make copies of my letters. Vidia, however, saved all of them. They are in the Naipaul Collection at the University of Oklahoma at Tulsa, with the rest of Vidia's papers. In writing this reminiscence, I asked to see the letters I wrote to Vidia, and some other material. Permission was not granted.

Writers were steadily canceling themselves out, the new replacing the old. The paradox was that the better they were, the more likely they were to be rejected, for they created a standard that would be revised and superseded. That was the saddest part. 'Really how unfair we are today to writers who educated us when we were young and sharpened our minds and gave us a new way of looking at the world and made us want to be writers.'

The worst aspect of the study of literature was that it dealt with the past, because literature was alive and mattered, or else it was nothing.

He urged me to consider the notion of time and tradition in relation to Charles Dickens and Rudyard Kipling. They had each been immensely successful, yet in their writing they had described a much older version of their culture. This version had been ignored because lesser writers – copycats, missing the point – had simply gone on working in a literary tradition. For example, Kipling wrote about an India that was twenty years out of date, but Kipling's contemporaries were still imitating Dickens, who himself had set his own books in an earlier period.

With this wise lesson in literature, Vidia sent his love.

I was encouraged to have him as a friend, and what he said was helpful to me, because I felt cut off in my house in Uganda, writing my third novel. The implication I drew from his air letter was that he saw me as a promising modernist, at a frontier in Africa, writing about what I knew. He was encouraging me; he wanted me to understand the paradoxes.

I needed the help. It was June 1968. My first novel, *Waldo*, had gotten good reviews. *Fong and the Indians* was about to appear. I was at work on another novel with an African setting, *Girls at Play*. My first child, a son, had just been born. I had resigned from my job in Uganda and had been hired to teach in Singapore. I was flying by the seat of my pants.

Departing from the blue Chinese-style air-letter forms, Vidia wrote across two sheets of note paper to congratulate us on our new baby. He also congratulated me on leaving Africa after more than five years. He frankly disapproved of the fact that I was going to Singapore to teach English literature, and he claimed never to have heard of the course I was to teach: Jacobean literature –

Shakespeare's contemporaries in the age of James I. But – and here came a Naipaul curve ball – 'perhaps you might get me out there as a visiting idler.'

It was just like Vidia to scorn the job I had taken in desperation, and to repeat his contempt for the study of literature, but at the same time to ask me to find him a slot as a visiting writer of the sort he had been, disastrously, in Uganda. It was a paradox he himself admitted. He tried to be high-minded, yet he was the first to confess his contradictions. The example of his candor was his greatest lesson.

Knowing that I needed to establish myself in England, he suggested to the literary editor of *The Times* that I become a regular reviewer. The money was not the point – I would get £10 for each review – it was, rather, the chance to become part of the London reviewing and writing coterie. I had to be seen as someone who was serious, who had judgment and wit, who was not above reviewing books.

Vidia said that he was traveling, leaving London, but not sure where he was going. He had sold his house. He still wanted to go to the United States. He repeated his request for my brother to find him a house, somewhere in rural America. He still had some journalism to do.

My wife and I moved from Uganda to Singapore with our baby son. This was in the autumn of 1968. I resumed teaching. I wrote some short stories and published them. I began reviewing books for *The Times*. My third novel was done, and I had an idea for another, more ambitious novel, about life in an African dictatorship. I still had no money. But it was not only poverty that kept me from returning to the States; it was also my curiosity about Southeast Asia – the echo of the gunfire from Vietnam, the effects of the war on nearby countries. And I found that I could teach and write. Teaching was not difficult; I found Shakespeare's contemporaries illuminating and undemanding, and the violent vengefulness in the plays made sense to my Chinese students, some of whom were ardent supporters of the Cultural Revolution.

Even in Singapore I had regular air letters from my friend Naipaul, who believed in me.

'What lovely Bongo-Wongo addresses you are picking up on the way!' he wrote in a letter with my exotic Singapore street address. A Trinidad stamp on that letter looked equally exotic to me.

In the past, when he was feeling frail from having worked hard, he said, 'I feel like a bird with a broken wing.' Now his broken wing was healing, he said. He was in Port of Spain. He had finished his historical narrative, pleased with it for being so contemporary. Even Pat had liked it. He implied that she was often one of his worst detractors. After two years, *The Loss of El Dorado* was done, and when it appeared it would explain a great deal about the modern world, in which race and class were primary issues. 'The book is good.'

From Trinidad, he was embarking on some journalistic assignments in the United States. Needing a visa, he had gone to the US consulate in Port of Spain and been treated with lavish courtesy and deference. He said to me, 'Guilt will make my hand shake if I ever write an unkind word about the US.'

He was granted two visas: one to enter the country, the other to work as a journalist for four years – he underlined the four. The visas had been presented with style, the consul-general emerging from his office to extend his congratulations, the whole consulate staff beaming.

It mattered a lot to him that he had been singled out from the other islanders and treated with respect. He did not take it for granted. He said he left the consulate feeling weak.

He reported that the literary editor of *The Times* liked my work and was using the reviews regularly, in spite of having to send the books all the way to Singapore. But the *Washington Post* was doing the same thing. What with my teaching and my short stories and the novel I had started, I had never worked so hard for so little money. My wife got a job at the Chinese university to keep us afloat, but still we had no savings.

Money was on Vidia's mind. He complained of high taxes and low standards in Trinidad. He would soon be leaving for New York City. A few months later, in March 1969, he wrote me from the New York apartment of Robert Lowell, where he was a houseguest. Lowell, he said, was the only writer in New York who had read his work. One of his bits of journalism was an interview with Lowell.

Vidia felt awkward being in New York, where no one cared about his work. He said. 'It makes me feel an intruder.'

He was out of sympathy with the writers and intellectuals he met in New York: Baldwin, Bellow, Roth, Trilling. He had no patience with their views. He saw them as obsessed and, ultimately, trivial-minded. Half the time he had no idea what they were writing about. They were publicity seekers, he said; their writing was wordy. It was better to grow slowly as a writer and to build a reputation book by book. He meant himself, and I guessed it was also a hint to me.

There were aspects of New York that he liked. The wine was good and inexpensive. The city had energy. He envisioned making a life in New York, buying an apartment and spending part of every year there. Indians – not 'dot Indians' but 'feather Indians' – were on his mind. 'I alternate between great happiness and great rage at the violence done to the American Indians,' he said. 'I feel the land very much as theirs at dusk, the sky high above Central Park.'

I had told him that I was getting on in Singapore; in spite of the financial narrowness, it was a new place with new people, and it gave me the chance to travel in Burma and Indonesia. I had begun to write *Jungle Lovers*. *Fong* had appeared – a small advance, good reviews, but no steady income. I said to myself, If I write a book every year for the next ten years, I am sure I can make a living. I could not think beyond ten years.

Vidia wrote back from New York to wish me well. He said he had been thinking fondly about my wife and son. That touched me at a time when I felt burdened and overworked. I lived in a small, hot semidetached house and wrote in an airless upstairs room. I could write only after my lectures had been delivered, my papers marked, and my wife and child were contented. After eight months in Singapore I had settled into a routine, but this, I swore, would be my last job. I fantasized about quitting, but I had no place to go. I had no plans, except that I was embarked on my fourth novel. My third, *Girls at Play*, was about to be published in England.

Vidia had plans, he said. He had written a piece for the *Telegraph* in London and another for *The New York Review of Books*, about

Anguilla. He was planning to spend the spring and summer in the United States and then travel back to London in September, when *The Loss of El Dorado* came out – not return for his own sake but to give some moral support to his publishers. Then, after London, perhaps Spain, to work on a book – he did not say what he had in mind – because Spain would be inexpensive.

He took an oblique and somewhat credulous interest in astrology and palmistry. The lines on my palm had impressed him. In New York he had met an astrologer who, noting that Vidia was a Leo, gave him a reading and predicted unending travel, both mental and physical. Vidia welcomed the prophecy. He was eager for a phone call that would send him abroad. The astrologer had said that no sooner would Vidia put his suitcase down than he would pick it up again.

Accompanying Norman Mailer in his campaign to be mayor of New York had occupied some weeks of Vidia's time. That was another piece of journalism. Vidia found Mailer energetic and attractive. He was reading Mailer's book about the political conventions, *Miami and the Siege of Chicago*. Mailer had called it 'a bazaar of metaphors.' Vidia corrected this: surely Mailer meant similes. Nevertheless, Vidia liked the book, and he liked Mailer. It was strange to hear Vidia praising a living writer and a new book. I had never heard him do this before.

By the way, he wondered, had I read Henry James's study of Hawthorne? I immediately got it out of the library and read it with pleasure. I wrote back, thanking him for the suggestion. He was still my teacher, my friend.

A month later, he read my new novel and praised me extravagantly. This was the middle of 1969. The book had just appeared in London, but a copy had been sent to Vidia in New York. *Girls at Play* was a dark book, set in a girls' school in upcountry Kenya. Though I denied the fact for legal reasons, the school was based on the one where my then fiancée had taught in Embu, in the bush about eighty miles northeast of Nairobi.

Vidia told me he had pounced on the book, and he congratulated me and said it was 'very very good' – all this in the first two lines of his air letter.

He had praised me before, but this was different – he said that the book was wonderful and liberating to him. He praised details – that was the best of it, his close reading. In Singapore on hot buggy nights with the ceiling fan croaking, I needed this encouragement. I had written a few chapters of what I expected to be a long novel. I was still writing short stories. I was doing book reviews. I was teaching. How was it possible to work so hard and earn so little?

Never mind, my book was good. V. S. Naipaul said so. He was even grateful to me for having written it – that sounded odd – but he said he would explain this gratitude some other time. He promised that I would get good reviews.

I had managed to please the one person who mattered. And he was more than pleased. He was impressed by its fluency, the transparency of the prose, the dialogue, the opening paragraphs – nearly all of it he found arresting and powerful.

Music to my ears. And there was more: 'Above all, this is the work of a man who has come to a *resolution* about a particular experience . . . There is an attitude that comprehends and absorbs all the experience that is given.'

This seemed the greatest praise possible. Knowing what one was doing was an insight – so he said – that Norman Mailer did not have. He had apparently changed his mind about Mailer. He now said he found Mailer's writing supremely egotistical. I had gone beyond my ego to a stronger objectivity, 'the true artist's detachment – which is not unconcern, far from it.'

He liked the passion, the humor, the nuances, the peculiar characters, the aspects of English decline and African strangeness, the landscape, the emotion. Because he was so positive, he said, he was confident that he could tell me what was less successful. He singled out the confessions. He said they were 'stagey.'

I reread his letter. It was the best review I had ever had, from a wise man, who knew me, the man who always said, 'Are you sure you want to show this to me? I'm brutal, you know.' Not only brutal but stingy and snobbish. Yet this was Vidia at his best, a subtle and generous man.

'Many congratulations again and again' was his way of signing off.

In the Singapore heat, on my low salary, battling with a new novel and feeling old at the age of twenty-eight, I was very happy.

The letter lifted my spirits and sustained me for the next two years in Singapore. I worked with a will. I had been told I was doing the right thing.

I had written *Girls at Play* off my own bat, without a contract, starting it in Africa, finishing it in Singapore. Here I was, still in Singapore on publication day. Vidia's letter prepared me for good reviews, and over the following months I got them – praise in the London papers first, then in the provinces, and finally in the United States. The sales were modest, not substantial enough to liberate me from teaching, but it was all a good omen.

His next air letter came from Canada and was dated August 18. It was the day after his thirty-seventh birthday, but he didn't mention it. Again he had money on his mind. He didn't have enough, he wanted more, he was insulted when a fee was low. Money was a theme with him, which was fine with me – I needed consolation on that score too. He had invested a small amount in the stock market, but he failed to make a killing. 'What I need now is a lot of money,' he said, explaining that if he became rich he would not have to write ever again.

For Vidia, as for me, journalism was money; fiction had to be supported by other work. We were paid for our books, but that money represented only a year's income at best. I had been turned down by the Guggenheim Foundation, I won no prizes, my advances were low – £250 for *Girls at Play* in England, a few thousand dollars from my American publisher. I published a book-length novella, *Murder in Mount Holly*, but that had not earned me much. Therefore, I needed my teaching job and my hack work.

Vidia was the soul of sympathy. He had no cash either. I put some money into stocks and they crashed. I moaned to Vidia. He said that the stock exchange underpinned Western civilization. You had to invest, but you needed to be wise. He analyzed the market, he denounced taxes, he described the fickleness of stocks, he deconstructed inflation, he cursed the necessity to spend.

He had just been in California, writing about John Steinbeck's Monterey. He doubted that I would like California. San Francisco was atmospheric but no match for New York. He had decided that New York was for him. He loved living in great cities – he was frank in his liking for the nightlife, the dinner parties, famous friends. The word 'glamour' was used approvingly throughout his Mailer-for-Mayor piece. He found New York humor profoundly amusing. He put one such exchange into the article.

'I was talking to an old Jew in Brooklyn yesterday,' a Mailer staffer says. 'I told him about Mailer. He said, "Isn't he the guy stabbed his wife?" Nine years, and he's talking about it like he'd read it in the paper that morning.'

'He probably gets his papers late,' another staffer says.

Vidia said, 'New Yorkers protest too much about their problems; in fact it is their problems that give the city its special life and tone.'

Vidia's Mailer piece appeared in the *Telegraph Magazine*. He had written a dozen such articles since I had met him, mostly long, discursive pieces of intense analysis. He had traveled in India, the West Indies, Japan, Canada, and the United States. He had published seven novels and three works of nonfiction. Although he had published in the United States, he was hardly known there and his books soon went out of print. Even Vidia admitted he was nowhere – poor and overworked, like me. This was late in 1969.

With Vidia's plight in mind, I combed through the University of Singapore library's reference section. I found bound sets of *The Spectator* and *The New Statesman*, in which there were scores of book reviews Vidia had written. They were hugely funny, some wickedly so. He was brutal, as he always said; he turned the books inside out, and he was harshest on West Indian authors. He had been writing book reviews since 1957. I read all these uncollected and obscure reviews and as many articles as I could find.

I decided to write a book about his work and proposed the idea to him in an air letter. He welcomed the proposal by opening his heart and telling me that he felt lost, he felt sad. I had to understand this, he said: he had come from nowhere, from nothing. He had been a 'barefoot colonial.'

'Think of it like this,' he said. And what followed was a startling illumination of his writing dilemma, as he used time's light to give me a glimpse of his remote past. 'Imagine the despair to which the barefoot colonial is reduced when, wanting to write, and reading the pattern books of Tolstoy, Balzac et al., he looks at his own world and discovers that it almost doesn't exist. Hemingway? The barefoot colonial in Paris? Where the Hemingway adventure for him? Try to understand this and see the effort to make art out of this destitution and alienation.'

Writing on his air letter in small script, his return address a loaned house in Gloucestershire, he was experiencing a personal crisis, he said. It related to his being in that house. He was feeling like an exile.

He felt miserable. He wanted to buy a house but did not know where, 'what physical area of the earth.' He wanted to write a book but his sense of crisis told him it would never find its audience. He felt that no one really cared about his dilemma.

I had dilemmas of my own: no money, a book in progress, the plays and poems of Shakespeare's contemporaries to teach, an awful house with no air conditioning on a Singapore back street. My son was almost two; my wife was pregnant again and wondering whether she had the strength to go on working. As if I didn't have enough to worry about, the vice-chancellor of the university, Dr Toh Chin Chye, stopped me outside the library one day and told me my hair was too long.

I was in the right mood to explicate Vidia's deepening sense of exile. Vidia agreed: he said it was opportune that I had suggested a book about his work. It eased his mind to know that I was eager to write something. In talking about his island, his sadness, his sense of exile, his uncertainty, he was preparing me. He was saying plainly that I had to know his background or else I would misinterpret him.

I took this as encouragement to write a book about his work. I made a bibliography. I read everything he had written, including all the incidental pieces – his 1958 review of Gustie Herrigel's *Zen in the Art of Flower Arrangement*, his profile of Graham Greene, pieces in *Vogue* and *Punch*, his many London Letters in the *Illustrated Weekly of India*. Even his journalism sparkled.

In another air letter from Gloucestershire, Vidia stressed how temporary his residence was, how he was shuttling around. He also urged me to get out of Singapore and find a place that was intellectually congenial. He saw me having to endure in Singapore the sort of second-rate society he had known in Trinidad. He was interested that we were having a second child – he seemed a trifle dubious. He said he was pleased that I was writing a new book ('you really are a worker'). He looked forward to my study of his work. He gave me total freedom to criticize, deplore, dismiss anything I wished.

'You must give me the pleasure of seeing what I look like,' he said. 'It would be like hearing one's own voice, seeing oneself walk down the street. Show me!'

Did he want me to be brutal? I didn't think so. I had told him how much I had liked *The Loss of El Dorado*. The Italian historian Benedetto Croce had said, 'All history is contemporary,' that the present was part of all history that was written. So Vidia's book explained much of what was going on in the year of its publication, 1970: the issues of race and violence and colonialism. A colony was by its very nature dependent and inferior. Vidia believed that a colony did not have the intelligence or concentration to rebel, which was why colonials had a self-destructive instinct for chaos.

He had been proven right about East Africa. Idi Amin had taken over and threatened to expel the Indians. 'What will you do when the crunch comes?' Vidia had asked almost five years before. The crunch was coming in Uganda.

The reviews of *El Dorado* had been good, though Graham Greene had reservations, finding the prose 'airless.' Vidia was unmoved. Reviews did not really help a book, nor did publicity matter. If a book was good it would sell, and it would last.

'The only consolation of the writing profession is that it is fair,' Vidia said in another air letter to me. This was his watchword, that literary excellence was always rewarded, in spite of everything.

He then explained something that he had not had time to go into when he first mentioned it in an air letter almost a year before: how he had been grateful to me for having written *Girls at Play*. He said that my confidence and forthrightness in the book had encouraged him to think seriously about setting a novel in Africa. It had been something he felt was impossible for him.

Five months after reading my African novel, he had started an African novel of his own. He was happy with its progress. It was a short novel. Writing it, he said, he thought constantly of me.

That was a great compliment: something I had written about Africa had had a positive influence on Vidia. The result was *In a*

Free State, which would not be published for another year.

Around this time I had word from London that B. S. Johnson ('Remember, you're first a poet') had committed suicide. In a fit of depression he had sat before a mirror, slashed his wrists, and watched himself bleed to death. He had been just a few years older than me and one of the most optimistic writers I knew. I never found out what went wrong.

Vidia kept me confident, and he filled me with such hope that I began to think of leaving Singapore, taking my wife and two children – my second son, Louis, had been born in Singapore in 1970 – somewhere and never again working for a salary, never having a boss or employees. Vidia had always emphasized the freedom of a writer. It was something I badly wanted. I finished *Jungle Lovers* and decided to take off for a few weeks, to get on a ship to Borneo and climb Mount Kinabalu. My wife said, 'If that's what you want . . .'

So I went to Borneo by sea. In the town of Kota Kinabalu I hired a Malay man to guide me. We went up and down the mountain without any technical equipment, hiking through jungles and upwards through forests of ferns and carnivorous plants. The pitcher plants were pitcher-sized, and purple orchids hung in clusters from wet trees. We spent several nights in mountainside shelters. On my way home I decided to give Singapore one more year and then resign.

I asked Vidia where I should go.

Think carefully about what you are planning, he said in his next air letter. I had mentioned the English countryside, but he said I was too young to retreat there. I needed to have connections to society. I should not cut myself off. 'Life appears very long; but no one does much creative work of a *new* sort after fifty; and the next twenty years are of great importance to you.' I was twenty-nine.

He doubted that England was a good place to live. It was sterile; there was no intellectual debate; English writers were cliquey. A writer had to be a part of the world if his work was to matter. 'Hemingway, Fitzgerald and the others, who were outside the world, are bad writers, for their inability to see beyond their careers as "writers."'

It was only possible, he said, to live in the English countryside if I had a book to write. Otherwise it was dreary and pointless. In any case, I would need to go to London once a week to see people, buy books, keep in touch. He advised me not to buy a house but simply to see what England was like. I should not commit myself, because essentially a house in the country was a place to write, a retreat. The world was elsewhere. He had been living in Gloucestershire for ten months, but as soon as he finished *In a Free State* he was getting out, he said, 'to see the world again.'

A month later there was another air letter. He had been brooding over my expression 'cottage in Dorset,' which was what I had in mind. He satirized my words, saying that I was thinking in clichés about the English countryside – 'milkmaids, spring mornings, polite rural greetings,' and also the absurd daydream of writing in the bosom of England on a sunny day behind the bright mullioned windows of my library.

Yet I had no fantasies of this kind. I was looking for an inexpensive house in a rural setting because I had a book to write. I had finished with Africa. I was making notes for a new novel, set in Singapore, about a man who becomes stuck there, working for a cruel Chinese boss ('Get a haircut') – my nightmare – and how he survives by pimping. Vietnam was to be part of it, since American soldiers came to Singapore all the time on R and R. I mentioned Dorset as a possibility because my in-laws now lived there and were looking for a house we might rent. I was itching to quit my job; I longed to spend my whole day writing.

In Singapore I was the last of the Mohicans: all the other expatriates in my department had left. The new policy was to hire only Chinese lecturers. I was asked when I would be leaving; they wanted to replace me with an ethnic Chinese person.

'I'm staying,' I said, just to annoy them. Privately I vowed to leave as soon as I could.

It was not merely that I felt overworked. I was also sick of Staff Club drunks, grousing expats, rude Singaporeans, high humidity, and monsoon rain. I hated our house, the stinks from the storm drain, the way my pen slipped through my perspiring fingers. There was no hinterland in Singapore. To cure myself of this sense of confinement, I traveled, taking turns with my wife in looking after the two children. But I had the better of it. I took the train from Singapore to Bangkok, then went to Burma, to Bali, and hiked in northern Sumatra, among the Batak people. In Bali late in 1970, I seriously considered dropping out, disappearing with my family, taking to the hills. But that was the effect of a brief experiment in smoking heroin. I was soon back at my desk.

When *In a Free State* was done, Vidia said in an air letter from London, 'This book will be of special interest to you: you and you alone, for reasons you will understand when you read it, are able to say certain things about it.'

He is my friend, I thought. I have a friend. I was a part of his writing life now, and he was certainly part of mine. In the dedicated diaristic activity of letter writing, I reported my progress – and he praised it; I sought his advice – and he obliged me; and we talked about the world. He was right about his book. I read it with special interest. I recognized many faces and landscapes.

Vidia went to Jamaica early in 1971. He sent me an air letter from Kingston to say that he had found some of his early articles back home in Trinidad and was struck by how hard he had worked and how quickly time had passed. He said, 'I had the curious feeling that I was looking over the relics of a dead man.'

He urged me to press on with the book about his work. He listed all the obscure magazines he had written for, including *The Illustrated Weekly of India, The Economic Weekly* (Bombay), and *London Life, Twentieth Century*, and *Queen*. He wanted me to succeed with my book. He was sure there was a market for it. Still he was nowhere in the United States, and in spite of the prizes he had won in Britain, his sales were small.

In the middle of May 1971, he reported in an air letter that he was at a very low ebb. He had retreated to Wiltshire, to a bungalow on a large estate. The bungalow was another borrowed address that made him feel like an exile. He had been sick and depressed for five months and had not written anything and so had earned nothing, which he underlined.

'A terrible intimation of age, failing powers, mortality. I suppose I fell ill because I have been deeply depressed these past two and a half years, after the mind-bending labor of *El Dorado*.' *In a Free State* had been 'a great triumph of will' but had exhausted him.

He felt 'a very deep fatigue and a great anxiety about the future.' He was thirty-nine.

I did not understand, though I was sympathetic. I had handed in my resignation in Singapore and given six months' notice. I also felt anxiety about the future and had no idea where I should go. I was determined to live by my writing. I had two tiny children and no savings. My wife gamely said that she would get a job, but still I was uneasy. My novel *Jungle Lovers* was about to appear in Britain.

Vidia reported from his bungalow: 'Marvelous reviews!'

What a pal, I thought, passing on this great news. All the reviews were good – he included the quotes, he underlined the praise, he said that though writing was agony, such reviews were its reward. He was happy for me. 'I cannot tell you how your success delights me.'

My novel was taken seriously by the critics. Such a reception boded well for its US publication a few months away. I was heartened, on the verge of leaving Singapore for good. Another piece of news was that we had found a house to rent in Dorset, not in a village ('polite rural greetings') but in the depths of the countryside, an old forge on a back road.

Vidia said the place was not far from his Wiltshire bungalow. He looked forward in the autumn to our visiting him and walking to Stonehenge. When I visited him we could have 'an editorial discussion,' he said. In researching my Naipaul book, I had told him I had found many essays and pieces that would comprise a collection of his nonfiction. The countryside was 'ridiculously Hardyesque.' One day while out walking he had come upon a sheep-shearing ceremony, which he described in detail: giant shearer, farm laborers, intimidated sheep, cluttered shearing shed, masses of wool grease, ritualistic wrapping of fleece. He made it sound like Act 4, Scene 3 of *The Winter's Tale*. And he concluded, 'So many things survive even in our polluted world.'

Not long after this, I nervously disengaged myself from Singapore. My wife encouraged me. She had helped locate the house in Dorset. We left Singapore on November 1, 1971, exactly three years after arriving there. In that time I had not left Southeast Asia, nor had

I made a single phone call – no phone. But then I had not had a phone in Africa either. Eight years without a telephone had sharpened my letter writing. I had published five novels.

The disorienting experience of going halfway around the world with two young children – overnight in Karachi, a delay in Beirut, the fireworks and bonfires on our arrival in London on Guy Fawkes Day – left me with a sense of vertigo – dizziness and a feeling that I was falling down, my legs liquefying under me. In London my older son, who was three, begged to be carried. I picked him up and he puked on my shoulder.

London was cold and damp, black streets, black buildings. I had not been cold for eight years. I was distracted, and in the confusion of Waterloo station, heading for the train to Dorset, burdened with boxes and suitcases, the children pale and limp with fatigue, I was approached by a porter pulling an iron baggage cart. He was black, some of the travelers were black, the sweepers I saw were black.

'*Jambo, kitu gani?*' I said, because the porter had hesitated.

He drew back further and did not greet me in return.

'*Mimi nataka mipagazi awiri,*' I went on. '*Sasa hivi.*'

He did not seem to care that another porter was needed right now, as my boxes and cases were tottering.

'*Kasha ume anguka,*' I said, drawing his attention to a tipped-over box, and wishing for him to fasten them all on his cart, I directed him, '*Fungo mizigo hii.*' But where was my umbrella? '*Mwavulo uko wapi?*'

The man was smiling, not helping, not moving.

'*Jina lako nani?*' I asked, because it sometimes helped if you knew a porter's name.

But he said nothing. The children began to fuss. My wife was tugging my arm. At that point I lost it and decided to tell him to bugger off.

'*Twende,*' I said. 'Let's go.'

'Are you out of your mind?' my wife said.

Only then did I realize that I had been mumbling to the man in Swahili. Not out of my mind, but out of my element.

A three-hour train ride brought us to the depths of the country-side. It was visibly different from and preferable to the parklike countryside nearer London. Here the hills were rougher, higher, and continuous; the trees were taller, the stone walls wider and more tumbled. Nothing was manicured. In our stone house a fire was burning in the fireplace. I found a room to write in at the top of the house. The wind pressed on the window glass, and when it came from the south it had the tang of the sea, which was seven miles away. Big bare oak trees, sodden green fields, muddy lanes, a low sky of tufty clouds. It was hardly three o'clock and already dark.

I thought: We can stay here about ten years. Then go home.

A week later, a note from Vidia, not an air letter but a thick white envelope. Please telephone, he wrote, and, frugal as ever, he added, 'It's cheap at weekends and after 6 P.M.'

8

The 9:50 to Waterloo

His bungalow he called The Bungalow, though many years after I first saw it, I discovered that its real name was Teasel Cottage. The truth was important to Vidia, but who could blame him for suppressing the fact of that silly name?

Small and squat and bad for his asthma, The Bungalow was the sort of contrived structure he usually called bogus and hated for its distressed flint and its quaintness – and here he was living in one. But this bungalow was on the grounds of a famous estate, Wilsford Manor, which I suspected Vidia liked for its old-fashioned glamour and its history of house parties. Wilsford's owner, known as an eccentric – as wealthy lunatics are always described – was so completely crazy that the manor house was little more than an asylum in which he was the sole inmate.

The manor house of the estate was an expensive fraud, made to look ancient but actually fairly new, built around 1900 by Lord Glenconner and anticipating Disneyland fakery in its late-seventeenth-century style of checkered flint and stone. It had ornate gables, and even the sort of mullioned windows that Vidia had scorned in an air letter. It was surrounded by made-to-look-old walls and phony gates, and it was secluded, on a side road that looked more like a lane, near Amesbury, outside a village called Lake (the mythical home of Sir Launcelot). There was no lake but there was a river, the Avon – another Avon, one of very many, for 'avon' in Old English means river.

The river ran through Wilsford Manor. Earlier generations who had lived on the land had created water meadows in the low boggy ground near the river. In full daylight the sky was a high and wide dome over Salisbury Plain, and Stonehenge was an hour's walk through farmers' fields. 'Stoners,' Vidia called it, and sometimes 'the Henge.' What was striking about Wilsford Manor were its trees, nearly all of them dead, having been throttled by dense climbing ivy, clumps and clusters of it. From the windows of The Bungalow these dead black trees were visible, strangled but still standing, thickly bandaged with ivy.

'He loves to look at ivy,' Vidia said. 'He doesn't care that it kills the trees.'

Stephen Tennant, he meant, the lord of Wilsford Manor. Teasel Cottage had been built for him but he had never used it. Tennant had various hearty ancestors and a few well-known relatives, some of them having titles. He himself was 'The Honorable,' which was decisive proof that Vidia was right when he guffawed over 'crooked aristocrats' and mocked English titles as meaningless.

Tennant had been out of his mind for years. 'I am the Prince Youssoupoff of England!' he sometimes screamed. His hair was dyed purple, and sometimes hennaed. He put on makeup every morning, crimson lipstick, rouge for his cheeks, and eye shadow – he was said to have sixty-six shades of eye shadow. He never went anywhere without his teddy bear and his toy plush monkey. Though he seldom stirred outside his house, he was not a recluse; he sometimes traveled to Bournemouth to buy cosmetics, and now and then went to London and even New York. He wrote bad poems. Before he went completely off his head, he had been a socialite. He had known Willa Cather and E. M. Forster, and one of his lovers had been the war poet Siegfried Sassoon. He also painted. His childishly hyperbolic pictures were of cartoonish men, sailors mostly, lascars, matelots, with the faces of lecherous cherubs, big biceps, and improbable bulges in their trousers, some like cucumbers and some like cantaloupes.

An idle, silly queen, Stephen Tennant was upper class and rich, so people laughed at his jokes and called him marvelous. He was looked after by a couple, Mr and Mrs Skull – 'the Skulls,' Vidia called them, always referring to John and Mary Skull as a pair. In protecting Tennant and attending to him, the Skulls, kindly and long-suffering, had become the sort of English servants who were indistinguishable from masters. They had power – nanny power, butler boldness, 'Begging your pardon, sir, but . . .' – and they stood between sad, giggling Stephen and the world. Were anyone to attempt to remove the strangling ivy from the trees on the estate, the Skulls would put a stop to that, smartish, as they might say. 'We'll have none of that here.'

But the black ivy made the place spooky and gave the trees an asymmetrical shape. The density and damage of the ivy obscured the varieties and species of the trees. They had the starkness of gallows, all standing in the soggy water meadows.

After almost nine years in the tropics, I could not believe how dark and unfriendly this landscape looked. Haunted was a perfect word for it. It seemed to me the weirdest place I had ever been. I felt a stronger sense of alienation than I had ever known in Bundibugyo. I looked at the dead and decaying trees and thought of Tennant.

The oddest thing was that Vidia had not set eyes on Tennant. In the event, after fifteen years Vidia had only a glimpse of the man, and he never spoke to him. Of all the strange places Vidia had lived, this was by far the strangest. But The Bungalow was cheap: Vidia paid his nominal rent to Lord Glenconner, Stephen's brother Christopher Tennant, and Vidia became the writer at the bottom of the garden, living within shouting distance of a crackpot who often said, 'Some people think I'm a genius.'

The Bungalow was poorly lit, with a low ceiling and thick cold walls and small windows. The flatness of Wiltshire was unlike anything in the west of Dorset, the neighbor county, where we lived. We were seventy miles away, in the rugged hills at the lip of Marshwood Vale, among the hedgerows, hardly hedgerows, sportive briars, and crumbling rock walls and earthworks. Near our house, called The Forge, there were old hill forts and small dark churches. The nearest church, in the village of Stoke Abbott, had been built in the eleventh century. The Forge had five rooms. I sat in the smallest one upstairs, writing my novel *Saint Jack*. Singapore and sunlight and mischief on my inky pages; and outside my window dark skies, wet lumpy fields, and black leafless trees, all oaks, which howled when the salt wind tore through their branches.

Please telephone, please visit, Vidia had written.

'You are phoning at the most expensive time of day!' he said when I spoke to him. It was eleven in the morning. I was not extravagant but careless. I was eager to see him again. We agreed on a day.

Vidia had prepared me for the social rituals of English life, the
stages of getting acquainted, which started with a cup-of-coffee
meeting and progressed, as the friendship ripened, to drinks at five
and then the greater commitment of lunch. Dinner was the highest
level of intimacy. 'Dinner is grand,' Vidia said. 'Dinner is important.' Meals and rituals meant a great deal to him. He always
insisted on choosing the wine, though he seldom paid for it. ('People
enjoy paying. I don't want to spoil their pleasure.') He noticed the
quality of the food, even if he did not eat much. He judged people
by what they offered him – the restaurant, the meal, the wine, the
conversation, even the way that people dressed. If they were badly
dressed he was insulted. He took everything personally. Your shoes
not shined? That was a comment on him. Your scruffiness was
rudeness.

I had bought a bottle of wine in our market town of Bridport,
on the river Brit, and set off with my wife, leaving plenty of time
for the trip, knowing Vidia to be an obsessive timekeeper. Lateness
was also rudeness.

Preparing for such a visit, I was always reminded of his once
saying about someone, 'You see? He is afraid he is going to do
something wrong and therefore he does everything wrong. Anxious
about failing, he fails. It is almost deliberate.'

But Vidia was also my friend. The last time we had been together,
I was in Uganda and had published nothing. Five years had passed.
I had published *Waldo*, *Fong and the Indians*, *Girls at Play*, *Murder
in Mount Holly*, *Jungle Lovers*. I was done with *V. S. Naipaul: An
Introduction to His Work*. I had just received an advance copy of
my collection of short stories, *Sinning with Annie*. I was half done
with *Saint Jack*. Eight books: I was thirty.

My advances had been small, my sales modest; still, I knew I
had done the right thing in chucking my Singapore job and striking
out on my own. I had done it with Vidia's encouragement. He had
insisted there was no middle way. A writer had to be a free man.
Anyone with a salary and a boss and office obligations was not free.

This subject came up on the way to Vidia's.

'I want to get a job,' my wife said. She had an Oxford education,
she was intelligent, and to her – to many women at that time – a
job represented a sort of freedom.

'What will you do in Dorset?'

'We'll have to move to London. There are no jobs here.'

But I liked Dorset, liked its darkness most of all – I wanted to write about it. This remote part of Dorset had pagan roots, witch stories, and on its prettiest churches ugly-faced gargoyles known locally as hunky-punks; it was deeply rural, snug and distant and cozy. The rent was low, and the hinterland was full of dropouts, potters and painters, farm laborers, rat catchers, and farriers. I met them at the pub, playing darts and skittles and bar billiards, at the Gollop Arms in South Bowood, which was not even a hamlet, just a crossroads. Up the road, at Four Ashes, another crossroads, there was a haunted house, called The Black House.

We traveled east on the road to Vidia's, talking about jobs; from Powerstock to Evershot and Wynford Eagle and Toller Porcorum and Puddletown near Tolpuddle, and onward past East Coker, where T. S. Eliot was buried.

'This is so beautiful,' I said.

'I'd rather be in London,' she said.

The thought of sooty bricks and filthy air and sour faces in London only depressed me, and in this mood of disagreement we arrived at Wilsford Manor and rolled up to The Bungalow. Vidia, who was a keen receptor of vibrations, definitely sensed the unresolved conflict, a sense of static and clatter in the air. I could tell, because he was so solicitous. He also knew a thing or two about marital quarrels. He was chirping, glad to see us.

'Before we go in – look. You see that wall?'

It was a thick cracked battlement near The Bungalow.

'It's not real,' Vidia said. 'One is supposed to see it from the window, but up close – look! It is just a folly. It tricks the eye.'

Pat emerged, chafing her red hands, looking harassed, always the nervous cook: she was obviously flustered in her cooking.

'This is for you, Vidia.' I gave him the bottle of Beaune and my advance copy of *Sinning with Annie*, inscribed *To Vidia and Pat, with love*, *Paul*.

'Paul, Paul.' He glanced at the label. His phrase for such a gesture was 'swiftly assessed.' He saw everything in a flash. The wine passed. He commented on the car, a Singer, and on my shirt, my jacket.

'How well you look,' Vidia said. 'So young, and you are working so hard.'

'Such a long way,' Pat was saying to my wife in her purring voice as she led her into the house. Women with women, men with men.

'Vidia, you have something on your nose.'

I did not want to say 'in your nostrils,' but his fingers went to his nostrils.

'Snuff,' he said. 'I'm passionate about it. Want to try some?'

The snuff was in small tins that looked like pillboxes. Vidia had five or six of them – different flavors. But this was not the time for snuff; that was for after lunch. He was tapping the containers of snuff and puffing his pipe as Pat finished setting the table, my wife helping. Vidia and I, the men, were kicking our heels, waiting to be fed. I felt awkward doing nothing, but Vidia chatted happily about snuff. He always converted an enthusiasm into a study. Last year it had been muesli, next year it would be vintage port or the stock market or his garden.

'Do sit down,' Pat said.

We had soup, then poached salmon and potatoes and brussels sprouts. There was a green salad in a bowl that went untouched. Pat was too frazzled and anxious to meet the implacable demands of a kitchen, too unconfident to juggle cookbooks. An insecure person is lost in front of a stove. Cooking requires confident guesswork and improvisation – experimentation and substitution, dealing with failure and uncertainty in a creative way. And Vidia was a challenge: a vegetarian food snob who could not cook and who never helped. He sat and was served.

'I want you to try some of this, Paul.'

He poured. I sipped.

'Hold it in your mouth. There – do you taste the almonds, the peaches? It's a complex finish, oaken with a hint of chalk. Do you get it? Isn't it delicious? It must be savored.'

He tipped some into my wife's glass.

'I won't have any,' Pat said.

He sipped from his own glass. 'And just the slightest hint of rose petals.'

'It's very good,' my wife said.

'Have some salad,' Pat said. 'Vidia is so difficult. He won't eat salad. Just fusses.'

Vidia shrugged. He was fastidious, unyielding, always on the look-out for any sign of meat. Meat disgusted him. It was flesh, it was sinew, it reduced the eater to the level of a cannibal. I always had the sense that he was talking about much more than meat when he was talking about meat. Gravy was just as bad, for the way it tainted vegetables. 'Tainted' was a favorite word.

'Do you get up to London much?' my wife asked.

'When I need a haircut,' Vidia said.

'But you must miss your London house,' I said.

'It's over. I have been paid. It's in the bank. My "house money," I call it.'

'We'd love to move. All our things are in storage,' Pat said.

That explained the starkness of The Bungalow, the small book-case, the few pictures, the bed-sitter atmosphere.

'Where to live?' Vidia said. He raised his arms in the Italian way. 'Where?'

My wife said, 'Swinging London.'

'London does not swing for me,' Vidia said. 'This is serious, man. Where can one live? Tell me, Paul. Do you think I should live in America?'

'You might like it. You said you liked New York City.'

'I have been thinking of something wild, someplace rugged. Mountains. Large tracts of land.'

'Montana?'

'Montana! I shall go to Montana.'

'Cold winters,' I said.

'Lovely.'

'Snow. Ice storms. Blizzards.'

'I adore snow. I adore dramatic weather.'

'What about me?' I asked. 'Where should I go?'

Vidia was never flippant. He frowned, he thought a moment, he stopped eating. 'You must make your name here,' he said. 'Forget America for the moment. It's just depressing. The display of ego. The Mailer business. Roth – the sour grapes of Roth. And what these people don't understand when they praise Hemingway and

Fitzgerald is that Hemingway and Fitzgerald are bad writers, man. Bad, bad!'

My wife said, 'I quite like *Tender Is the Night*.'

'Bogus emotion. Bogus style. All forced. His letters to his daughter are excellent – no bogus display there. Just a father addressing his daughter. But his novels say nothing. And all this nonsense about his wife.'

'Zelda,' my wife said.

'She was crazy,' Vidia said. 'Out of her mind.'

'Oh, Vidia,' Pat said, beginning to scold.

'I am explaining to Paul why he will find a greater degree of appreciation of his work in England. He does not indulge in bogus displays of ego.'

'I am not talking about that,' Pat said.

'Can I pass anyone the salad?' I said.

'Zelda,' Vidia said. 'I am so bored with the self-dramatization of the female soul. It is really just a way of pleasuring the body.'

'She wrote a novel, *Save Me the Waltz*,' my wife said.

'I am speaking in general, not about any particular book. I am speaking about this bogus feminism, the way it makes women trivial-minded.'

My wife said quietly, 'Women are trying to liberate themselves from traditional roles that have confined them. That's why a job –'

'Women long for witnesses, that is all,' Vidia said. 'Witnesses to their pleasure or their distress.'

'Vidia, do stop,' said Pat. 'You are being such a bore.'

He smiled and said, 'Why are women so obsessed with their bodies? Men are like that in adolescence, but these women are adults.'

'A lot of women are unhappy, I suppose,' I said.

'No, no. Deep down they are very happy. Give them their witnesses and they will be even happier.'

My wife had fallen silent.

Pat said, 'I have a lovely apple pie that Mrs Griggs made.'

Vidia said, 'Where is Griggs? I haven't seen her today.'

'She's got the brasses today at the church. There's a christening, one of her nieces. She's polishing the brasses.'

'I won't have any pie, thank you,' my wife said.

'Coffee then,' Pat said. 'Now Vidia, go into the parlor. I won't have you ranting.'

'What are you chuntering on about?' Vidia got up from the table. 'Paul, let's try some snuff.'

Again I was acutely aware that Pat and my wife had been left behind to clear the table and make coffee. I made an attempt to help, but Pat waved me away. She said, 'Vidia has been dying to see you.'

He showed me how to take snuff. I tried several flavors, tapped some on the back of my hand and snorted it, and I sneezed explosively.

Vidia did not sneeze. The snuff vanished into his nose. He could not explain the anticlimax. He just laughed. Then he and I went for a walk to the old water meadows, and he explained how they had been made. He had become acquainted with the shrubs, he knew the names of the wildflowers, the different grasses, and even the trees that were dead and covered with ivy. He knew which were oaks and which were yews and which were ash. He talked a bit about his landlord, but in the most respectful way; he mentioned the Skulls.

'There isn't time to go to the Henge,' he said. 'But you'll come again, won't you?'

'Oh, yes.'

'We'll walk to Stoners.'

It was growing dark: the November dusk, which seemed to rise from the ground like the vapor of night, brimming and blackening; not a dying light but a dark tide of mist that made you think you were going blind at three o'clock on an English afternoon in late autumn.

Using the bathroom back at The Bungalow, I saw that, as in London, Vidia and Pat had separate bedrooms. I knew it from glimpses of certain books and clothes. They were the sort of bedrooms that suggested insomnia and loneliness.

'We must go,' I said.

'Please have some tea,' Pat said. 'And there's cake.'

We had tea and plates of fruitcake, and I tried Mrs Griggs's apple pie. Vidia speculated about Montana. He said he would be going to Trinidad in the new year. When we put our coats on he said, 'It is so good to see you. You're going to be all right.'

'Come back and see us again,' Pat said.

In the darkness outside, I heard Vidia whimper. Then he said, 'I don't want you to go. I'll be depressed after you leave.'

'Vidia,' Pat said in a soothing voice.

He looked small and blurred in this rural darkness, and the wall of Wilsford Manor made the darkness greater, like a door closing behind us.

It was dark the whole way – no streetlights on these country roads. My wife was silent, ruminating.

'You said they were so happy,' she said after a while. 'I don't think they're happy at all.'

'Aren't you glad we came?'

'Yes. I pity Pat, but I'm glad I saw her. I never want to end up like that.'

She was silent all through Wiltshire and well into Dorset. In the lights of Dorchester she seemed to waken, and she spoke again.

'But he isn't interested in me.'

'He is.'

'He never once asked me what I did. He didn't ask about the children. Just you two, the boys, talking about their writing.'

'I think Vidia feels awkward around women.'

'No, not awkward. They irritate him. He mocked Zelda, and what does he know about her? He mocked feminism. That could mean he's madly attracted to women but that he hates the thought of it.'

In the six years I had known Vidia, I had never thought about him in this way.

'Never mind,' my wife said. 'He's your friend, not mine.'

Back at The Forge, I buried myself in my novel, *Saint Jack*. I also wrote several book reviews a week, one for the *Washington Post*, one for *The Times*. But the money was poor. I began to live on my small savings. My wife said, 'See?' I was hopeful I would sell *Saint Jack* and be solvent again. I had applied once more for a Guggenheim. A letter to me at The Forge said that I had been turned down. Why did it bother me so much that the Guggenheim

Foundation had spelled my name wrong in their letter of rejection? I complained to Vidia.

'Be glad they turned you down,' he said. 'Those foundation grants are for second-raters, people playing with art. You don't need them. You're going to be all right.'

We spoke by phone. At the age of thirty, I had my first telephone. The Bungalow was a long way by road from The Forge – hours of winding roads and country lanes clogged with tractors, slow drivers, elderly cyclists, and herds of cows. But we were on the same railway line, the Exeter line to Waterloo. My nearest station, Crewkerne, was just over the county line in Somerset; Vidia's was Salisbury.

Winter had come. A housing boom in London meant that we would probably never be able to afford a house there. Never mind, I was happy to stay in the countryside, working all day, kids at the nursery school in Beaminster, up at the pub at night playing bar billiards. I marveled at the farm laborers who drank in the pub. They were full of vicious opinions and xenophobia. 'I says to the bugger, "Well, you can fuck off back to where you come from."' One day there was news that a party of children on a school trip had become lost in a sudden snow squall in the Cairngorms, and seven of them had frozen to death in the snow.

Old Fred, sitting by the Gollop Arms fireplace, said, 'Serve 'em right. When I was at school we never went on these fancy trips to Scotland.'

Every two weeks I took the train to London, turned in a review, sold my review copies for cash at Gaston's as Vidia had done five years before, had lunch, mooched, walked the streets, and got a late train back to Dorset. Dinner on the train: 'More roast potatoes, sir?' The lights flying past, villages twinkling in the blackness.

'Let's have lunch in London,' Vidia said during one of our phone calls.

'What about Wheeler's?' We'd had lunch there on my first visit to London. It was the only restaurant I knew, and even so I avoided it, because of the expense.

'The Connaught is better,' Vidia said. 'Although many of your fellow countrymen eat there, it really is quite satisfactory. Shall we say the Connaught?'

'Fine,' I said.

'You'll have to book it,' he said.

He met me on the train, boarding the 9:50 to Waterloo, which I had boarded an hour and a half earlier at Crewkerne. Yeovil, Sherborne, Gillingham, Shaftesbury, then Salisbury, where he appeared on the platform, a small, dapper man with thick black hair, wrapped up against the cold – muffler, collar up, gloves – yet looking exotic, almost a spectacle, a small Indian in Salisbury station in 1971, all the English people towering over him and deliberately not seeing him. Nor did he take any notice of them.

Seeing me, he nodded and looked relieved. He slid the compartment door open and took a seat opposite. The other passengers averted their eyes, which made them look even more attentive. A tall man I had seen boarding at Sherborne, probably from the school there, was holding a small faded clothbound book close to his face. He was not reading but listening, for Vidia had already started to speak to me.

'Paul, Paul, you have something on your mind. I can tell.'

'No. I'm fine.'

'Your wife is not happy. I have a vibration.'

'She wants to get a job.'

'Good! Earn a few pence.'

'What about you? How's things?'

'I have a broken wing,' he said. It was his usual expression for exhaustion and near collapse. But he explained. 'For the past fifteen years I have been driven by an enormous tension.' He stiffened and grimaced in illustration, and then he went limp. 'I am now so exhausted that the act of creation scares me. I'm tired. I'm idle. Insomnia, man. But look at you. Full of ideas, writing your novels. Tell me, who are you seeing in London?'

I told him.

Vidia said, 'But he is no one.'

I mentioned another name.

Vidia said, 'Who is he? Is he anybody?'

I told him a third name.

Vidia said, 'Bogus, man. All bogus. They do not exist.'

'They've been pretty good to me – I mean, giving me work.'

'Of course. You do your work. You are busy. You have ideas. But these people will draw off your energy. After you see them you are very tired, aren't you?'

'I suppose so.' But what did that prove? After I saw Vidia, I was very tired too, and sometimes my head hurt, my brain feeling nagged at.

'They are sucking your energy.'

At the word 'sucking,' the schoolmaster from Sherborne in the corner seat glanced up from his book, then quickly covered his face with it.

'They will destroy you,' Vidia said. 'They are playing with art. I'll tell you a story. The first man you mentioned' – out of delicacy, Vidia did not repeat his name – 'he has no gift, yet he wrote a novel. "I am a novelist." He wrote his bogus novel. Just playing with art. He wrote another – farmers, provincials. He begins to move in grander circles, still playing with art. His provincial wife is very unhappy. She thinks he is a genius. She doesn't know he is playing with art. He is caught with another woman. It is his right. He is an artist, a novelist, he can do such things. But his wife is in despair. She kills herself. Why?'

Now the schoolmaster was frankly gaping and so was I.

'Because he played with art.'

Green fields, greener than the summer fields of Africa, and clumps of trees moved past the windows, a bouncing belt of scenery. Crows flew up.

'Don't play with art.'

We stopped at Andover. No one got off. The last seat in our compartment was taken by a woman who seemed startled when I spoke.

'I'll keep that in mind,' I said. 'I see *In a Free State* everywhere.'

'Do you? I'm afraid I have no interest in that.'

'It's sure to be shortlisted for the Booker Prize.'

'Prizes are such a con. I think the Americans have the right idea. Sell the book, don't go looking for prizes.'

'I mean, you were so prescient about the East African Indians being thrown out.'

'The book is important.'

'I wonder what they made of it in Africa.'

'Tommy McCoon wouldn't like it.'

The man in the corner seat looked up again.

'But it's a big book.'

A large, neat sign lettered *Stop Coloured Immigration* was painted on the stonework under a bridge near Basingstoke.

Vidia stared straight ahead. 'And you booked a table at the Connaught. Oh, good.'

At Waterloo the compartment emptied fast, and as we were leaving I saw on the seat the faded book the man I had taken to be a schoolmaster had been reading. Yes, I had been right in guessing he was a schoolmaster. The book was Cicero's *Select Orations*, a Latin text, no name on the flyleaf but many pencil marks in the margins.

'We'll take it to Lost Property,' Vidia said.

On the way to Lost Property, Vidia recited an imagined dialogue between the book's owner and someone else. *It's gone, I'm sure of it.* Then, *Have a look at Lost Property. Someone might just have turned it in.* And, *Couldn't possibly.* Then, *Do let's look. There's just a chance ...*

We left the book with the clerk who sat among all the umbrellas and sinister-looking parcels.

Vidia had books to sell. We made the circuit: a taxi to Gaston's, the tobacconist for Player's Navy Cut, the newsagent, then a taxi to the Connaught, in Carlos Place. It puzzled me slightly that I had paid for both taxis.

The doorman at the Connaught was dressed in a top hat and a dark caped ulster with green piping at the seams. He had a red face and side-whiskers. The porter was mustached and alert; he wore a frock coat and striped trousers. There were fresh flowers in a vase near the entrance. The etched mirrors gleamed. All these Dickensian touches were distinct signs that the Connaught was expensive.

We were met at the entrance to the Grill Room and shown to a table. The waiter was subservient in the bossy English way – that was a bad sign too. We were given menus. Vidia asked for the wine list. He pinched his glasses to get the right angle and looked at the list with serious concentration for a full minute. Seeming to have found the right bottle, he looked up at me.

'You will do well here,' he said. 'Michael Ratcliffe is very pleased with your reviews.'

Ratcliffe was the literary editor of *The Times*.

I said, 'I hate doing them.'

'They force you to make a judgment on a book. It's important to reach conclusions. Most people have no idea what they think of a book after they've read it.'

The sommelier came over to us. He was dressed in black and wore a chain around his neck and could have passed for a mayor wearing the gold insignia of his office. He saw Vidia with the wine list.

'Have you made a choice, sir?'

Vidia said to me, 'Let's get a real wine. Let's get a classic. A white burgundy.' He put his finger on his selection. 'Number seventy-eight.'

'Very good, sir. An excellent choice. Shall I bring it now?'

Vidia nodded. The sweating silver bucket was set up and the bottle opened, the cork sniffed. It was a Puligny-Montrachet. Vidia sipped some and worked it around his teeth.

'It's good,' he said. 'So many flavors. The roots of these vines go very deep. It gives complexity – taste the chalk?'

I sipped it. Was that what chalk tasted like?

'What was that name again?' I asked. I picked up the wine list and, pretending to examine the name, I glanced at the price. It was eleven pounds. The review I was about to turn in would net me ten pounds.

'The roots of your California vines are much shallower, because of the rainfall. It's not bad – different virtues. Savor their differences. These French wines have deep roots.' He sipped again.

A beef trolley was wheeled over. It contained the Thursday 'luncheon dish,' boiled silverside. Vidia waved it away. Thinking that it might offend him if I chose meat, I looked at Poissons. The menu was mostly in French.

'The English recruit people,' Vidia said. 'That is not widely understood. They often take on new people. They make room. It is not exclusive – it is selective.'

He was ignoring the waiter who hovered near him. The man was making me nervous.

My finger was on Truite Grillée ou aux Amandes. I said, 'I'll have the grilled trout.'

'Something to start with?'

'Bisque d'Homard.'

As the waiter noted this, Vidia said, 'That's a nice idea. I will also have the bisque, followed by Quenelles d'Aiglefin Monte-Carlo.'

'Any vegetables? Shall I make up a selection?'

'That will be lovely,' Vidia said. He sipped some more wine, sucked it past his gums, and said, 'For a writer like yourself, even an American, there is a kind of recruitment, and you will be part of it. You will be coopted. I think it has started already for you. Your name is growing. What happens next is up to you.'

'Did that happen to Robert Lowell?'

'I think Lowell is fraudulent, don't you?'

This was not the moment to mention that he had been Lowell's houseguest in New York; Lowell's was the return address on a number of Vidia's letters to me. And Vidia had interviewed him for *The Listener*. In researching my book I had read the interview.

'His poems are very good,' I said. '*Lord Weary's Castle. Life Studies*.'

'I am sure I am a very bad judge of American poetry,' Vidia said, which was his way of saying he disliked Lowell's poems. But he had not said so in his interview.

Our lobster bisque was served. Swallowing some, I said, 'But Lowell's crazy, isn't he?'

'That's the one thing he's not.'

'You think it's a con.'

'Total con, total con.' Vidia was concentrating on his soup, which he ate neatly, his spoon at a studied angle.

I said, 'He goes to mental hospitals, gibbering.'

'He's playing,' Vidia said. 'Hospitals are wonderful places for people to act out their fantasies of infantilism. I think Lowell adores being in a hospital.'

'His hospital poems are pretty scary.'

'I don't know them. Should I read them?'

'It's up to you. What about his wife, Lady Caroline?'

Vidia rested his spoon, leaned over, and said, 'I was sitting next to her a month ago at a dinner.' He made his disgusted face, and his features were so distorted it looked like a Kali mask. 'She *pongs!*'

I laughed out loud, but Vidia was still frowning and sniffing.

'The title means a lot to Lowell,' he said. 'What is it about titles? Americans are so glamoured by titles.'

'That's because we don't have them,' I said. 'Anyway, it's a big deal, isn't it?'

'A title is nothing,' Vidia said.

The waiter was listening, and it was hard to tell whether he approved. He was obviously torn because, being a flunky in such a classy place, he had been trained to admire something that was for him unattainable.

'Careful, gentlemen, the plates are very hot,' he said, positioning my trout in front of me and serving Vidia his quenelles. He then made a business of serving us four different vegetables, working two spoons in his fingers like tongs.

When he was gone, Vidia began eating. I waited for him to say something about the food. He said nothing.

'I have the idea that they should sell titles at the post office,' he said. 'You'd pay for it the way you'd pay for a television license. You go in, buy some stamps, and paste them into a little book. Save up. Buy some more stamps. Fill up books. Three books of stamps would get you an MBE. Six for an OBE. A dozen books of stamps would be worth a knighthood.'

'That's what it's worth?'

'That's what it's worth.'

We went on eating and Vidia went on denouncing the Honours List over the food-splashed table.

The waiter returned to whisk our plates away and hand us the dessert menu, which was also Frenchified: Pêche Melba, Glaces, Framboises, and a selection of Fromages.

'I won't,' Vidia said.

'Coffee?'

'Black,' Vidia said.

A child began to cry in the foyer, the cries diminishing as the child descended the staircase in someone's arms. I was touched by hearing a child's wailing amid all this pomposity.

'God,' Vidia said, 'who would bring a child here?'

'In Italy they bring children to restaurants.'

'A low peasant habit,' Vidia said, and he ranted. But I knew this rant, about all the articles that were written about children. Why didn't someone write a piece about people who, like Vidia, had made a conscious decision never to have children?

I shrugged, but I felt like a coward for not telling him how fiercely I loved my children. Just before I had left The Forge, Marcel, my older son, had said, 'Buy me a Ladybird book in London!' and his brother, Louis, had echoed him, 'Book!' Just thinking about them in the restaurant, I felt a pang. I missed them.

'A workman came the other day.' Vidia was smiling at the thought of what he was about to say. 'He told me that when he is at work he misses his children. Can you believe that?'

'Yes. I miss my children now.'

'Really.'

While he had been talking, the waiter had approached and put a white plate on the edge of the table. On this white plate was the bill, folded in half. It now lay between us. Vidia's 'Really' had produced a silence – such apparent interest on his part always indicated its opposite: disbelief, incomprehension, boredom – and in that silence I poked at the bill with my fingers and tweaked it open.

Seeing me looking at it, Vidia became preoccupied. He sat back, his expression altered to a glow of serenity. He was lost in his thoughts.

'Seventeen pounds and sixty-four pence,' I said.

Vidia was smiling. He was deaf. He heard an American at a nearby table saying, 'I'd be happy to pay you for it. It's just that my wife saves menus from all the foreign places we eat, especially when we're traveling in Yerp.'

'You see? One of your fellow countrymen.'

I took out four five-pound notes from my wallet. Only two one-pound notes remained.

'Oh, good,' Vidia said.

'What about the tip?'

'That's plenty,' he said, meaning that the twenty would cover it. 'That will make him very happy. Anthony Burgess is frightened of waiters and tips them extravagantly. Taxi drivers, too.'

My twenty pounds was carried away on the plate by the now deferential waiter. I had bus fare and enough left over for a pint of Double Diamond on the train. But dinner was out of the question, and so was the Ladybird book.

'Shall we go?' Vidia said.

We walked through Berkeley Square to Piccadilly, talking about books some more. I listened without hearing or understanding. I felt that peculiar weakness, almost a frailty, familiar to me whenever I lost a bet or discovered an overdraft. This time it was the effect of having spent all my money on lunch. Vidia was sprightly, for the opposite reason: I was broke, but he was restored. He was actually energized, and it was almost worth what it had cost me to see him so bright and to hear him.

'Don't worry about your book,' he said. He was chatty and encouraging. 'You won't know what it is about until you finish it.'

He was jaunty, but this was also his old intense teaching method, which had helped me in Africa. He was well fed, he had drunk most of the white burgundy, it had cost him nothing. His chatter was a form of gratitude.

'Each day you will make breakthroughs as you write. You'll make discoveries all along the way. When you finish you'll be amazed to see where you've got to – you'll probably have to go back and fix the first part of your book, because you'll have discovered what your subject really is.'

At Duke Street, near Fortnum & Mason, he turned and urged me to go partway down the hill, where an art dealer had two Indian prints in his shop window.

'I want you to come back here sometime and look at these pictures. Buy some when you have the money. They are Daniells, aquatints of India. Aren't they delicious?'

But I could not concentrate. I still felt weaker, lamer, frailer, even slightly deaf, the loss of twenty pounds like an amputation.

'What are your plans, Vidia?'

'I am going to the London Library. It's just round the corner in St James's Square.'

'I mean future.'

'Trinidad,' he said. 'Queen-beeing it there. Then South America. Argentina.'

He went glum and uncertain, looking ahead, seeing nothing discernible in the mist.

'I would like to write nothing. I feel I have said all I wished to say.'

Taxis clattered down Duke Street as we stood on the narrow sidewalk. An auction had just ended at Christie's down the street, Vidia said, and there was a commotion, like an audience leaving a theater, a sudden mob, dressed alike.

'I may fall silent,' Vidia said.

He looked at the pair of aquatints. One showed the Union Jack flying in an Indian landscape: a handsome building, like a pavilion, with Indians, Europeans, and horses around it. *The Assembly Rooms on the Race Grounds, Near Madras.*

'Yes, I may fall silent.'

'I'll be in Dorset,' I said. My fists were jammed into my empty pockets.

'You're going to be all right, Paul.'

'If I don't see you . . .'

I put out my hand, but Vidia was preoccupied with the possibility of falling silent. Anyway, he seldom shook hands, and when he did his grip was limp and reluctant, as though fearing a taint.

'I'm going down this way,' he said.

'I'll hop a taxi to *The Times*.'

That was bluster on my part – I didn't have the money. I took a bus to Blackfriars and turned in my review, and then I walked from Blackfriars to Waterloo along the Thames, to save my bus fare. With no money for dinner, I took an early train to Dorset so that I could eat at home. It puzzled me that I had spent so much on lunch. I hated having to think about such things. That single lunch had cost me the equivalent of one month's rent.

Back to The Forge and my lovely clamoring family, back to my room upstairs, back to my novel. Vidia was right. I wanted to finish the book to discover what it was about.

But that night, without the new Ladybird book, I lay between my children and read them a story from one of their older books of fairy tales, this one by Hans Christian Andersen. Outside, the wind from the sea at the end of the road tore at the bare boughs of our black oaks.

With the children snuggled against me, I read, '"You don't understand the world, that's what's the matter with you. You ought to travel." And so they traveled, the shadow as master and the master as shadow, always side by side.'

9

'I Must Keep Some Secrets'

Vidia spoke about finding me, yet my conceit was that I had discovered him. Both could have been true. Friendship is often a case of mutual rescue. The previous year, in Singapore, I had written a book about his work because he was unknown in the United States. He had no American publisher; his American editions were out of print; there had never been paperbacks. I was grateful to him for his help in my writing, but I also thought he could use my help. And publishing my book in the States might bring both of us to the attention of readers. So *V. S. Naipaul: An Introduction to His Work* was a labor of love, done out of friendship, but like many gifts it was also self-serving.

The book was accepted by Vidia's publisher. The advance was small, surprisingly small – say, four lunches at the Connaught. I was counting on my novel *Saint Jack* to restore me to solvency.

Writing to me at The Forge from Trinidad, Vidia expressed his pleasure that the book about him was to be published. In spite of the tiny advance, he said, his publisher would stand by the book. If it sold well I would benefit; if it was a good book, it would cause many things to happen. A worthy book made its own way, and a gifted author never failed to be rewarded. And, sometimes, miracles happened.

I had complained to him that I was working too hard, combining work on my novel with writing book reviews. He said he understood my dilemma.

'You need to appear more often in the English papers, to broaden the base of your reputation,' he said. Practical as always, sound advice. 'But they do pay appallingly.'

On the subject of drudging as a freelance, Vidia knew what he was talking about. He had trodden this same road, hacking away on Grub Street, twelve years before: the small rented house, tight money, the weekly review, hack work and honorariums. I knew from the bibliography I had made that he had reviewed many books while writing *A House for Mr Biswas*. If he could write a masterpiece and review books at the same time, surely I could follow his example. He was sensitive to this burden, which was part of a writer's independence. Writers in residence never faced it, salaried magazine staffers and writers on fat contracts were oblivious of it, but for the freelance writer it is a constant dilemma, because the freelancer hates to say no to any request, for fear that the requests will vanish. At the same time, the freelancer knows that the true meaning of 'hack' is 'workhorse.'

A similar sort of problem had just arisen in Vidia's writing life. He intended to go to South America, on assignment for *The New York Review of Books*. But its rates were low. He wanted to write about Argentina – and the *Review* would print anything he cared to write – yet he felt there was no profit in it. So he was inclined to remain in Trinidad, at his sister's, queen-beeing it, so he said.

His usual discursive medical report was appended to this letter. He tended to go into minute detail when the subject was money or health. He anatomized insomnia, and his dealings on the stock market were another sort of fever chart. Writing exhausted him. Each time he finished a book he was close to collapse. He said he had been working steadily from 1965 to 1971, and he felt depleted by *The Mimic Men*, *The Loss of El Dorado*, and *In a Free State*, as well as by all the journalism – enough to fill another book. The potted history of his physical effort was just the inspiration I needed, though I was alarmed by the consequences he described: extreme torpor, fatigue, dizzy spells in public places, frayed nerves – 'the mind, rather than the body, calling for rest and still more rest.'

In this burned-out state he stopped writing, and I remembered his saying, 'I may fall silent.' I still wrote to him in Trinidad. I had more time now. I had finished *Saint Jack* and sold it to The Bodley Head in London. It had not solved my problems. My English advance was £250, half on signature, half on publication. For my year's work on the novel I now had £125, minus the agent's ten percent – five meals at the Connaught. 'We wish it were more,' my editor had said. So did I.

All these tiddly, trifling numbers – but they mattered to me at the time because my life depended on them.

'And you say you don't want me to get a job?' my wife said. But she did not recriminate; she was gentle. This was a delicate subject.

She got a job with the BBC and we moved to London, wrenched from Dorset in the clammy English spring, with a damp summer looming. Instead of rural poverty, which I found bearable for its downrightness and sufficiently dignified for the amount of space we had – a whole house, the surrounding woods and meadows – we were now plunged into a dreary inner suburb, in a small apartment. It was nasty and uncomfortable, narrow, dirty, mean, and noisy. It smelled, it was cold. The seedy grumbling neighbors, the big cars flashing loudly past on the main road – every bit of it was like a reminder of failure.

I wanted to start another novel. I had a good idea, based on a ghost story I had been told in Dorset by an old man in the Gollop Arms. My first impression of Dorset was of a weird landscape. I wanted to write about that, a place darker and stranger than anything I had known in Africa. Beyond the ghost story, the germ of my idea was of an English anthropologist who has thrived in Africa and then retires and returns home to this haunted place.

But in London I had no place to work. We lived in two rooms in a noisy, much subdivided house. I tried to write on a table in the bedroom but was disturbed by all the ambiguous memories and associations: a bedroom is charged with dreams and slumber and sex, and this one had all the residue of its previous tenants. It stank, too, as bedrooms in rented houses often do.

It was at ground level, and from where I sat, with my back to the room, I could see beyond the weedy front yard to Gordon Road, Ealing, under a gray sky. My two children were in the other room, staring at the rented television set. I could not work. I felt idle. I complained of this idleness to Vidia. His response was friendly and wise.

'The essence of the freelance life is freedom,' he wrote. And he spoke of indolence as an aspect of freedom, one that I should accept. He said that any freelancer needed the confidence to believe that in spite of occasional setbacks, everything was going to be fine in the end. But of course that was a problem. 'This faith your friends cannot give you: it is something you have to discover in yourself.'

He went on to speak approvingly of my wife's job with the BBC World Service, which he listened to all the time. This second letter from Trinidad was more allusive than any I had received from him lately. He seemed refreshed by his trip to Argentina – he had taken the assignment after all. He had been back in Port of Spain for only two days and he was making plans. He would first write his pieces, one on the Argentine writer Jorge Luis Borges, the other on Argentina itself, Evita and Peronism figuring strongly. After that, he had to choose whether to go to Brazil or New Zealand, or head straight back to The Bungalow. He had recently turned down trips to Canada and Nigeria.

Perversely, being in demand reminded him of rejection. The very fact of this friendly attention and the many invitations gave him a gloomy vision of his future, when he would get no attention, nor any invitations. He could not contemplate acceptance without anticipating his being superfluous. In this mood he regarded good-will as a curse and praise as the Evil Eye.

Preparing the collection of pieces that he was planning to call *The Overcrowded Barracoon and Other Articles*, he was opposed by Pat on his intention to include his pieces about India. She said that no one would be interested in them. The reviewers would use those pieces to attack the book for its monotonous insistence on Indian subjects, Indian elections, Indian deficiencies. Pat was correct, India was his obsessive subject, but the act of writing was obsessive and often irrational. So he resisted. He felt that in the end he would be all right. He often said so.

That was his greatest strength, his unwavering belief that writing was fair – that a good book cannot fail, that it will ultimately be recognized as good; that a bad book will eventually be seen as junk, no matter what happens in the short run. Only the long run mattered. There was justice in writing. If you failed, you deserved to fail. You had to accept your failure.

This belief was both armor and a sword, and by repetition he instilled this belief in me and made me strong. It was a little early to tell whether we would be rewarded for our work. The external signs were still ambiguous. He was living in a room at his sister's house, in 3 Woodlands Road, Valsayn Park, Port of Spain, Trinidad; and I inhabited, with my family of four, a pair of narrow rooms in 80 Gordon Road, Ealing, West London, with someone's radio playing and a child crying upstairs. It helped that I believed in my writing, and it helped as much – perhaps more – that he believed in me.

Even his asking favors was a form of giving me confidence. He wondered whether I would be willing to look over the proofs of his collection of articles. This was the book I had suggested to him after I read all his magazine pieces in Singapore. I had made a list. He used some from the list but in the end did not include any of the book reviews I had found. That was another lesson. He said that book reviews served their purpose but had no lasting value, except for the jokes. 'Too bad we can't keep the jokes and get rid of the rest.' He chose long, solid pieces. He had put enormous effort into his journalism, bringing to it the intensity of fiction writing. In this period, as he put it, no novel offered itself to him.

He had no ideas for a novel. 'Creatively, I continue barren.' He was healthier than he had felt for a while, but he feared the future. He maintained that my most productive years and best work were ahead of me – I had that to look forward to. That promise excited me. As for himself, 'At forty, I have the sickening sensation that my work is behind me.'

The very sight of his books irritated him. He hated talking about them. He felt like a fraud. He was pretty gloomy, he said. 'In this profession, is satisfaction ever attained?'

The words were harsher than the tone he used in the rest of the letter. He seemed energetic, like a mountaineer cheerfully grumbling about the steepness of the ascent as he skipped from ledge to ledge. He even sounded hopeful. 'If I write again, though, I think it will be a new man writing.' Up till then, writing had been his 'therapy.' It had given him confidence, he said. Now he suggested that he was starting over.

Already he seemed like a new man. No novel, true, but he had pieces to write and travel plans. And he was full of insights. He said that a girl he had met in Argentina had copied two pages from a Thomas Hardy novel in which a heroine reflects on the melancholy of her life and situation. One of the Hardy lines, 'meanest kisses were at famine prices,' was frightening, Vidia said, commenting on the shocking juxtaposition of 'famine' and 'prices' and 'kisses.'

He did not quote more than this, and he gave me only the title of the novel, *The Return of the Native*, but I found the pages and, moved by what I read, marked several paragraphs with a red pen.

To be loved to madness – such was her great desire. Love was the one cordial which could drive away the eating loneliness of her days. And she seemed to long for the abstraction called passionate love more than for any particular lover.

She could show a most reproachful look at times, but it was directed less against human beings than against certain creatures of her mind, the chief of these being Destiny, through whose interference she dimly fancied it arose that love alighted only on gliding youth – that any love she might win would sink simultaneously with the sand in the glass. She thought of it with an ever-growing consciousness of cruelty, which tended to breed actions of reckless unconventionality, framed to snatch a year's, a week's, even an hour's passion from anywhere while it could be won. Through want of it she had sung without being merry, possessed without enjoying, outshone without triumphing. Her loneliness deepened her desire. On Egdon, coldest and meanest kisses were at famine prices; and where was a mouth matching hers to be found?

Fidelity in love for fidelity's sake had less attraction for her than for most women: fidelity because of love's grip had much. A blaze of love, and extinction, was better than a lantern glimmer of the same which should last long years. On this head she knew by prevision what most women learn only by experience: she had mentally walked round love, told the towers thereof, considered its palaces; and concluded that love was but a doleful joy. Yet she desired it, as one in a desert would be thankful for brackish water.

She often repeated her prayers; not at particular times, but, like the unaffected devout, when she desired to pray. Her prayer was always spontaneous, and often ran thus, 'O deliver my heart from this fearful gloom and loneliness: send me great love from somewhere, else I shall die.'

'So I feel about love and writing,' Vidia wrote to me. Waxing uncharacteristically lyrical, he said he needed passion and comedy and relief from the past. If he were not vitalized, he feared he would die at a time when he was capable of writing brilliantly.

This astonished me – the sudden outburst, the yearning, the passion, the appeal. It sounded like the fear of unrequited love. He then quoted some lines from Derek Walcott. He had quoted Walcott before; the man was a neighbor islander, a man close to his own age. He said the words had scared him in 1954 when he had first read them: 'But my talent grew bad and my wit turned stale / – but I sprang from my mind –'

I reread the lines. I reread the Hardy: 'meanest kisses.' Vidia closed, saying, 'See how this jolly letter has turned out. Strange things happen when a writer sits down on an off day to write to a friend.'

That was like a poem ('See how . . .'). Vidia's lines were more mellifluous and rhythmic and meaningful than Walcott's, with its weak second line. Once again, by his using the word 'friend' and his affirmation of friendship, I was bucked up. That same day, in spite of the radio and the squawking child and my debts, I had the confidence to work. I began plotting my next novel, *The Black House*.

One other thing I noticed. His letter had been tampered with. He had done the tampering, had torn off half a page. He explained it in a teasing parenthesis: 'Last half of that first page censored. I must keep *some* secrets.'

When Pat wrote a month later from Trinidad to say that she liked my book about Vidia's work, I was pleased; and she added, 'Vidia cannot be detached from it. He read with great absorption and smiled or laughed often,' which delighted me.

Yet I continued to worry about what was to become of me. My strategy had been to write and survive that way; my strategy was not working. A novel, a book of criticism, scores of book reviews, a collection of short stories – this in less than a year had produced such a paltry income that I was grateful to my wife for getting a job. Now I was at work on my seventh novel, and still doing journalism, and it did not seem as though I could make a living. All this in spite of burning the midnight oil and getting wonderful reviews.

In this profession, is satisfaction ever attained?

I thought, Yes. I was satisfied, but I had no money. It was all the more important that I had Vidia as a friend.

Pat said she saw the love and understanding in my book *V. S. Naipaul*, and the depth of this feeling had given me unusual insights into Vidia's work. She confessed that she had thought of writing something personal about Vidia. During the writing of *In a Free State*, he had read a biography of Tolstoy and a book about Dorothy Wordsworth and other writers' lives. Literary biography was something Vidia often read, as if peering through a window to compare his life with the lives of fellow sufferers. Listening to him read aloud from the diaries of Dorothy Wordsworth and Sonya Tolstoy, Pat Naipaul marveled at the perceptions, and she thought she might do something similar.

She began making notes, describing Vidia's progress on his book, keeping a diary, writing down his comments. But she lost heart. She had never been strong, and it was hard to write in a household where the central figure was V. S. Naipaul. She felt she lacked profundity and passion; she suspected that she was trivial. There was something wrong about her – Vidia's wife – using him as the subject for a candid or intimate portrait. It was intrusive and bordered on vulgarity.

That was why, she said, my book meant so much to her, because I expressed many of her own feelings about Vidia's work. She said she was delighted I had done the book, since she was so similarly affected by his writing.

Another success, another good review, but I had no income. I was angry and bewildered. I had not asked for much, only a simple living. I did not dare think about getting rich. I wanted to get by, nothing more.

In the midst of my bewilderment, a letter was pushed through the letter slot of this rented place, asking me if I would consider being a writer in residence at the University of Virginia, starting in two months. I said yes. If I went alone and lived like a monk, I could finish my novel and pocket most of my salary. I would be away four months, the first semester.

My wife said, 'I'll miss you.'

She understood. She was happy working at the BBC, and this

fulfillment made her sympathetic about my frustration. But there was something especially galling about returning to a university a year after quitting my Singapore job and saying I would never teach again. I should have been consoled by my grandiose job title, writer in residence, but it mocked me. A writer was supposed to be free of any employer – Vidia had said so.

In Virginia, living my monkish life, I received a letter from Vidia describing his trip to New Zealand. He was back at The Bungalow. He had passed through Trinidad again, visited Argentina again, finished writing his pieces. He had read my book and wanted to reread it, because he had been distracted by work. He had also felt self-conscious, being written about. He was his usual paradoxical self: 'But I don't think it matters what I think (and I don't know what I think).'

He wanted to meet, to talk about England and how I was adapting. Was I disappointed? After my eight years in the tropics, what did I think of this 'industrial reality'?

Africa was on his mind, because the Indians had been thrown out of Uganda by Idi Amin. As he had predicted so often, he said, Uganda was turning into a jungle. He blamed the white expatriates, who would take no responsibility for Amin – yet they had created the situation that had produced Amin. In the end they would go away and allow Uganda to become a forgotten horror.

I had not heard Vidia denounce a situation so thoroughly for years, but his anger was doubtless deepened by the fact that all his dire warnings had been fulfilled. He had predicted the rise of the dictatorship, the expulsion of the Indians, the bolting of the whites, the decline of Kampala into bush.

'It is an obscene continent, fit only for second-rate people. Second-rate whites with second-rate ambitions, who are prepared, as in South Africa, to indulge in the obscenity of disciplining Africans.' You either stayed away or you remained, with a whip in your hand. Uganda proved that the only survivors in Africa were second-raters and savages, masters and slaves.

This was the most severe condemnation he had ever made. He was raging as eighty thousand Indians – men, women, and children – were being loaded onto planes, their valuables being snatched from them by African soldiers. They were losing homes and land

and businesses, and in many cases their life savings. Most were allowed into Britain, but they really did not want to live in a cold and hostile climate. They had few defenders in Britain and the United States; they had none in Africa. Africans heckled them, and the white expatriates, as Vidia had said, stood by and watched.

'The melancholy thing about the world is that it is full of stupid and common people; and the world is run for the benefit of the stupid and the common.'

As for plans, Vidia had none. He had been back in England for only four days, and he felt he was living through an uncertain, purgatorial period. He spoke of his four years without a house. He feared a stock market crash. He wanted to write a book but had no ideas. It was his old feeling of emptiness and insecurity, of his life's being over, the dusty intimation of the scrap heap.

He was low and feeling adrift. It was his alienated mood of *What country? What passport?* He was placeless in The Bungalow and this was another reason he wanted to talk about England with me. He wanted to find out what I liked and didn't like. He saw me as another wanderer.

But I was in Virginia, dreaming of my wife and two children, like a sailor in a storm at sea, vowing that I would never do this again. Vidia spoke of going back to Trinidad to cover the violent murders that had taken place at a Black Power commune.

His verdict on my book about his work was just what I wanted. He said he had read it 'with amazement, delight and great humility. It seems marvelously responsive and humane; it reminds me and informs me of things that I had forgotten and perhaps had never realized.' He spoke of my generosity and thoroughness. Reflecting on so much labor in the past ('gone, gone'), he became apprehensive about the future. He was sad and fearful, he said.

He had won the John Llewelyn Rhys Memorial Prize, the Somerset Maugham Award, the Hawthornden Prize, the W. H. Smith Award, and, with *In a Free State*, the Booker Prize. Already he was being spoken of as the greatest living writer in the English language. Yet it was little comfort to him to know that his reputation was formidable. He pined for better sales and more money.

While he regarded his life as over, mine had, I felt, hardly begun. He made a few corrections in my book, small ones, all of them factual. He talked about *In a Free State*, how 'tightly constructed' it was. He wrote about a dream the main character had that he decided to leave out. 'I dreamed all the dreams myself, for him, during the writing.' The book had possessed him; he had been 'deeply immersed – almost to the point of neurosis' in it.

I had felt so close to *In a Free State* that I could not evaluate it. In the book I recognized Haji Hallsmith and the besieged African king; I knew some of the Africans; Vidia's Colonel was the Major of the Kaptagat Arms – the same man, the same shouting; the waiters were his waiters, and, as Vidia had remarked at the time, 'The boy was big and he moved briskly, creating little turbulences of stink.' The roads were the roads we had traveled down; the well-marked sign the same *Beware of Fallen Rocks*; the coming-of-age boys I had seen myself. I had been frightened by those same dogs barking. Much of it was our safari in Rwanda, but made into a quilt: I saw the stitches, and what another reader would see as a large, harmonious design seemed to me a mass of patches. But that is what happens when you have a writer for a friend and you travel the same road.

He said, 'I do hope that your book will show you some reward for your great sensitivity, labor and love.'

My reward was his saying that. I had begun the book as a labor of love, a favor to him, a lesson for me. I learned a great deal in the writing, but there was no material gain. Perhaps it interested some people in his work and found him new readers. But I suspected that in many ways Vidia's life was even more interesting than his work. He had made this observation about Somerset Maugham, how Maugham's life was complex and rich, even though the old man always denied it. As for *V. S. Naipaul: An Introduction to His Work*, it hardly sold and was not reprinted. Twenty-five years later it was still out of print. The advance was spent the day I received it. There were no royalties in twenty-five years, nor did I ever get a sales statement from the publisher. I never discovered how many copies were printed. A few thousand, perhaps. It met the worst fate that can befall a book: it became a collector's item, pretty much unread and uncirculated, celebrated only for its scarcity.

*

Vidia also needed money at this time, so he said. He had no assets apart from his manuscripts and papers, an entire record of his career to date. He had gone to the British Museum and discussed the matter, mentioning a figure of £40,000, which would include letters, manuscripts, pictures, mementos, maps, sketches, note-books, everything in his paper-rich life. It was quite a large stack, for he had told me he was superstitious and never threw away a piece of paper with his handwriting on it, as one might keep nail parings or locks of hair. It was possible that after his gathering up all his papers, the British Museum would change its mind and not pay even the agreed-upon minimum. He needed a backup plan.

Would I please, therefore, spread the word that he was thinking of selling his archives? An American university would be convenient because he wished to consult them in the future. In a cardboard box in Trinidad he had found letters and notes he had written in the distant past: 'penciled notes I made in the PAA aeroplane as soon as I got off the ground in July, 1950.' Rereading the many letters had suggested to him that he might write an autobiography. But what if the papers were destroyed in a riot ('not unlikely in Trinidad')? He needed them to be in a safe place.

Also, the money. He wanted to convert the papers into a flat in central London.

The chairman of the English Department at the University of Virginia was also a friend. He was the man who had offered me the writer-in-residence job. I asked his advice. He said I should see the university's librarian. The librarian was the assiduously orderly sort of person – more orderly than intellectual – you find running libraries. He had the peculiar baldness that went with an orderly disposition; he was close-shaven, with pink cheeks, and so tidy and well turned out that I doubted he was much of a reader.

'I wonder if you'd be interested in buying the archives of V. S. Naipaul,' I said.

'I know that name,' the librarian said. 'He wrote *The Man-Eater of Malgudi*.'

'That was R. K. Narayan,' I said. So I was right: this clean, clear-eyed man was really thick. I listed Vidia's book titles, none of which rang a bell, though the man kept smiling.

'What is he selling?'

'Everything. Every piece of paper he has. Letters, books, manuscripts, pictures, the lot.'

'Would he have any interesting letters from well-known writers? Those are usually pretty valuable.'

I felt this conversation was not going well, and I was glad that Vidia was being spared the indignity of explaining that he was not R. K. Narayan.

'I'm sure he has lots of letters of that kind. Anthony Powell is one of his closest friends.'

The librarian smiled, but not with pleasure. It was the uneasy smile that indicates incomprehension, as if I had slipped unconsciously into a foreign language.

'What sort of figure does he have in mind?'

'Forty thousand pounds.'

'How much is that in real money?'

'Maybe ninety grand.'

'You're joking.'

I said nothing. The librarian clamped his jaw shut and bit on his teeth. The university didn't have that kind of money, he said. I sensed his triumphant smile grimly heating my back as I left his office.

Surely other libraries or universities would be interested. I wrote letters. I made phone calls. Sometimes I mentioned the price, other times I solicited a price. There were no takers. Many people I spoke to were only dimly aware of the name Naipaul. How was this possible? It did not surprise me that Vidia was little known in the United States; it was the reason I had written my book about his work. But I was astounded that academics and librarians were so clueless.

I broke the news gently to Vidia, but perhaps it was my delicacy and tact that made it obvious I had been rebuffed. Sensitive to rejection, Vidia took it badly. He sent a brief note and lapsed into silence.

Judging from my classes at the University of Virginia, American universities were vastly inferior to Makerere University and the University of Singapore. My Charlottesville students had read little – hardly any of them had read the short stories of Joyce or Chekhov, but they wanted to write short stories themselves. Sometimes they handed in work they had done the previous year, for another course. Usually they handed in nothing. They were pleasant but intellectually lazy. Some were graduate students. When I gave them low marks they objected.

'Hey, Paul. You don't get it. I need a B in this course,' one grad student said to me.

I told him that his C was generosity on my part. He was in the master's program. He had done very little work.

'Look, I need a B,' he said in the snarling voice of someone demanding my wallet.

This was new to me: teachers who did not read, students who could not write. One semester of this was enough. I took my savings and went back to London.

We moved from west London to south London. We had a whole house in Catford, but the area was much grimmer than Ealing. It was full of lawbreakers – petty burglars, pickpockets, car thieves, bag boosters, second-story men, muggers, and hoisters of all descriptions. But Catford was so poor these villains had to take a train to other boroughs or up to the West End, the more salubrious parts of London where the pickings were better, to commit their crimes.

In the spring of 1973, having finished *The Black House*, I cycled to Waterloo, put my bike on the train, and went to Salisbury, cycling from there to Wilsford Manor. Vidia could see that my finances were as miserable as ever, but I told him why I had left the University of Virginia.

'You had said you'd never teach again,' Vidia said. 'You broke your own rule. If you make a rule, keep to it.'

We walked to Stonehenge, through the fields, and he explained the water meadows once more.

'You'd like Virginia,' I said. 'The countryside is beautiful – rolling hills and meadows.'

'I'm afraid that America is not for me. I don't think I could live in a rural setting.'

'In some ways it's a bit like this.'

But I was thinking: It is much more beautiful than this funny fenced-off part of Salisbury Plain, with a highway running alongside this weird ancient monument, belittling it.

'I have to stick with what I have,' Vidia said. 'It's too late for me to transfer to another country.'

We kept walking toward the big biscuit-colored cromlech that lay on the other side of the whizzing cars on the motorway.

'So what's the plan?'

'I'm still looking for money,' he said.

'Are you serious about buying a place in London?'

'Yes. I think it's just what I need.'

'I'm sure you could get something for less than forty thousand.'

He said, 'No. I want something uncompromisingly fashionable.'

He said this while looking at the sky.

A few days after I returned to London, my editor at The Bodley Head, a cigar-smoking Scotsman and sometime poet named James Michie, invited me to lunch at Chez Victor. He said he wanted to discuss *The Black House*. He was very friendly when I met him, but it seemed ominous that we had finished the first course and most of the bottle of wine before he mentioned my book, and then he told me he did not like it at all.

'I'm afraid I can't publish it,' Michie said.

'You mean you're turning it down?' I could not believe this.

'It will hurt your reputation,' he said.

'I have no reputation.'

'I think if you reread the book you will agree with me,' he said.

'I don't have to reread the book. I wrote the book. If I thought it was no good I wouldn't have submitted it.'

My voice was shrill, and I think that surprised him. I was hurt and angry. Probably he thought he was softening the blow, because Londoners are such eager lunchers, but it seemed callous to turn lunch into an occasion for such a rejection. And why was I being rejected? The novel was good, surely?

'I let William Trevor look at it. He agreed with me.'*

Trevor was one of his authors, a talented one, I thought.

I said, 'My last novel got great reviews. You paid me two hundred and fifty pounds. I assumed you'd give me the same for this. You'd be getting it for a pittance.'

---

* William Trevor is bewildered by this; he has never read *The Black House*. The book he read in typescript – and liked – was *Sinning with Annie*.

'It's the principle of the thing,' he said. He had lit a cigar and, feeling defensive, he had stopped eating. 'I don't believe in the book. I can't publish something I don't believe in.'

'You publish lots of crappy books,' I said.

I guessed he saw the truth of this, because he hesitated, at least looked uncertain.

I said, 'If you turn this down you'll lose me as an author. I'll go to another publisher. I'll never let you publish another book of mine. And all it's costing you is two hundred and fifty quid. This lunch is costing you thirty!'

Michie was bald but he had a hank of hair that grew from the side of his head that he arranged over his pate to give the semblance of hair. This damp, fussed-with strand had slipped down and hung by the side of his ear like a strange Hassidic sidecurl. It made him look desperate.

'If you twist my arm, I'll publish it,' he said.

'That's it, then. That's all. Forget it – I want my manuscript back.'

Feeling ill, I finished my meal and walked back to his office, wishing the whole way I could push him in the path of a car. He gave me the typescript and still seemed surprised and somewhat embarrassed by my anger.

I found another publisher, but in the meantime seriously wondered how I would ever make a living as a writer. I told Vidia. He invited me to tea at the Charing Cross Hotel.

'You should have shown the book to me. Why didn't you?' he said.

'I didn't want to bother you with my problems.'

'That's what friends are for,' Vidia said.

He could not have said anything truer or kinder. After eight years he was still on my side, still a well-wisher.

'He gave it to William Trevor to read. Apparently Trevor didn't like it either.'

'Who is William Trevor?'

That was what I needed, the old corrosive contempt.

'He is no one,' Vidia said coldly. 'Something similar happened to me when I was starting out. Deutsch told me to put the book aside. It was *Miguel Street*. He didn't know what to do with it.

And one still gets the odd foolish remark about one's work.'

'Why do they do it?'

'They do it because they are common, lying, low class, and foolish. That is why they do it.'

He was so angry he could not continue the conversation. He sipped his tea, looking around at the other tables. He saw a heavily pregnant woman moving slowly across the shabby room, bracing herself by resting on chairs and with one hand pressed for balance on the small of her back.

'To me, one of the ugliest sights on earth is a pregnant woman.'

This astonished me. I did not know what to say. He turned away from the woman.

'I have an idea for a book,' I said.

'Tell me.'

'A long railway trip.'

I explained how, in Virginia, I had read Mark Twain's *Following the Equator*, an obscure and out-of-print travel book, but lovable for its geographical non sequiturs and incidental mishaps. I liked the spirited jokes and the long journey. It was about nothing but his trip. A lot of it was dialogue. Twain did not pretend to be knowledgeable about the countries he passed through – Australia, India, and South Africa, among many others.

'I checked the maps,' I said. 'I can leave Victoria Station and go to Paris, to Istanbul – to the border of Afghanistan. Then there's the Khyber Pass, and trains all through India. Burma has railways, so does Thailand. Even Vietnam has trains. I would travel around Japan and come home on the Trans-Siberian, and then write about it.'

'That's a lovely idea,' Vidia said. He was seriously concentrating on it, looking for a flaw or something suspect. But it was too simple an idea to have a flaw. Taking trains from London to Japan and back: it was surprising that no one had done it before.

'I'm thinking of leaving in September,' I said. 'I would be in India in October. What's the weather like then?'

'Delicious.'

He seemed distracted; he was still thinking about my book, my trip. He saw something I did not see – I could tell from his reaction. He knew it was a good idea, but he saw something more. He saw a hugely successful book.

'Who do you think I should visit in India?'

He thought a moment. He frowned. 'You'll find your way.'

For the first time in the years I had known him, I sensed a reluctance on his part to help me. Only a few minutes before he had said, 'That's what friends are for.'

'Isn't there anyone you could introduce me to?'

He had been to India six or seven times recently and had lived there for a year. He had written about it many times. It was his obsessive subject. He knew India intimately.

'I don't know. You might see Mrs Jhabvala when you're in Delhi.'

As he was speaking, giving me the name with such reluctance, I vowed that I would not visit Ruth Prawer Jhabvala.

'You'll be all right,' he said. But this time the statement was tinged with self-pity, almost resentment, a feeling I had never detected in him before. It was as though I were abandoning him. And why? This train-riding idea I had conceived out of sheer desperation, in the urgency to have a book to write and money from a publisher.

The bill was brought. I paid it, I left the tip. Vidia had not seen it. He did not see bills even when they were brought on the most expensive china and folded like origami and presented to him. It was one of his survival skills that a bill could come and go without ever being visible. Still, he looked disgusted.

'This hotel used to be quite grand,' he said in his pained voice. Perhaps the pain was due to the idea I had just divulged. 'Having tea here was once something special. One was glamoured by it.' He made a face. 'No longer.'

I took the trip. I left London on September 19, 1973, on the train to Paris. I changed trains and went to Istanbul, changed again for Ankara, for Tehran, and for the holy city of fanatics, Meshed. And onward, through Afghanistan (by bus, no trains) and down the Khyber, up to Simla, down to Madras and to Sri Lanka, on the train and on the ferry. To Burma and Thailand and Singapore, along the coast of Vietnam (heavily bombed and still smoking), up and down Japan, a boat to Nakhodka, and the Trans-Siberian home. My heart was in my mouth the whole time. Out of fear I wrote everything down; in my misery I mocked myself, and a febrile humor crept into the narrative. In January of the following year I returned to London, still feeling miserable. I had missed Christmas. Everyone howled at me, 'Where have you been?' I propped up my notebooks and wrote the book, made a single narrative out of all those train trips. The title came from a road in Kanpur: the Railway Bazaar.

Sometimes miracles happen to a writer, Vidia had said. *The Great Railway Bazaar* was a small miracle. I was not prepared for it. While I was working on it, *The Black House* was published – the reviews were respectful – and I started *The Family Arsenal* after I finished the travel book. Even before publication, *The Great Railway Bazaar* was reprinted three times, to accommodate bookstore demand. It was an immediate bestseller. It was my tenth book. I had known Vidia for ten years. In that time I had published about a million words.

'An agonizing profession,' Vidia said. 'But there are rewards.'

All windfalls are relative. I did not become rich with that book, but at last I was making a living. I paid my debts. I had enough to support me in my next book. I was out from under. I never again worried about money – that freedom from worry was wealth to me. No more drudging. I was free. I was thirty-two.

And at last I understood what Vidia meant when he had written, 'I have never had to work for hire; I made a vow at an early age never to work, never to become involved with people in that way. That has given me a freedom from people, from entanglements, from rivalries, from competition. I have no enemies, no rivals, no masters; I fear no one.'

10

Lunch Party

'I can see it all now,' my wife said in a fantasizing voice, though she was not looking at anything except a loose sock on the floor. She snatched at it. 'The boys talking about their books. The girls talking about cooking.'

It was Saturday. She was busy with the week's laundry, moving through the house while I followed her. It was one of those maddening married people's conversations, one spouse chasing the other with questions, the dialogue shifting from room to room. We had moved to a much bigger house; we had many rooms now. Why didn't she want to go to Vidia's lunch party with me?

'Sunday is my only free day. Besides, he's really your friend.'

Such a discussion was supposed to end when one of the parties stopped pursuing, or the other, pretending to be too busy, hid.

'Hey, I often socialize with your friends.'

Dodging me, dodging the question, seeking more laundry, she said, 'I specifically asked whether we could bring the boys. Pat said that Hugh and Antonia Fraser will be there and are not bringing their kids. I took the hint.'

'We can go alone. It's a lunch party. It might be fun.'

'I don't think he likes me one bit.' She was shaking out clothes to be washed. 'But I don't take it personally. I doubt that he likes any women.'

'That's unfair.'

'Look at the women in his books. They disgust him. They're awful. He's the man who wrote "wife is a terrible word."'

I laughed at her and said, 'There's a nice woman in *The Mimic Men*. Lady Stella. Remember sex and fairy tales? "Goosey-goosey Gander"?'

'You might know that the only decent woman would be posh

... Oh, do go,' she said, looking hardworking and virtuous, burdened with an armload of laundry. 'Enjoy yourself. But please don't ask me to go with you. He won't miss me. I'll bet he won't even ask about me.'

The children, hearing us, crept to the upstairs landing to listen.

'You can take the train,' she said. She called up to the boys. 'Dad likes trains, doesn't he?'

'Dad likes trains!'

Trines, they said, a consequence of our living in London.

The empty ones on Sunday morning going west out of London were the trains I liked best. The Salisbury train from Waterloo racketed through Clapham Junction without stopping, past the very houses and back gardens I had looked at with horror when I first came to London, asking myself, Who could possibly live among these black bricks and broken chimneys and dim lights and gleaming slate roofs and grim gates and the sootiness that crept into the nostrils? The answer was me. I lived in one of those houses. All of them looked dismal except my own.

To the triphammer sound of the train wheels as they tapped the joints of the rails, I read the Sunday papers, looking up from time to time to rest my eyes on the green meadows and the trees, some bare and others with yellowing leaves. The leaves flew up singly like startled birds when the wind strengthened. Autumn made me thoughtful. Four years ago, in just this season, I had arrived and seen the trees like this, the fields sodden and green, mist on ponds, and dead leaves stuck flat to wet roads.

'I'll send a car for you,' Vidia had said, and he had given me the name of the driver. It was Walters. He was outside Salisbury station, waiting beside his car.

'You must be Mr Furrow,' he said.

'That's me.'

We drove to Wilsford in silence down roads with dense drifts and piles of leaves while I reflected on Vidia's thoughtfulness in sending a car. At The Bungalow, Walters opened the door for me, chauffeur fashion, and said, 'That will be four pounds.'

The gravel driveway announced every car with a rolling crunch like a chain being drawn on a pulley. Vidia came out and greeted me. Behind him was a small elfin-faced man wearing tight velvet trousers and a red and gold waistcoat.

'Do you know Julian Jebb?' Vidia asked.

'I've heard of you,' I said, shaking the man's hand.

'People say dreadful things about me. But take no notice,' Jebb said. 'I'm mad, bad, and dangerous to know.' He looked aside and in an American accent said, 'Hey, that's enough of that crap!'

He was the sort of Englishman who could express his humorous side only by speaking in an exaggerated American accent. It was not unusual. Many American academics I had known could only theorize in a precise way by using a fake English accent. Parody so often resulted from simple self-consciousness.

'Yes, yes,' Vidia said, looking impatient at Jebb's foolery. 'Come inside. Have something to drink.'

'I was telling Vidia how much I hate his gramophone,' Jebb said, stepping through the door. 'Look, isn't it hideous? It belongs in the V and A. It's just a silly contraption for distorting sounds.' He put his hands to his cheeks. 'I hate it!'

Just then we heard the serious and sudden crunch of the driveway, a thoroughly satisfying sound that reminded me now of molars and nuts. This continuous grinding was caused by the broad tires of a brown Jaguar. Closer, it even sounded like a big-pawed animal hungrily padding through gravel.

'Hugh and Antonia,' Vidia said. 'Yes. Yes. Yes.'

Jebb went to greet them. His voice was teasing and friendly but growly from his chain-smoking. He smoked French cigarettes from a blue pack.

The Frasers were introduced to me. I said, 'I met you almost ten years ago, around Christmas.'

'I distinctly remember you,' Lady Antonia said.

I loved her lisp on the word 'distinctly.' She had beautiful eyes and pale skin, and when she spoke, her tongue and teeth, slightly out of alignment, made her awkward, and sexier, and drew attention to her pretty mouth.

'Your book has done so well,' she said. 'I've given copies of it away as presents.'

Hugh Fraser, hearing this, turned to me. He was very tall and slow in his movements, with a large, thoughtful face that looked both apprehensive and domineering. His shoulders were lopsided, one higher than the other, which gave him a weary posture. It was a letter from Hugh Fraser that Vidia the graphologist had once shown me, saying of his handwriting, 'Look, even upside down it's still tormented.'

'The Welsh are the only people who bring out my racial prejudice,' Jebb was saying to Lady Antonia.

Hugh Fraser's bigness and aura of helpless authority filled The Bungalow. He was a Conservative Member of Parliament, and he made me wonder why anyone so judicious and reflective had wanted to go into politics. I could not imagine him giving speeches or stumping for votes. He represented Stafford and Stone, in the Midlands. I knew those places from the train window, the stops before Crewe and Stoke, on the way to Liverpool. His was a safe Tory seat and the towns looked dreary, but that could have been misleading: riding trains in England was an experience of the back yards and open windows you rarely saw. And if you said to an English person that a certain place was dreary, he'd respond, with an indulgent chuckle, 'Oh, the Potteries,' as if its dreariness were irrelevant.

'Sherry?'

Vidia was pouring and also describing the merits of this particular sherry, a suggestion of walnuts and oak.

'I always feel like Alice here,' Jebb said, and then he laughed and made a monkey face. 'Of course, I feel like Alice in lots of places!'

In his overloud laugh there was a scream of disturbance, yet he was funny and much friendlier than the others.

'Stephen Tennant is the March Hare and the Red Queen rolled into one,' Jebb said, and cupped his hand close to his mouth and whispered in my ear in his affected American accent, 'Faggot.'

Jebb's breath against my head made me so uncomfortable I said, 'He's a recluse, isn't he?'

'I don't know whether I would call someone who goes to America as much as he does a recluse. He loves Bournemouth. He never misses the Christmas pantomime. Stephen is savagely peripatetic compared to Vidia, the true recluse.'

'This is a fantastic place,' Lady Antonia said. 'It's like a cottage in an enchanted forest.'

She was dressed like a shepherdess, her soft skin set off by a frilly lavender blouse and a velvet peasant skirt with brightly embroidered bib and shoulder straps. Her greenish-blue eyes were beautiful, as was her somewhat tousled blond hair. With her big soft lips she seemed half girl, half woman, laughing as she disagreed.

'If I lived here I would never leave,' she said. 'You talk such rubbish, Julian.'

'About Stephen?' Julian pretended to be indignant, puffing pompously on his French cigarette. 'I am probably the only person in this room who's met him. I think of him as a sort of Oriental potentate. He greets all his visitors by lying on a lovely couch, draped in silk shawls. Something terribly Oriental about that – and of course something frightfully epicene too,' he said, cackling.

'There is something magical here,' said Lady Antonia.

'Stephen had the cottage built for himself,' Jebb said. 'He never set foot in it. He's just over there, you know, giggling over something very naughty.'

I wondered whether Vidia would tell Lady Antonia why the ivy-strangled trees were dead, but he said nothing. He had heard more guests arrive – the gravel again in the driveway. He was alert to the crunching. This was a taxi.

'Yes, yes,' he said, and went to the door. A young couple entered, and Vidia introduced them as Malcolm and Robin, visiting from New Zealand. Vidia had met them there on a lecturing visit. Malcolm had dark hair and a face so ruddy it looked like a higher form of embarrassment, the kind of color only English farm boys and some Scotsmen had – a naturally pale person's rude health. Robin was sweet and square-shouldered, wearing a soft, unnecessary hat, as New Zealanders seemed habitually to do.

'Beaut book, Paul,' Malcolm said to me. 'When we met Vidia in Auckland, I told him that it was a dream of mine to meet you when we came to England. So this is a pleasure.'

Jebb said mockingly, 'A real fan!'

I ignored him. Being a pest was part of his humor. 'My pleasure. Are you a writer?'

'I do some writing. I'm on the English faculty at the uni. I took Vidia around when he visited. Sort of smoothed the way.'

He was younger than me, and I knew exactly what his role had been, because it was the role I had played ten years before. I saw him as a Vidia protégé and seemed to be looking at my younger self, when I had visited England and Vidia had rewarded me for smoothing the way for him in Africa.

'It gets dark so early here,' Robin said. 'And listen to that wind.'

If I had not heard New Zealand in her nasalized *dahk* I would surely have heard it in her *weend*. But I had made the same observation of English weather when I had first arrived.

'Quite right,' Hugh Fraser said, but he was speaking about something else to Vidia. He had stood up. His head was near the ceiling. He looked awkward in the room's smallness, but then he probably looked uncomfortable in most rooms. 'I knew him well,' Fraser said. 'I would have given anything to work with him again. He always showed up in these sort of marvelous suits. "Got it in India," he'd say. "Made from the chin hairs of a certain goat in Kashmir."'

'I felt I could eat that cloth,' Vidia said.

Who were they talking about? But I didn't ask. Parties in England were full of remarks like these, about colorful people you'd never heard of.

'Instead, why don't you eat some food?' Pat said, emerging from the kitchen. She greeted everyone and apologized for being preoccupied with the meal. She looked harassed, but I could see that she had help, a woman in a brown sweater and apron ladling soup into bowls.

Vidia poured the wine, saying, 'I think you'll like this. It's balanced, it's firm, perhaps a bit fleshy, but smooth and, I think you'll agree, round.'

'We are taking no notice of Vidia's diet today,' Pat said. 'This is Mrs Griggs's oxtail soup.'

Vidia was served a plate of smoked salmon, which he had to himself, and I knew when I saw it that everyone else at the table would have preferred it to the brown soup.

Jebb said, 'Vidia is such an absolute fanatic about food. There's a new restaurant in London called Cranks, for vegetarians. I always think of Vidia when I go by. I'm usually cottaging in that area – see, no one even knows what it means!'

'One is thinking of buying a car,' Vidia said, abruptly changing the subject. 'Tell me, what car should one buy?'

'I'm car-blind,' Jebb said. 'I can't tell them apart. I can't even drive. I hate them, really. I'm car-bored, rather.'

'We once made the finest motorcars on earth,' Hugh Fraser said. His voice was solemn and slow. We waited for more. 'And no doubt we shall again.' He paused and added, 'Perhaps you should wait until then, when these paragons of British workmanship are once more rolling off the assembly lines.'

'How do you like your Jaguar?' I asked.

'It's a bit of a tired old warhorse,' he said. 'Like its owner.'

'Except when you're out on the road and speeding and calling out, "Eat my dust!"' Jebb said, slipping into an American accent again. Then Jebb said to Malcolm with intense interest, 'Isn't there a fabulous native name for New Zealand?'

'I think you mean Maori.'

'I suppose one does,' Jebb said. He was smoking at the table, while everyone else was eating.

'Aotearoa,' Malcolm said. 'It means, The Land of the Long White Cloud.'

'Or, The Land of the Wrong White Crowd, more like,' Jebb said. He turned his back on the New Zealanders and smiled at Lady Antonia, who hadn't heard.

'There is nothing I would love more than living on one of those islands,' Lady Antonia was saying to Pat Naipaul. But they weren't talking about New Zealand. They were engaged in a separate conversation, about the West Indies. 'I would adore being absolutely idle.'

'You'd get tired of the heat.'

'I'd adore the heat.'

'You would be so bored.'

'Not at all,' Lady Antonia said. 'I would love it. Flowers. Heat. The sun. The sea. It's my idea of heaven.'

This lovely woman, naked under a loosely fitting white dress with frilly sleeves and a big floppy bonnet and a white parasol, came smiling towards me in a tropical garden while I sat on the verandah of a yellow stucco plantation house at a table set with tea things, including marmalade made from my own oranges. A jovial parrot squawked in a big cage and sunlight blazed from the blue sky, showing the veins in the large green leaves of my anthuriums and Lady Antonia's body silhouetted in her thin lacy dress. I was pouring tea for her and she was utterly at peace and fragrant with pheromones. Heat, idleness, and contentment were the combination that produced sensuality.

'I love those hot islands,' she was saying to Pat as my temperature went up. 'I love doing nothing.'

'You're the busiest woman I know,' Pat said. She had gotten up to pass the plates for the second course, poached fish and buttery leeks and salad.

Lady Antonia was protesting, but I didn't care. I had already eloped with her, and I was barefoot on the verandah in my planter's shorts and straw hat, living out my fantasy of bliss in a coconut paradise.

'How is your wine?' Vidia asked me.

'You were right. Fleshy. Round. Smooth.'

Jebb said, 'Are you talking about Princess Margaret?'

'Afterwards we're all going to try some snuff,' Vidia said, cutting him off.

'Harold Macmillan took snuff,' Hugh Fraser said. 'One was perpetually badgered to try.'

'I won't badger you,' Vidia said.

'I want to try,' Lady Antonia said eagerly.

On our tropical verandah she was always saying yes to my wild suggestions, and she needed only to sigh and twitch her dress with her fingers for me to say yes. I looked up and saw Mrs Griggs collecting the plates and realized that my fantasy had possessed me so completely, lunch was over.

'I'll have a go,' Malcolm said. 'Robin?'

Robin nodded, yes, she would try some snuff.

'What a pathetic lot of sheep,' Jebb said. 'I will not put that vile substance up my nose. I'd rather have a fag. Oh, look at Paul! He's so shocked.'

I said, 'I know "fag" means cigarette, Julian.'

'But I mean the other kind of fag,' Jebb said. He laughed at me, and in his American accent said, 'Faggot.'

The correct response, I knew, was to let yourself be teased and not get riled, and then merely smile in pity at the teaser to make him feel childish. Or else to say, You may well be right!

'That snuff just vanishes up Vidia's nose,' Pat said.

'Aren't you supposed to sneeze?' Robin asked.

'Vidia never sneezes,' said Pat.

'I love to sneeze,' Lady Antonia said. 'I wonder why that is.'

This was my chance. I said, 'The reason it's so pleasurable is that there is erectile tissue in the nose – even a woman's. The nose is also a sexual organ. It's very sensitive. I mean, it can become aroused and swollen. There are some people who can't breathe through their nose when they're sexually excited.'

Everyone stared at me.

'It says so in Krafft-Ebing,' I went on, blabbing. '*Psychopathia Sexualis*. Sneezing and sex.'

Lady Antonia smiled, but her husband was frowning in contemplation at his big hands, and his face was darker as an uneasy silence descended on the table. I had probably said too much, but I didn't mind. I was thinking of nakedness on a hot island.

'That sounds like the voice of experience, Paul,' Jebb said.

'If it sounds that way it's because I am boasting,' I said. 'But haven't you been told you have a virile nose?'

'All the time, but fortunately for me I am impotent,' Jebb said. 'I am "The Maimed Débauché."'

Malcolm put his elbows on the table, and his pink face grew pinker as he recited:

> So when my days of impotence approach,
> And I'm by pox and wine's unlucky chance
> Forced from the pleasing billows of debauch
> On the dull shore of lazy temperance . . .

'That sounds so lovely spoken in New Zealandish – is that right?' Jebb was puffing energetically and blowing smoke. 'Or do I say "Kiwi"?'

'That verse is terribly familiar,' Lady Antonia said. She was dabbing her pretty lips.

'John Wilmot, Earl of Rochester,' Malcolm said.

'Malcolm's doctoral dissertation was about the Augustans and court wits,' Robin said. 'I typed every word, so I should know.'

'Rochester is delightful,' Lady Antonia said. 'Do you still read him, Vidia?'

Before Vidia could answer, Malcolm stuck his pink face into Antonia's pale one and said, '"Delightful" is a strange word for porno.'

'I don't find Rochester in the least pornographic. You New Zealanders must be rather easily shocked.'

I liked that. We would read Rochester on our verandah, Lady A. and I. Instead of giving her a direct reply, Malcolm propped himself up on his elbows again, a beaky Kiwi in the throes of pedantry, proving his point to the Poms, and declaimed:

> By all love's soft yet mighty powers
> It is a thing unfit
> That men should fuck in time of flowers
> Or when the smock's beshit.

'I think you've just proved my point – you've certainly revealed something about your own shockability,' Lady Antonia said. 'Rochester is a moralist, really, and very funny for being a wee bit naughty.'

'A wee bit naughty!' Malcolm cried. Speaking in his New Zealand accent he could not make much of a point; he sounded as if he were satirizing himself. He angrily recited again:

> You ladies all of merry England
> Who have been to kiss the Duchess's hand,
> Pray, did you lately observe in the show
> A noble Italian called Signor Dildo?

'"Naughty" is precisely how I would describe that,' Lady Antonia said.

Vidia was fidgeting, made uncomfortable by the turn in the conversation. I knew he was impatient to leave the table and end this talk. He had taken out his pipe and was smoothing it and sticking his thumb in the bowl.

'Malcolm can go on all night,' Robin said, and patted her husband's rigid arm.

'Rochester is all foreplay,' Jebb said. 'Who was it who said foreplay is terribly middle class?'

Malcolm's eyes were glassy with rage, and I guessed it was because Lady Antonia was smiling and turned slightly away from him, her hands primly in her lap. Malcolm set his jaw at her and said:

> So a proud bitch does lead about
> Of humble curs the amorous rout
> Who most obsequiously do hunt
> The savory scent of salt-swollen c—

'Language, I hear!' Jebb shouted in glee, and then, 'Your New Zealand accent lends piquancy and incredible nuance to Augustan poetry.'

'Shall we have coffee?' Pat said.

'Is this another branch of the awful study of English?' Vidia said.

Jebb said, 'My grandfather hated that poetry. Do you know my grandfather?'

I said, 'No. Do you know mine?'

'Mine was Hilaire Belloc. Who was yours?'

Lady Antonia was smiling directly at Malcolm now. He looked fussed and breathless and indignant. She put her lisp to dramatic advantage as she said,

> Then talk not of inconstancy,
> False hearts and broken vows;
> If I, by miracle can be
> This live-long minute true to thee,
> 'Tis all that heaven allows.

'Rochester wrote that as a lame excuse, because he found it impossible to be faithful,' Malcolm said.

'I think it's lovely and lyrical,' Lady Antonia said. 'I don't know those poems you're quoting. But maybe that's because we invent the writer we want. I know why I think Vidia is brilliant. I'm sure you could quote something against him. But Rochester is for me a lyric poet with heaps and heaps of charm.'

The dispute was probably less about Lord Rochester than it was about class and accents. It created a staleness in the air around the lunch table and an awkwardness for all that remained unspoken. Vidia got up, Malcolm and Robin whispered to each other in a wound-licking way, and Jebb giggled. Hugh Fraser was frowning as though listening for an echo that would reveal a meaning. At that point I heard Lady Antonia sneeze, and saw tawny snuff-dust around her nostrils. She smiled at me with watery eyes. I wanted her to ask me about erectile tissue.

'I have just thought of it, Vidia,' Hugh Fraser said, returning to an interrupted conversation. 'It's that odd racial contradiction you get with so much intermarriage. Black becomes white and white becomes black.'

'I have written about that,' Vidia said. He went to a bookshelf, picked out a leatherbound copy of *The Mimic Men*, and read the concentrated paragraph about the fable 'The Niger and the Seine.'

As soon as he began speaking – and he spoke clearly and well, knowing just how to emphasize each word, knowing what was coming, timing his pauses – the lunch guests stopped talking. Vidia sat upright, holding the book straight, his thumb in the gutter of the spine, and read on, carefully, as if giving a lesson in recitation to Malcolm, who had blurted out the rude Lord Rochester stanzas. When Vidia was done, he shut the book like a vicar shutting a Bible after a homily.

'You see?'

We went for a walk behind The Bungalow so that Vidia could show us the water meadows and the trees.

Robin and Malcolm were walking together, wife reassuring husband, who still looked flustered. Pat went over to them, to walk along with them – it was only now, outside, that it was obvious there had been a scene at lunch; Pat was being a pleasant peace-making hostess. I jostled onward to walk next to Lady Antonia.

We talked about nothing – the delightful woods, the overhanging branches, the thicknesses of ivy.

'Your fantasy is my fantasy,' I finally said. 'A hot island and idleness, clear sky and a blue lagoon.'

'I am so glad you agree with me. Everyone thinks I'm absolutely mad.'

'No, no.' I could see the white dress, the parasol, the hat – and the thrashing legs and damp flanks.

Hugh Fraser was walking up front with Vidia, both men talking about a weighty matter – I could see it from the way they held their heads, tilted at an angle that indicated seriousness.

'I also like your "seize the day" lines of Rochester,' I said.

'That's so sweet of you to say,' Lady Antonia said. 'What are you writing at the moment?'

'A novel, set in London.'

'I am sure it will be a great hit. Vidia is so proud of your success.'

I wanted to hug her and bury my face against her neck – she looked so soft and warm, her lips so pretty. I wanted to clutch her shepherdess costume. She skipped slightly to avoid stepping on muddy ground.

For that brief orderly moment we were eight people moving down a path by an old water meadow, a path so narrow that most of the time we followed in single file. It seemed to me that it was no more than a live-long minute of harmony and vitality, a happy convergence, all of us different people together, like dancers around a Maypole.

Jebb fell in with us, and he turned to me and said, 'I've got a title for my novel at last. Want to hear it?' He spread his hands before him, laying it out in the air. 'I'm going to call it *Light*.'

He hurried ahead, perhaps to tell Vidia. He walked in a jaunty way, in his bright red waistcoat with the gold piping, a little clownish, a bit like a circus performer, but eager to please.

'I didn't know Julian was a novelist,' I said.

'He's not,' Lady Antonia said. 'But he is awfully sweet.'

My mind was elsewhere. I was considering the thought that the obscene poems of Rochester had aroused me, especially at the point I had seen Lady Antonia smile and shrug. I wanted to tell her how I imagined the two of us on the tropical island. But the day would soon end, and I thought, What's the use? I was just fantasizing. It was the habit of a lifetime.

Back at the house, Pat served tea outside on a little wicker table. Vidia got his air rifle. We took turns shooting at a paper target. Robin scored the highest. She said, two or three times, 'I've never even tried this before!' Lady Antonia looked beautiful holding the rifle and squinting when she fired. She was not a shrinking violet; she was a game-for-anything woman. I loved that. Another reason she would be great company on a tropical island. When she raised the rifle again and pressed her lips together, I wanted her to spin around and shoot me.

It was Jebb's turn next. He said, in his American accent, 'Okay, drop your guns!' He fired four times and missed the target entirely. He posed with the rifle while Vidia snapped a picture with his Kampala camera.

'Vidia, this has been just the most super treat,' Hugh Fraser said, turning the drinking of the last of his tea into a gesture of farewell. He pulled his car keys from his pocket and raised his hand to signal to Lady Antonia.

I wanted to go back to London with them in their car, to be with her. But it was useless yearning. They did not offer anyone a lift. I had the feeling they were planning to use the return trip to discuss something serious and domestic.

'I'm going to be late,' Jebb said. 'Will you call me a taxi?'

Jebb left. I lingered a little. The New Zealanders lingered also. Perhaps Jebb had been a protégé before me – he had a confident, teasing friendship with Vidia that suggested this might have been the case. My protégé days were over: I was making a good living now and had a family and another book to finish. Malcolm was perhaps the new protégé, but it seemed to me he would not last; he was too contrary. You got nowhere arguing with Vidia. You needed to listen, to indulge him, not to debate every illogical point, and to remember. If he said, 'The Italians make cheese out of dirt,' you didn't say, 'No, milk.' You laughed. You surely did not quote the scatology of Lord Rochester.

'And you're saying I'm mistaken for telling them what to read?' Vidia said to Malcolm.

'No, I only said that the majority of New Zealanders see their national history as a benign colonial model.'

They were reliving a Kiwi encounter. Vidia seemed cross and looked misunderstood. Pat was pale from overwork and sleeplessness and too many luncheon guests.

'I must go,' I said.

'I'll call Mr Walters,' Pat said.

'We'll talk, we'll talk.' Vidia seemed rattled by something Malcolm had said.

Malcolm and Robin were conferring, looking like foreigners again.

We all left separately, and it was as though, out of sight and separated in the dark, we became much smaller in our destinies; wandering off to be disloyal, to disintegrate, and die. But for that lunch party, a matter of hours, we were bright.

On the train to London, I tried to look out the window, but all I saw was my own reflection, framed by the night, looking in: my other self staring at me for one and a half hours.

'Well, did he ask about me?' my wife said. She smiled and did not wait for a reply, because she knew the answer. It was a trivial question, and she knew it. Time took care of it.

Fiction depends on revelations to make you turn the page. It is often a matter of timing. But this is another sort of narrative, a different shape, unsuspenseful, just a chronicle of a friendship, spanning the years.

Time took care of us too. Lady Antonia left her husband and married the playwright Harold Pinter. Hugh Fraser, sick with sorrow, moved out of the family house and lived with friends, who later said he died of a broken heart. Pat Naipaul was diagnosed with cancer. She had a mastectomy. It did no good. She died too. I left my wife, I lost my family. Jebb committed suicide, with a mixture of vodka and pills. No news of the New Zealanders.

But all that was much later. The lunch was the most minute interval in this, just one sunny day.

Part Three

Sir Vidia's Shadow

11

The Householder

Vidia's joke, early on, was that he would one day Anglicize his name, from Naipaul to Nye-Powell, and stride around Kensington wearing a floppy tweed hat and Norfolk jacket, brandishing a walking stick. Heigh-ho, I say! Jolly fine day, what?

'V. S. Nye-Powell,' he repeated, as though announcing a distinguished guest. He pronounced Powell 'Pole,' in the manner of Anthony Powell, whom he knew well, and kept in touch with, and relentlessly patronized, in spite of the vast difference in age and class and (so Vidia believed) literary ability.

I loved hearing Vidia's jokes. His laughter was a sign of health. It mattered more than anything that after ten years we were still friendly enough to swap jokes, or anything else. I could say what I wanted to him. *What are friends for?*

He also said, 'People who see one as a little brown Englishman are making the biggest mistake of all. One reads it. One hears it. One is somewhat appalled.'

But what was he? Loathing self-definition, and especially hating the description 'West Indian writer,' he wished to be appreciated for his gifts – who doesn't? – but as an ethnic Indian it was his fate to be one out of many (the title of one of his stories): owing to his racial coloration, he was indistinguishable from the billion or so Indians in the world. Most Indians in Britain, a new class, lived simple, humble lives. Vidia on a London street was less likely a Nobel Prize candidate than a shopkeeper, the very *dukawallah* he despaired of: a London newsagent hurrying from the bank back to his shop, where he hawked cigarettes, chewing gum, and the daily newspapers, keeping the tit-and-bum magazines on the top shelf. That place was now a national institution, known throughout Britain as 'the Paki shop.'

The most maddening thing for any Indian in England was that

they were not called Indians but 'Pakis' – short for Pakistani. Just as few English people troubled to make serious distinctions when they saw a brown face, Indians did the same when they saw a white one. Vidia celebrated himself as unique. He once spoke of his pleasure, years ago, in standing out and seeming exotic on an English street ('Recognition of my difference was necessary to me'). That was before the deluge. Now, purely on the basis of his physical characteristics, Vidia was no one – that is to say, just a Paki.

The idea of an address – a place of his own – preoccupied him, sometimes to the point of obsession. Not owning a house made him yearn for one. He always said he had no home, owned nothing, belonged nowhere. I surmised that his satisfactory but chaotic childhood – he is Anand in *A House for Mr Biswas*, the novel that is the chronicle of his family – had given him no firm footing in Trinidad, and he often suggested that the Indians had been disenfranchised on the island.

His return addresses on letters were usually care-ofs and the poste restantes of publishers and agents. Sad, I thought. For years he had seen The Bungalow as temporary. He hoped for better, and he kept most of his belongings in a warehouse. But time passed and still he did not have a house. He was Anand in the book, but more and more he resembled Mohun Biswas, his hero, who longed for a place he could call his own.

I had bought and sold two houses in London, and so these days we talked more of real estate than of books. I was a property owner and he liked the solid practicality of that: no more hand-to-mouth living, the rented flat, the rented TV. Anyway, he seldom talked about books and was especially reticent about the one he happened to be writing, except to nod and say confidentially, but with noticeable astonishment, 'I think what I am writing now is very important and has never been said.'

That he never mentioned my work I took as approval, not indifference. He now said, 'You're all right. You see?'

But property was on his mind. Place, too.

'Some snowy place. I see a cabin, a log fire. Boots.' He smiled at the thought. 'I love the snow.'

He had written about the snow, always with the dreamy hyperbole of a person from a tropical island for whom snow is decoration

– like icing on a cake – if not magic, weightless, crystalline, never having to be shoveled or driven through. But he had gone to several snowy places and had not liked them. Cross 'snowy places' off the list.

For a few years he had fantasized about Montana. He liked the name; he imagined big skies, high mountains, dense forests. He did not know the 'badlands' image. But he decided without ever going there that Montana was not for him.

California attracted him. He asked me for names, addresses, and telephone numbers of Californians who might show him around and also treat him to meals. He was a conscientious looker-up of people. He liked being met, enjoyed occupying the place of honor – where, of course, he belonged. My contacts served him. But he disliked California. He found that Californians cultivated the body but not the mind; he saw them as selfish and materialistic and smug.

He liked New York City. He liked New York humor and New York acceptance. No one stared at him in New York. He had once spoken of buying an apartment and living there for several months a year. But he did not act on this.

An islander, a country boy, as he thought of himself – though he had moved from his small rural hometown of Chaguanas to Port of Spain when he was seven – he said certain aspects of the Caribbean made him nostalgic to return: his memory of the cool cocoa plantations, the big shady villas with wide verandahs. The thought of disorder beyond the plantation gates, of the sort he wrote about analytically in 'The Killings in Trinidad' and imaginatively in *Guerrillas*, kept him from ever making this move.

All these places were far from his English addresses: the not very distant county of Wiltshire, and London, which he knew well, having lived as far north of the river as Muswell Hill and as far south as Streatham.

'What did you pay for your house in Clapham?'

I told him.

'And what is it worth now?'

I guessed at its value.

'You see? You're part of the market, you're in the housing spiral. All the time I have spent chuntering and dithering I have been losing money. One should have bought something years ago. Just let it quietly appreciate. Then make one's move. But one dithered.'

He was gloomy, feeling worse than houseless: he was placeless and a little hopeless.

'And you have a place in America?'

'A house on Cape Cod.'

'I don't want to see it,' Vidia said. 'It would just remind me of all the mistakes I have made in my life.'

There were large Victorian houses in Clapham, I told him. The inflated prices of Chelsea had not crossed the river. This made him smile.

'But, you know, one wants something fashionable,' he said. 'Uncompromisingly fashionable.'

Kensington or Knightsbridge, he said. They were places that I associated with Arabic graffiti in different colors, and scrawled-upon posters, and no parking spaces, and Arabs dressed in galabiehs as though for the Empty Quarter, and businesses that catered to London Arabs: kebab shops, fruiterers, juice parlors, liquor stores, massage and escort services, and undisguised brothels. Every public phone booth was plastered with the explicit calling cards of prostitutes ('Young buxom blonde at your command').

Instead of telling him this – which he knew – I made other suggestions.

'What about Chelsea?'

'Pretentious.'

'Lord Weidenfeld lives there.'

'I think you have just proven my point.'

'St John's Wood is fashionable, isn't it?'

'St John's Wood, my dear Paul, is suburban.'

'Richmond is lovely. I'd like to live there, by the river.'

'It's nice. People do live there. But it is suburban. And one would need a monkey wagon.'

The idea of buying a small car and riding up and down in it was just ridiculous to him.

'Mayfair must be the height of fashion.'

'Mayfair is corrupt. It's a con. It's full of prostitutes. I know Americans are glamoured by it, but I am sorry, Paul, it is not for me.'

'You've lived all over London.'

'Not really. Muswell Hill. The flat had previously been occupied by a Nigerian. It was unspeakable, but Patsy and I managed to disinfect it.' He made a face. 'Streatham. I wrote *Biswas*. That was a wonderful period. Then Stockwell Park Crescent. Very modest accommodation, really. I have been a nomad.'

'You lived at Edna O'Brien's house in Putney.'

'Briefly,' he said. 'But Putney wouldn't do. I want something fashionable.'

He found a flat off Gloucester Road, in a white Victorian canyon of apartment blocks with ornate façades, balconies, and Greek pillars. Queen's Gate Terrace. It might be bad luck to talk about it, he said. He did not say much more until after he bought it.

'Come for tea,' he said, after he had furnished it.

It was tiny, the smallest habitable space I had so far seen in London. I came to realize that these imposing edifices had been intensively subdivided, so that what he had bought was a small corner – the pantry, the inglenook, the maid's bedroom – of what had once been a roomy apartment.

The elevator was narrow; only two people could fit inside at a time. 'I'll walk, you ride,' someone would say, if there were three. If voices were audible, the language was Arabic.

'This is a bijou flat,' Vidia said. 'This is my luck.'

He liked it for the neighborhood and, perhaps, for its odd shape and size. It was one small, incomplete room – a roomette – that was interrupted by half a wall and an entryway. One more step and you were in the kitchen, a one-person nook. The bedroom was up four stairs in a kind of loft that was filled by the bed. That was it: so small that, inside, you had to assume all sorts of economical postures, sitting compactly, standing with caution, no abrupt moves or you'd hit something. A russet Hokusai print on one wall, some small shelves, a bronze dancing Shiva. Everything had been chosen for its small size; everything fitted. But two people filled the sitting area. Out the one north-facing window were the backs of houses.

Vidia could be the greatest enthusiast. He was often depressed or low, but he was capable – as he said – of enormous happiness. When he had something he liked or had longed for, he was delightful to be with.

'You'll have to dress fashionably here,' I said. 'You'll really have to change your name to V. S. Nye-Powell.'

'V. S. Nye-Powell, OBE,' he said, and laughed.

Having this home made him hopeful and confident. He said that his spirits were high when he was in the flat – it was his nest, as I saw it, and the way he described it suggested that he saw it that way too. It may have been small, but it was high and hidden. He felt protected. It was quiet. For a writer, any house or apartment is judged by how suitable it is for work. Certain places seem perfect for their silence and their light and for the harder-to-define elements of their *feng shui*.

'I see myself doing good work here. Something big, something important.'

Meanwhile, I was sitting on a chair so low my knees were under my chin, my hands folded. I was afraid that if I moved suddenly I would knock something over.

'Later, in a few years, if the market moves up as it has done, I will get something bigger.'

Happiness helped him imagine another flat – larger, roomier, just as fashionable – although 'fashionable' was a word that always made me smile, because fashion was something the writer (irrational, rebellious, manipulative, innovative, as I saw myself and Vidia) turned his back on, or even attacked, for being the enemy of the creative imagination.

Vidia did not see being fashionable as conformist; he saw it as something else that put him out of reach. Being out of reach – 'unassailable' was his word for it – was the most desirable position. He disliked being visible and proximate, within shouting distance. It eased his mind to be remote, a little mysterious and detached, while at the same time remaining at the center of things. It was obviously the reason he had rejected Montana in favor of Kensington. This was not a literary part of London. He knew no one here. That was a plus. It was disconcerting, if not vulgar, to be in a place where he could accidentally bump into people he knew: he had the manipulator's horror of the sudden and the unplanned.

'I see Patsy giving lunches.' He was still talking about the larger flat he envisioned when he traded up, the one with many rooms. 'And I am in my study, working.'

He was setting the scene, which was some years away. He is working on an important book in this big flat, and guests are assembling in the lounge while the table is being laid (by a devoted old woman in mob cap and smock, Wickett, an absolute treasure). Pat is in the kitchen supervising, or is she in the parlor pouring drinks? In any case, it is lunchtime, and Vidia is working in his book-lined study.

'And then' – he made a two-armed gesture of double doors opening, swinging apart, as he buttoned his jacket and made his entrance – 'I go through to lunch.'

I wish he had been smiling, but he wasn't. Nor was I, though at the back of my smiling mind I saw the master summoned from his study to a roomful of expectant and admiring lunch guests. It was the kind of scene I associated with Tennyson at Freshwater, or Henry James at Lamb House, or Maugham at the Villa Mauresque, the category of writer whom Larkin satirized as 'the shit in the shuttered château.'

Because of this flat, I saw Vidia more often. That pleased me, because I had so few other friends in London. At the end of my writing day it was pleasant to get out of the house – my arms ached, my back was kinked, my legs were knotted from sitting too long. I rode my bike over Battersea Bridge and kept going north through Chelsea and Fulham to Kensington, where I chained my bike to the black railing outside Vidia's white apartment block and listened for his voice on the squawk box: 'Yes, yes.'

One day I happened to have a paperback jammed into my pocket. He noticed it and asked me what it was.

'*The Go-Between*. I've never read it before.'

Vidia suddenly remembered something ironic. I could see it in the set of his lips and in his eyes.

'Hartley was mad about the Queen,' he said. 'Absolutely adored her. Then the day came – he is offered an OBE. He accepts it at once. His chance to meet the Queen.'

We were drinking tea. Vidia swallowed and smiled at the same time.

'All his preparations are made. He is in Bath. He hires a car and is driven to London in his morning suit – tails, top hat. Filled with excitement. Big day. His work recognized at last. The Queen awaits.'

Now Vidia was nodding, teacup in hand, and his posture suggested this was a moral tale.

'Hartley is at the palace. He is in the queue of people accepting their honors. The Queen approaches. Hartley is very nervous, but grateful. At last he has the Queen's approval. She stands before him and glances at her note cards and says, "Hartley, yes. And what do you do, Mr Hartley?"'

Vidia put his teacup down and lowered his head and looked humble.

'"A writer, Your Majesty."'

And he laughed at the absurdity of it.

'As you say, Vidia, people should get their knighthoods and OBEs at the post office.'

'Books of stamps. Buy some each time and stick them into the book.' He made licking and sticking gestures. 'Hartley was crushed, and I imagine it was a very long trip back to Bath.'

On another bike ride to Vidia's flat, a few days after a riot in Clapham, I passed through Clapham Junction and saw boarded-up shop windows and looted shops; there was shattered glass in the street and dented cars. It was much worse than I had been told. The riot had started as a racial incident in Brixton and had spread up the High Road and across the Common to the Junction, where the rioters had converged and spent hours breaking windows and vandalizing cars.

I described the scene to Vidia when I got to his flat.

'That was not a riot,' he said. 'That was a disturbance. Frightening, I grant you. But not a riot.'

'Hundreds of people. Angry West Indians.'

'Not angry,' he said. 'Why would they be angry? They were jubilant. They wanted witnesses, and people took notice. They succeeded in destroying something. Windows, whatever. I suppose they stole some television sets.'

'It looked serious.'

'It's all for show.'

'If that's not a riot, what would you call it?'

'High spirits,' Vidia said.

He was afraid of mobs, he avoided large crowds, he did not use public transportation. But his general feeling was that it had all been done for cameras and publicity. If no one had taken any notice, nothing would have happened.

But when the riots – for they were riots and not high spirits – continued, Vidia was asked by a BBC news program to comment on the violence. He said all right, he had been thinking about it. The BBC would provide a car to take him to the studio, but Vidia said that such a trip was out of the question. With great reluctance, the producer agreed to come to Vidia's flat with a camera crew.

I was at Vidia's the next day while, smiling, he told me what had happened.

'There were three of them,' he said. 'I must say, it was rather crowded. They wanted to get started immediately, and of course I had prepared my remarks. I wanted to talk about the excitement of this sort of affair, how it stirs people to see destruction and makes them spirited. I was going to quote from that lovely Louis MacNeice poem "Brother Fire." Do you know it? "When our Brother Fire was having his dog's day / Jumping the London streets . . ." It's about London being blitzed by German bombs, the perverse thrill of someone watching it. It is perfect for what is happening now.

'"Shall we get started?" the producer said.

'I said, "You haven't mentioned money."

'This clearly threw him. Money? But I told him I do not work for nothing, and that I must be paid. He asked me what I wanted. I said, "What you would pay a world-class doctor or lawyer."

'"I'll telephone my department," he said. At the end of a very long call he said, "I can offer you three hundred pounds."

'"Out of the question," I said.

'"It's the best we can do."

'I simply turned my back on him. I noticed that one of the crew was looking at my bronze of Shiva. I said, "Do you know how each arm is positioned in a particular upraised way and the whole figure gives the dynamic impression of movement?"'

I said, 'What about the BBC?'

'They stood around for a while and then went away. I won't

work for three hundred pounds. The figure I had in mind was a thousand.'

'I wonder why they wouldn't pay more.'

'Because they hold a writer in contempt.'

'But why did the man come all the way over, thinking you would do it?'

'Because he was a common, lying, low-class boy.'

'What about the others?'

'Epicene young men.'

He knew I was baiting him. He did not mind. He was glad to have a chance to vent his feelings. Pat tended to sigh or become fearful when Vidia fumed, but his anger was a loud broadcast of what was on his mind.

A writer must not let himself be presumed upon, he said. The TV crew had come and unpacked; the TV crew was sent away, having filmed nothing. A weaker person might have said (I am sure I would have said), 'Since you've come all this way, we might as well do it. But this will be the last time.'

To relent in that way, Vidia would have had to break one of his cardinal rules, which was: Never allow yourself to be undervalued.

'Do lawyers allow it?' he said. 'I say to these presumptuous people, "What would you pay a lawyer? What would you pay an architect, or a doctor at the height of his profession?"' On this subject he was unshakable. 'An architect or a doctor would command thousands of pounds for a consultation. That is my fee. I am at the frontier of my profession as a writer. My fee must be no different from a doctor's, or a scientist's, or a lawyer's. Anything less is an insult.'

Around this time, the first year of his little flat, the Public Lending Right movement had gained a following in London. The moving force was one person, the writer Brigid Brophy. The campaign called for a parliamentary bill to establish a government department that would determine, on the basis of random sampling, the number of times a writer's books had been loaned from libraries. Using a formula, an amount would be worked out, and the writer would be sent an annual check. There would be a ceiling of about £2,500. Public Lending Right – authors compensated for library borrowings – was an enlightened scheme for which I became a strong advocate.

In its early stages, signatures were needed to bring the idea to the attention of the minister for the arts. I pedaled up to Vidia's for a signature.

'No,' he said. Never mind that it was a worthy cause. He hated petitions. And he could not bear to see his name on something he had not written. 'I sign nothing.'

The push of his dignity, the force of his friendship, made me think of him vividly whenever I wrote anything. He hovered over my desk; he was the reader over my shoulder. His criticism had nothing to do with friendship. He might approve, but he was almost impossible to impress. Now and then he quoted a poem, but these were single lines. Really, there was not a living writer he praised, nor any dead ones he acknowledged as exemplars. I had mentioned his uniqueness, the apparent absence of influences, in my book about him, and was criticized for this by scholars and other writers. Perhaps I should have said his influences were minimal, and internalized to the point of their being untraceable. After a time, Vidia acknowledged his father's writing as a strong influence. But he always said: You're on your own.

Even knowing that he probably would not read what I had written, still he was the reader I had in mind whenever I framed a sentence. It gave me confidence to have his approval, but his approval was anything but casual. He hated inattention and intellectual laziness and received opinion. In conversation, he often said sharply, 'What do you mean by that?' to the most offhand remark. When we were together I had his full attention, which was a demanding scrutiny. Usually I listened: I was Boswell, he was Johnson. I was still learning. I knew that I had to be at my best whenever I was with him, and that I got much more out of him as a listener than when I interrupted to argue with something he said. Challenge only infuriated him, so what was the use? He could be uncannily prescient, if not psychic, in some matters; at other times he was wrong and unfair and frighteningly intolerant.

Vidia tended to have something on his mind, always. While in England, as a householder, he did not get out much or see many people. He hardly talked on the phone. He ruminated when he was not working. World events and public people nagged at his solitary mind. In any encounter, he first fretted and explained what he had been thinking, whatever pent-up issue he had been worrying over during his long nights of insomnia. 'This nonsense about South Africa,' he would say, and after that, with the matter ventilated, he could talk more easily. In his presence, my concentration was complete. Working alone, I was also intensely aware of his intelligence, and did not write a word without wondering what he would say about it, nor a paragraph without imagining his pen point striking through it ('I'm brutal, you know') – even now, this one for example, ragged as it is.

'I am an exile,' he always said. In his own prim little flat in Queen's Gate Terrace he said it more often, as though the flat were visible proof of the absurd delusion – and the settled belief of many foreigners in England – that owning property was the same as belonging. The more he became a householder, the stronger his sense of alienation.

Living precariously in rented places, his earthly possessions in a warehouse, he did not speak so often of exile; and traveling in India, the United States, the Caribbean, and frequently to Argentina, he did not seem to have the time to mention exile, either. He was on the move. But with a tidy and secure place in central London, and some of his goods at last out of storage – favorite prints and books, comfy chair, dancing Shiva – he said with more force and greater solemnity, 'I have no country to call my own. I am placeless.'

Out of politeness, I did not mention that he was the one with the British passport, while I carried an Alien Registration Card. I drank my tea and encouraged him to go on.

'Exile is not a figure of speech to me. It is something real. I am an exile.'

After tea we sometimes went over to the V and A, a ten-minute walk, to look at the Mogul paintings. Vidia pointed out how some of those small lozenge-shaped portraits looked like the miniatures of Nicholas Hilliard.

I still visited him in the country, at The Bungalow. One day he showed me an estate agent's flier: a tiny snapshot of a brick house, some specifications ('in need of modernization'), and 'To be sold at auction.' It was not far away, in Salterton, on the way to Old

Sarum, nearer Salisbury, and seemed from the picture to be no more than a semi-derelict cottage.

'Pat's going to bid on it.'

Auctions made Vidia anxious, even the picture auctions in London. I liked them for their surprising bargains. In his mind they were frenzied free-for-alls; the intensity unnerved him. It was so easy in bidding to get in over your head. Someone else always did the bidding for him.

But he did not want to talk about the house auction for another reason. Talk might jinx his chances.

Pat went and bid and was successful, getting the place for a relatively modest price. A long period followed during which the house was renovated. This was a real house, set in a sloping meadow. Vidia added a brick terrace with a balustraded stone wall, gave it a new tiled roof, a garage, a wine cellar, and new windows, double glazed so that he would never hear the cows mooing in the meadow or the overflying jets from the RAF base on Salisbury Plain. He landscaped it, enclosed it in high hedges, gave it a gravel drive and a steel gate. It was late Victorian, possibly Edwardian, very pretty, and because it was not at all grand, it looked like a home. It was called Dairy Cottage.

'People use the term "exile" all the time,' Vidia said. '"Robert Lowell is an exile." But Robert Lowell is not an exile. The airfare from London to New York is a few hundred pounds. He is an American. He has a substantial house in New York. What does "exile" mean in a world of cheap airfares? He can go home!'

Vidia was sitting on his sofa at Dairy Cottage, his legs crossed, smoking his pipe, the sun streaming through the windows. Crows in the sky were framed by the windows, an Emperor Jahangir portrait on one wall, another wall of books, a Hockney etching of a hairy naked man in bed.

'But I can't go home,' Vidia said. 'I have no home.'

India I understood to be an area of darkness for him, and England – well, no one *became* English, though they might acquire a British passport. But what about Trinidad?

'Trinidad, man – Trinidad!'

He had recently been there to write a series of articles about the trial of Michael X, a Black Power advocate convicted of murdering a number of members of his motley commune, including his white girlfriend. The plot was violent, race-driven, full of deception and sexual ambiguity and double-crossing.

'Cuffy has taken over Trinidad. Cuffy doesn't want me.' He puffed his pipe. 'But does Cuffy really know what he wants?'

This 'Cuffy' was a curious word, obsolete, found in the older travel books in which blacks were in the background, and based on the name Kofi, a Ghanaian (Akan) word for Friday, given to a male child born on that day. Vidia was not using the word because he was racist, nor did he intend to give offense. He liked to appear old-fashioned in these matters, regarding 'Cuffy,' and another favorite, 'Mr Woggy,' as playful.

'Exile is something real to me,' Vidia said. He got up from the sofa and looked out the window, gloomily regarding his seven-foot hedge.

'This house is in a bower,' I said, to change the subject from 'Cuffy.'

Halfway down a narrow lane that had no name – just a footpath, really – Dairy Cottage was entirely surrounded by dense shrubbery and low trees.

'Yes. A bower.'

He liked the word, and the idea. It was true. He had planted the shrubs and trees so as to create a blind and hide the house. Going past it on the Salterton road, you saw the newly tiled roof peak and no more.

Vidia threw open the double doors to the terrace, led me outside – probably thinking, Bower, bower – and explained his landscaping scheme.

'What do you notice about the garden?'

'No flowers?'

'Yes, partly. But more than that. It is green, all of it,' he said. 'You see? Green.'

No flowers at all, none even in pots or planters. Flowers were a distraction and a nuisance and implied fussy attention. And they were a national obsession. It was an English thing to create a rock garden, an irregular slope of lungworts and fuchsias, pansies and pulmonaria, alyssum and lobelia straggling around mossy boulders. Such a garden as Vidia's, all green, a mass of leaves, was unknown

244

in the England I knew, and it might well have been unique. Who had ever crowed, 'Behold my green garden'?

This monochrome was the opposite of the herbaceous border and the lily pond and the window box, the succession of rose arches, the climbing clematis and wisteria. Yet in spite of the single color, here were numerous different shrubs. Vidia knew each one's name and characteristics.

'How did you decide to have your garden all the same color?'

'No, Paul,' Vidia said, smiling at my mistake. 'Green is not one color. Green is many colors. It ranges from the palest pinkish green to almost black. There is enormous variation here, every possible shade.'

Hardly any grass, however, and no lawn to speak of. I remarked on this.

'True. Very little grass. No lawn. Part of my plan.' He smiled again. 'I have a theory that it is exhausting for anyone to look at a large expanse of lawn. The viewer becomes tired reflecting on the effort that goes into cutting all that grass. A lawn is not restful to look at. A lawn represents great labor and noise, hours of rackety lawn mowers. A lawn is exhausting.'

Who would have thought that?

My blunder was in having brought him a wholly unsuitable redleafed Japanese maple, a dwarf tree, as a housewarming present. Vidia was doubtful but thanked me, and he instructed an aged kindly man he called Budden to put the sapling into the ground. The deep red leaves stood out in all the greenery. How was I to know he had banned all other colors from his garden?

A few months later he reported with pleasure, 'Your tree is not red all the time. Late in the season the leaves become greenish.'

Dairy Cottage was on its own, not near any other houses, not in the village, unmarked, no house sign, hardly visible, in its own green bower. To be remote and hidden was, in Vidia's mind, to be safe.

One of the few snags was the jet aircraft from the fighter squadrons of the RAF base that constantly flew overhead. The planes engaged in surprising maneuvers, flew vertically, stopped in midair, tumbled, descended like helicopters, even flew backwards. Outside Vidia's double glazing they were ear-splitting.

'I suppose Saudi Arabians and Chinese come down to see the fighter planes put through their paces,' I said. 'The defense ministers.'

'No,' Vidia said. 'Mr Woggy doesn't come down here.'

'But they buy these planes, don't they?'

'Mr Woggy stays in London. Mr Woggy goes to an airfield near London for his demonstration.'

'So you don't see them?' I could not bring myself to say 'Mr Woggy.'

'Mr Woggy does not know this exists.'

He meant the meadow, the little river, the farm on the opposite hill, Wiltshire.

Most of Vidia's possessions, everything except his papers, had been liberated from the warehouse and now furnished Dairy Cottage. Pieces of furniture I had seen years ago in his house in Stockwell had now reappeared, dusted and polished and gleaming, and pictures, and some artifacts from Uganda and India. And with all he owned surrounding him, in the comfort of his home, he returned to the old subject.

'I am an exile,' he said. 'You can go home. You have a large, strong country. I have nothing. No home for me. Yes, "exile" seems an out-of-date word. But for me it has a meaning.'

I went on visiting, pedaling from Salisbury station on my bicycle, uphill on the way to Vidia's, downhill on the return. I kept my bike in the guard's van and felt freer for having it. I loved taking it out on a spring morning, heading to my friend Vidia's house past banks of bluebells, or later when the poppies were in bloom. At a certain bend in the road there were always pheasants flying up.

'I had a telephone call from America this morning,' Vidia said. 'I picked up the phone and heard the voice. American.'

It was clear from his tone that the call was unwelcome, yet he looked serene.

'I did not say hello. I said, "Don't ever do this again."'

Vidia looked so pleased with himself, uttering this stern sentence of rebuke, that I started to laugh.

'"Don't ever do this again," and I put the phone down.'

Pat said, 'I knew Paul would like that.'

246

Yes, because of the sudden hostility of the greeting and also because it interested me to know what anyone's limits were, and particularly the limits of a friend. It helped to know what was deemed going too far. A stranger's calling him was unacceptable.

'How did he get your number?'

'I have no idea.'

Vidia's telephone number was known to only few people. His reasoning was this: a strange voice on the phone had to be someone asking a favor or importuning him.

'I want to be sure when I pick up the phone that the person is someone I know and like,' he said. 'I don't want to hear a strange voice.'

His wine cellar was almost full, and that collection was one of his oddest passions because these days he seldom drank wine, and when he did, it wasn't much. He said wine gave him a headache. But each time I visited he showed me new crates and filled racks, he told me the vintages, he explained the complex flavors.

Walking past Dairy Cottage's garage one day I saw a car. *A car?*

'Vidia, you have a car. What kind is it?'

'I don't know. One of these little European monkey wagons.'

It was a brand-new Saab. It was green. I never saw him drive it, nor did I ever see it outside the garage.

Time passed. He bought another flat in London, much bigger than the one at Queen's Gate Terrace. This flat was off the Brompton Road. It was the sort of place that suited his fantasy of the lunch, when he would be summoned from his study to meet his friends and admirers. He kept the little flat in Queen's Gate Terrace. He continued to live in Dairy Cottage. He paid occasional visits to the new flat, sometimes wearing a floppy tweed hat and carrying a walking stick, and he wondered aloud how it should be furnished. And more than ever he began monologues by saying, with passion and sadness, 'The word "exile" has a meaning for me. I am an exile.'

12

My Friend's Friend

Vidia was phoning from his flat, the tiny one – I could tell from the squashed acoustics, like a murmuring man trapped in an elevator: 'Are you free for a coffee after lunch? There is someone I want you to meet.'

'Someone' meant a friend. Yes, I wanted to meet my friend's friend.

It was the hot English summer of 1976. Even the London heat did not diminish my happiness, spending days in pure invention, writing my novel *Picture Palace*. In the voice of a smart old woman, Maude Coffin Pratt, I wrote about the contradictions of writing by describing the life of a photographer. I promised myself that after I finished the book I would take a long trip, as an antidote to the several years I had spent in novel-writing confinement.

Still, it was not easy to write on the hottest days in London. Open windows made it noisy, the slate roofs blazed with glare, the bricks became crumbly and overbaked. The very earth underneath the city shrank, because London is built on thirsty clay. Subsiding houses began to split and crack, jagged seams opened in the pointing, and the masonry over windows collapsed. It was the intense heat.

Londoners cracked too. Unused to the heat, they became skittish and self-conscious and dressed more sloppily, and there were more of them on the street. You saw women in parks stripped to their underwear, sunning themselves, grinning at the sky. Bare-chested men with pink arms competed for space with tourists, who kept saying, 'We expected rain!' People were generally merrier, but it was the wrong city for sun: not enough space, too narrow, only a few public pools, and they were dire. The city had been made for work and indoor pleasures and pedestrian exertions in big parks. It was unusual to have so much sunshine, and there was no way to use it – only rented rowboats in the Serpentine, rented deck-chairs in the parks at twenty pence an hour, and benches on the Embankment. The sun and swelter would soon become demoralizing, with nothing much to do except sit in it and drink pints of lager.

I saw these people all over; so many turned out that the traffic was affected. I went by bike in order to be on time for punctual Vidia: downhill to the river, uphill to the café near the Green Park tube station, where we had agreed to meet. Piccadilly was crowded with workers on their lunch break, smiling – even the people walking alone were smiling – because of the sunshine. Londoners habitually bowed their heads and hurried in the rain, but walked more slowly and much straighter in the sunshine, holding their heads up on days like this. You had to live through every phase of English weather to know the English traits: so many English moods and turns of phrase could be ascribed to the weather.

I locked my bike and looked around. No Vidia.

When he arrived at the café a few minutes after me, his face puckered in remorse, the energetic apology he made for his lateness was his way of reminding me that his standard of punctuality was as high as ever. I must not think from this single lapse that he was becoming lax. He still bluntly boasted of never giving anyone a second chance, especially someone who had been otherwise loyal; when a dear friend lets you down once, that must be the end. The relationship had run its course. A single instance of lateness might be all that was needed to fracture it. So I took his 'Sorry, sorry, sorry' to be a scolding for both of us.

A smiling woman was with him. She was slim, about my age, thirty-six or so, and wore a fluttery light dress because of the weather. She had some of Pat's features, the paleness, the pretty lips, the same posture and figure, full breasts – a taller Pat, the Pat of ten years before, but far more confident.

'Paul, this is Margaret.'

'I know all about you,' she said. 'From Vidia.'

So this was my friend's friend. Had she been a male protégé, like Jebb or Malcolm the New Zealander, I would have compared myself to her; I might have been anxious. But anyway, I was alert. Was she a writer? From your friend's friend you understand your friend better and notice qualities you might otherwise miss – aspects of tenderness, humors, and responses. Always, no matter the sex, it is like meeting a rival lover.

We talked about tennis. Wimbledon was in full swing.

'I hate Wimbledon,' Vidia said. 'I loathe tennis. It's nonsense.'

'He doesn't mean that. I taught him how to play,' Margaret said, and I thought she was pretty feisty to oppose him.

'I play sometimes,' I said.

'But you don't make a fetish of it like these other people,' Vidia said.

'He's simply being contrary,' Margaret said.

'When everyone was cheering Francis Chichester, Vidia wanted him to drown,' I said.

'Did I?' Vidia said, pleased to be reminded. 'Did I really?'

'Who is Francis Chichester?' Margaret asked.

From that remark, and her slight accent, which I could not place, I gathered that she might not be English, yet she certainly looked English. I studied her accent as we talked about the weather – the sunshine, the heat. Vidia said it brought out the rabble. We ordered coffee at the bar and stood there, Vidia enumerating the errands he had to run that afternoon.

'I very much liked the piece you wrote about Vidia in the *Telegraph*,' Margaret said.

It was a portrait. I had thought: I will do what Vidia would do, write the truth, be impartial, let the peculiarities speak for themselves. He was an original, but it was annoying to read that word over and over. Better to be anecdotal and set down aspects of his originality. Some people had come to like him on the basis of the piece, others had said they found him insufferable, on the same evidence.

'I recognized him in it,' she said. 'I have read so many pieces about him and never recognized him. They don't ring true. But yours – even Vidia's mother said she recognized him.'

Vidia was smiling a bit impatiently, perhaps because of this mention of his mother. He was devoted to the memory of his father, Seepersad, who had died relatively young, but had more complicated feelings towards his mother, matriarch of many Naipauls and still alive, a tenacious Indian widow in Trinidad.

I liked the praise, but I was still baffled by Margaret's accent, the rhythm and intonation of her speech: the careful way she gave weight to each syllable, the manner in which her voice trailed off, the insistent, almost Latin way she spoke. Maybe she was Welsh-speaking? I didn't ask.

'Your review of *Guerrillas* in the *New York Times* was also very good. Vidia was pleased.'

This embarrassed me. Vidia and I never spoke of the reviews I had written of his books. There was no need to. A review was not an act of friendship; it was a literary matter, an intellectual judgment. As Vidia himself said, writing a review meant having to reach a conclusion about a book, something the casual reader seldom did.

I said, 'That novel really frightened me. It doesn't happen often. But I was also scared by "The Killings in Trinidad" – the Michael X piece.'

'It's scary stuff, man,' Vidia said.

'I thought it was too long,' Margaret said.

'What was too long?' I asked. It seemed a strange and even audacious way to describe the piece. I would not have dared say this. But she was his friend.

'Those articles. The *New York Review* should have made them a bit shorter.'

I glanced at Vidia. He was sipping his coffee, yet he had heard.

'And the woman in *Guerrillas*. She was so naive. I thought she was awful.'

'I think maybe that was the point,' I said.

She had dragged out the word, making it sound even worse: *awwwwwwfool*. Vidia didn't blink, and I did not dare to smile.

Vidia said, 'I won't be a moment,' and headed for the rear of the café.

'So where are you from, Margaret?'

'The Argentine.'

'You live there?'

'Yes. In BA,' she said.

'I'd love to go there.'

'You must. Vidia's a bit unfair about it, all this business about "a whited sepulcher." Really!' She had a beautiful laugh. 'And you live here in London?'

'At the moment. I'm working on a book. I'll be heading for the States as soon as my kids get out of school,' I said.

'The school year is so long here. In BA it's much shorter.'

'You have children?'

'Three. But –' She was going to say something more, and thought better of it. She lost her smile and looked into the middle distance.

I said, 'The place I like best is Dorset. I lived there when I first came to England. Do you know it?'

'No. Just from books. Thomas Hardy.'

'You're pretty well read if you know Hardy.'

'Not at all. Vidia says, "You know nothing!" And it's true. What else do I read? Mills and Boon!'

'Sometimes Hardy is Mills-and-Boonish.'

'I don't think so,' Margaret said.

'There's that passage in *Jude the Obscure* where the heroine laments her fate.'

Margaret shook her head, smiled again, but in confusion. The conversation was moving too fast for her. She looked in the direction that Vidia had gone.

I said, 'She says, "To be loved to madness – such was her great desire. Love was the one cordial which could drive away the eating loneliness of her days." Something like that.'

Margaret had begun to look closely at me.

I said, 'And it ends –'

'It ends with a prayer,' Margaret said. And she said the prayer, enunciating it prayerfully in her foreign-sounding accent, clasping her hands: '"O deliver my heart from this fearful gloom and loneliness: send me great love from somewhere, else I shall die."'

'You know it.'

'It's *The Return of the Native*, not the other one you said.'

'We must go,' Vidia said when he got back to us. He hesitated a moment, perhaps realizing he had reappeared at an important moment, yet he had no idea what had been said. He looked as if he wanted to leave, in order to separate us. He said, 'Are you all right, Paul?'

'I'm fine. Working on a novel.'

'He's full of ideas,' Vidia said to Margaret.

But the idea in my mind was linked to the long-ago letter in which he had written that a girl he'd met in Argentina had copied out two pages from *The Return of the Native*.

Back home, I got the novel out and read the passage again. It was longer than I remembered. I had marked the pages the day I received Vidia's letter about the 'coldest and meanest kisses . . . at famine prices.' They had meant little to me. They meant much more to me now.

After the sentences about kisses, it went on, 'Fidelity in love for fidelity's sake had less attraction for her than for most women: fidelity because of love's grip had much. A blaze of love, and extinction, was better than a lantern glimmer of the same which should last long years.' It continued, evoking Eustacia Vye's yearning to be loved, and ended, 'she desired it, as one in a desert would be thankful for brackish water.'

The passage was like another of Vidia's lessons in literature. The first time I read it, I thought only of Thomas Hardy; the second time, I thought only of Margaret in Argentina.

A year went by, and no Vidia, or very little Vidia. But in friendship, time is meaningless and silences insignificant, because you are sure of each other. Not at all weakened by the insecurities of a love affair, you pick up where you left off. And I was also Boswell, listening to Dr Johnson say, 'Do not fancy that an intermission of writing is a decay of kindness. No man is always in a disposition to write, nor has any man at all times something to say.'

He was away, then I was away. I saw Pat sometimes, and she apologized for Vidia's absence, apologized for showing up alone; and I labored to reassure her that I liked seeing her, my old almost lover. She was more easily confused these days, got flustered over insignificant things she had forgotten, and she would struggle and sigh with something as small as extracting the right coins from her purse. The insomnia that had taken hold of her like a virus that would not let her sleep made her pale and gave her sunken eyes. Her face was lined and her hair had gone totally white. In her forties she became a little old lady and had all the fret and frailty of someone afflicted with a chronic illness. No matter how little her handbag or the parcel she was carrying – it could be as simple as a book – she looked overburdened, seeming to lug whatever thing was in her hand.

She came to dinner on her own and seemed frailer for being alone.

'Vidia's away,' she said in a faltering voice. 'He has taken one of those jobs in America at . . . would it be called Wesleyan?'

'Vidia? Teaching?'

'I'm afraid so.' Her smile was a smile of pure worry. 'He's awfully good and the people were terribly nice to him. And you know he gets standing ovations when he speaks sometimes – he did in New Zealand that time. But' – she paused and turned her pale eyes away – 'he does get ever so cross if the students don't do their work.'

I knew that 'ever so cross.' It was purple, tight-faced rage.

'Do you have his number? I have to go to the States in a few weeks.'

It was the snowiest day I had ever known in New York, so snowy the city had shut down – stopped cold, brimming with drifts, no cars at all moving down Fifth Avenue, only people in the deep white street. Such conditions always made me think of Vidia's saying, 'I love dramatic weather.' He meant hail, high winds, monsoon rain, ice storms, snow like this.

New York was transformed. It was muffled and made natural again, silenced, simplified, made safer even, for in the worst weather villains and muggers stay home in stinking rooms and lie snoring in bed. The soft white city was beautiful and wild, the blurred mist-shrouded skyscrapers like the north face of a mountain range of glaciated canyons and ledges, where icicles drooped like dragon fangs.

Having just come from Vermont, I was dressed for this snow. I trudged to several appointments – though most businesses and offices were closed – and at noon called Vidia at Wesleyan.

A woman answered the phone.

'Vido, it's for you.'

Veedo?

'Yes, yes, yes,' Vidia said in the old way when he recognized my voice. He was glad I had called, he said. He wanted to drive into New York. We could have dinner.

'What sort of car do you have?'

Always finding absurdity in technical description, he clearly enjoyed telling me it was a 'subcompact,' and he repeated it twice, chuckling.

'Will it make it through the snow?'

'It will be fine.'

He was never prouder of his punctuality: he made it from the snowdrifts of Middletown, Connecticut, to Manhattan at the appointed time, six o'clock.

'Americans fuss so about the snow,' he said. 'It stopped just after you rang. All the roads were sanded and plowed. The road crews are marvelous. People exaggerate the danger. I loved the drive.'

'You drove the whole way?'

'Of course.'

Dressed warmly, he looked more Asiatic, not Indian at all but like one of those tiny, flint-eyed nomadic descendants of the Golden Horde you see hunkered on horses in central Asia. He was alone. His hair was long and, as always when he was tired, his eyes were more slanted and hooded.

'I thought we might go to the Oyster Bar at Grand Central station,' he said. 'I'm told it's all right.'

'But let's have a drink first.'

We were at my hotel on Central Park South, in my room. I had been drinking a beer when he arrived. I finished that one and was halfway through another. Vidia noticed.

'It's the heat,' he said, defending me. 'You need that beer because you're dehydrated from the central heating. They overdo it here. And American walls are so thin you can always hear someone chuntering.' And he laughed, because I was opening a third beer. 'Are you going to drink another one, really?'

I poured him a glass of wine. 'How's teaching?'

The tables were turned. Twelve years before, I had been the teacher and he the writer. He had warned me against teaching jobs. It was acceptable to travel to Singapore, but teach there? *As you know, I disapprove of the means. . .* A writer ought to have no job, no boss, no teacher, no students; ought to follow no one else's routine; ought to have no masters, no servants. The essential point was that writing was not a job at all but, in his own phrase, a process of life.

I knew from eight years of slogging in the tropics that it was not possible for me to teach and also to write well. Many people did it, and some succeeded, but even when the writing was fluent, something was missing, because colleges were so far from the world. Vidia himself had taught me this lesson – Vidia now a poorly paid writer in residence and teacher of creative writing in a snooty college. He had recently given an interview in the London *Sunday Telegraph* in which he had said, 'I would take poison rather than do this for a living.'

All this went through my mind because Vidia had not answered my question. He was frowning at his glass of wine.

'I didn't know that writing courses were a soft option!' he said in a voice of mock astonishment, slightly overdoing it out of anger.

'Neither did I,' I said. 'You're a tough teacher, aren't you?'

'Not tough enough,' Vidia said. 'The students take my course because they want A's without having to work. They seldom do the assignment. They hardly write. They lie to me. I try to goad them into work and they glare at me. They are deeply offended. "But this is a writing course! This is supposed to be easy! You are making us work!"'

He raised his hand in resignation, and sipped, and looked miserable. In the *Telegraph* piece, one of his students had described her reason for dropping out of his course: 'He was simply the worst, most close-minded, inconsiderate, uninteresting and incompetent professor I have ever met.'

'That's supposed to be a good university,' I said.

'They're all corrupt. It's all a con.' The students were lazy, the other teachers were inferior, the place was intolerable. His own mind was being damaged from being in close contact with people so inferior.

'What about the weather?'

'The weather is very nice,' he said. 'Let's not talk about the corruption. This wine is not bad. May I see the cork?'

Twitching the cork with his thumb and forefinger, he uncovered the details of the vineyard. He revolved the cork again, and again twitched the dusty residue, like an archeologist with a helpful artifact.

'California wine is vastly underrated,' he said, almost to himself, and then, 'What brings you to New York?'

'I was in Vermont, visiting Kipling's house outside Brattleboro,' I said. 'I want to write about him – his American wife, his American residence, the way it ended.'

'And how did it end?'

'In a huge kerfuffle. His drunken brother-in-law threatened to kill him. It was just bluster, but Kipling decided to bring a case against him. His brother-in-law was popular, a good old boy. Kipling was regarded as a snob and an interloper, a limey. It ended badly. Kipling went back to England and sulked.'

'He was immensely famous,' Vidia said. '*Immensely* famous.'

'I think it would make a terrific play – the arguments, the rivalries, the court hearing, all that. I have a transcript of the case. And he was writing *The Jungle Book* at the time – you know, the law of the jungle.'

'It's a lovely idea,' Vidia said. 'Very attractive.' He brooded a bit. He sniffed the cork.

'Shall we eat? There are some restaurants near here that aren't bad. An Indian one near the Plaza.'

'Let's try the Oyster Bar, shall we?' he said with a note of insistence.

We walked out of the hotel and the fifteen blocks to Grand Central station, all the while marveling at the silence. By now some streets had been cleared, and a few taxis moved slowly through the whiteness.

'I have an idea for a play,' Vidia said. 'Raleigh is sixty-four, in Guyana. He has been let out of the Tower so that he can find El Dorado and redeem himself. It is a risk, and now he has found himself at a dead end. But he can't admit defeat. He is old and lost.'

He told me the story of Raleigh on the Orinoco, the play he intended, as we kicked through the snow.

In the light of a building entrance, a woman stood waiting in an area that had been shoveled. She wore a fur hat and a coat with a fur collar, so her foxlike face was framed by the soft pelts, the warmth of fur and skin. She turned away from us, not wishing to make eye contact, and just as we passed, an important-looking car swung to the curb and she rushed to it, seeming relieved.

'Did you see that woman? Pretty, don't you think?'

When he did not answer me, I took his silence to mean that I had asked a silly question. But no, he was thinking.

'All women are built differently.' He spoke slowly, as though delivering a piece of news.

Closing his fingers, like a man plucking fruit, he made a scooping gesture with his hand. I took 'built' to mean something more complex than their shape. He was suggesting contours, not an interior mechanism peculiar to each woman; he was implying something more urological.

'But you knew that, didn't you?'

It was pleasant to be in a big city with him. We were both free, the snowfall had given New York a holiday, emptied of people and most cars. So the city was ours.

And after all these years I never took this friendship for granted. I felt lucky to know him, privileged to be with him, blessed for all his good advice, cautioned by his mistakes, stimulated by his intellect, enlightened by his work. I was aware of his contradictions. More than anything, I was inspired by the dignity of his struggle. Writing tormented him, he suffered through each book. And where were we now? I was thirty-six, he was forty-five, we were both working hard. I was writing a play and contemplating a trip to South America, and he was teaching – though he had said 'Never be a teacher,' here he was, a creative-writing teacher in Connecticut. There could be only one reason: he needed the money. Our positions had been reversed so dramatically, I had to be careful not to wound his dignity by mentioning it or saying to him (as he had said to me so often), 'You teachers make lots of money!'

We walked along – he was thinking about Raleigh, I was thinking about Kipling – and we told each other that these were great ideas.

The reassurance, the intellectual vigor of his friendship, made me happy. What perhaps mattered most was the trust, the mutual compassion, which was also forgiveness, and the fact that we understood one another. By now we knew each other well and had arrived at that point at which friends realize they cannot know each other any better. His friendship was a pleasure and a relief.

I was still reflecting on 'All women are built differently' when he said, 'So you see, we are seriously talking about whether the president of the United States knows how to read a book!'

'Jimmy Carter?' He must have been gabbling about Carter while I was thinking.

'Yes. Does he know how to read? I have seen no indication of it.'

'He talks about Dylan Thomas a little.'

'Oh, God.'

The philistinism of the US government occupied us for the time it took to travel the short distance east from Fifth Avenue to Grand Central. We descended the stairs to the warmth and light of the Oyster Bar – not busy, another casualty of the blizzard.

We ordered. We talked. We drank. We ate. Vidia kept returning to the subject of Wesleyan. It was corrupt, a con, a cheat, the soft option of writing courses, the laziness of students.

'It's crummy, man. Crummy. I should never have come.'

'Why did you?'

'I believed they were doing some good. And the pence, of course.' He made his rueful face. 'But, you see, I have only myself to blame. I broke one of my rules.'

From time to time he lifted his eyes to look behind me, at a table where some people were speaking excitedly. I thought he might go over and tell them to shut up or stop smoking. But he was considerate: just a glance and then we kept talking, now about New York writers and how they were self-regarding. Vidia saw New York writers as shallow, cliquey, and envious, uninterested in the world, needing local witnesses, frenzied, not even very bright.

'I have my students reading Conrad. They don't know him at all. They read – who? Kurt Vonnegut? But they respond to "An Outpost of Progress" and *The Secret Agent*. Some nice things in that.'

'I used to teach it in Singapore. Winnie's a good character.'

'Of Winnie, Conrad says, "She felt profoundly that things do not stand much looking into."'

'I also used to have the students read your *Mr Stone and the Knights Companion.* I love that book.'

'You're so kind, Paul. You know, I am assigning my students your *Family Arsenal*, for its depiction of London and bombers – excuse me.'

Interrupting himself as he looked up, he went to the table behind me while I held my breath and prayed that he would not make a scene.

When I looked around, I saw three people sitting at a table, sharing a bottle of wine, not eating, but all of them smoking cigarettes. A man and two women, and one of the women was Margaret from Argentina.

'Hello.'

She smiled and raised her glass. She looked a bit tipsy and rumpled. I had last seen her on a hot day in London, wearing a summer dress. On this freezing night in New York she was blotchy from the cold air and wore a thick dress. Her hair was windblown and damp. Yet with all this dishevelment she was as pretty as ever – perhaps prettier, the way some women look when their clothes are slightly awry, a blouse untucked, a button undone.

I got up to speak to her, and when I approached she introduced me to the others, her brother and sister-in-law. Vidia said nothing.

'How about this snow?' I said.

'Vidia adores it, but it makes life impossible,' Margaret said. 'We live so far in Connecticut.'

Vidia said, 'Paul, this has been splendid, but I think we must be going. We do have a long way to go. Margaret?'

'Just a minute.'

'Shall I see to the bill?' Vidia said, a trifle wearily.

'No. I'll get it,' I said.

'Oh, good.'

Margaret frowned at him.

'I'll be back in a moment,' he said.

Once again, Margaret and I were together, but unexpectedly. I gave the waitress my credit card.

'It must have been quite a ride from Connecticut,' I said.

'I did the driving. Vidia hates to drive.'

Really? But I said, 'If I had known you were here, I would have asked you to join us.'

'Vidia wanted to talk to you. You're his friend. You never quarrel!'

'That's us. *Dos amigos.*'

'*Claro.*' She laughed. 'He has the students reading your book. I don't know which one, I'm afraid.'

'I used to tell my students to read *Mr Stone.*'

'It's one of his books he doesn't like.'

This was news to me. 'Which others doesn't he like?'

'*Suffrage of Elvira. A Flag on the Island.*'

'I thought he liked those. And *Mr Stone*'s a little masterpiece.'

'He doesn't think so.'

Seeing Vidia hurrying toward us, I thought of asking him: What was it that he didn't like about these novels of his? But it was late and they were leaving, and I was the wiser for seeing my friend's friend materialize in this distant place.

We said goodbye in the snow outside and I left wondering, but also feeling profoundly that some things do not stand much looking into.

Later that year, in London, I visited him at his tiny apartment and we had tea. Pat was in the country, at Dairy Cottage. I did not mention New York, or Wesleyan.

'I'm going to South America,' I said.

'I am thinking of going to the Congo,' he said.

'A travel book?'

'Not exactly that. Call it travel with a theme.'

I said, 'I'm planning to leave my house in Medford, Massachusetts, and just take trains, heading south, until I get to Patagonia.'

'It's a delicious idea. I know you'll do it well.'

'I'll be spending some time in Buenos Aires,' I said. He did not react, and so I went on, 'I don't know a soul there.'

'Really.'

'Or in Argentina, for that matter.'

This seemed a natural inquiry, because Vidia had been to Argentina many times over the past seven years, had written about it extensively – about Borges and Evita and the culture of politics and terrorism. He had been fierce in some of his statements: 'There is a certain "scum" quality in Latin America. They imagine that if you kill the right people everything will work. Genocide is their history.' But he was frowning at me now, as if I had mentioned a place that was foreign to him.

'Do you know anyone there I might meet?'

'There are so many fraudulent people there,' he said. 'Stay away from the ones that wear white shoes. And the ones who wear wristwatches that light up.'

'I was thinking of particular people I might call on.'

He thought hard. At last he said, 'No. No.' And he stood up. Tea was over, the visit was at an end. He said with a trace of bitterness, 'You'll be all right, Paul. You'll be all right.'

I took my Patagonia trip. I wrote my book. He took his trip. He wrote his Congolese pieces – journalism. After a time, he wrote a novel, *A Bend in the River*, set in Africa, about an Indian there who has a passionate affair with a married woman. And he wrote something else. I saw it listed in a bookseller's catalogue, a privately printed book called *Congo Diary*: 'In a limited edition of 330 copies. Three hundred are numbered, twenty-six lettered, and four bear the printed name of a recipient.'

Mine was not one of the printed names. I bought copy number 46 for $200. It was signed by Vidia. The dedication was 'M. M.'

13

Death is the Motif

Brothers are versions of each other, a suggestion implicit in the word itself, the 'other' in 'brother.' Seeing Shiva Naipaul was always an oblique encounter with Vidia, as though I had bumped into someone similar, not an identical twin; the rough draft, not the finished article.

Brothers are like that. The wit in one is craziness in another; one is an original sculptor, another is 'good with his hands,' a third is a klutz who drops things, and a fourth might be a brutish criminal, even a destroyer. Three or four flawed prototypes for the man of achievement. You discern the thin one in the fat one, the artist in the con man. What are the roots of this variety, so many exotic blossoms on the same stem? No one knows their past; and the brothers resent the blurring of these convergent echoes and resemblances, because such resemblances can be so misleading.

The history of scribbling brothers is full of conflict, which ranges from hurt feelings and petty grumbling ('Why does *he* get all the attention?') to vicious attempts at literary fratricide ('Take that, you bastard!'). One of the brothers is always the other's inferior. Look at the brothers William and Henry James, Oscar and Willie Wilde, James and Stanislaus Joyce, Thomas and Heinrich Mann, Anton and Nikolai Chekhov, Lawrence and Gerald Durrell – there are no intellectual equals here, and, being writers, they are borderline nutcases.

Such brothers are often fratricidal from birth and babyish in their battling, for there are nearly always aspects of lingering infantilism in sibling rivalry. When brothers fight, family secrets are revealed and the shaming revelations often make forgiveness irrelevant – the damage is done. In the literature of sibling rivalry, an enthralling spectator sport but pure hell on the fraternal rivals, the cry is usually 'He hit me first!' or 'Choose me!' It is also typical for one sibling to feign an utter lack of interest in the other; inevitably you end up admiring one and pitying the other. The larger family – the cause of it all – winces and tries not to choose sides. The nicer-seeming brother is not necessarily the better writer, nor even necessarily nicer.

Shiva Naipaul never had news of his brother, and was insulted if you asked: they seldom met. In the way of a brother, Shiva's presence rang bells like mad and was full of reminders of Vidia – turns of speech, Trinidadian eccentricities, Hindu fastidiousness, and chance remarks that at times added to my understanding of Vidia; but in the impatient and rivalrous manner of a brother, Shiva more often obscured it, even undermined those insights.

Meanwhile, Shiva protested his love for Vidia, yet he said his brother had hurt him. 'I had vulnerabilities he did not always find easy to understand,' Shiva wrote in an essay, 'My Brother and I.' 'For a long time there was mutual distress.' That was putting it mildly, and 'distress' was a Vidia word, an understatement he used often to indicate outrage or fury. There was anger on Shiva's part, indifference – or disparagement – on Vidia's.

'Shiva was raised by women,' Vidia had said. He repeated this formula often, shaking his head at the imagined damage from female attention.

More softly and with feeling Vidia had also said, 'When my father had his heart attack, Shiva found him alone. My father was dead. Shiva just stood there, frozen, mute. He could not speak.'

I saw Vidia occasionally, talked with him on the phone quite often, and corresponded. I bumped into Shiva all the time, never spoke on the phone, never wrote him a letter, nor did I ever receive one from him. This bumping into him characterized the randomness of his life. He said he didn't make plans – that seemed a luxury to me. I felt I was overworked and stuck in a routine, but if I complained, it was dishonest of me – I liked the grind, I was happiest when I was writing, creation to me was pure joy. Shiva, echoing Vidia, said writing was misery. All the same, he could seem quite jolly.

I had run into Shiva in the middle of my period of financial uncertainty, in 1973 – 'I'll take a trip and find a book to write.' It was to be *The Great Railway Bazaar*. After leaving the Punjab in Pakistan, I went to New Delhi. I met Shiva by chance in a guesthouse there. He told me he had flown to India. I said I had come overland on trains from London.

'God, how long did that take?'

'About five weeks.' I thought I had made pretty good time.

'Five weeks!' He sat like a pasha on cushions, smoking and drinking tea. His chubby cheeks shook as he laughed. 'You're a masochist.'

'Some of it was fun,' I said. 'The Orient Express. Some of the Turkish trains. The mosques in Herat, in Afghanistan. The Khyber Pass.'

'Carry on, up the Khyber!' And he laughed again.

His mockery made conversation futile. It was nothing new. I always felt there was envy in his jeering, and I knew that if I jeered at him, he would be furious.

I smiled, defying him to mock. October in Delhi, twenty-five years ago. Two thirty-year-olds in a garden, each with a book in mind. He had a famous brother – he'd be all right. But if I didn't bring home a book I was sunk.

'Why are you putting yourself through this?'

'A travel book,' I said.

'I didn't think you wrote travel books.'

'It's just an attempt. I need the money.'

'So you're going to write about India like everyone else?'

'No. This is a whole trip. I'm going to Sri Lanka by train, via Madras. Then all over – Calcutta, Rangoon, Vietnam, Japan. And home on the Trans-Siberian.'

I should not have told him this. He exploded with laughter, gagging and choking, smoke shooting out of his nostrils, his big face going red.

'I think I'll be home by Christmas.'

He said, 'I'll be home on Wednesday.'

Today was Monday. I wanted to go home. Feeling demoralized, I went to a hotel and tried to call my wife but got nothing, just the sound of surf and a feeble voice on the line. I was horribly homesick and could not sleep.

Shiva and I met the next day, also by accident. He had one of the good rooms in the guesthouse, and I passed it on my way out. He called to me and ordered coffee. Among the papers on his coffee

table was a telegram: CONGRATULATIONS ON THE HAW-
THORNDEN. LONGING TO SEE YOU WEDNESDAY. LOVE,
JENNY.

He had won a literary prize. He was going home. His wife loved
him. This was bliss – beyond bliss.

'What do you think of India?' I asked.

'I don't think much!' He howled again.

This was how he conversed. Was it aggressive? He made you
ask the questions, and he would give an unhelpful answer and then
laugh in a mirthless way.

'This is paradise compared to some places I've been,' I said.
'Iran. Kabul. Peshawar.'

'This is the Turd World!'

And that laugh again, like a form of punctuation, a jeering
exclamation mark. I took it to be nervousness, or obstinacy. The
young companion of my London Christmas long ago had become
a rather prickly man.

He had become very heavy, and in the heat of India his bulk
made him slow and clumsy. He looked uncomfortable. He chain-
smoked. He drank whiskey. Instead of a fat, contented drunkard,
I had the impression of a dissatisfied sot, confused, unhappy, and
angry. Nothing was angrier than his laughter.

He lived in Vidia's shadow, as I did, but no shadow is darker
than a clever brother's. Yet he had started his intellectual life
idolizing Vidia, who left Trinidad in 1950, when Shiva was five,
and who was always absent. Shiva became a devotee, and was so
deeply influenced that his writing often looked like a parody of
Vidia's. Attempting subtlety, Shiva ended up sounding pompous
and convoluted, though he was seen to be the 'warmer' brother,
in the shorthand of magazine profilers and portraitists. And there
was that act of piety which even Vidia marveled at: the memorizing
of *The Mystic Masseur*. Veneration could go no further than
reciting the sacred texts by heart, but it was death for Shiva's prose
style. In spite of his mockery of me, it was impossible for me not
to feel a bit sorry for him.

Yet at that moment in India I envied him his swift return to
London. I cursed my luck at being on this long trip alone. The
phones didn't work. I got no mail. I was like an old out-of-touch

explorer. True, it was the reason I saw so much, and the reason I was changed by the experience. But if someone had said, 'Here's ten thousand dollars, scrap the trip,' I would not have hesitated to join Shiva on the London-bound plane.

There was a young Indian woman who hung around the guesthouse. She stared at me. Why? Indian women never did that. She touched my arm. 'Hey, I've been to the States.' She took my hand and squeezed it. In Indian terms, this was as if she had said, 'Take me, I'm yours.' She looked me straight in the eye.

'I won't bite you,' she said. Her powdered face and red lips and kohl-darkened eyes gave her a lecherous mask that made me desire her and fear her at the same time.

'You are afraid of me,' she said.

'Right.'

Her red betel-stained teeth were straight out of a 'Kali, Goddess of Destruction' picture. She plucked at her sari and laughed again. I was not afraid of making love to her – I sensed she was wild; I was afraid of everything that would come after – indignant relatives with swords and daggers, my goolies in great danger. Everything in India had a price, and pleasure usually had a penalty.

That night, having a farewell drink with Shiva, I saw the Kali woman again in the courtyard.

'See that girl?' Shiva said. 'I slept with her this morning.' His laughter was more ambiguous than ever. 'She's crazy. I mean, really crazy.'

In the morning he left for London to collect his literary prize and resume his life – lucky dog. That same day I took a train to Nagpur. I put 'the Turd World' into my diary, and the remark found its way into my book, without Shiva's name attached to it. After Madras in southern India, I went to Sri Lanka and beyond, way beyond: Burma, Vietnam, Japan – onward, going slowly into the unknown.

Christmas came. I was in Siberia, it was winter. I was still on my goddamn trip! I battled on. At last, around the New Year, I returned home. I wrote my book and it was published a year later. I paid my bills.

And I saw Shiva at parties.

'Taking any more trains, Paul? Ha! Ha! Ha!'

Now I was sure it was envy, and I pitied him, and his laughter defied interpretation.

Vidia's image of himself as a struggler against the odds and of Shiva as an overprotected child of privilege might have been accurate, but it made their relationship touchy. I knew little about their childhoods. It was clear that Shiva had had a smoother ride at Oxford, and when he decided to make a living as a writer, he was welcomed by publishers. His older brother was a writer, so surely he too had to have talent. Shiva hated that sort of reasoning but profited by it nevertheless.

'He's a complainer, always making excuses. My father was like that,' Vidia said.

The father, Seepersad, was an enigma to me, but the fact that the fictional Mr Biswas had been modeled on him helped to understand the man. Some of those Biswas traits were recognizable in the Naipaul brothers. Mostly I saw Shiva as a suffering parody of a much younger Vidia – prickly and slow, hating the shadow that had been cast over him by his famous and formidable brother, who could be so bluntly present or silently absent.

Taking Vidia's cue that writing was an ordeal, each sentence a hideous labor (I always wanted to jeer at them and say, 'Isn't it much worse for men at sea?'), Shiva went Vidia one further and did no writing at all for long periods. He used his inactivity as an example of the uniqueness of his gift, yet the writing he did manage to scratch off, while perhaps the result of extraordinary labor, did not seem so extraordinary in itself. He just talked more about it. Vidia said he was lazy and drank too much. He said Shiva's fatness was self-indulgence. If I winced at his description, Vidia admitted he was being brutal. Wasn't it simpler than this, that Shiva found it very hard to write? But who finds it easy?

'In Vidia's eyes, Shiva couldn't do anything right,' Vidia's longtime editor, Diana Athill, said some time later. 'He had this picture in his mind that Shiva was going utterly to disgrace himself and the family and that he was going to become a drug addict, was going to be useless. It was intense anxiety.' And she went on to describe how Vidia's scolding would reach a point where Shiva was sitting there not daring to speak, because if he said anything, he was snipped at.

'He's not happy,' Vidia said. 'And why?'

What kept Vidia most serene was his often stated belief that there is justice in all things – in human effort as in nature and art: nothing arbitrary or random but always an elemental fairness. The good you did was rewarded, and you were improved by your act. Good writing always succeeded, dishonest writing was always found out – though with all writing, time was a factor; it might take a while for the work to rise or fall. If an apparently inferior writer made a hit, there was always a reason. Vidia did not dismiss popular novelists. He said, 'Perhaps there's something there.' He meant an illumination or a truth, however crudely expressed. He felt George Wallace's remark about 'pointy-headed intellectuals' expressed an essential truth about the corruption in academic life, and he took satisfaction in taunting Americans by quoting Wallace with approval. Evelyn Waugh had managed to infuriate many Americans in a similar way by saying, 'Erle Stanley Gardner is your finest novelist.'

But Vidia was only half teasing. He believed there were few real accidents in life. What you took to be an accident was undoubtedly well deserved, a kind of karma. Vidia was the first person I had ever heard use that word, as he was the first in my experience to use 'vibration' to mean intimation. He also believed that some people's inner disturbance and confusion made them magnets for ill fortune; others simply begged for it. Things not going well? Vidia was seldom sympathetic to anyone's moaning. It had to be your own fault. Literary fellowships and free money and patronage did not get books written; writers did, and a good writer was dauntless. It was not an expression of fatalism or pitiless indifference but rather a belief in cosmic harmony on Vidia's part when he repeated that in life people got pretty much what they deserved.

Shiva did complain, as Vidia said. Vidia didn't listen. He saw the complaints as unjustified, merely Shiva's indulging himself. 'He is seeking attention. It's theater. Stop listening and he'll stop complaining.'

It did not help that Vidia praised me, and did so for the same reason. It was not by luck or accident that I was doing well, he said. It was application, hard work. 'And you see, Paul, you have something to say.' I did not usually complain, but really, what had

I to complain about? Even before my books sold in any numbers, I had found a way of making a living as a writer: publish a book a year and never say no to a magazine assignment. And, out of a horror of destitution, I lived within my means.

The irony was that I saw Shiva much more often than I saw Vidia. We were nearer in age – he was about four years younger than me – so we had more in common and knew many of the same people – Jonathan Raban, for example, who said he found Shiva Bunterish and nervous and inexplicably giggly. Shiva was not as strong as Vidia, but it was his fate, as the younger brother of a distinguished writer, to have his path to publication smoothed. Understandably, Shiva wanted to be judged separately from his brother, to be seen clearly, without that obscuring fraternal shadow. Yet he seemed self-destructive in his choice of subjects, which served only to make the brothers more intensely like versions of each other, alike in their concerns. Both of them wrote about colonialism as outrageous farce, the futility of African travel, the corruption of power in the Caribbean, the dead end of the Third World, the stagnating complexities of India, and, relentlessly, the question of alienation: where do I belong? And in this they were each deluded in believing that anyone cared.

Some of Shiva's literary obsessions verged on mimicry. Shiva's attack on calypso sounded like a parody of Vidia. There was a definite resemblance in their prose styles, even in the adoption by Shiva of some of Vidia's favorite words – 'tainted,' 'fantasy,' 'distress,' 'loss,' 'fraudulence' – and even the same fastidiousness, expressed in an almost identical way, calling attention to its similarity by the use of exaggeration.

Here is Shiva Naipaul having lunch in a Chinese restaurant in Sri Lanka, not an unusual event for a traveler anywhere. He is in the seaside town of Galle, a pretty little place. But for Shiva it is a disgusting experience of unimaginable uncleanness:

'I ate sparingly and nervously, avoiding the thumb-printed tumbler of water that had been brought me. Now, walking across the vacated Green, with the taint of sewage rising from the seashore, it was hard not to be apprehensive, not to recall, with rising alarm, the abandon with which carelessly tended hands had soiled my plate, my knife, my fork.'

The inhabited world is fairly dirty. It did not seem to occur to Shiva that his pompous description said nothing about the world and everything about his squeamishness. Vidia's horror of dirt was a legendary revelation of his anal compulsiveness, but when he wrote about it he sometimes made a larger point, about caste or culture. Shiva merely revealed himself as a timid fusspot.

Vidia, the true colonial, made a convincing case for his sense of alienation, although any reader could reply, 'So what? We all have problems.' After all, he wasn't writing about the human condition so much as the privileged life of a prosperous middle-aged and middle-class shuttler between Wiltshire and Kensington – himself and no one else. Shiva, the postcolonial sixties rebel and seventies conservative, was unconvincing in depicting himself as an exile and a wanderer. Anyway, what wanderer? He frankly hated travel. His idea of the Worst Journey in the World was a junket to a Chinese restaurant. His trips were very short. He had married into a family of distinguished journalists and lived well in London, where he was known as a partygoer.

He went to parties alone and usually got tipsy, if not drunk, in a sad, giggly way. At his drunkest he indulged in weird confrontations with women in which he would compliment their beauty in a babu accent ('Goodness gracious, you are wery beautifool'), and with such insistence the women did not know whether they were being wooed or insulted.

Whatever Shiva happened to be writing was never going well. He paraphrased Vidia's complaint about the difficulty of writing and made it into a form of boasting. 'I haven't written a word. It's such a struggle.' What was the problem? He had wide recognition for his first book, a generous publisher, and hospitality in all the London papers.

I tried not to argue, for fear it would have seemed that I was minimizing his pain.

'A book is like an illness with me,' he said.

'Of course.'

'But you just churn them out, Paul.'

'You think so?'

That belittling word 'churn' brought to mind a stick and a keg.

'What are you churning out now?'

That laugh of his, barking and too loud, was pure misery and perhaps was meant as another interruption, which kept me from replying.

'Writing's easy for you,' he said.

This sort of insult I had begun to hear more and more in London – though not in the States – for envy gave the English a reckless confidence in giving offense. It had started with Shiva, probably as the result of his resentment of Vidia's avuncular attention and pointed praise. My not complaining about the difficulty of writing was a sure sign I was second-rate; Shiva's struggle was clear evidence of his genius.

'He drinks too much,' Vidia said. 'The body is going. He is fat. Notice how puffy his face is? He gets no exercise. It is a lazy, selfish body.'

That was another aspect of Vidia's sense of justice: you got the body you deserved. And in Vidia's judgment people's bodies told everything about them, even to the extent of bad skin making you a villain and obesity being like a moral fault. The fat characters in Vidia's books were nearly always unreliable, if not outright crooks.

'I am very proud of having a beautiful physique,' Vidia had told an interviewer. 'The body is the one thing we can control. It's a kind of envelope that contains the soul.' In spite of this, several people had mentioned to me how Vidia, because of his small size and his asthma, had a deep sense of physical inferiority.

Anyone could see that Shiva was unhappy. I did not know why, but there had to be a connection with Vidia. I still felt that knowing Shiva better was a way of knowing Vidia, because – though Vidia might deny it – one brother was often the key to understanding the other. The paradox was that, more and more, Shiva and I were fraternal, in the feuding, wrong-footing mode, and our relationship was undermined by the nearest thing to sibling rivalry.

'Come to tea on Sunday,' Shiva said at a party one night. 'Bring the family.'

That sounded all right. This was early on. Our wives and children had not met. Shiva was living in a house in Essex. On a map it seemed a straightforward drive, but on the day it was a three-hour slog in my small car because of rain and bad roads and the quaint and maddening bottlenecks of English villages ('This must be

Gosfield'). All the way I had promised my little family that this visit would be worth it. We met Shiva's father-in-law, a noted broadcaster. The house was crowded with people – Shiva was well connected. But he was on the telephone when we arrived, and when I managed to say hello, he smiled in exasperation.

'Can't you see I've got my hands full?'

And then that gloomy laugh.

We had our tea and left after an hour, because it was such a long way back to south London. He had hardly spoken to me.

'Which one was Shiva?' my wife said.

I mentioned this to Vidia, that we had gone all that way for tea but had felt unwelcome.

Vidia said, 'He told me he gets depressed when he sees you.'

'I can't imagine why. I never talk about my work. I just listen to him.'

'Perhaps that's the reason.'

'That I listen?'

'That he hates himself.'

At another period, Shiva had a large apartment in Earls Court, over a bookstore. It seemed very stylish, his living in the middle of things, especially the raffish multiculturalism of Earls Court. We lived narrowly in distant, lifeless Catford, an hour across London. By now we were unwilling regulars at each other's dinner parties.

The first time at dinner in his Earls Court flat, I noticed that Shiva was served a special meal: bigger, different, tastier-looking.

'What's that?' I asked.

'Shiva's a vegetarian,' his wife explained, as Shiva protected his full plate with his forearms.

'It looks like chicken to me,' someone said.

'It is chicken,' Shiva said. 'It's not as bad as beef.'

There was beef in our moussaka, and I felt at that moment all of us coveted Shiva's special meal. Shiva explained that he had been raised eating certain foods. I gathered that chicken was regarded as a vegetable in the Naipaul household, and I was able to understand a bit better Vidia's contradictory crankiness when it came to diet.

On another visit to Shiva's, helping to clear up after the meal, I put some leftovers into the refrigerator and saw many stacked containers, all precisely labeled: *Lunch Wednesday, Dinner Wednesday, Lunch Thursday*, and so forth.

'You're well organized,' I said to his wife, who was at the sink.

'Oh, that. I'm going away Tuesday.'

She explained that whenever she went away, she left meals for Shiva, all the meals he would need for the duration of her absence. They were all different, precooked, needing only to be heated up. Shiva was unable or unwilling to make a meal for himself, so this nannying – or mothering – was the elaborate answer.

Seeing me smile, his wife reacted defensively and said, 'Vidia doesn't cook either. He is waited on hand and foot by Pat.'

That was true, and it was a world away from my life and the lives of most of the people I knew. Was it that the Naipaul brothers' lives were well organized or that they had submissive wives? It spoke volumes about the family home in Trinidad. Surely they had been indulged, and all that had done was to make them seem helpless, if not infantile.

Even if someone had offered me meals and nannying, I would have refused. In the balancing act of working on *The Mosquito Coast*, I was progressing with such steadiness that I became superstitious: I wanted nothing in my life to change. I stayed in London. I ate the same lunch every day: fish fingers. I meditated intensely on the implications of my story and on the characters. I felt that any change in my circumstances would upset my narrative.

The month I finished my novel, April of 1981, I wrote to Vidia, who immediately and enthusiastically replied, praising me for the book.

It was what I wanted to hear after almost two years of working on the book. Vidia had never been more generous.

'Your energy is amazing; you seem vitalized by all your many successes. I run across your name and your books everywhere and I always feel slightly proprietorial.'

After all these years he was still my friend and my booster. I rejoiced in pleasing him. He read the new novel.

He said, 'This is a big book.'

*

Both Shiva and I had been shaken by the 1978 mass suicide, in Jonestown, Guyana, of members of the People's Temple commune. To me it was one of the ghastliest events that had occurred in my lifetime. Paranoia could not take a more violent or nightmarish form. The transplanted messiah, Jim Jones, creating madness among his followers, was someone who had triggered my thinking about *The Mosquito Coast*, though my book was very different. Shiva wrote a book about Jonestown, *Journey to Nowhere*. He often alluded to the grisly nature of his experience, for he had arrived in Jonestown before all the more than nine hundred bodies had been bagged and taken away. He said that he had never seen anything worse. He was dispirited by the experience, and for a while it rendered him mute. He suffered something akin to a nervous breakdown during the writing of the book. I understood then that it was not conceit or vanity or childishness that kept him so insecure, but something fundamental: he had emptied the goblet and in tipping it up had seen fear lurking on the bottom, as in the horrific line from the play I used to teach: 'I have drunk and seen the spider.'

In his depression Shiva's writing became turgid and verbose. Parties were 'revelries,' speeches were 'orations.' He would write, 'Machines had subverted the bondage of mass muscular exertion,' when he could have written, 'Machines had taken the place of workers.'

Speaking of Trinidadians, he wrote, 'We acknowledged, with unspoken candor, our humble status in the imperial dispensation,' a pretentious way of saying, 'We felt we didn't matter much in the British empire.'

When truth broke through pastiche the effect was vulgar, and what he attempted as style was forced and unrewarding. He admitted as much. He said he was frustrated. Now nearly everything he wrote was a form of fault-finding.

'I sit at my desk all day,' he told me. 'I do nothing. I try to write. It won't come.'

This was not the lazy artistic boast of ten years before, but a more imploring anguish. It was also fear.

'Sometimes I can't do anything until five o'clock. Sometimes there's nothing.'

With no one else listening, he didn't mock me, didn't giggle; he was solemn, and he looked terrible: pasty, swollen, almost deranged, holding a drink in one hand, a cigarette in the other.

'My brother thinks I'm lazy.'

Weariness was in his voice. He was a man burdened, and now I knew it was not an act. He seemed on the point of resignation. When Indira Gandhi was killed, in 1984, he flew to India and wrote an angry, grieving piece. As though evading the serious commitment of the book he had started, he wrote more articles: about the Third World – denying that such a place existed; about Australia – hating the whole country; about himself and his brother – wishing for his confusion to be understood and admitting that perhaps Vidia was the only person on earth who understood him.

After the least exertion, he became short of breath. He said, 'I get so tired,' and the way he said it convinced me something was truly wrong. I asked Vidia whether there was anything we might do to help. But he only repeated that Shiva had brought this misery on himself. He said it with sympathy, helplessly, not knowing what the remedy was.

And really, a man of thirty-nine or forty, when he speaks of fatigue you don't think that he is ill so much as overworked or even exaggerating – too many late nights, he must be neglecting himself. You never imagine that such a person is deathly ill. Yet Shiva was.

He was working on a section of his Australia book, writing about a comical Sinhalese named Tissa, who spoke to him about the futility of male ambition in Sri Lanka. Shiva wrote Tissa's question, 'Is it like that on your island as well?' and then he died.

His heart had been weak. It explained everything he said and did, everything he felt. It had taken away his strength; it had made him tired. It was why he panted and perspired, why he was often winded, why everything was so hard for him.

He was found slumped at his desk by his son, just as thirty-three years before, Shiva had found his own father dead.

I wrote to Vidia as tenderly as I could. He wrote back, saying, 'I am melancholy in a clinical, helpless kind of way. I get, or am attacked by, these bad dreams just before waking up. In fact they wake me up.'

And he ended the letter, 'How nice, in the middle of this, to get your hand of friendship.'

It was as though I were the brother who had survived. But Vidia went on mourning, and when he wrote *The Enigma of Arrival* and dedicated it to Shiva, he said of the book, 'Death is the motif.'

14

Tainted Vegetables

'At Oxford Circus, walk north until you come to the church with a spire like a sharpened pencil,' Vidia said, directing me in his precise way to the Indian restaurant where we were to have lunch. But I knew the church.

I was, as always, eager to see him. I needed to know what was on his mind, because he questioned everything, took nothing on faith, saw things differently from anyone else. His talk was unexpected and original. He was contrary and he was often right.

Long before, I had been with him while he listened to Indians in Uganda boasting of their wealth and security. 'They are dead men' was Vidia's verdict. Now most of London's newsagents and sub-post offices were run by those same Indians, refugees from Uganda. They comprised almost a whole shopkeeping class in the south of England.

Three years before Shiva died, in 1985, Vidia had been upbeat and funny. 'Intellectual pressure' was making his hair fall out, he said. But he was busy and happy. 'One seems to be extraordinarily full of affairs.' He was only fifty. He accurately predicted the outcome of the Falklands War, in a characteristic paradox. The Argentines had sworn they would fight to the end.

'When the Argentines say they will fight to the last drop of blood,' he said, 'it means they are on the point of surrender.'

And that happened, too. But with Shiva's death he grew sad. He sorrowed quietly; his grieving showed in his writing, in his choice of subject. He wrote of death and dying – his sister had also recently died; intimations of mortality and a sadness crept into his prose, the tones of deeper isolation, because there is a note of loneliness in all elegies – beyond the death, something of departure, a sense that he was being left behind.

It made us firmer friends. Now, after almost twenty years, we depended on one another – each of us could count on the other to listen and be sympathetic. We were chastened by Shiva's death. I realized how precious life was, how brief, how each day mattered.

If we were saddened, we were also vitalized, seeing what a waste it was not to live all we could. Vidia traveled more, but we were able to pick up the thread of friendship after weeks or even months of silence.

That was how I came to be rising from the Oxford Circus tube station to walk north on Upper Regent Street, toward the church with the pencil-like spire that I knew to be All Souls. We met on the sidewalk.

'Yes, yes, yes, Paul.'

Vidia placed a high value on physical characteristics, and especially on radical change. If someone had gotten very fat, or very thin, or pale or pimply, or had begun sporting a silly hat, Vidia took it as a danger sign, a mental lapse, depression, folly, vanity, something deeply wrong.

Watching him size me up swiftly, I could see that he was pleased I had not changed. Nor had he, I told him.

'I'm still doing my exercises every night,' he said.

In the Indian restaurant, the Gaylord, on Mortimer Street, Vidia began staring at the Indian waiter, a bespectacled young man, following him with his eyes around the room as though he had recognized him and was trying to think of his name. At last Vidia raised his hand and called him over.

'Do you know that you look like me?'

The waiter shook his cheeks and squinted, murmuring the question in disbelief. 'I am not knowing, sir.'

In his twenties, with crusted sleepless eyes, dark jowls, thick untidy hair, horn-rimmed glasses, and a scowling smile, he had that fatigued and impatient look of many Indian waiters in London. The news Vidia gave him seemed to unsettle him. It was clear that no one had ever made such an observation to the waiter before. He glanced at Vidia and appeared to be so disturbed by what he saw that he turned away and laughed in a chattering way, his mouth wide, his eyes dead.

'Yes, I look like you,' Vidia said.

He studied the young man's face closely and with such intensity the waiter backed away, giggling in anguish.

'Maybe, sir.'

'But you don't really think so.'

'No, sir.'

'And yet it's true. You look like me.'

This peculiar conversation bothered the waiter but was highly illuminating to Vidia, who seemed to see his younger self before him. The waiter was nervous, contemplating his face as represented by this fiftyish man grinning in satisfaction at him.

'Look in the mirror,' Vidia said. 'Go on, you'll see.'

The waiter, who could never have taken much pleasure in staring at his own reflection, waggled his head, Indian fashion, to mean yes he would. But I could tell that any resemblance was the last thing on which he wanted positive confirmation.

And it was all in Vidia's mind. I didn't see much of a likeness.

'All right,' Vidia said. 'We'll order, then.'

Over lunch Vidia told me that he had received his first Public Lending Right check, about £1,500. Mine was about the same, and the more popular authors got quite a bit more. This great scheme for compensating authors on the basis of library loans had finally been introduced in Britain. I had asked Vidia to sign a petition to support the PLR bill some years before. He had refused. *I sign nothing*. Now he was crowing over his check.

'Publishers want to cash in,' he said. 'But why should they? We're the ones who do the work.'

I said, 'That campaign for PLR was quite a struggle. Nothing like it exists in the States. For a long time, no one paid any attention.'

'Really.' He raised himself up slightly from his chair and looked around. 'I don't see anyone I know here.'

'Who are you thinking of, Vidia?'

'No one in particular. But it's nice when one sees someone one knows in a restaurant in London.'

'I saw Bruce Chatwin the other day in L'Escargot.'

'Who's Bruce Chatwin?'

It was how Vidia belittled anyone.

'The way he talks,' Vidia said. 'All those airs. That name-dropping. He is trying to live down the shame of being the son of a Birmingham solicitor.'

'I don't think he cares about that,' I said. Bruce was a friend of mine, and I suspected this to be the reason for Vidia's dismissing him.

'No. You're wrong. Look at Noël Coward. His mother kept a lodging house. And he pretended to be so grand – that theatrical English accent. All that posturing. He knew he was common. It was all a pretense. And think of his pain.'

He was still scanning the restaurant for a familiar face. Seeing none, he settled into his prawn curry, seeming disappointed, as if he had shown up but no one else had.

'How's your food?'

'It's all right, but lunch – lunch is such an intrusion. It fractures one's day. It takes over, makes the morning hectic, destroys the afternoon, and leaves one no appetite in the evening.'

'What's the answer?'

'One prefers to break the day into three distinct parts. Work in the morning. Light lunch. Something in the afternoon. Exercise. Prepare for the evening – the dinner. Dinner is grander.'

'Grand' was one of those words that Vidia could use in an almost satirical way. But if you smiled he might react, and then you knew he really meant it. 'Very grand' sometimes meant pompous and hollow, or it might mean important or powerful.

'Do you know Bibendum?' he asked.

It was a new restaurant in South Kensington, housed in a well-known art deco landmark usually referred to as the Michelin building. Bibendum had been started by the entrepreneur Sir Terence Conran, who insisted that people use his title. Vidia had met him once, and he hated Conran for his brashness and his flaunted knighthood.

'Do try to get a table there next time, Paul, won't you? One would be happier there.'

I said I would. What prevented me was the expense. It was a five-star restaurant. No matter where we went I ended up paying, and so I stayed away from the most expensive places, like Claridges, the Ritz, or the Connaught. I preferred the peacefulness of eating in relatively empty restaurants, which were always the less stylish ones.

Knowing of his interest in graphology, I showed him a page from a letter I had received that week. It was handwritten with black ballpoint on a yellow legal-sized sheet. There was no salutation, no signature, just a page of writing. I said, 'So what do you think?'

'Oh, God. Oh, God. Oh, God.' Vidia's face became a mask representing suffering and torment. He made passes with his fingers over the page. 'This man is in trouble.'

'It's from John Ehrlichman, the Watergate man. He sent me this from prison. He's writing a book.'

We finished lunch. I paid. Leaving the Gaylord, we walked toward All Souls Church, in Langham Place, near Broadcasting House. Vidia pointed out the Langham, once a hotel, then a BBC building, where parts of the Overseas Service had had offices.

'I had an office there,' Vidia said. 'I started writing there, in the Freelance Room. God!'

'What were you doing?'

'Caribbean Service. I did programs. One called *Caribbean Voices*. Went mad wondering whether I could write a book. I began writing *Miguel Street* there.'

Though I knew he had worked there, it was surprising to hear him mention it. He disapproved of a writer's working a regular job and was proud of the fact that he had worked only ten weeks on salary, as a copywriter for a company that sold cement. That, as his whole salaried career, was bound to have distorted his view of the working world.

'Such a lovely church,' he said as we entered Langham Place.

'All Souls,' I said. 'Thomas Nash.'

'It is Nash's only church,' Vidia said. 'So strong. Look what he does with the simplest lines. They ridiculed it when it was built in the 1820s. No one approved.'

'Kipling got married here,' I said.

Vidia smiled. He loved sparring.

'That was just before he went to America,' he said. 'Of course, his wife was American.'

'Henry James was his best man,' I said.

'And then Kipling came back to England, moved into a grand house, and wrote nothing,' Vidia said.

'He wrote some great short stories.'

'Nothing as great as *Plain Tales from the Hills*.'

'The late stories are much subtler,' I said.

'Everyone tells me that,' Vidia said. He shook his head. 'I have been seriously wondering about fiction. What is it now? What can it be?'

'What it has always been,' I said. 'A version of the truth. And I think that's what nonfiction is, too.'

'Yes, yes, yes,' Vidia said. He thought that was apt. 'But I am still wondering. I think the novel as we know it is dated.'

And so we walked along, up to Regents Park and along the footpaths by the flower beds, until it was time for his dental appointment in Harley Street, where we parted.

It seemed cruelly ironic that Vidia's developing interest in stylish restaurants coincided with serious dental problems – gum disease, a gingivectomy, and painful extractions. I sometimes met him at his dentist's office. He was one of the few people in England I knew who had a private dentist; most people made do with the impatient National Health Service dentists, who gave them fifteen minutes of attention every four months and, in their incompetent haste, were lax in detecting the sort of gum disease that was afflicting Vidia.

At another lunch, Vidia wincing with each bite from his sore teeth, we talked about money. We usually talked about money, as writers do – the futility of making it, the punishing British tax system, the way people presumed on writers by trying to underpay them, the fatuity of wealth, and could we have some more money, please?

'I know the solution – my solution,' Vidia said.

'Please tell me.'

'I want a million pounds in the bank,' he said. 'Not the equivalent of a million in real estate. Not valuables. Not stocks. I want a million in my account.'

'I suppose that's possible,' I said, so as not to discourage him. In fact, I had no idea how one would accumulate that amount.

'But you have a million, Paul.'

'You're joking.'

'You got a million for the *Mosquito Coast* film, surely.'

'Nowhere near it. Maybe a fifth of that.'

'Really.' He was surprised, even shocked.

'And I bought a house with it, so now it's gone.'

'Actors get paid in the millions, surely.'

'Yes,' I said. 'But not writers.'

'I will get my million,' he said, as I paid the bill for lunch.

After yet another lunch, we walked to the offices of his publisher so he could sign three hundred copies of *A House for Mr Biswas*, one of the titles in a series of signed books that were part of a book-club offer. I stood by him, opening them to the half-title page, and he wrote his signature. As always, he used a fountain pen and black ink.

'When I wrote this book I wore out a pen. The nib was worn down to the gold. It was a little stump. Imagine the labor.'

He signed, I stacked.

'What is the good of signing books? It simply inflates their value in a bogus way. I will never see the profits. Someone else will get it. All these people who call themselves publishers – they are no better than people who sell books off a barrow.'

I pushed the books at him. He signed quickly, making his initials and his surname into a single calligraphic flourish.

'These will go for big money,' he said. 'They will be resold. Why am I doing this?'

And he stopped signing. He put the cap on his pen and stood up. He was done.

'There's more,' I said.

'That's enough,' he said, having convinced himself that signing the books was a mistake.

Later that day, we went to my house for tea. My two boys were upstairs in their rooms, doing homework. I called them down so they could say hello. I was proud of them; I wanted Vidia to see them. Now they were the right age. Vidia could not deal with young children – he rather disliked children – but he took to my boys as he had taken to me, long before.

'And what homework are you doing, Marcel?'

'English prep. And a Russian essay.' He swallowed and went on. 'On Ivan the Terrible.'

'Tell me about Ivan the Terrible.'

Marcel said, 'I'm reading a book about him by Henri Troyat.'

'I know Troyat's *Tolstoy*. You say this book is about Ivan the Terrible?'

'It's his new one. It hasn't come out here yet.'

'You have the American edition?'

'No. The French one.'

'But this is your Russian essay?'

'My essay's in Russian. The book's in French.'

'Yes, yes, yes, yes,' Vidia said, liking the answer. 'And what about you, Louis?'

'English essay. My Phillimore.'

'What is a Phillimore?'

'It's the big essay of the year. It's supposed to be pretty long and serious.'

'Is yours long and serious?'

'It's not done yet. It's about the attraction of evil.'

'Yes,' Vidia said, concentrating hard and murmuring, 'the attraction of evil.'

'Ahab,' Louis said. 'Richard the Third.'

'You should read *Old Goriot*.'

Louis nodded, not sure whether a book or an author was being recommended.

After the boys had gone upstairs Vidia said, 'You are so lucky to have your sons. They're intelligent. They're polite. They are nice boys.'

Agreeing with him, I deliberately positioned myself near the shelf in the bookcase where all of Vidia's books were lined up, from the ones I had bought with Yomo, in Kampala, to the latest ones.

I said, 'Vidia, would you mind signing these books?'

'Not now. Some other time,' he said.

He had convinced himself in the course of signing all those copies of *Biswas* that book signing was a cheat. Other people made money from signed books, not the author, who was invariably swindled. He consoled me with a joke about the writer who had signed so many books that the rarest books of all, and the most valuable, were the ones without his signature.

*

Every October, around the time the Nobel Prize was announced, Vidia was named in confidently speculative articles as the likely recipient. He never mentioned the prize, nor commented on the speculation. On the contrary, he seemed to make a point of ignoring it. It was I who brought up the subject. In 1973, when Patrick White had won, I told Vidia how pleased I was – I liked Patrick White's fiction, his humorous and sometimes hallucinatory prose style. Besides, he conveyed very specific and vivid images of Australia.

Vidia said, 'I've read him. I don't think there's much there.'

Three years later, Saul Bellow won. Vidia claimed he had never read him. And he laughed when William Golding won in 1983.

'Tell me, what did Golding do to win it?'

The Nigerian writer Wole Soyinka won the Nobel Prize in 1986.

'What do you think, Vidia?'

'Did he write anything?'

Vidia did not wait for my reply. We happened to be walking down Cromwell Road toward the V and A, and from the way he stiffened his legs in a marching manner and planted his feet more firmly I gathered that he had something on his mind. Perhaps it had unsettled him to think of Wole Soyinka, wearing a crown of laurel leaves, with $190,000 in his pocket. In any case, Vidia became agitated or sad when he thought about Africa.

'The Nobel committee are doing it again,' he said, striding down the sidewalk.

'Doing what?'

'Pissing on literature, as they do every year.'

I started to laugh.

'Pissing from a great height,' he said. 'On books.'

In time, we changed from lunch to dinner. 'Dinner is grander.' Also, it did not break up the day, as lunch did. Yet our dinners were no more frequent than our lunches had been. One or two, then nothing for a year. He was away – on the long journey for his Islam book, or in India, or, quite often, in Buenos Aires.

I was traveling too, in China and Africa, in the United States, and on book tours. Almost everywhere I went I was asked about Vidia: What influence did V. S. Naipaul have on your writing? or

How did Naipaul help you as a writer? There was no simple answer, at least none shorter than would fill a four-hundred-page book. It was understood that we were friends, that we had had a teacher–student relationship when I had started writing. Because Vidia usually avoided book tours ('The book will find its own way'), people wondered what he was like. I told them truthfully that I had never met anyone like him.

'Writers are crankish,' Vidia said. 'You get crankish from being alone.'

Often, I heard stories about him – people sought me out to tell me the stories, believing that I had to know everything about my friend.

When something disgraceful was rumored of Vidia, there were often several versions of the story. Vidia's hasty exit from Amsterdam is a good example of the mutation of a simple tale. In the first version I heard, a Dutchman in Amsterdam told me of Vidia's disastrous visit of a year before. Vidia had arrived from London to see his Dutch publisher and had agreed to a week of publicity. About an hour after his arrival, a press conference was arranged: Naipaul on a stage, the Dutch audience waiting to ask him questions; cameras, tape recorders, journalists.

The first question, phrased as antagonism, was from a woman who asked him to explain his offensive attitude toward Africans.

Vidia said, 'I have no comment on this.'

The woman demanded an answer.

'I don't have to listen to this,' Vidia said.

With that, he walked off the stage. Cameras and lights followed his progress out of the hall. He went back to his taxi, which still held his bag, and back to the airport. He returned that same day to London, without ever having unpacked or seen his hotel, his whole visit torpedoed by a single question that he had found impertinent.

The second version of Vidia's Amsterdam exit was reported in the Dutch paper *Het Parool*, under the headline 'Naipaul Came, Got Angry and Disappeared.'

In this story Vidia was to have spent five days in the Netherlands, but departed 'in anger' after two days. For a public discussion at the Amsterdam PEN Center, Vidia asked that questions be submitted in writing, but he ridiculed them when he looked at them. A sample question he hooted at was 'How do you see the future of our world in ten or twenty years?' To save the situation, the Dutch host asked a question, about how terms like 'fascism' and 'communism' describe European ideas that cannot necessarily be transposed onto societies fundamentally different from our own. When Vidia expressed mild agreement, a woman from Amsterdam's Free University asked, 'If terms like "fascism" and "communism" are not applicable, then how about using "rich" and "poor" as yardsticks?'

'Why "rich" and "poor"?' Vidia said. 'Why not "lazy" and "ambitious," "learned" and "illiterate," "good" and "bad"? It's about time we started looking at other aspects of people.'

Hearing this blunt reply, a Dutch author, Margaretha Ferguson, began (so the paper said) 'an endless story about Naipaul's negative attitude towards Islam,' and attacked him for saying that Dutch had virtually disappeared from the Indonesian language.

'Why do you ask me such things?' Vidia said ('irritatedly'). 'To show that you know better? Of course you know better!'

'But if you are talking about intellectual clarity –' Miss Ferguson replied ('sputtered').

'I don't think you know what intellectual clarity is.'

Vidia rose from his chair, muttered something about the gathering's being 'senseless,' and decided to leave for the airport, where he handed back his fee for the afternoon (750 guilders) and flew home.

Which version was true?

'Does it matter when one is dealing with nonsense?' Vidia told me.

'What went wrong?'

I had had enjoyable experiences in Holland, where most people speak fluent English and are intellectually curious and widely traveled. They had not mythologized their colonial history, as the British and French sometimes had, making wog-bashing into a glorious mission to civilize. In the most provincial Dutch towns hundreds of people turned out to hear visiting novelists lecturing in English. But Vidia disagreed.

'The Dutch,' he said. 'Potato eaters.'

The famous image in the Van Gogh painting said everything about the culture, he believed: ugly, moronic, famished peasants in a greasy kitchen, crouched over a basin of spuds and cramming them into their mouths.

I heard other stories that I did not bother to verify, because they had the ring of truth. There were many complaints about his behavior and even his writing. Vidia was used to complaints. He said, 'I think unless one hears a little squeal of pain after one's done some writing, one has not really done much.' Any story related to fastidiousness, and especially food, was unquestionably true.

He was at a dinner party in New York City. He sipped his wine. It was satisfactory – he had insisted on choosing the wine. The dishes were passed by the waiter, people helping themselves. The main course was meat, but because Vidia was a guest, extra dishes of vegetables were also served. Vidia waved them away. He spent the entire meal sipping wine and nibbling a piece of bread.

'You haven't eaten anything, Mr Naipaul,' the woman next to him said. She was Dame Drue Heinz, patroness of the arts and part of the Heinz food fortune.

'Yes, I'm a vegetarian,' Vidia said.

'There are vegetables in that bowl,' she indicated.

Vidia explained that he had watched all the vegetables being served and had seen someone – he did not say whom – using a serving implement that had come into contact with the meat dish.

'Those vegetables are tainted.'

At another dinner party, in London, something similar happened. The dishes were passed, Vidia took nothing for himself. He sipped wine, he nibbled bread. The hostess was surprised by Vidia's indifference, for knowing that he was a vegetarian she had made an effort to provide extra vegetables. She watched Vidia waving the steaming dishes aside.

The host, tipped off by his wife, approached Vidia quietly after the meal.

'Was there anything wrong with the food?'

Vidia said, 'I didn't see anything for me.'

'There were vegetables,' the host said.

'Those were not my vegetables,' Vidia said. 'Those were every-one's vegetables.'

Only a non-Hindu would find this behavior strange. One day in India I was approached by a beggar. I was seated under a peepul tree, eating a coconut that had just been cracked open for me by a street vendor. The beggar asked me for some rupees. He was starving, he said, and he looked it: ragged dhoti, hollow eyes, clawlike hands.

'You are hungry?'

'Yes, sahib.'

'Have the rest of this coconut.'

He refused. He was a high-caste beggar. I was a foreigner, an Untouchable. He could not eat coconut that had been tainted by my fingers. He wanted his own coconut. If he had been dying of thirst, he would not have drunk out of a container that had touched my lips. He was a Brahmin.

Naipaul is a Brahmin. He is also proud of what he has achieved. On another occasion, he was guest of honor at a dinner in London to which a large number of people had been invited. Before the dinner, a woman came up to him and said, 'You wrote a dishonest book about London – *Mr Stone*. Nothing in that book is true. You totally misrepresented the way we live.'

Vidia did not reply. Instead, he immediately left the party, before all the guests had arrived, before any were seated or the meal was served.

'What about the hostess? Didn't you say anything to her?' I asked, because Vidia himself had told me this story.

Vidia shook his head. 'Let that foolish woman who insulted me explain why I wasn't there.'

At about the same time, he told an interviewer, 'I can't be interested in people who don't like what I write, because if you don't like what I write you're disliking me.' It was after such an encounter that he said, 'England is a country of second-rate people – bum politicians, scruffy writers, and crooked aristocrats.'

To people who found him demanding, insisting on high fees to speak or read, first-class airfares, five-star hotels, chauffeurs, minders, secretaries, and vintage wines, Vidia gave his usual reply:

290

Treat me as you would a world-class brain surgeon or astro-physicist.

His sweeping generalizations and cutting remarks were widely quoted. What about Africa? one interviewer asked him. What was the future for Africa?

'Africa has no future,' he said.

Indians were treated no more gently by him. They did not read, he said. 'If they read at all, they read for magic. They read holy books, they read sacred hymns – books of wisdom, books that will do them good.' He told me that it was very bad that Indian women kept their hair so long: 'It encourages rape.' He became noted for pointing out that the red-dot caste mark that Indians wear on their forehead means 'my head is empty.'

Asked about his book sales on his native island of Trinidad, he said, 'My books aren't read in Trinidad now. Drumbeating is a higher activity, a more satisfying activity.' Once he had written, 'I happen to like Spanish dancing,' but later in an interview he said he deplored dancing. 'Dance? I've never danced. I'd be ashamed of it. It is something out of the jungle. It's undignified. I dislike all those lower-class cultural manifestations.'

He was invited to San Francisco to read at two performances. He demanded, and received, his astrophysicist's fee. Both performances were sold out in advance. Vidia read. But the audience was dis-appointed that he took no questions afterwards. When his host tried to ask him why he would not relent, he pretended he had not heard the question and showed her his tweed jacket, saying, 'It's rather fine, don't you think? Made in South Africa.'

But he told me the reason. 'I was invited to read from my work, not to answer asinine questions.'

He was much more concerned by the movie shown on his incoming flight. He had hated it. He mentioned its name.

'Do you know that film, Paul?'

I said I didn't.

'The people responsible for making that film should be punished. They should be beaten. Whipped! No one should be allowed to make films like that. It was grotesque. Beat them!'

Another flight, this one to Trinidad, also enraged him. After take-off, he stood in the aisle to slip off his sweater. A flight attendant hurried toward him.

'Please don't take your shirt off,' she said.

'You see?' he told me. 'Here is this simple West Indian fellow. He is planning to fly to Trinidad with his shirt off – bare-chested – as they do on his island.'

'What did you do?'

'I'm afraid I raised my voice. I screamed at them. I said they were all cunts. Excuse me. I was very angry.'

He screamed in India, too, when he was told to remove his shoes before entering various temples, including the ancient Lord Jagannath Temple in Puri. Vidia pointed out that the temple floor was far dirtier and more disgusting than his shoes and that the idea of defiling such a filthy, unswept place was ridiculous. This story was repeated in *The Times* of London, which indicated that there had been 'an altercation.'

In Portland, Oregon, he was being driven to the airport the day after a reading, which had been arranged by his American publisher. His driver, a local woman, making small talk on the long drive, asked him his feelings about Portland, and, as he had just visited Seattle, she chitchatted about their differences.

'Seattle is an ocean city,' she said. 'Portland is definitely an inland place.'

'How would you characterize Portland?' Vidia asked.

'This is a small town,' she said.

Vidia suddenly became furious and turned on the woman, shouting, 'I don't go to small towns! I never go to small towns!'

He raged on as the nervous woman drove. It was as though he had been tricked into visiting Portland, conned into believing it was a real city – which of course it is, substantial and prosperous and bookloving, Seattle's younger sister.

Seeing that her driving had been seriously impaired by Vidia's outburst, the woman gripped the wheel and wondered what to say.

'Thank you for doing this, then,' she said at last. 'I really didn't expect you to come here. I don't expect you'll be doing it again.'

'By thanking me, you show me how stupid you are,' Vidia said.

I must not cry, the woman thought, negotiating the rush-hour freeway traffic and feeling that tears were filling her eyes. She had risen early, given her husband breakfast, seen her children off to school, and had hurried in the darkness to meet Vidia at his hotel, pay his hotel bill, and give him his fee and his lift to the airport. Now, so as not to rile Vidia further, she politely denied that she was stupid, and she kept driving.

Vidia said, 'You are stupid, because if you knew anything about me, you would not have invited me to your small town.'

'But you were sent here,' the woman said. 'You have to understand that it was your publicist who arranged this. She indicated that you wanted to come.'

'They don't know me!' Vidia howled. 'They don't know me!'

He was still ranting as the woman drove up the ramp to the airport terminal.

'They are stupid too. How dare they send me here!'

'That's their job, to put you in front of audiences,' the woman said, and brought her car to the curb. She was dazed. She told me later, 'It felt like being hit by a two-by-four.' She got out, took Vidia's bag from the back seat, and placed it on the sidewalk.

Vidia said, 'Please bring my bag in,' and turned away sharply.

Inside the terminal, the woman set the bag down on the scale at the check-in counter.

Just as Vidia was about to speak, the woman winced. She thought he was going to scream again. But he said, 'You have lovely fingers. So thin.'

Without a word, the woman left him. She went to her car and found a parking ticket on her windshield for $72. She drove home sobbing.

The woman was my friend. In telling me the story, she was also saying, Why did your friend Naipaul do this to me? I winced at these stories. I had no answer.

Such stories that people volunteered, saying 'You must hear this,' Vidia always said were true. It was sometimes hard for me to imagine his fury or his cold cruelty, because we had never quarreled, nor had I ever witnessed a scene as awful as those I heard described.

There was a story I never asked Vidia to verify – didn't dare ask, because I wanted it to be true. If it was not true, it ought to have been.

Ved Mehta is a distinguished Indian writer. Vidia knew of him. Speaking of *The New Yorker* once, how under the editorship of William Shawn he could not interest the magazine in his writing, Vidia said, 'Of course, they already have a tame Indian.'

Ved Mehta is also famously blind. A certain New Yorker doubted his blindness. Seeing Mehta at a New York party, speaking to a group of attentive people, holding court, the man decided to test it. He had always been skeptical that Mehta was totally blind, since in his writing he minutely described people's faces and wrote about the nuances of color and texture with elaborate subtlety, making precise distinctions.

The man crept over to where Mehta was sitting, and as the writer continued to speak, the doubting man began making faces at him. He leaned over and waved his hands at Ved Mehta's eyes. He thumbed his nose at Ved Mehta. He wagged his fingers in Ved Mehta's face.

Still, Mehta went on speaking, calmly and in perfectly enunciated sentences, never faltering in his expansive monologue.

The man made a last attempt: he put his own face a foot away and stuck his tongue out. But Mehta spoke without pause, as if the man did not exist.

Realizing how wrong he had been, the man felt uncomfortable and wanted to go home. Leaving the party, he said to the hostess, 'I had always thought Ved Mehta was faking his blindness, or at least exaggerating. I am now convinced that Ved Mehta is blind.'

'That's not Ved Mehta,' the hostess said. 'It's V. S. Naipaul.'

15

'It's Major'

At some point in these late middle years, when Vidia was working on a book, hiding and making himself ill from hunching over it as his handwriting grew tinier with concentration and anxiety, he would interrupt himself in describing what he was writing and say, 'It's Major.' His pompous certainty gave the word a capital letter.

In the past he had said, 'It's Important,' or 'It's a Big Book,' and raised his eyes and seemed to see it hovering in the air, like the prophet Joseph Smith contemplating the gold plates of Mormonism glittering in the hands of the angel Moroni. Several times, Vidia had applied this praise to me. *The Mosquito Coast* was a Big Book. My Africa books were Big Books. They might even have been Important Books. But they weren't Major. *A Bend in the River* was Major. Being Vidia, he repeated it: 'It's Major. It's Major.'

Was he satirizing himself? Not so far as I knew. He never spoke about his work except in tones of the utmost solemnity. No one I had ever met was so devoted to the act of writing. That was his lesson. His dedication and belief had attracted and inspired me, so I had followed him, uttering my own humble equivalent of 'Good Master, what good thing shall I do, that I may have eternal life?' Vidia was almost mystical in his belief in writing, for literary creation was a form of prayer, a disturbing prayer. He was not the writer as equal, the reader's buddy, but rather the writer as priestly figure. Nor did he deviate from his vows: if he said something was Major, he meant it.

Much of Vidia's writing is like a literary shadowgraph, full of the starkly textured silhouettes of keenly observed shadows, as though the penumbra for Vidia has more meaning than the person or thing that shapes it. *Miguel Street*, the first book he wrote (though not the first published), ends with a dramatic departure, as the narrator says, 'I left them all and walked briskly towards the aeroplane, not looking back, only looking at my shadow before me, a dancing dwarf on the tarmac.'

There is also adumbration in the last sentence of *In a Free State*: 'Seventeen months later these men, or men like them, were to know total defeat in the desert; and news photographs taken from helicopters flying down low were to show them lost, trying to walk back home, casting long shadows on the sand.'

Perhaps because of its shadowy title, there are many shadows in *An Area of Darkness*, but the best image occurs in New Delhi: 'Each Sikh [was] attached to a brisk black shadow.' And in his latest, *Beyond Belief*, a book that is almost devoid of landscape and weather and color, he writes particularly of shadows, how in Iran 'on sunny days light and cloud shadows constantly modeled and remodeled the ridges and the dips of the bare, beige-colored mountains.' In that same book, trees are judged less by their foliage than by their shadows, as with the trees he describes on the outskirts of Peshawar, Pakistan: 'a spindly hybrid poplar that cast little shadow.' And the racecourse in Kuala Lumpur, 'green and sun-struck, with still, black shadows.' And the wall in Tehran that 'cast a broad diagonal of shadow tapering up to the top and there disappearing.' Even people can be shadows, like the servants in Pakistan, 'the thin and dingy shadow people of every Pakistani household.'

It is as if, for Vidia, shadows have substance.

He did not, of course, use language casually. He was particular in his choice of words, which made him a demanding listener, too. Any word he used was intended, and considered; he sought simplicity, and one of his gifts was finding ambiguity and subtle meaning using primary colors. It was unusual for him to use a word such as 'deliquesce,' though he did once, in *An Area of Darkness*; 'nigrescent' he used only in *The Mystic Masseur*. He would say 'cushion-shaped' rather than 'pulvinate,' and 'strong as leather' instead of 'coriaceous,' and would always choose 'delay' over 'cunctation.' Anything that smacked of show, or style, or display, or falsity, anything that was used purely for effect, he disdained. Writing must never call attention to itself. 'I just wish my prose to be very transparent. I don't want the reader to stumble over me.' He was such a stickler for the truth, and so determined to root out any pretense in his work, that a style evolved made of favorite words, a way of expressing an idea and the ideas themselves, a tone of voice, recognizable sentence structures. His style came naturally and was the more distinct because it was a rejection of style. No one wrote like him.

The lightness of his early books was gone. Much of the humor was gone. His writing was denser, plainer, devoid of ornamentation. His gift for summing up a landscape was as strong as ever, but even more abbreviated, the effects concentrated in just a few words, a flash of light, an intrusion of weather, the texture of stone or wood or fading light sharply rendered. His writing acquired a wintry stoicism, full of fine shadings of a single color, powerful for its being monochromatic; a lushness was lost, but he had never trusted lushness. And now, in travel, he let people speak for themselves – sometimes for a dozen pages of monologue, in his attempt to devise a new sort of travel book, which was a chorus of people talking about their lives, a chain of voices, with hardly any intervention on his part.

There was always a lesson for me. I was not so sure that native monologues were the best way to write about a distant country. Vidia always said, 'Make the reader see.' All that talking, like those ten-page confessional speeches in a Russian novel, blurred my vision. His more recent books were shaped like Studs Terkel's tape-recorded narratives, but of a heartless and selective sort – tendentious, a word that Vidia hardly ever used.

He did not parody himself, but he had kept to his habit of thinking out loud. Saying 'It's Major' was his way of testing the possibility on me.

I took it that way. He was trying it out, and also, in his heart, he believed it to be true.

Another day he said, 'Can you meet me in Kensington?'

I said yes, and met Vidia at the appointed place, a crimson telephone booth on a side street.

'Please make a phone call for me,' he said.

Following his instructions, I dialed the number, made the call, and asked for a certain woman; I had made no comment when Vidia told me the woman's name was Margaret. She was summoned to the phone by the man who had answered me in a chilly voice, as though he suspected the ruse. I told Margaret that Vidia would call at a particular time.

'It's much too boring to explain,' Vidia said after I hung up.

He did not have to explain. It was no mystery to me that such a wonderful writer could speak of his present work as Major, and be a guest at a Garden Party at Buckingham Palace (*The Lord Chamberlain is commanded by Her Majesty to invite . . .*), and the next moment would implore me like a child to dial a telephone number, because – surely? – he feared his own undisguisable voice might provoke an unwelcome reaction. He didn't want to be told off. He was human.

Now I knew, as only a friend can, that for all his apparent strength, he could also be weak and unsure, and even unfair, with a coldly sarcastic streak. He looked at the populous continent of Africa and said, 'Bow-and-arrow men!' or 'Cuffy!' He glanced across the English Channel at Holland and said, 'Potato eaters!' He frowned at the whole of the Middle East and grunted, 'Mr Woggy.'

But he had also written subtly of Africa, and appreciatively of Europe, and as for the Middle East, he had written an entire book about Islam. So, while I tried to see him clearly, I kept from judging what I did not understand.

At its most profound, friendship is not a hearty, matey celebration of linked arms and vigorous toasts; it is, rather, a solemn understanding that is hardly ever discussed. Friends rarely use the word 'friendship' and seldom speak of how they are linked. There is a sort of trust that is offered by very few people; there are favors very few can grant: such instances are the test of friendship. With your ego switched off, you accept this person – his demands, his silences – and it is reciprocal. The relationship does not have the hideous complexity of a family's sibling rivalry – that struggling like crabs in a basket. Nor does it have the heat of romantic love or the contractual connection of marriage. Yet a sympathy as deep as love springs from the moment you detect any disturbance or intimation of inadequacy in this other person. You take the rest on faith. It is not belief but acceptance, and even a kind of protection.

Friendship arises less from an admiring love of strength than a sense of gentleness, a suspicion of weakness. It is compassionate intimacy, a powerful kindness, and a knowledge of imperfection. Conversely, the attraction of power seems to me purely sexual in origin, something to do with advancing and strengthening the symmetry in the species, and with animals looking for mates. In the natural world the weak or wounded are outrun and eaten by predators. There are plenty of robust courtships among animals, and the strong have flocking instincts and a pack mentality: animal species succeed because they reject the lame and the halt. Geeks and wimps in the animal world are left to die. Friendship is peculiarly human, and all the implications of friendship lead inevitably to the conclusion that friends make bad mates.

Humans like each other for opposite reasons, because although we might be weak and ineffectual, we are still kind. We have that in common, and much else: our intelligence and sympathy and self-respect. Vidia had liked me long ago in Africa. Before I had dared to admit that I wanted to write a book, he had said, 'You're a writer.'

How helpless I must have seemed. But he saw other strengths in me, something in my heart. He saw my soul in my face, my art in the lines of my palm, my ambition and moods in the slope and stroke of my handwriting.

I had thought he was very strong. We became friends. I saw that he had many weaknesses – and he saw mine. It made us better friends. Most writers are cranks, so friendship among them is rare, and they end up loners. I was lucky.

Friendship means favors. Our friendship had started with a favor, Vidia's saying 'Do you have a motorcar?' And soon after, he did me the favor of reading some things I had written. He was under no obligation; he hardly knew me; I was not his student. The favors were reciprocal. Often the same favor helped both of us. I read *The Mimic Men* in proof form for typos; that was my favor to him. He allowed me the first glimpse of *The Mimic Men* and I learned a great deal; that was his favor to me.

As the years passed, he would ask me for simple mysterious favors, like dialing the telephone number. Now and then he asked me to read the typescript of a book.

A writer asks a friend to read something in typescript – a smudged provisional form – in order to be encouraged. In this lonely and paranoia-inducing job we need friendly words. And unless a writer already thinks a piece of writing is very good, he does not hand it over for inspection and favorable comment. After that, with publication, there are many judgments, but by then the writer has moved on to something else. So the first look and the first praise is crucial, and often it is all that matters. It is a privileged peep into the heart of a writer at his most vulnerable. No writer would allow it unless praise was expected.

'I would like you to look at my new book,' Vidia said. 'It's Major.'

It was *A Bend in the River*, a bundle of typed pages. It was set in Africa. Even before I began reading it, I was apprehensive. Vidia was afraid of 'bush people,' as he said, of 'bow-and-arrow men.' Most of Africa seemed to represent his worst nightmare of brutishness and illiteracy. He was without much hope. 'Africa has no future.'

I opened the book. I read, 'Nazruddin, who sold me the shop cheap, didn't think I would have it easy when I took over.'

The narrator of this perversely plain opening sentence, Salim, was a Muslim. That was something new. As a Brahmin, a half-believing Hindu, Vidia had never shown much interest in Muslims, and he had often been distinctly unsympathetic, blaming Islamic nationalists for the partition of India and for a repressive Pakistan. In Africa he had gravitated to the Hindu *dukawallahs*.

Right away I felt something was wrong, not just with that opening sentence but with some details. Salim ate nothing but beans. Surely a Muslim would eat meat and would make sure the animal had been slaughtered in the proper way, so that it was *halal*, the Islamic equivalent of kosher. Vidia had unconsciously imposed his own bean-eating on his narrator. I made a note in the margin: *Eats only beans?*

The novel showed an intimate knowledge of Kisangani, at a bend in the Zaire River. In an earlier magazine piece about the Congo, 'A New King for the Congo,' Vidia had written of how Stanleyville — Stanley Falls Station — had been the actual haunt of Mr Kurtz, the heart of darkness, and 'seventy years later at this bend in the river, something like Conrad's fantasy came to pass.' He meant the tyrannical reign of Mobutu.

I found myself reading the typescript quickly, finding little to comment upon. It was a good book. It contained the somnolence as well as the random violence of Africa, and Vidia's nose anatomized the stinks and putrefaction, the atmosphere of imperial failure and ruin. It was also a love story. Salim has an affair with Yvette, the wife of an expatriate. Salim is also a very prickly fellow. One day he feels slighted by Yvette, so he kicks her. She cries. Moments later she gets into bed, inviting him to join her. He realizes that it is the end of their affair. 'Her body had a softness, a pliability, and a great warmth.' One expects that he will make love to her. He holds her legs apart. What Salim did next made me swing the typescript away from my face: 'I spat at her between the legs until I had no more spit.' *What?* Yvette objects – naturally – and she shouts and struggles. So Salim hits her again. 'Bone struck against bone again; my hand ached at every blow.'

I spat at her between the legs until I had no more spit.

The difficulty I always had with Vidia's scenes of sex or violence became almost overwhelming. Vidia's scenes were aggressive, strange, joyless. Women's bodies were pathetic and frail; they smelled. He was forever finding women leaky and damp, in sadly wrinkled clothes, creases at the crotch, stains at the armpits. Even when they tried to correct the condition, they could not win. In *In a Free State*, Bobby finds a sachet in Linda's room. 'It was a vaginal deodorant with an appalling name. The slut, Bobby thought, the slut.'

And in *The Mimic Men* there had been the whore in Spain whom Ralph Singh brought to his hotel room: 'A figure from hell with a smiling child's face.' She is very fat. The act of love is like a visit from a proctologist. 'Nails, tongue, breath and lips were the instruments of this disembodied probing ... The probing went lower. I was turned over on my belly. The probing continued with the same instruments.'

Disgust and desire were mingled with a distinct hostility toward women in *Guerrillas*. The 'white liberal' woman, Jane, becomes aroused when she is viciously slapped, 'so hard that her jaw jarred ... and then she was slapped again.' She discovers 'to her dismay and disgust that she was moist.' Odd that Vidia, of all people, found any veracity in the misogynistic cliché of slapping as foreplay and a beating as an aphrodisiac. Later, in a Black Power commune,

Jane is raped by Jimmy Ahmed, who is the commune's leader. Jimmy has a hair-trigger problem: 'Just like that, without convulsions, his little strained strength leaked out of him, and it was all over.' But forget hanky-panky: Jane is more aroused by being slapped around. And Jimmy is actually homosexual: 'He longed for the feel of Bryant's warm firm flesh and his relieving mouth and tongue.' Nevertheless, Jane stays in the commune, only to be violently sodomized by Jimmy, who taunts her: 'You didn't bring your Vaseline.' In this act, his *ejaculatio praecox* is apparently cured: 'He drove deeper and deeper until he was almost sitting upright on her.' Very soon after, at Jimmy's command, Jane is hacked to death with machetes.

In his essay on Evita Peron, Vidia mentions Evita's full red lips, hinting at 'her reputed skill in fellatio.' He describes the machismo of Argentine males and their single-mindedness on the subject of sodomy. 'The macho's conquest of a woman is complete only when he has buggered her . . . *La tuve en el culo*, I've had her in the arse . . . a kind of sexual black mass.' Elsewhere in his writing he would describe a man with a complexion 'like risen dough' and imply, and sometimes assert, it to be the clear indication that the man was an ardent masturbator, much as Dickens had implied the same nocturnal autoeroticism by giving Uriah Heep circles around his eyes. If it is fair to regard the passions and fantasies of a writer's characters as those of the writer himself – and why not? – then I found Vidia's observations unsettling.

'In the old days I would have grown dizzy with excitement here,' Vidia wrote recently in *Beyond Belief*, describing the crowds of Pakistani whores in the red-light district of Lahore. 'Up to my mid-thirties I had been attracted to prostitutes and sought them out.' If that was true, how did it square with his looking me in the eye in Kampala, when he was thirty-four, and saying, 'I have given up sex'? It did not square at all, of course, and I now believed the later statement, of his having been a whore-hopper, which was why I was convinced that only with the passage of time did one know the truth.

But I had *A Bend in the River* in my hand. The spitting scene stayed in my mind, as well as that unpromising first sentence. The rest I liked. We met for tea. I brought the typescript.

'What do you think, Paul?'

'You're right. It's Major.'

'No suggestions?'

'The first sentence is wonderful,' I said. 'But there is an even better one in the sixth paragraph.'

'Show me.'

It was in the middle of the paragraph. It ran, 'The world is what it is; men who are nothing, who allow themselves to become nothing, have no place in it.'

It was certainly a mouthful for a semi-educated Indian shop-keeper in the Congolese bush, yet it seemed to me the most effective way of starting the novel.

Vidia circled it, made a balloon for it, and indicated where it should be inserted, at the top of the first paragraph.

'You're right, Paul,' he said. 'I'm sure that's better. It will sell more copies this way.'

'One other thing. Salim eats an awful lot of beans. He never eats meat.'

'Patsy said something about that.'

'Give him some meat, I think.'

A Bend in the River was shortlisted for the Booker Prize that year. I was one of the Booker judges. I reread the book, one of many submissions for the important prize, and saw that Vidia had transposed the sentence, as I had suggested. He had also made Salim a credible carnivore. But when it came to the decision, I voted against it. Mine was the deciding vote. I preferred Patrick White's novel, *The Twyborn Affair*.

'Patrick White? Over my dead body,' one of the panelists said.

Another said to me, 'I thought Naipaul was your friend.'

'So what? I didn't like the spitting. I wasn't convinced by the ending – all that to-ing and fro-ing, the visit to London.'

In the end, we compromised on *Offshore*, by Penelope Fitzgerald, and most people jeered at our choice. They said Naipaul should have won. But Vidia had already won the Booker Prize with *In a Free State*. It was thought that because I was a judge, Vidia would be a shoo-in. Not at all.

Though Vidia maintained that writing was fair and that books always made their own way, he had been impressed by the effectiveness of Shiva's agent. I had introduced Shiva to this agent, who was also my agent. Vidia asked for an introduction and very soon afterwards became a client. Vidia's advances and the terms of his contracts were greatly improved. He might soon have his million.

'I am not happy with my publisher,' Vidia said on another occasion.

I introduced him to my publisher.

'What can I do to tempt him?' my publisher said.

'Give him a million pounds.'

'Out of the question.'

'Then get a table at a fabulous restaurant for dinner. Not lunch. "Dinner is grander." Then let Vidia order the wine. It's not a guarantee of success, but at least he won't get up in the middle and stalk away.'

'Do you think he would have the temerity to do that?'

'It has happened before.'

I was invited to the dinner. My publisher was nervous. Vidia ordered a white Burgundy and a prawn entrée. But the prawns were bad. Vidia said he had to leave. I drove him back to Kensington just in time for him to be nauseated in the privacy of his own home. He found another publisher. It wasn't the food, however, it was the money – he was still aiming at a million.

One of the chores of book publication is the writing of jacket copy. This copy is also recycled in the publisher's catalogue. When he received the proposed jacket copy for *A Turn in the South*, Vidia pronounced it unsuitable. He did not rage. He wrote a long, patient letter to his publisher, Viking, explaining his intentions. He closed the letter: 'A writer sets out to do a particular thing. He should do that thing, and should feel that he has done it. But every real book catches fire, goes beyond a writer's intention. So it happens that readers and critics find other meanings in a real book. I was hoping that someone at Viking might have said something interesting in the blurb.'

But no one had, and the agent called me, saying, 'Paul, Vidia asked me to ring you. We need a favor.'

This was in the month of August. I had just ended a book tour for *Riding the Iron Rooster*, my book about China. I was working on a novel, *My Secret History*. I listened with a sinking heart.

'Would you, as a favor, write the jacket blurb for *A Turn in the South*?'

It meant putting my novel aside to perform the most menial and thankless work in publishing. It meant closely reading Vidia's entire book, then writing the blurb – in effect a short, insightful, and persuasive rave – and sending it to the publisher, who was probably on vacation. It was a monumental intrusion into my writing life, something no writer – and certainly not Vidia – would consider for an instant.

'I'll do it,' I said.

The agent laughed at my pliability. He was grateful, of course, and also surprised. But Vidia felt he was in a spot, and I remembered his saying years before, 'That's what friends are for.'

A bound proof was sent to me. I read it with interest and I liked it, the apparent simplicity of the journey in the American South: Vidia's appreciation, something resembling humility in his approach, with no bombast and a genuine curiosity. He defined the sort of travel book he was writing and in so doing made helpful distinctions between other sorts. It was not possible to write a conventional travel book about the United States – a book in which, as Vidia explained, the traveler said, 'This is me here. This is me getting off the old native bus and being led by strange boys, making improper proposals, to some squalid lodging. This is me having a drink in a bar with some local characters. This is me getting lost later that night.'

That kind of book, very common, depicted the traveler 'defining himself against a foreign background.' He added that 'depending on who he is, the book can be attractive,' but it worked only if the traveler was 'alien or outlandish in some way.' Yet this method seldom worked for the traveler in the United States. 'The place is not and cannot be alien in the simple way an African country is alien. It is too well known, too photographed, too written about; and, being more organized and less informal, it is not so open to casual inspection.'

This was to me an inspired lesson in the varieties of travel writing. Vidia also seemed, once again, to be speaking directly to me, a traveler on native buses, a buyer of drinks for local characters, making a meal of my losing my way. Twenty-three years on, I was still learning from him.

So I began my blurb, '*A Turn in the South* is a completely fresh look at an area and a situation which have become caricaturish for some and incomprehensible for others.'

Knowing that Vidia would be scrutinizing every word, I wrote carefully, self-consciously, with the sort of precision and invention Vidia expected, struggling to make it right: a forty-eight-year-old man revisiting the humility and strain of his apprenticeship. The three hundred words took me two days. I sent the piece, via the agent, to Vidia, like a student submitting a crucial essay to his professor. It was both a test of friendship and a test of skill.

The reply came back from the agent, a scribble: *V. very grateful.*

A more unusual favor was asked of me by Vidia when he was writing *The Enigma of Arrival*. The germ of the book was old. In 1966 Vidia had shown me some pages of a story he intended to return to again. 'I warm up this way,' he said. To get into a writing mood, he copied and recopied the pages, describing a classical scene pictured in a painting by de Chirico. After two decades he was using those same pages as part of a novel.

I met him for tea in his tiny flat in Queen's Gate Terrace.

'I was assaulted in Gloucester Road,' he said. 'A Negro approached me. He made as if to walk by and then hit me hard on the side of the head – *whack*!'

'That's terrible, Vidia.'

'It was a shock.'

But he was calm. Beside him was a large file folder containing a four-inch stack of paper, undoubtedly a typescript.

'I am at a very delicate point in my book,' Vidia said. He glanced at the file folder.

'Is that it?'

He nodded gravely. 'It's Major.'

He did not say that it was a continuation of his old story; he said nothing about it other than that it was Major. He only mentioned that he had not finished it.

'I may never finish it.'

What a funny thing to say, I thought. I said, 'But you have to.'

'What if my brain is damaged?'

'Your brain is fine, Vidia.'

'What if someone else assaults me? One of these idlers one sees on the Gloucester Road. He might do serious damage. I would then be incapable of finishing the book. How could I, with a damaged brain?'

'In that case, I see, you'd be mentally unfit. But that's just speculation.'

'It is a real possibility! I tell you, I was attacked by a Negro!'

'Maybe you should stay in Wiltshire.'

'I shall. But one comes up for the odd errand. One's bank manager. One's publishers. One's haircut,' he said. 'Paul, I want you to read this typescript. Read it closely.'

'Of course. I'd be happy to.'

'And if my brain is damaged and I cannot continue, I want you to finish writing the book.'

I leaned back to give myself perspective and to see whether he was smiling. But no, he was stern and certain, and he was brisk in his certainty, like a warrior making a will.

'You'll notice there are many repetitions. Those are intentional. Keep the repetitions. And the rhythm, the way the sentences flow – keep that. You'll see how the narrative builds. Keep building, let it flow.'

From the way he spoke, I had already, it seemed, been commissioned to finish writing *The Enigma of Arrival*, and he was brain damaged, sitting by while I scribbled, the ultimate test of the Sorcerer's Apprentice, his snarelike shadow falling over me.

'What do you think, Paul?'

'It would be an honor, of course. And a challenge. A bit like Ford Madox Ford and Conrad collaborating on a novel, or Stevenson and his stepson Lloyd writing something together.'

'No, no. This is Major.'

I went home with the heavy typescript. I read it – three quarters of the book – and at the end my confidence was gone. There was no way I could finish the book or comment on it. I didn't even like it. It seemed a studied monotony – repetitive, as he had said; indistinct, allusive, but fogbound, enigmatic in every way, a ponderous agglomeration of the dullest rural incidents. I had never read anything like it. It might be a masterpiece like *Finnegans Wake*, the sort of book people studied but could not read consecutively, an ambitious failure, something for the English Department to explicate and defend.

The Bungalow and Wilsford were in it, and so was a glimpse of Stephen Tennant – his plump pink thigh, his straw hat. Not very funny, though. The nutter seemed to represent the decline of Englishness rather than (as I thought) the apogee of the landlord as drag queen. Julian Jebb was in the book. He was unmistakable, his 'little old woman's face.' He was called Alan. I knew him to be an accomplished television producer. Vidia depicted him as a drunken flatterer, rather pathetic and hollow. He was 'theatrical.' Jebb's suicide was in it, in the middle of a dismissive paragraph, with less compassion than if Jebb had passed a kidney stone. 'And then one day I heard – some days after the event – that he had taken some pills one night after a bout of hard drinking and died. It was a theatrical kind of death.'

But what threw me was this: 'One autumn afternoon I had a slight choking fit as I walked past Jack's old cottage and the derelict farmyard. The fit passed by the time I had got around the corner, cleared the farmyard, and left behind the old metal and tangled wire and timber junk below the beeches. (Not the birches near the firepit; they were on the other side of the way. These beeches were at the edge of the farmyard, big trees now in their prime, their lowest branches very low, providing a wonderful rich, enclosing shade in the summer that made me think of George Borrow in *The Romany Rye* and *Lavengro*.) Past the beeches and the farm, in the familiar solitude of the grassy way, I began to breathe easily again . . .'

It was at this point that I had a choking fit of my own. I could never enter into this narrative. I did not understand it. My bafflement made me anxious. What was this book about? The writing was so deliberately plain, so humorless, so obstinate in denying itself pleasure that even when it was being particular it was indistinct, as in the choking-fit passage, with the beeches and the birches. But I had only part of the novel. When Vidia finished it I would understand, I was sure. There was no way on earth that I could write a word of this.

'You must finish this yourself,' I said when I saw Vidia again. 'It's beyond me.'

'What if my brain is damaged?'

'It won't be damaged in Wiltshire by anyone. Just stay there and work. Please, Vidia, I can't do this.'

'You can see that it's Major.'

'Absolutely.'

He knew I admired V. S. Pritchett. He told me the proof that Pritchett was second-rate was that he was still writing short stories as he approached the age of ninety and still found writing enjoyable: 'It's frightfully easy for him!' Vidia announced in an interview, 'I have done an immense amount of work,' and speaking of the quality of his writing, he said, 'It's a great achievement we're talking about.'

Pritchett himself had said – truly, I think – that all writers were at heart fanatical.

The Enigma of Arrival was published and was found by many reviewers to be enigmatic. Vidia said he paid no attention to reviewers. One English reviewer, known for his oldfangledness and his pipestuffing rusticity, hailed the novel as a masterpiece. Derek Walcott disagreed. He did not like it at all. This was a change. Vidia had quoted Derek Walcott to me with approval many times. Walcott had dedicated an early poem, 'Laventille,' to Vidia – it was about a visit to a poor district in rural Trinidad. I had understood the two writers to be friends, and I had admired Walcott's poetry as much as I admired Vidia's prose.

Walcott attacked Vidia in his review. 'The myth of Naipaul as a phenomenon, as a singular, contradictory genius . . . has long been a farce. It is a myth he chooses to encourage – though he alone knows why . . . There is something alarmingly venal in all this dislocation and despair. Besides, it is not true. There is instead another truth. Naipaul's prejudice.'

Walcott went on to say that Vidia's frankness was nothing more than bigotry. 'If Naipaul's attitude towards Negroes, with its nasty little sneers . . . was turned on Jews, for example, how many people would praise him for his frankness?' Privately, he called him V. S. Nightfall.

Being black himself, Walcott had some authority in this matter, but Vidia was also a man of color. Speaking strictly of tinctures, Vidia was a double espresso to Derek's café au lait, which was why from time to time Vidia had been discriminated against in England for showing this face. The charge of racism was serious, but it was odd, too, given Vidia's race. And Walcott was attacking someone who admired him: one of the few living writers whom Vidia praised. Though he had been born on St Lucia, in the Windward Islands, Walcott had become a permanent resident (and prominent writer) of Trinidad in 1958, when he was still in his twenties. He was a near contemporary of Vidia's, a fellow islander, and in many respects a brother writer. Two brown men from the same dot on the map.

I did not mention the review to Vidia. It was my favor to him.

A few years later, Derek Walcott won the Nobel Prize for literature. Because the prize is essentially political (a Pole this year, a South American next year, a Trinidadian the year after), it meant that Vidia had missed his chance. He would probably never get it. Two Trinidadian Nobel laureates? It was as unlikely as two Albanians.

Vidia might have muttered, 'There they go, pissing on literature,' but I doubted it. Derek Walcott was someone he read and remembered.

So I did not mention the Nobel Prize ever again. Another favor.

Part Four

Reversals

16

Poetry of Departures

Suddenly Vidia was honored – at fifty-eight a knight, and Pat a lady by association. Such gongs in England were mostly granted to older people – Angus Wilson at seventy, V. S. Pritchett and Stephen Spender at eighty, P. G. Wodehouse at ninety – and to nearly everyone else they never came at all. It was especially rare to find a writer's name on the Honours List, because writers were suspect, had nothing to give to the politicians who helped draw up the list, had no allies in the government, were notorious carpers and boat-rockers. Actors were a better bet and much more popular. As Vidia had once said, titles were usually awarded to the more devious of the Queen's subjects. Even so, Vidia got the lowest order of knighthood, the Knight Batchelor, rather than the grander Knight of the Thistle (KT) or, the grandest of all, Knight Commander of the Order of St Michael and St George (KCMG, which to insiders stood for 'the King Calls Me God').

It might have come about, as happens in Britain, because Vidia knew a lord or two. One was the plain Hugh Thomas I had met at Vidia's house in Stockwell thirty years before; he had been elevated to the Baron Thomas of Swynnerton, and as his peerage showed, he was thick with Thatcher. One of the pleasures of my seventeen years as an alien bystander in Britain was seeing how the ordinary names of familiar people were festooned by titles and sometimes transformed by baronetcies and lordships. Simple Smith or Jones in his brown suit, his knees shiny from his being arse-creeper to the party in power, now bore a title befitting a twelfth-century crusader and became the unapproachable Lord Futtock of Shallow Bowels, waving a banner with a strange device. 'You're just envious,' English people whinnied at me when I shared these skeptical sentiments, and of course I was envious, for while the honorees said it made no difference, it manifestly did. Among other things, a title assured the bearer an excellent table in a restaurant.

When she knighted Vidia at Buckingham Palace (for reasons he did not explain, Vidia left Pat at home), the Queen bobbled her notes and said vaguely, 'Naipaul. You're in books.'

Dissolve in a flashback to a food-splashed table at the Connaught and the remains of lunch, the last of the wine, bread crusts, sticky spoons, the white bill primly folded in half on a white saucer, Vidia still chewing and saying, *A title is nothing . . . I have the idea that they should sell titles at the post office . . . You go in, buy some stamps, and paste them into a little book . . . Three books of stamps would get you an MBE. Six for an OBE. A dozen books of stamps would be worth a knighthood.*

'Yes, Your Majesty,' Vidia said, bowing deeply. But Vidia's cut-price knighthood, by his own calculation, was perhaps worth only eight books of stamps.

The conglobated Sanskritic syllables that made up his almost unpronounceable name did not easily attach to the archaic Anglo-Saxon handle of a knighthood. Nevertheless, he was now Sir Vidiadhar Surajprasad Naipaul. The only precedents of his sort were Indian cricketers and politicians and the oiliest Indian tycoons. It was impossible to know how he would style himself, but after some experimentation he settled on Sir Vidia. Pat was the Lady Naipaul. And it can't have escaped her sense of the absurd to reflect on how one day she was peeling the sprouts and a little tearful over the stale sponge cake she had bought at Tesco, and the next day, with her name change, she sounded like the heroine of an Arthurian legend.

I was transformed too, or at least I understood the role I had played from my earliest days with Vidia, for in a sense he had always been a knight. I saw that I had always been his squire – driver, sidekick, spear carrier, flunky, gofer; diligent, tactful, helpful – delicately finessing the occasional intervention. *Paul, I want you to deal with this.* It was my luck. I had never contradicted him; we had never quarreled. Because he was not the perfect knight, I had to be the perfect squire, Sir Vidia's shadow.

It seemed to me he knew that. When he bought his first computer and got some lessons in using it, he wrote to me, just rambling, to test the printer. He was delighted that he had managed to make it work, another technological triumph for the man who had begun his writing life with a dunk-and-scratch quill pen in a little school in Trinidad.

On the bottom of the crisply printed page of the letter, he wrote in black ink – unbidden, voluntarily, what was he thinking? – *Your work is such an example and an encouragement to me.*

Hadn't I many times said or suggested those same words to him? His repeating them back to me was a gift, particularly now, at the moment of his greatest eminence.

'I'd like to visit you,' I said to him on the phone.

I had news. Again I put my bike on the train and rode second class to Salisbury. I had been feeling ill that day, the sense of a wasting disease that depression seems to bring on, a spiritless and leaden feeling that was deepened by the sight of bare branches and wet fields, coots and moorhens toiling frantically across muddy ponds. Hopelessness had robbed me of my strength, and cycling uphill from Salisbury to Salterton just made me feel worse.

'Tell me, tell me, tell me,' Vidia said at the gate of his house. There were no obvious signs of knightliness in his demeanor. 'What's wrong?'

He had the strongest intuition of anyone I had ever known. He was sometimes wrong, but more often he had an unnerving ability to detect my moods, particularly my low spirits. This may have been because they so closely reflected his own moods and matched his own low spirits, his intuition an example of a known echo, perhaps often the case when a person is prescient – prescience being the ringing of a familiar bell. It helped that he was always so solitary. In one of the few works Vidia ever recommended to me, *Death in Venice*, Thomas Mann had written, 'Solitude gives birth to the original in us, to beauty unfamiliar and perilous – to poetry. But also, it gives birth to the opposite; to the perverse, the illicit, the absurd.' Vidia's solitude had similarly driven him in both directions.

I parked my bike. I said, 'My wife and I are splitting up.'

'God.'

Pat appeared, smiling wanly at the kitchen door. She looked so ill that I could say nothing more about myself. She was like an apparition, ghostly white – white hair, white skin, no color in her lips, and her whiteness was a kind of translucence almost, the papery skin traced with spidery veins like lines in parchment. She was breathless, stoop-shouldered, a tottering insomniac, and she looked at me with colorless eyes. I kissed her and, holding her, I could feel her bones, all her frailty in my hands. The Lady Naipaul.

'How are you, Paul?'

'I'm fine.'

I had just biked fifteen miles and had my health, so what was I complaining about?

In the wine cellar, choosing a bottle while Pat made lunch, Vidia and I talked about my situation. My wife and I had agreed to separate. I would be leaving England.

I said, 'I always thought I would stay ten years. Look, it's almost eighteen now that I've been here.'

'Good things have happened to you,' he said. His back was turned. He was looking at the wine bottles in the racks. 'Haven't you felt that people have been kind?'

'Yes,' I said.

People had been kind, yet I had never felt like anything but an alien bystander in their midst. I could not help thinking of all the English people I knew in the States who, in much less than eighteen years, had been accepted and become established. They were bureaucrats, politicians, businessmen, educators, local writers: the bossy Scotsman in his employment agency, the Ulsterman flush with real estate, the pushy Liverpudlian on the planning board, denying me permission to subdivide some land in Massachusetts, where I was born and he wasn't. I saw them on television, or met them. I knew the accents, they couldn't fool me – London, Birmingham, the West Country, Cornwall, Wales, the North. They were important in America and part of the system and moaned or boasted like everyone else. When had I ever been part of the English system? I had always been an alien, like almost every other immigrant. The people who had been kind to me had also been waiting for me to leave.

I said some of this to Vidia. He was crouched near the wine racks, hovering over his selection.

'But England has been good to you,' he said.

'Of course. I suppose it's been the making of me.'

'About the other thing,' he said. He meant the separation. 'You don't have to leave. It's your house. Your property. You can stay.'

'I don't care about the house. Why do material things seem so sad just now? I get depressed just being in it.'

'God.'

He was so shocked by my news that I felt awkward pursuing it. I said, 'This has become quite a wine cellar. It's so much bigger than the last time I saw it.'

'These are my clarets,' Vidia said, sounding relieved that I had changed the subject. He indicated bottles on racks and in cut-open cases, the necks protruding. 'These are my Burgundies – white Burgundy here, red there. This year's reds are big fruity wines. My Bordeaux are tannic. I'm laying them down. Last year's Sauternes are perfect – rich, concentrated.' He picked out a bottle. 'This is big.'

I looked at the label: a Bordeaux.

'This is fleshy. I am waiting a bit,' he said. He replaced it. He brought out another bottle. 'This is crisp. A little fruity but soft. You'll like it. It's classic.'

That word an echo from the Connaught lunch all those years ago. Easy to remember the day, not because we discussed knighthoods but because the bill had cleaned me out and I had gone back to Dorset broke. This classic was also a white Burgundy, each sip a taste of destitution.

'It might be better not to say anything to Patsy,' he said. 'About the other thing.'

'She's not looking well.'

'She's all right,' Vidia said.

Lunch was the same meal we always had: poached fish, parsleyed potatoes, salad. And the wine, small measures of it. Vidia sipped. He kept the bottle out of my reach. He was the pourer. He ate with precise manipulation of knife and fork, and it was apparent that he was still having trouble with his teeth. Just behind him on the wall was the Hockney etching of the hairy naked man in the rumpled bed.

As at so many other meals with Vidia, I used the occasion to verify stories I had heard: *Did you really say that? Did you really do that?* And he usually said yes, or he corrected the elaboration that gossip had given a story. I wanted to ask him finally about the Ved Mehta tale, but something held me back, my old wish to believe that every word was true. I asked him about the dinners: *Those are not my vegetables*, and *Those vegetables are tainted*. Totally true. A mutual friend had reported Vidia's saying over and over, *I want to be immensely famous!* But that was too sensitive an utterance to ask him to verify.

Talk about cricket turned to talk of cricket fans, and then Harold Pinter. Vidia had been to Pinter's recently; their link was Lady Antonia. Pinter's son, he said, was very unhappy – and wouldn't you be, with a case of alopecia as bad as his? Pinter had shown Vidia a photo of the boy as much younger, years before, with all his hair, smiling, the son he had once been, now a fantasy. Vidia found this a telling denial.

'How are your boys?'

'Marcel got a First at Cambridge and is now at Yale. Louis is at Oxford.'

'God.'

We talked about a newspaper owner. Vidia said, 'He is a very stupid man. His problem, of course, is that he can't read. He is a monkey.'

Pat said, 'He has done some very good things. Everyone predicted he would fail.'

'His successes mean nothing. He thinks publishing is the same as printing. He might as well be selling bags of rice as newspapers. Or shoes. He has no idea.'

Pat was protesting, and in seconds tears were running down her cheeks. She sobbed, telling Vidia he was unfair, while he continued his meal, using his knife and fork like a lab technician, dissecting the fish.

The first time I had witnessed such a quarrel was in Uganda twenty-five years before, and it had been repeated at various times in the intervening years. It was always a surprise, always upsetting. Tears made me helpless. And to see a woman so obviously ill in tears was much worse, because the tears seemed to arise from a different source, not the petty argument but something deeper that was almost despair.

'I won't have a row,' Vidia said sternly. 'Do stop chuntering.'

'Let's change the subject,' I said. 'Have you been to any art auctions, Vidia?'

'Just to look,' Vidia said, while Pat sniffled. 'Christie's had some delicious botanical things. I've changed my mind about all that company art. I've seen so much that's rubbish.'

He was expert on the subject of Indian art, all periods, from the Moguls to the East India Company to the last years of the raj. He had a large collection. This was not only a safe subject, but also one in which I wanted enlightenment. I had learned from him in the past and had myself bought watercolors and aquatints.

I maintained this conversation until Pat recovered. Even as I sat there, it seemed the basis of a good short story. A man goes to his best friend to tell him of his marital woes and that he will soon be separated. The friend protests – he must stay married, it is the best outcome – but all the while the friend quarrels with his wife in a more acrimonious way than the man has ever done with the wife from whom he is separating. Perhaps he changes his mind . . .

'Excuse me,' I said.

'It's at the top of the stairs,' Vidia said, having divined the purpose of my apology.

Heading to the bathroom, passing Pat's room, I saw on her bedside table Ibn Battuta's *Travels* and John Locke's *Two Treatises on Government*. I had read Ibn Battuta, one of the world's greatest travelers, but I did not know the Locke book. If I read it, I thought, I might know Pat better.

She was in the kitchen when I came downstairs.

Vidia said, returning to my troubles, 'You will know what to do when the time comes.'

Once before, after a heart-to-heart talk, he had written to say, 'The sexual nature of the relationship that is exercising you does, I fear, go with the fatigue and the irritation. The fatigue and the irritation prove the strength of the relationship . . . You simply have to live with it, as you have lived so far; there is no way now that it can be neatened.'

We had coffee in the living room – Pat, very quiet now, serving; Vidia, thoughtful; and I felt simply desperate. I needed a formula from him, not the old one of 'You'll be all right,' but something subtler.

Pat said, 'Why don't you take Paul for a walk? It will be dark soon.'

'Paul has expressed not the slightest interest in going for a walk.'

'I'd like to go for a walk,' I said.

The last time I visited, I had come by car. Vidia had suggested a drive, and we went up the road to Wilsford Manor. Barmy Stephen Tennant had died and the manor had been sold. It was being torn down and the estate bulldozed to be turned into a housing development. Seeing us surveying the property, a woman approached Vidia and said, 'Are you Mr Naipaul?' Vidia shook his head and said 'No.'

The little red Japanese maple I had given him to plant had been on my mind. I sometimes laughed when I thought of it. How was I to have known that he had planted a green garden? A green garden was unheard of, and so was his dictum that large lawns make the viewer feel tired at the thought of all the grass that has to be cut.

We looked at the tree, no longer little but now spreading, with a thickening trunk and strong limbs and spindly branches.

'The leaves start out red, of course, but their final color is green. So that's lovely.'

We walked behind the house, down the narrow descending track to boggy land and the small swift stream that flowed under the flat wooden footbridge.

'Things will work out,' Vidia said.

'I've lost my way.'

'This is a natural thing. It is not a calamity. Look at your life.'

'It doesn't look like anything. It doesn't seem to matter.'

He was staring at the stream. 'All that water, rushing. It simply gathers here. There are good-sized fish in it.'

I said, 'I feel dreadful. I shouldn't have come.'

'No,' Vidia said. 'You have something on your mind. Very well, leave her.'

'He was relieved,' Vidia used to say after he had given someone advice like this: 'Don't ever write again,' or 'Go away from Uganda,' or 'Leave her.' He wanted me to say I was relieved. What had at first seemed a depressing possibility had, with his encouragement, become an act of liberation.

'You will gain perspective,' Vidia said.
I thought,

> Sometimes you hear, fifth hand,
> As epitaph:
> *He chucked up everything*
> *And just cleared off,*
> And always the voice will sound
> Certain you approve
> This audacious, purifying,
> Elemental move.

We were walking along a path beside the dark, greasy-looking stream. I wondered whether my presence had provoked his quarrel with Pat, for Pat felt weak and needed witnesses. Perhaps she felt overpowered when she was alone with him.

Vidia walked ahead. I had the sense I would never see him again, never see Pat, would never come back. The English had been right to keep me at arm's length. I was unreliable, uncommitted, hideously skeptical, a mocker. And now I was bolting.

On the riverbank I remembered walking with him in Africa in places like this – sodden, untidy grass flopped over and flattened; twisted trees and a brimming river gurgling past – like the highlands of Kenya and those walks on the Rwanda trip and in fields outside Kampala, up the Bombo road. We had grown older and closer in age, the way middle age converges, and now never talked about writing. He hated hearing about writers and books, and I did too.

Out of the blue I said, 'I have never had a worse problem than this.'

Vidia said, 'Problems are good. You're a writer. You'll do something with them.'

'I'd rather not have them,' I said. Something in me was protesting.

'Problems are good,' he said again, and kept walking through the damp grass.

I took this to mean he did not want to hear about it. I did not blame him. It was not that he had refused to offer a solution. There was no solution, except for me to go.

'Leave her,' he said. 'You know my rule.'

His rule was: Never give anyone a second chance. It had been explained by his narrator Ralph Singh, in *The Mimic Men*. It stated that if someone let you down – failed you, offended you, broke a promise – you sent the person away. It was over. And if the person who let you down had been a dear friend or lover or a great employee, there was even more reason to end the relationship, because there had been so much more at stake. Friends were the last people who should fail you and so were the last people to whom you should give another chance.

Vidia seemed preoccupied, or perhaps he was being cautious. I was uncertain of his mood and somewhat wary. We were now, twenty-five years later, still strangers to each other in some respects – still had secrets. That kept us watchful and a little remote when we were alone with each other.

I said, 'I like the way your trees are filling in. It's beautiful.'

'That was my plan. To hide the house with some shrubs and trees and that high hedge.'

Hiding was what all of us did, so that we could work. I had lived here once, not far away, in Dorset. That was the past. I had visited him with the sense of something beginning for me, and on this last visit my life here was ending.

Cake had been cut for us at the house, apportioned on plates, with tea and a tray. Pat poured and apologized, a white-faced old lady now, whom I had once desired in the garden of the Kaptagat Arms, long ago in Africa.

Vidia showed me some slides he had taken on the Rwanda trip. I had never seen them before. One showed me in my horn-rimmed glasses and tweed jacket, when I had scorned travelers in Africa who wore desert boots and safari khakis. I was twenty-something, among the Virunga volcanoes.

Vidia said, 'It is an amazing image, not only for the background, but also because you have changed so little.'

That proved one of his theories, that I was truthful and still had all my marbles. If I had gotten fat or changed physically in any other way, it would have showed I was morally weak.

'Don't be sad,' Vidia said when I left, wheeling my bike to the gate. 'You'll be all right.'

But as I went down the country lane at dusk, I thought: Problems are not good. I don't need them. I don't want them. I have had enough problems.

There was something so melancholy on this dark afternoon. It was me, a big man on his bicycle, trying to lull myself with the faint click inside the axle as I pedaled alongside the battered briars and hedgerows and black trees, under a sky like cat fur. At the same curve in the road a pair of pheasants flew up, and this time they frightened me. I uttered a cry, and a pain creased my heart. But just after that I saw the birds flying. I felt better and a little hopeful.

17

A Wedding is a Happy Funeral

I seemed to evaporate. I died. I disappeared. I left London, left my home and family. As the ghost of the man I had been, I traveled across half the world looking for a simpler place and sunshine and no memories. Two years I spent wandering the Pacific. I went back to Africa to look at where my writing life had begun – but before Vidia, before Yomo even – no specific memories, only the reminder of big dusty African plains and dusty faces and mud huts. A slim, quiet girl I had taught in Malawi was now enormous and jolly in a wide loose dress, three of her seven children goggling at me from the door of her hut. I could not find Yomo. In the north of Malawi I saw elephants, a family herd, devouring the bush, chewing on trees. I went to Mexico and Ecuador. I did no writing. I asked myself, Are problems good?

The Pacific drew me back. I paddled a kayak among whales and slipped into the sea to hear them singing. Dawn over the volcano cone on Haleakala; a Trobriand Islander whispering 'Meesta Boll'; the fragrance of gardenias, the total eclipse of the sun, the taste of honey from my own bees, the heat in my bones from sleeping at noon on the sand at Waimea Bay; birdsong, blue skies. I saw the connections in all this and thought, God is a fish. And so I came back from the dead.

But everything else had ended, not just my other life but – was it my age? – friends and relations began to die. In the past, people fell ill and recovered, but now they got sick, they declined, and the next thing I knew they were dead. Five women from breast cancer, one from leukemia, and my best friend in Hawaii, ailing but saying 'I'll be fine,' and dropping dead. After long illnesses two uncles and two aunts; several neighbors – heart attacks, cancer, and AIDS.

None of these were drownings or road accidents or plane crashes or blunders in the home. They were not preventable. In each case the body failed: it was death as doom, the limit of mortality. I never went to so many funerals. And still I was not prepared for what was to come.

One morning my mother called me in Hawaii to say that my father, who had been frail for some years, had been taken to the hospital on Cape Cod. I had gotten out of bed to answer the phone. She would keep me posted, she said. I lay down again and the piercing fragrance of a gardenia in a dish near my bed sweetened a reverie of my father. It was a real reverie, a dreamlike sequence of images: my father's face, the aroma like a sunburst of pollen, the perfumed flower (a bouquet of which my mother had held, next to my father, in their wedding portrait), the whiteness of the petals, the fullness of the blossom, the dark green leaves, the sweetness of the dish near me – following the whole sequence of associations from my father to the cut stem.

When I got to the image of the snipped-off stem and ached remembering my father's sweet nature, I realized that no matter how vital he might seem, he was dying.

The phone rang again, my mother. 'Come quickly. He hasn't got much time.'

My father was smiling the day he died. He even laughed proudly. He said, 'You look good, Paul,' and seeing the whole family gathered near his bed, grateful at the moment of his death – could anyone be more humble? – he said, 'What a wonderful reunion.'

I stayed with him to the end, with my brothers Gene and Joe, and after twenty minutes of agonal breathing he drew his last breath, almost on the stroke of nine o'clock. Nothing on earth I had ever seen had filled me with such desolation as watching my father die in his hospital bed in Hyannis.

'Grief is pure and holy,' a woman of ninety-seven wrote to me. 'You will find out that your father has not left you but will continue to live within you and seem to guide you.'

This was accurate. I felt my father's presence strongly afterwards. But I missed him as a friend. We had had no 'issues.' He was proud of me, and I loved him – loved him most of all because he had set me free. When I told him I was going to Africa for two years, he was delighted for me. And: 'No one owes you a thing.' He wrote to me often. I was in Africa more than five years. He encouraged me to explore. He had freed me because he was free himself. He had been loved by his parents. He knew how to love.

Vidia wrote. I had sent him my father's obituary. 'He sounded an immensely strong man, and his going will create a gap, whatever age he was.'

We were discussing by mail the appearance in *The New Yorker* of a number of letters Vidia had written me. They were 'Letters to a Young Writer.' He reported the reactions. Only two. One letter from a friend. Another from a fool.

He had published *A Way in the World.* In it was the story about Raleigh, an old man on the Orinoco, under siege by the Spanish, hoping to find gold so that he would not be executed. Vidia had told me this story in New York, that snowy day twenty years before. He said he was planning a new journey for a book. It was to be a sequel to his Islamic travels of 1979 which resulted in *Among the Believers* – peregrinations in Malaysia, Indonesia, Iran, Pakistan.

He hoped he had the stomach to write the book. He had been visited again by the intimation that he was a has-been. He complained that in his writing life he had had few well-wishers and little practical help. He said that his had been a solitary struggle. 'I have had to do it all out of my own reserves.'

That last part was inexplicable. Hadn't he had plenty of encouragement? Not just the literary prizes – every English book prize that was winnable he had won. His friends were distinguished and adoring. His advances were substantial, far outweighing his sales, which were never great. With this prestige he had sold his archives, including hundreds of my letters, to the University of Oklahoma at Tulsa for $640,000.

One of his American acquaintances had said to me, in a reproving way, 'Vidia wants everything.'

But everything means everything, for when wishes are granted, answered prayers are not sorted into two piles, good and bad, and always there are consequences: you had forgotten that asking for everything in the sack includes the sack itself. Vidia said this was the lesson of Salman Rushdie. He had set out to be original and shocking. He wished for fame. He became the most famous writer in the world, the origin of his fame the price on his head, like a cruel fable of wishes granted.

At this point, Vidia – Sir Vidia – had his wish: he too had everything. He had been very specific. He had wished for a place to call home. He now had three, two flats in London and a house in Wiltshire. He had wished to live in a manner that was 'uncompromisingly fashionable' and to be 'immensely famous.' He had Kensington and his knighthood. He had wished for a million pounds in the bank. Surely he had his million now.

When he returned from his Islamic journey, he was devastated by what he had found. He wrote urgently to tell me that Pat was on her deathbed. 'It is more than I can bear,' he said. 'She has been with me since January or February 1952. I cannot endure the knowledge that in another room of this house she is suffering without any hope of relief, except the very final one.' He implored me to write her obituary, in the form of a reminiscence. He reminded me that I had known her a very long time. He knew of my affection for her. He did not want her to be forgotten. His implication was that he himself was incapable of writing anything about her. Yet it seemed to me that we study the art of writing for, among other things, moments like this.

Now I understood the quarrels. 'We row all the time now,' Vidia had told me. Pat, whose mocking maiden name was Hale, knew she was dying; she was raging – sorrowful, indignant. How unfair that someone who had asked so little of life, who had spent so much time waiting, attending, being silent, speaking ill of no one, constantly apologizing, excusing herself – the very model of intelligence and simplicity; frugal, frail, humble, full of compliments, saying sweetly, *I thought of you*, and almost the only person on earth who sent me a birthday card; modest, a little timid, always indoors – how unfair that death was stalking her.

More than anyone, Pat had had the darkest experience of Vidia's shadow. Even if she had not known about his passion for prostitutes, which Vidia had claimed had lasted into his mid-thirties, she had been painfully acquainted with the facts of his relationship with Margaret, how he had traveled with her and taken her to parties. Everyone knew. Vidia did not conceal his affair with Margaret, and it had lasted as love.

Why didn't the Naipauls just split up? Was it purely because Pat allowed him to have a lover, and his lover had not made marriage a condition? But life was more complicated than that.

In every sense, Pat was left behind. I had suspected this early on, seeing her as a worried woman of an old-fashioned sort who in another century would have been called neurasthenic. Her ill health was the result of the way she lived, as a captive wife, a shut-in, fluttering in whatever cage of a house Vidia devised for her. And of course, because the way she lived made her ill, and her lifestyle never changed, she got worse. 'A case of nerves,' a quack would say. She was trembly, she was inward, introverted, a stay-at-home, afflicted with insomnia, a fretful and hesitant sort, and yet in the same room with Vidia she could seem maternal toward him – overprotective, solicitous, weepy, long-suffering. Vidia played the wayward demanding child to this wounded mother.

Everyone liked her, with an affection that bordered on pity. When Vidia was away – and he was probably with Margaret – Pat ran his affairs. It made me think that Pat was stronger than most people guessed. It was Vidia who could not function alone. What bothered me most about his 'travel books' was that he seldom traveled by himself and never revealed his traveling companion. I suspected Vidia's travel narratives to be extensively varnished, because Margaret was nowhere in them.

What was the challenge in traveling with a loving woman? To me, all such travel was just a holiday, no matter the destination. There were no alien places on earth for the man who had his lover to cling to at night and tell him he was a genius. I had always avoided reading about the journey in which Mr and Mrs First-Class Traveler were embarked on a satisfying adventure ('My wife found an exquisite carving . . .'). That sort of vacation interested me only if it truthfully reported the cannibalism in the marital woe of the traveling couple: bitter arguments, jealousy, sex, pettiness, infidelity, unfounded accusations, culture shock, or pained silences.

If Pat was dismayed to be left out of Vidia's trips and Vidia's writing, she never spoke about it to anyone except Vidia. She covered for him. She was the Lady Naipaul the newspapers mentioned. She stuck by him like the steadfast wife of a prominent politician, fulfilling her role as the loyal helpmate, letting no criticism show. Vidia often told me about their quarrels, and I imagined floods of tears, but in spite of that friction, and considering the circumstances, they seemed to get on remarkably well.

Pat was well educated and extremely well read. She did little but read books. She had had an ambition to write, but the few finished pieces I saw – a visit to Trinidad, an account of a political meeting in London – were not very effective. They were like her, bloodless and a bit pedestrian and terribly nice; she had no guile, not much humor, she was shy. Vidia was the shouter and the prima donna. She was not as weak as she seemed, however, nor was he as strong as he pretended to be. They were mutually dependent. Perhaps he needed her to be at home in the way that some men can be sexual only if they are unfaithful: it was the need to betray Mommy and, in a larger sense, the need for Mommy to know it and permit it.

Pat loved him – loved him without condition – praised him, lived for him, delighted in his success in the most unselfish way. She had lived through each book, and even when Vidia was traveling with Margaret – in the Islamic world and in the American South – she took pride in the books that resulted, *Among the Believers* and *A Turn in the South*. She stayed home, she read, she tended to the household – hired painters, oversaw renovations, did donkey work, paid bills – and prepared for Vidia's return. She awaited him in a way that suggested all the quaint and comforting props of the hearthside: roomy slippers, the favorite cushion, the pipe and hand-knitted comforter, the kettle of vegetable soup simmering on the hob.

In Africa years before, in his disarming fashion, relying on his shocking candor to do the job, Vidia volunteered the fact to me that there was no sex in the marriage. I knew they slept in separate rooms. I did not want to know more than that. But how was it that, knowing what she knew, she still spoke of his books in terms of great praise, and that the marriage had worked for so many years – indeed was still working?

The answer was that she adored him. Possibly there was an element of fear in it – the fear of losing him, the fear of her own futility and her being rejected. More than that, she was unselfish; love sustained her, which was why anyone who pitied her was misled. Pat had strength – that was evident in her ability to be alone. She was discreet. She was kind, she was generous, she was restrained and magnanimous; she was the soul of politeness, she was grateful; she was all the things Vidia was not. It was no accident that they had been married for forty years.

Death does not discriminate, but as the most efficient predators demonstrate – the lion, the hyena, and, most successful of all, the wild dogs of central Africa – victims are chosen for their weakness. Death shadows the innocent, the ones who stumble or look the wrong way. Death, the opportunist, skips past the strong to pounce on the feeble and the unwary.

A death watch began, and soon after that letter sending news of Pat's illness, Vidia wrote again: 'Now just five days on, her brain has gone. It can focus on only the most immediate thing.' Though she was almost a corpse, she seemed to Vidia almost youthful – there was still a brightness in her face. He was remorseful. He said, 'I took her too much for granted. I am surprised [by] my own grief – even while she is silent and alive in her room.'

That was all it took to make me hurry my piece. *Her brain has gone*. I wrote and faxed my memory of Pat and told Vidia to give her my love.

Two days later it happened. I read it on the paper headed *Dairy Cottage* scrolling through my chattering fax machine: Pat had died just a matter of hours before. Vidia had been summoned by the nurse to witness Pat's final moment of life. 'It was shattering.' After that, the funereal functionaries took over – the night nurse, the day nurse, the doctor, and very soon the undertaker's assistant, who seemed to Vidia 'Dickensian.' Vidia did not watch, not even when Pat's body was taken from the house in the coffin. Only a week before, Pat and he had visited the doctor in Southampton.

'I felt relieved when she left,' Vidia wrote. 'I telephoned some people. I even thought I would start working. But then I felt very tired, and it occurred to me to send this note to you.'

My obituary appeared in the *Daily Telegraph,* under the heading 'Lady Naipaul.'

In the many books that V. S. Naipaul has published, Pat Naipaul is mentioned only once, and obliquely (the prologue to *An Area of Darkness,* where she is referred to as 'my companion'). But her intelligence, her encouragement, her love and her discernment are behind every book that Naipaul has written.

'She is my heart,' he told me once. She was also that most valued person in any writer's life, the first reader.

In Uganda, 30 years ago, in what I considered to be highly unusual circumstances, I met Pat Naipaul and was immediately impressed. The Naipauls had been given a house in the grounds of Makerere University in Kampala, and Vidia was asked by the Building Department how he wished his name to read on the sign. He said he did not want his name on any sign. He was told he had to have something. He said, 'All right then, letter it "TEAS."'

As he told me the story, Pat burst out in appreciative isn't-he-awful? laughter. And then – this is the unusual part – Vidia continued to do what I had interrupted. He was reading to Pat from the last chapter of *The Mimic Men*, a novel he was just finishing.

I felt privileged to be a part of this intimate ritual. He read about two pages – a marvellous account of a bitter-sweet celebratory dinner shared by the guests in a hotel in south London. Brilliant, I was thinking, when the reading was over.

'Patsy?' Vidia said, inquiring because she had said nothing in response. Pat was thinking hard.

Finally she said, 'I'm not sure about all those tears.'

She was tough-minded and she was tender. For more than 40 years, in spite of delicate health and in latter years serious illness, she remained a devoted companion. It is a better description than wife. (In *The Mimic Men*, the narrator says that wife is 'an awful word.') The Naipauls made a practice of not reminiscing, at least in front of me, but I knew from casual remarks that in those early years they had to put up with the serious inconvenience of a small and uncertain income and no capital; Vidia used to laugh about the only job he had ever held as a salaried employee lasting just six weeks. Pat laughed too, but she had worked for a number of years as a history mistress at a girls' school.

While she was still in her thirties, she resigned from her teaching post to spend more time with Vidia, which she did as a householder in Muswell Hill, in Stockwell, and in Wiltshire; as a traveler in India, in Africa, in Trinidad, and America. She helped in the research for *The Loss of El*

Dorado, and she became involved in the complex issue that Vidia described in *The Killings in Trinidad.*

As the first reader, highly intelligent, strong-willed and profoundly moral, Pat played an active part in Vidia's work. She understood that a writer needs a loyal opposition as much as praise. She enjoyed intellectual combat and used to say, when Vidia and I were engaged on a topic, 'I love to see you two sparring.' She always said it in a maternal way, and it touched me.

I loved her for her sweetness and her unselfishness, for the way she prized great writing and fine weather and kind people. She had no time for their opposites. ('Life's too short,' she said.)

I see her always as I first knew her, in the garden of the Kaptagat Arms in up-country Kenya, where Vidia took refuge from our political troubles in Uganda, to finish his novel. Pat sat smiling, reading in the sunshine, sometimes writing, and always alert to – just beyond the hedge of purple and pink bougainvilleas – the sound of typing.

'Thank you for the lovely and generous note about Pat,' Vidia wrote. 'I told her you had sent your love. I will write more later.'

But there were no more letters, only rumors. I dismissed them as outrageous. I should have known better. In the rumors that circulated about Vidia, the most outrageous ones were usually the truest.

A little over two months after Pat Naipaul died, Vidia married again. He had fallen in love. He was unembarrassed about such passions. Even while Pat was alive, he had spoken publicly – in *The New Yorker* – of his pleasure in having found sexual satisfaction in middle age with Margaret in Argentina. In this same piece he also delivered himself of some choice Naipaulisms: 'I have an interesting mind' and 'I can't bear flowers' and 'I have no more than a hundred months left' (that was in 1994; in 1979 he had also said he had only a hundred months left) and 'I can't stand the sound of women's voices.'

Margaret was actually named in the *New Yorker* piece as Vidia's long-time lover, and was then still in the picture. 'The sexual ease came quite late to me,' Vidia said to the interviewer, of Margaret, while Pat toiled in the kitchen making lunch. 'And it came as an immense passion. Conrad has a lovely line: "A man to whom love comes late, not as the most splendid of illusions, but like an enlightening and priceless misfortune."'

But the new Lady Naipaul was not Margaret. She was Nadira Khannum Alvi, who had begun life in Kenya, the daughter of two transplanted Pakistanis. More than thirty years before, Vidia and I had encountered a small girl who resembled her on the verandah of a *dukawallah*'s shop in Nairobi. Vidia had loathed her on sight, but then, he disliked most children.

Nadira was now forty-two, a divorced mother of two teenagers. Vidia had met her at a dinner party at the home of the American consul-general in Lahore, Pakistan, in October 1995, as Pat lay dying in Wiltshire.

As with many stories about Vidia, at least two versions of their meeting existed. The first described Mrs Alvi as an admirer of his work who approached him at the party and said, 'Can I kiss you?'

'I think we should sit down,' Vidia said.

Three weeks later they decided to get married. It only remained for Pat to die before the marriage date could be fixed. In the event, it was to be April 15, 1996.

All this – the place, the name of the woman, the admiration, and 'Can I kiss you?' – I read in the *Daily Telegraph*, which published an account by a reporter, Amit Roy, of the wedding lunch in London. The piece was neither corrected nor contradicted, something the scrupulous and insistent Vidia would have done if he had been misrepresented, so I took it as a record of facts, until someone who had been at the party in Lahore, the man who had brought them together, told me the second version.

'I introduced them at the US consul's dinner,' he said. 'I wanted Naipaul to meet some characters for his book. I saw Nadira sitting at another table. I went up to her and said, "Guess who is here?" and "I want to introduce you to him." She told me she did not know the name V. S. Naipaul and had never read anything by him. I then accompanied her to meet him. She went up to him at the dinner table where he was serving himself, and as I introduced them, she said, "How fantastic" and "What an honor" and "I know your work" and then plonked a big kiss on his cheek. He blushed, but he was taken. They were together for the whole evening. The very next day he phoned me and said, "I don't need your help because Nadira is taking me around and we are leaving for Bahawalpur." Nadira was with Naipaul in the hotel when he phoned me.'

The marriage lunch was at an Indian restaurant in South Kensington. Vidia and his new wife sat holding hands at the table. This was a new Vidia. I had never seen him hold Pat's hand. This was a smitten Vidia, a far cry from the man who once said to me that he turned away if he saw two people kissing on television. He was also a reticent Vidia. The new Lady Naipaul did most of the talking, and her talk sounded very similar to what Vidia always referred to as 'chuntering.'

'It was amazing for him to have a woman in an Islamic country walk up and kiss him,' Nadira said, explaining her unorthodox manner of introduction. 'I astounded a lot of people, but I tend to do that a lot in Pakistan anyway.' (This kiss received further revision two years later in an interview in London's *Sunday Times* of May 10, 1998, in which Nadira was quoted as saying, 'My kiss was not some silly bimbo, fluff-headed thing . . . It was an act of reverence.') Going on to describe their travels in Pakistan after they met, she said, 'I think we fell terribly in love with each other.'

Nadira was a bit surprised by the suddenness. 'There can be dichotomy between the writer and the person, someone you don't want to meet again. I found the writer was the person. Here I had met a combination of a wonderful man and a man who had a vision, tremendous compassion, someone who reminded me of my past. He was my soul-mate. He was someone I had always looked for. I am madly in love with him. I think I shall always be madly in love with him.'

There was more. But knowing Vidia, this was the moment for him to cry, 'Stop chuntering!'

Instead, Vidia said to the man from the *Telegraph*, 'Do you know about Nadira, her reputation and her work? She is very famous.'

During the wedding lunch Nadira clutched Vidia's hand and whispered, 'I want you,' as the guests tucked into King Prawn Curry and Chicken Badami Korma. Among them were his agent, his old Oxford tutor, a couple of literary critics, a fellow whom

Vidia unfailingly referred to as 'that epicene young man,' and Harold Pinter and Lady Antonia Fraser. I was ten thousand miles away, on the slopes of Mount Haleakala.

Vidia and I had often talked about Philip Larkin. We had both bought *High Windows* when it was published, in the summer of 1974. Larkin's poetry – mordant, sour, funny, right wing, cynical, elegiac, mocking, contemptuous of fame, fearful of death – matched exactly many of Vidia's moods. In 'The Whitsun Weddings,' Larkin had written of the faces at weddings,

> . . . each face seemed to define
> Just what it saw departing: children frowned
> At something dull; fathers had never known
> Success so huge and wholly farcical;
> The women shared
> The secret like a happy funeral . . .

Vidia had referred to Nadira's 'reputation and her work,' and had said, 'She is very famous.' But surely Nadira's celebrity was similar to that which I had enjoyed when I had been famous in Kampala and in Bundibugyo. Nadira had been famous in Bahawalpur, a small town on the Sutlej River about two hundred miles south of Lahore. She wrote a 'Letter from Bahawalpur,' which appeared each week in *The Nation* (Lahore). Her picture accompanied the column, a passport-quality full-face halftone of a vague, unsmiling woman with bobbed hair and dark raised brows like diacritical marks over her staring eyes.

To verify Vidia's high opinion, I got hold of a sequence of Nadira's dispatches from Bahawalpur.

In 'Pardon Sir, Your Slip Is Showing!' she wrote, 'Words are wonderful things. They are extremely useful, even indispensable at times; you can use them to communicate, to beguile, to frustrate, to berate, to admire, to flatter, to fool . . .' And she ended, 'If words loose [*sic*] their meaning, life looses [*sic*] its meaning.'

'Remembering the Old of the Sadiqians' was Nadira's lament for the fact that the retired teachers of Sadiq Public School in Bahawalpur had small pensions or none at all. Conclusion: 'No wonder our education system is in shambles.'

A week later, in 'Computer Blues,' Nadira deplored the rise of computer technology. Her then husband made an appearance in this piece: 'The early days of his computer mania were quite a strain on our marriage.' Nadira hated her computer. Nothing worked as it should – disks, printer, fonts, spell checker; power outages in Bahawalpur did not help. Also, 'I keep loosing [*sic*] articles from the disks, sometimes loosing [*sic*] the disks,' and so on.

Lovable, ungrammatical, clumsy, audacious – had such pieces turned Vidia's head? Nadira had been married to a man who was living the more or less feudal existence of a wealthy Pakistani farmer-landlord. That sort of life – you see it in India also – is like a glimpse of old Russia, something Tolstoyan in the landlord's experimental farm, with his many peasants and tenants and his money, for this man lived on the same premises with Nadira and his first wife, a German woman, and the children from both marriages.

The rest of the story, too, is like a Russian novel. Nadira acquires some local fame as a columnist. She revolts. She leaves for Lahore. She is squired around town by several men, who woo her but stop short of being suitors. She has no money except for the insignificant fees for her 'Letter from Bahawalpur,' and she no longer lives in her town. On her divorce, it is said that her husband does not even return her dowry. She is living precariously when she receives an invitation to meet Sir Vidia Naipaul.

She says to my friend in Lahore, 'Who is he? Has he written anything?'

It is impossible not to admire her pluck.

Later, people said, 'Have you heard about Vidia? He got *married*.'

Vidia had sounded happy in the piece describing his wedding curry lunch. It did not surprise me that I hadn't been invited. I was in Hawaii, half a world away, and I had still not gotten over the death of Pat or the sad news that there had been only a handful of people at her funeral.

A month after Vidia's wedding, I had a call from Bill Buford, the literary editor of *The New Yorker*, telling me that the magazine was sponsoring an event at Hay-on-Wye, a well-known literary festival, in a pretty part of the Welsh border country.

'We want you and Vidia to appear,' Buford said. 'Do a sort of literary dialogue.'

'Vidia hates literary festivals,' I said. 'He has never been to one. And they seem like dog shows to me. Have you asked him?'

'We were hoping that you would, Paul.'

'Never. He'll just scream.'

'He's been very mellow since he got married. It's a new Vidia, honestly.'

'He won't do it,' I said.

'We figure he might if you ask him. He'll listen to you. You're his friend.'

'Believe me, he does what he wants.'

'Salman Rushdie will be there.'

'That's no incentive to Vidia. He laughed when the ayatollah announced his *fatwa*. I tell you, he won't want to go.'

'But Vidia's new wife might.'

'I don't know Vidia's new wife.'

'Paul, if you ask Vidia to attend it will mean a lot to us.'

'He'll want to be paid.'

'We'll pay him. Within reason, of course. Will he want a lot?'

'Yes.'

'Paul, please . . .'

I cannot bear it when people plead with me. Perhaps they know that. Pleading always has the intended effect.

It was a deep-voiced woman who answered the telephone at Dairy Cottage. I knew just where she was: on the white sofa by the window, which gave onto the western side of the hedge, the green shrubs, the green trees, the red maple. It was where Pat always sat, because Vidia disliked answering the phone.

'And who is speaking?' she asked.

I told her my name.

As she passed the phone to Vidia, I heard her say, 'It's Paul Theroux. I want to meet him.'

I should have known that would be enough, but even then, I was not certain that Vidia would say yes to the festival.

18

Literature is for the Wounded and the Damaged

It happens to be a tic of mine as a traveler, on returning to any distant city, to take the same walk, make the same stops, eat the same meals at the same restaurants, look into the same stores, verify the faces of clerks or doormen, even touch the same posts and gates – go through a ritualistic renewal of familiarity along a known route before striking out and doing anything new. It is not compulsive. It eases my spirit. And in any new city I make a route and remember it.

It was a sunny morning at the end of May in England's never-disappointing springtime. I was just a tourist now. Christie's salesrooms were on my London trail. I walked from Brown's Hotel to King Street in time to see the 'Visions of India' pre-auction show.

'Your friend Naipaul was just here,' a Christie's man said, greeting me. He knew me as a sometime bidder and Naipaul as a connoisseur. 'He might still be somewhere in the building.'

We looked among the pictures but didn't see him. I had wanted to surprise him, perhaps have lunch. He had agreed to go to Hay-on-Wye to do the staged dialogue. I would have enjoyed looking at these pictures with Vidia, who had a discerning eye for paintings of Indian landscapes. But he had gone.

I continued on my quasi-Tourettic walk, feeling like a prac-titioner of advanced mazecraft. I had arrived in London that morn-ing and was happy with my first-class rail ticket to Newport, Wales, in my pocket. I left the next day from Paddington station, first reading the newspaper and then looking over the first chapter of *Kowloon Tong*, which I had just started to write. I had spent part of the winter in Hong Kong.

If things had been different in my life, I might have been writing the book in one of those Oxfordshire or Somerset houses – the Old Vicarage or Stride Manor, say. The house filled with the aromas of log fires and baking bread. 'Dad's working in the library.' It had been a dream of mine to end up in the West Country as a solvent escapee from London and part-time patriarch, my kids coming down with girlfriends or wives, maybe even grandchildren, on weekends. Wearing muddy wellingtons, I would meet them at the local railway station with the other parents and country squires, leaning against our Land Rovers and listening for the train. I would be known as 'the American' in the village and greeted with insincere and resentful jollity by the gruff locals in the pub, the Black Horse – 'Evenin', squire.' They would patronize me with archaisms and bore me stiff with country lore they'd got out of books. Behind my back I'd be called 'the Yank.'

No matter! The West Country was one of the prettiest places in the world. I knew that now. I had been looking at it, off and on, for thirty-four years, but now I knew it would never happen. Just thinking of the word 'never' and seeing these blue remembered hills made my eyes prickle with regret.

A taxi met me at Newport. The driver, a former teacher and Welsh speaker, took me to Abergavenny and across the Black Mountains past jumbled villages. Too far from London to be within commuting distance, the countryside looked unmodernized, like the England of the sixties and seventies. The village of Hay was on a hill, the river Wye below it. I dropped my bag at the innlike hotel and after lunch, on that afternoon of June 1, 1996, went to the festival.

Vidia and Nadira had arrived, having left Dairy Cottage that morning.

'Paul, this is Nadira.'

The skinny, scowling seven-year-old girl in her little-princess sari on the Nairobi verandah had become a big woman. She was dark and tall – taller than Vidia – and watchful, with the sort of frank sizing-you-up stare that is never seen on the faces of Pakistani women. Her sari was loose at the hips, as if she had just lost some weight. She was waiting for me to say something. I spoke to Vidia.

'I just missed you at that Indian show at Christie's yesterday.'

Before Vidia could reply, Nadira slapped his shoulder and said, 'You bad man! You did not tell me you went there!'

She slapped his arm again and scolded him. This seemed a trifle presumptuous in a woman who had been married only a month. I had never seen anyone touch Vidia before.

'You will not buy any more pictures!'

'You're telling my secrets, Paul,' Vidia said quietly, looking a little grim.

Salman Rushdie was being introduced to Vidia as I stepped up to a table to get myself a cup of coffee, and then I saw Bill Buford from *The New Yorker* beckoning, and we all headed to a big white circus tent.

As I passed Salman, he was smiling and shaking his head. He said, 'I have never met him before.'

'What did he say?'

'He said, "Are you all right?" I told him yes, I am all right. He said, "Good, good, good."' Salman began to laugh.

We took our seats, Vidia, Bill Buford, and I, on the stage in the big circus tent. The audience was large, but still the atmosphere was that of a dog show. We were being asked to perform, to walk on our hind legs, jump through hoops, create a spectacle for the readers. Buford said, 'What about questions afterwards?'

'No questions,' Vidia said. I felt sure he hated doing this, but had agreed; I had not twisted his arm. His general philosophy was 'The writer should never precede the work.' Or even: 'The writer should remain invisible.' Books were the things. But there were no books in sight, only goggling faces in the sold-out tent and the sense of scrutiny, all those faces like light bulbs.

In his rambling introduction – Vidia fidgeting irritatedly as my new book was mentioned – Bill said, 'Paul, you're two decades younger than Vidia,' and finally asked, 'What did Vidia give you as a writer?'

I thanked him and said, 'A couple of corrections, Bill. I am not two decades younger than Vidia. I am fifty-five, Vidia's sixty-four. And we met over thirty years ago, when I actually did feel more than twenty years younger. I felt very young. I felt that I was meeting a much older, much wiser, much more experienced person. A person much more than nine or ten years older than I was.'

Vidia sat looking meditative. He had not said a word, and we had hardly spoken beforehand. He was wearing a dark jacket and a sweater under it, dark wool trousers, dark shoes. He seemed to be listening carefully, and I was grateful to have this chance to pay tribute to him.

'And you ask what he gave me?' I said. 'I feel that he gave me everything. The main thing that he gave me was the confidence that I was a writer. He said that every writer was different, and if you were great, you were a new man. I had to write my own book, but that it would not resemble anyone else's book. My writing had to come from inside me, and that every book needed a reason to be written.'

To my left, I could see Vidia nodding. I was annoyed that I had had to speak first, and I felt I was rambling.

'In 1966 in Kampala, when I met Vidia, I had not published a book. Vidia was the first writer I had met who had a total sense of mission, a total sense of self, an uncompromising attitude towards himself, towards the novel. If he made a rule, he kept to the rule. He said that a writer has to make his own way in the world. He asked me once or twice, "Are you sure you're up for it? Are you sure you want to be a writer? Are you sure you want to live this terrible life?" I was twenty-four years old. I said, "I'm up for it."'

Vidia was sitting next to me, near enough for me to hear him sighing in impatience – or perhaps he was simply breathing asthmatically. Near as he was, he was not looking at me or at the audience. He sat at an angle and stared into space while, on his other side, Bill Buford spoke to him – spoke to his shoulder, for Vidia remained turned away. His body language said bluntly that he wished he was elsewhere.

Bill began to ask me another question when, out of self-consciousness – for Vidia, the star of this show, still had not spoken – I turned to Vidia and asked, 'You once wrote, "To be a victim is to be absurd." What did you mean by this?'

Vidia cleared his throat and said, 'Well, I think the word "victim" has probably been extended. I was thinking about people who were utterly helpless politically and had no rights, no one to turn to, and I thought: They were always absurd. This was in a note to a study of slavery and revolution that I spent some years in working on. The slaves had no rights – and I am thinking about the Caribbean slavery – and to be a victim *is* to be absurd. Slaves are absurd people. That is the truth. The current use of the word is an extension of that. I haven't thought about it like that. I was thinking about it in a very practical, realistic way. I don't make generalizations.'

'So you don't mean it in the modern sense,' I said.

'No, not in the sense of someone in a university who can't get a job,' Vidia said with the sort of snappish energy he had when he was irritable. I had noticed the awkward way he sat and could see that he had something on his mind. 'No, that's another kind of victim.'

People in the audience laughed at his seeming to mock universities, and over their laughter I persisted, hoping to draw him out.

Vidia lifted his head, looked at nothing, and said, 'I don't think like this about myself. I deal with material at hand and I don't make generalizations like this.'

Feeling rebuffed, I said no more and let the silence descend. Time for Vidia to offer something. Perhaps he was right: it seemed in my question that I was embarrassed by his discomfort and trying to ingratiate myself.

He giggled confidently in the silence and said, 'Sorry, I don't want to stump the conversation.'

Buford rescued the faltering moment, saying, 'Paul, if I can intercept. I arrived from New York last night, and as I got here on the train I was thinking of your books. In some ways no two writers could be more different, and yet there are some similarities. And one is that both of you became writers in Britain. In your case, Vidia, you actively became a writer when you came to Britain and started studying at Oxford. And in Paul's case – you, Paul, also became a writer when you lived here. What was the effect of being in Britain for you?'

I gestured for Vidia to answer.

'This is a very important question,' Vidia said.

He coiled on his chair, concentrating hard, and lifted his gaze again, speaking to the heights of the circus tent.

'It has to be considered,' he said. 'Writing is a physical business. Books are real physical objects. They have to be printed, published, reviewed, read, distributed – it's a physical object, it's a commercial enterprise. It's an effect of the industrial society. You can't beat a book out on a drum.' He let this sink in. 'So, in the 1950s, when I started, if you were writing in English, there was only one place where you could be a writer. It was here. It couldn't be the United States, because I had no link with America. I had a link only with here. It certainly couldn't be any other English-speaking country, because I don't think they even had publishing industries.'

He frowned and folded his arms, looking defiant. 'The thing was different in 1950. It has changed considerably. There's a publishing industry in Australia, Canada – India has developed a publishing industry. And to write always as an exotic is a very awful thing to have to do.'

'Why is it awful?' Buford asked.

'Because you seldom have people who can share your experience, your background,' Vidia said. 'My brother, while he lived, said to me one day that probably he was the only man who could truly understand what I was writing. And I understood a little bit more of what he was trying to do as well, because we shared the background. If we were addressing audiences of people like ourselves, we would have been different writers. I am always aware of writing in a vacuum, almost always for myself, and almost not having an audience. That wonderful relationship that I felt an American writer would always have with his American readers, or a French writer with his French readers – I was always writing for people who were indifferent to my material.'

Buford said, 'Why could you not return to Trinidad?'

'You cannot beat books out on the drum!' Vidia cried. 'It's as simple as that. What would I have done?' He moved heavily in his chair and looked pleadingly at Buford, mocking him with incomprehension. 'I mean, enter into it imaginatively – that question. Who would have published your books? Who would have read them? Who would have reviewed them? Who would have bought them? Who would have paid you for the effort? It's not a question.'

Over the nervous laughter from the audience at seeing Vidia's hackles rise, Buford said that surely the source of Vidia's fiction was the richness of Trinidad.

'Yes, yes, inevitably, because that's the material you have when you're starting out,' Vidia said. 'It's the material you carry for your first twenty years or so. And it is very important, because it's a complete experience. Experience later will be modified. But that's very pure.'

'I was just wondering, regarding this question of an audience,' I said. 'When did you develop this sense of people reading your work?'

'I don't have that sense at all. I've seldom met people who have,' he said, and there was laughter. 'I've met an awful lot of people who come and bluff their way through interviews with me.' There was more laughter, and silence when the laughter died down. In that silence Vidia smirked and said, 'But again, I don't want to stump the conversation.'

'No, you're not stumping it.'

'Oh, good.'

'But circumstances of writing do change,' I said.

It was obvious that he had no questions for me. So I was obliged to assume the humble position of interviewer and petition him with questions. Once again his shadow fell across me. Did I mind? Not at all, for here we were, occupying a stage in front of an attentive audience of readers. Yet I had a vibration – yes, a vibration – that Vidia objected to sharing the stage.

'Now, you said once that writing *Mr Biswas* was your Eden,' I said. 'I just imagine a kind of paradise – in quotation marks. I think I know what you mean, but would you explain that?'

Vidia frowned and said, 'Well, great anxiety. Great poverty. Extraordinarily squalid conditions in London, especially for people like myself. Very hard to get accommodation.'

The audience became very attentive at hearing Vidia refer to racism in Britain as personally affecting him. Vidia was usually seen to be the snob, the excluder, the mutterer.

'Miraculously, in 1958, I found a lady in Streatham Hill who let me have the top part of her house,' he said. 'She worked all day, so I had the house to myself. This was a wonderful experience for me. I was in the second year of this book, and I began to feel the strength in myself as a writer. I was extremely happy. It didn't matter to me what was said about the book afterwards.'

He seemed happy saying this, speaking about the work of writing and its satisfaction to him almost forty years ago. I sat back and listened and tried to think of a new question.

'And it was an Eden,' he said, 'because there was a kind of innocence about the purity of that dedication and that happiness. And in those days – you know, people have probably forgotten – in those days when you published a book, nothing happened. There were no interviews. There was no radio. No television. Books were published – they made their way. That was a thing in many ways. There wasn't this element of the show about it. That was a kind of purity.'

'Were you aware that you were writing a very ambitious book?' I asked.

'Yes, I knew that I was writing an immensely ambitious work, and the knowledge of this grew on me. The book began simply in conception and developed as I wrote it.'

I said, 'I'd like to pursue this a bit, because I read all the early reviews of *A House for Mr Biswas*, and this is the first time I have heard you say that reviews would not have mattered to you. The reviews were good, but they weren't ecstatic. They welcomed the book. *The New Statesman* –'

'Bad review! Bad review in the *Statesman*. My own paper!'

'How did you feel?'

'Didn't mind!' Vidia crowed. 'I knew it was going to be all right. I had to comfort my editors. I used to say, "Forget it – it's going to be all right."' He laughed at the thought of consoling his editors. 'Certainly in the United States I had to comfort a series of broken editors. "It will be all right! It will be all right!" And they were in tears, if they were women, and saying, "We should be doing this for you, and here you are comforting me."'

'Not too long after that you went to India,' I said.

He nodded and awaited my question. Now I was firmly in the position of pedestrian interviewer, and Vidia was the immensely famous interviewee, the focal point of this event. It was better this way: he was happier, I was happier. He did not want to listen to me, or anyone, talk about writing. It bored him. But he had become animated talking about *Biswas*.

'You have written three books about India, directly about experiences of living and traveling in India. Most people write about a place once, then go away and don't come back.'

'Paul, you were one of the people I consulted. I said, "Should I

345

do it?" It was an idea from another source. I asked you, and you said, "They're thirteen years apart. You should do the book."'

I had no recollection of saying that. But if I had, then I suppose I could take some credit for his return to India and his writing *A Wounded Civilization*.

'It was an entirely different book,' he said. 'The first book was personal. It was – you know, our family had left India in the 1880s. We were really ragged dirt-poor people from the eastern Uttar Pradesh, Bihar area, wretched after the Mutiny and everything else. India was a subject full of nerves. Nerves was the subject of the first book. The second book was more analytical, so there's always more distance, and I just wanted to go and write another kind of book. In the third book, I had arrived at this new way of writing, the travel books, which would make the word "travel" a little odd. Exploring civilizations not through what one thought of them but through what the people had lived through, and making a pattern of that.'

I said, 'To me, the most interesting thing one can do is to go back to a country, to look at it again, write it again.'

'The world has changed, I have changed,' Vidia said. 'I wish to add new knowledge to the old. I don't wish to do a repeat. I would like every book to be different from the ones that have gone before. I'm not stirred to write a book unless it is different from the ones that have gone before. This thing about travel books – I find what I do very interesting, taking human narratives and sticking to the truth as far as possible. It seems to me preferable to taking an adventure which you stumbled upon and falsifying it in fiction, to do a Maugham sort of novel.'

Realizing that I needed to prod him with a question, I said, 'There was something I was going to ask you. Yesterday when I was in London, I went to the Christie's preview of "Visions of India" and someone said that I had just missed you.'

'Oh, my God. My secrets given away,' Vidia said, and I knew it was a mistake to begin that way. But I kept on. 'I wanted to ask you about pictures and writing. How is your imagination fed by images and a love of the pictorial and your writing?'

Sounding stubborn and doubtful, Vidia said, 'I don't think there's any relation. I think words and the pictures of words are quite different. And the thoughts of words and the things that occur in the brain are different from the pictorial impressions. The talents are entirely different. I don't think I'm a judge of art.'

'I think you're being modest. You are a good judge of art. You've bought it, you have it on your walls. So?'

'But I don't think it's related, Paul.'

He was stumping me again, but I could not understand why he denied his pictorial gift. I said, 'The images in your books are made out of words, but they begin as observations – describing some one's shadow, the texture of skin, hair, sunlight, color, the shapes of things. Obviously the talent is different: Landseer could draw fur, but you can describe fur.'

'I think it is an intensity for observation with which I was born,' he said, admitting this. 'I remember being aware of it when I was very young. Studying a face very carefully, for what it said. Studying hands and the shape of bodies, the parts of people.'

'Isn't that what painters do?'

'I don't know. I like the line in a painting. I like Hokusai's invention. Velázquez, the way he handles paint. It's quite different from writing a sentence or shaping a narrative.'

'But how can you write if you can't observe? The gift of observation is transformed into writing.'

'You must observe,' he said, at last agreeing with what I had been hinting at all along. 'I'll tell you a story of the observing gift. One of the earliest memories I have, probably when I was about six or seven. I was at my grandmother's house in a country town in Trinidad during the school holidays. And there's a teacher, an Indian teacher from the school, and he's moving his possessions in a box cart. My father stops him and they exchange a few words. And the teacher says, "I'm not like some people who will show off and get a proper cart or get a van to move my goods. I will move them and let people look at me and let them laugh!" And I thought, "That is how the poor behave." A boy of six made this sad observation. "He's like this because he's a poor man. He's a teacher whom one respects, but really he's a poor man." So, it's deep inside one. And it's also related, perhaps, to my feeling for handwriting. You know, one judges people by their handwriting, or their parents, or the way you look, the way you walk, the way you talk. The whole person. No mysteries for me.'

'Aren't those surfaces you're talking about?' I asked.

'No, not surfaces, because we carry our life in our face. We carry our experiences in our face.'

'But they are surfaces – surfaces that reveal inner states?'

'Yes, we make ourselves.'

More confident over the flow of talk that had developed, something like a conversation, even if it was all made of my impatient questions and his reluctant answers, I said, 'I want to ask you about universities. You once said that you were disappointed at Oxford. How do you think you would fare at a university these days?'

'I think they're calamitous, these English courses,' Vidia said angrily. He shifted in his chair, looking combative, shooting from the hip. 'They're actively destructive of civilization and thought. When I was at Oxford in 1950, I think we all knew that English was not a serious subject for study, not worth a serious degree, not worth a physics degree. It was not worth a man doing medical research.'

The audience was restless, suspecting heresy but half agreeing with it, as Vidia warmed to his theme. Obviously I had struck a nerve.

'We knew that this business of doing English was a very soft option, an extension of the divinity courses of the last century. But that was what people went to Oxford for, to learn to hunt and to live this great social life, and later, endless divinity people were produced. Probably a hundred years ago or less, Professor Sweet – you know, who is the origin of Professor Higgins in the Shaw play' (he meant Henry Sweet, 1845–1912, phonetician and philologist) – 'he and some other people established this English course, a form of idleness for simple people. So it was a kind of imperial statement about English literature, like English history, so it was a brand-new study. In 1950 the study stopped at 1830, people weren't encouraged to go beyond that, and very few wanted to. They were content with the shallows of the eighteenth century.'

Vidia sat very erect, folded his arms again, and his voice became almost a shout.

'So that now what has happened is that this *non*-course, this *non*-subject, has been taken over by politically motivated people.

Universities have become places where free thinking is not allowed, where your tutor does not ask for an original thought about a work. But it's a political line! We were told at Oxford in 1950 that the best thing that happened to you occurred in the holidays. That's when you did a lot of reading. The point of this course was that it allowed you to do an infinite amount of reading. Nowadays people read very, very little, and they have elaborate theories. And there have emerged whole generations from the universities who can't think and who just parrot the phrases.'

There was applause from several sections of the audience. Who had ever heard English departments being attacked or subjects being evaluated this way? Physics more important than English – indeed, English study vastly inferior to all others.

'This has particularly damaged the newer countries, the lesser cultures, who at great cost have produced intellectuals. They send them to Oxford, Cambridge, they send them to American universities, and they come back parroting dreadful political tripe. They're corrupt!'

The response, as his voice broke on the word 'corrupt,' was tumultuous applause from every side of the circus tent. At last they had a performance worthy of such a tent, a raging novelist in full cry, an Indian performing an authentic rope trick.

'And I think that an English course ought to be recognized as a silly course!' he called out. 'Not worth a physics course, or a medical research course, or astronomy! And there should be no support for it, and all the professors and all the lecturers should be withdrawn from that kind of work and put into some other job. I wonder what work they'll do? What work will they do! In the old days we'd say, "Get them on the buses!" But now we know that conducting a bus is a form of idleness.'

There was no point in my saying anything now. I waited for the laughter and applause to die down and then crept into his shadow once again and asked, 'So you think that literature courses should be disbanded?'

'I think literature should be read privately,' Vidia said. 'Literature is not for the young. Literature is for the old, the experienced, the wounded, the damaged, who read literature to find echoes of their own experience and balm of a certain sort.'

'The old and the damaged,' I said.

Vidia had begun to laugh in a triumphant way. 'Contented tribal societies don't need literature. They pound their yams and they're quite happy!'

'But people can't abandon literacy, can they?'

'No, you can't go back. You can't pretend, you can't unlearn what you've learned.'

'A moment earlier you sounded like Chairman Mao.'

Laughing, relaxing a bit after having delivered his tirade, Vidia said, 'When did I sound like Chairman Mao? You mean "Get them on the buses"?'

'Learning by doing,' I said. 'It's one of his thoughts.'

'Like Mr Squeers.'

'And also: Go into the countryside and learn how to pound yams.'

Vidia said, in a reasonable voice, 'Literature will look after itself. People will have to read it. Now, apart from the universities you have the dreadful pressures of the prizes, which are a dreadful kind of corruption of publishing. As I said, when my first books were published there were no interviews, nothing, and books just trickled down and made their own way. If there had been all these prizes, and my books hadn't got the prizes I would have been run out of town by the publishers.'

'But that is part of the selling mechanism,' I said. 'Interestingly, universities are also a business.'

'And part of the contraction of the reading habit, because of certain approved texts,' Vidia said. 'I am told that Francis Parkman is no longer taught, no longer approved in America. People are no longer encouraged to read his work. He's a great writer. *The Oregon Trail* is a great work. But he's not there, not available, because he is politically unacceptable. There is a kind of tyranny which this bogus English course has imposed on whole civilizations.'

'So reading should be a private activity.'

'Yes. A private activity. And your friends will tell you to read a book. And you'll read it quietly. You don't want people telling you what to think.'

'But if you went back to Oxford now, what would you study?'

'I would have to do something equally idle,' Vidia said, laughing softly, sounding West Indian again. 'The whole point of doing English was a form of idleness, you know. It was a way of spending time – it wasn't serious. So we need a place as a kind of decompression chamber, from adolescence to adulthood.'

I said, 'But it was a crucial period for you as a writer.'

'No. No. No. It was not. Except if you consider what perhaps are the effects of solitude, or long solitude, or long unhappiness, but that probably would have occurred elsewhere.'

'You didn't need to go to Oxford for that?'

'Didn't need to go to Oxford for that, to be unhappy, or to be poor.'

Buford had been sitting by, laughing and occasionally looking shocked. He said, 'You said something earlier which I found interesting, when you described travel writing as somehow more authentic than some fiction. Do you find your nonfiction now more honest or more satisfying to write?'

'Yes. I'd have a lot of trouble writing straight fiction now, because I've done my fiction,' Vidia said. 'And I've been writing for forty years. I've handled my experience as best as I can. I can't go back to doing this thing which I now reject, because I want to know why one should falsify a perfectly valid experience. Why, for the sake of drama, should one dress it up? In the last century, things moved quickly because of this swift modification that occurred, writer by writer, book by book, and the forms developed quickly. I think now that if your material is so varied, so many cultures meet, and the novel works best when you're dealing with a monoculture – one culture with a set of norms that everyone can appreciate, almost like Jane Austen. It's easier to write fiction like that. But when the world is moving together in all kinds of ways, that form doesn't absolutely answer, and the ability to lie is so immense. When I read books from Southeast Asia, I worry about it. I think, "Where is this lie from? Why is this a lie?" It's like reading an autobiography, where you think, "What is being left out? What is being distorted?"'

I said, 'So your response to this need for a new form is *The Enigma of Arrival* and *A Way in the World*?'

He said, 'All great writing has its own new form. Montaigne's essays – completely new. He began writing classical essays, and then it develops, he writes about himself, he writes about the war around him, he writes about cruelty, he writes about the discoveries of the world, and he writes in his mocking way about himself as well, this new modern man – absolutely new. That is why Montaigne is Montaigne. All great writers are new. They are not like other people.'

I liked this observation, not only for what it said about great writers but for what it revealed of Vidia's own conceit about himself. He saw himself as one of these new men, and now I saw his reason: his role model was Michel Eyquem de Montaigne (1533–1592).

He said, 'At the universities and the schools, people are not taught to be new. They are taught to copy other people. Copying becomes the highest virtue, and I don't know how you can judge a derivative form. I don't know how, if you get forms that are not original, not delivering new visions, how to go about judging them. People say, "Judge for the style. Judge for the characters." I don't know.'

Buford said, 'Both of you have written strongly autobiographical novels. The thing about the autobiographical novel, whether it's *The Enigma of Arrival* or *A House for Mr Biswas*, *My Secret History* or *My Other Life*, is that once those stories are told, they're told. The autobiographical novel is spent, therefore that kind of novel's possibilities are exhausted.'

Vidia made a magisterial gesture, doing his Gradgrind impersonation, and said, 'I feel I want to say that I am not against narratives fundamentally. We must deal in narrative. Without narrative there is no point.' He grimaced, he invited attention. He said, 'So what can I say about novels now? Narrative writing is what we need, whatever form it takes. The reason Paul probably had to go in for the autobiographical fiction is that his experience has been unique. It has not been a simple Massachusetts childhood. He has traveled, he has gathered experience in different cultures, he has ventured and absorbed other cultures. And because of this special experience, he has to define himself in the books he is writing. He just can't write a third-person narrative without defining who the participant, the viewer, who the "I" and the "eye" are. And probably more and more people, as the world gets more confused, will feel the need to define exactly who they are. Otherwise, with the third-person narrative one wonders, "Who is writing this?"'

It seemed a strange observation, a loss of faith in fiction that was akin to saying the novel was misleading and mendacious, if not dead. But it was not news. Almost three hundred years ago, Daniel Defoe had said as much in one of the sequels to *Robinson Crusoe*, after the first volume became a huge hit: 'This supplying a story by invention is certainly a most scandalous crime, and yet very little regarded in that part. It is a sort of lying that makes a great hole in the heart, at which by degrees a habit of lying enters in.' I did not agree at all with this, and I felt that, like Vidia, Defoe was being self-serving, as well as pandering to puritanism.

I said, 'But in *The Mystic Masseur*, your first book, you're sometimes writing in the third person and sometimes in the first person. I thought that was the most amazing innovation. I had never read a book in which that happened. Where did that come from?'

'Ignorance!' Vidia shouted, and laughed. 'And both people were fictions – that is, the narrator was an artificial figure too.'

'Could I ask you how your father influenced you?' Bill asked.

'We can't go into this, Bill, because the subject of one's writing – it's too profound, and too personal.'

Almost an hour had passed. Buford thanked us, and as the audience applauded, Vidia repeated to Buford, 'No questions.'

As we were led out, I said, 'Are you staying at the hotel, Vidia?'

'I'm not staying. I'm going back to Wiltshire,' he said.

He looked pained – less irritated and edgy than he had onstage, but tired and unforthcoming.

'It seems quite a nice hotel,' I said. 'We could have dinner later.'

'I get so lonely in hotel rooms.'

He spotted Nadira coming towards him through the departing crowd. He motioned to her, and seeing him, she picked up her pace. She moved quickly, marching like a soldier, swinging her arms. Her hands were fists.

'We'll talk,' he said.

As Vidia and Nadira were escorted to their car, Salman Rushdie came up to me. His heavy-lidded eyes gave him a perpetually mocking look, and he had never looked more disdainful. He was holding a small notebook and peering at a scribbled-on page. Vidia would have read a great deal in Salman's handwriting: it was upright, confident, closely printed, very black, un-English, linear on a page without lines. Even upside down it looks arrogant, Vidia might have said. He would have been impressed.

'I learned two things,' Salman said. 'One, close the English departments. Two, literature is for the wounded and the damaged. Ha-ha!'

19

Exchanges

'We'll talk,' Vidia had said, but it was not possible. I wrote to him, but for almost a year I was seldom in one place long enough to receive a letter or a fax. I was on the move – more than two months in the African bush, drinking the rivers again: on the Angola border of the upper Zambezi, in Barotseland, camped in the compound of the Litunga, the Lozi king; sick in a tent in the remote Dinde Marsh of southern Malawi, with acute dehydration, not drinking enough of the muddy river; and paddling in Mozambique, near where Mrs Livingstone lay buried under a baobab tree at Chupanga. On the lower Zambezi I saw a lion's paw prints in the dust of the riverbank. The creature had paused to relieve herself.

'Female,' I said.

My observation was challenged by one of those aggressively skeptical Australian women you meet in such places.

'How do you know that?'

'Females are retromingent. You probably are.'

'What's that supposed to mean?'

'Piss backwards.'

Then I was in Hong Kong, mugging up on the Chinese take-away. I had kidney problems and gout brought on by the African dehydration.

All this I faithfully reported to Vidia in my usual way: postcards, air letters. I could not phone. It did not strike me as unusual that Vidia did not respond. I knew he was still writing *Beyond Belief*, the sequel to his Islam book. You will say: But you corresponded with him and wrote his blurbs and read his manuscripts while *you* were working on a book. Yes, but he had different rules. I found rules, in general, an inconvenience.

We no longer had any friends in common. I had no idea what was happening in his life. This was strange, since for thirty years

I had had a pretty good idea of the ebb and flow of his affairs.

There was a piece in the magazine supplement of *India Today* (Delhi) early in 1997, an interview with Vidia and Nadira, a portrait of their new life together. Nadira had taken charge. For one thing, she had closed his archives in Tulsa. Vidia said, 'Nadira is more encouraging. Pat could be very stubborn and critical.' And: 'I think I made a great error. I took writing far too seriously.' The author of the article found Nadira imperious and wrote, 'She likes to be called Lady Naipaul.'

Then, about a year after Hay-on-Wye, when I was in Hawaii in an angle of repose, I received by mail a catalogue from a Massachusetts bookseller who specialized in modern first editions. Some items caught my attention:

#336 THEROUX, Paul. *Fong and the Indians*. Boston: Houghton Mifflin, 1968. His second book . . . This copy is *inscribed by Theroux to writer V. S. Naipaul*: 'For Vidia/ & Pat/ with love/ Paul.' Near fine in a very good dust jacket . . . Theroux and Naipaul met in east Africa in 1966, presumably about the time and place that constitute the setting for this novel, and their friendship extends over three decades, dating from a time when both were relatively young writers, and neither had achieved the degree of literary renown that both enjoy today . . . An excellent association copy. $1500.

#337 THEROUX, Paul. *Sinning with Annie*. Boston: Houghton Mifflin, 1972. His first collection of stories. This copy is *inscribed by Theroux to V. S. Naipaul in the month of publication*: 'To Vidia & Pat/ with love/ Paul.' . . . An excellent association copy, inscribed at approximately the time that Theroux's book on Naipaul would have been approaching publication. $1500.

#338 THEROUX, Paul. *V. S. Naipaul: An Introduction to His Work*. (London): Deutsch (1972). An early book of criticism of Trinidadian author V. S. Naipaul . . . Scarce . . . $850.

No inscription on that last one. I had sent it through the publisher, who was Vidia's friend, so that Vidia could see the earliest possible copy. I hoped that he would like it. He had, as he had said in several effusive letters. There were several more of my books in the catalogue, and probably they too were from the shelves of Dairy Cottage, Salterton, Wiltshire. Someone was cleaning house.

The prices were extortionate. And I knew that Vidia would have received only a fraction of that – modern firsts is one of the adjuncts to the rag-and-bone trade, and its practitioners are little better than junk dealers. To twit him about this, I faxed him the bookseller's catalogue pages, and I asked, 'How are you?'

The reply came from his new wife. It was one of the strangest looking messages I had ever received, printed in big wobbly letters like a child's school essay. I watched, squinnying at it, as it scrolled out of my fax machine. My first thought was that the chuntering woman from Pakistan had lost her marbles.

Just the look of it, the way it was set out on the page – the oversized printing, the crazily toppling paragraphs, the random punctuation and nineteenth-century notion of capitalizing, the odd locutions and even odder grammar – was slipshod even by Bahawalpur standards. There was another telling thing. You can judge a person by the manner in which, over the course of a two- or three-page letter, the handwriting breaks down. Vidia had taught me that. Nadira's began at the top of the first page as big accusatory capitals and then sloped and tottered and, as though a new person had taken over the scribble on page two, collapsed into a slant, which I read as the sort of italics you would use to indicate a hoarse nagging. And I could see that it was indeed a nagging letter.

My immediate reaction was deep embarrassment for Vidia.

She began with a startling non sequitur, asserting that I would not be writing her obituary. As I was murmuring 'What?' I read on. She wanted to make a few things clear, and she rambled a bit. It was babu English, but I got the point.

The obituary I had written of Pat Naipaul was a pretty poor job, Nadira said. It was not an obituary at all. It belonged in the realm of fiction and was more about me than about 'poor Pat.' And I reread 'poor Pat' in the block letters of the woman who had been with Vidia in Lahore as the unlucky woman lay dying in Wiltshire.

If my writing the obituary had been a favor, Nadira went on, the favor was reciprocated by Vidia's agreeing to appear at the Hay-on-Wye festival. She then rubbished Bill Buford, who had arranged the event. She rubbished the event. She accused me of trying to make Vidia seem fanatical and extreme on the subject of Africa. In two novels, she said, Vidia had told the truth about

Africa. I had not followed his example. I had misrepresented Africa.

Elaborating on this last point, she said that she had read something I had written about Africa – she did not identify the work by name. She implied that I had quoted Vidia out of context. I had to understand that his life would soon be made public. She hinted at a forthcoming biography. Therefore – and this constituted a type of warning – I should be a better and more responsible friend, for did I not know that Vidia set himself apart from the pettiness of liberals?

Affirming her friendship for Vidia's literary agent, she signed off, 'Nadira.'

This was crazy, I thought, and I began to laugh and crinkle the fax paper in my hand. She's nuts! Going absolutely barking mad in Wiltshire! It was predictable. The woman was a highly visible person who would have been denounced or ridiculed on sight as 'colored' or a 'Paki' in most of Britain. Wiltshire was the haven of crusty right-wing retired military men and xenophobic farmers. This was, surely, a kind of nightmare for the lady letter writer from Bahawalpur.

This was crazy, for there was nothing I had done to provoke the letter. Certainly my role as Patricia Naipaul's obituarist did not justify this abuse. And the festival business was misdirected – since when did anyone force Vidia to say or do something against his will? He was a man of iron resolve. Vidia had asked for the obituary. He had thanked me afterwards. I had his letter – only gratitude and grief in it.

At first I put her letter down to a need to prove herself to Vidia. She had decided to take charge, to clean house in all senses. She had to have been the one to get rid of the books with the loving dedications that had predated her. This was the inevitable revisionism of the new wife. She had turned into Carrie Kipling, Fanny Stevenson, and was aiming at being Jane Carlyle, the martyr of Craigenputtock, humoring and defending her wayward husband. Nadira was seeing me off.

The more I reflected on her letter, the louder I laughed. Its obsessional style and bad grammar and clumsy handwriting were proof that Vidia had not seen it before she sent it. He was scrupulous in matters of punctuation. Poor grammar set his teeth on edge. I had seen him scream at such an ill-conceived thing, like a man howling at a filthy rag. He was put off by the slightest gaucheries. I remembered how, in Stockwell, he had whimperingly told Pat and me that he had seen a workman sit on his bed – the thought of the man putting his bum on the place where Vidia slept was too much, and he nearly sobbed. This abusive note would be just such a horror to a man who saw English departments as representing corruption and the decline of civilization. It was a weird, shame-making letter. I thought he should see it.

I faxed it to him with this message: 'I have just received the attached fax from your wife. I will reply to her, but of course am rather puzzled about it and wonder what could possibly have motivated her to write to me in this way.'

There was no reply from him. That was odd, but at least – unless she had intercepted the fax – he had seen her crazy letter, accusing me of writing a self-serving obituary and browbeating him into going to Hay-on-Wye more than a year before.

He was my friend. He had been my friend for over thirty years! He was not by nature a bridge burner – there weren't enough bridges in his life for him to develop any skills of this sort. He was, if anything, a mushy soul afflicted with a cruel streak, and like many severe men, something of a sentimentalist. He was depressive. He cried easily.

After a suitable interval, I wrote to Nadira. I curbed my instinct to fill my letter with sarcasm or write a parody of one of her Letters from Bahawalpur, a name I had begun childishly to enjoy murmuring for its nearness to the word 'bowel' – 'Bowelpur,' as I thought of it, the quintessential shitty little town. She would not find that funny. And if I parodied her in the style of the Bowelpur columns, with their sententious theorizing and garbled English and frequent references to her husband and her characteristic 'loose' for 'lose' and the shortage of definite and indefinite articles, she would, I was sure, miss the point. So I wrote:

Dear Mrs Naipaul,

I had not written to you, but to Vidia, and was therefore surprised to receive your fax today, and rather startled by its confused and rather combative tone.

You object to my obituary of Pat Naipaul. I wonder why. She was a woman I loved deeply; the piece was not 'a favor,' as you put it, but a labor of love. You accused me of writing a self-serving obituary of, as you termed her, 'poor Pat.' How inappropriate that you should mention her name in this way, since you were associated with Vidia as the woman lay dying. I attach a letter written to me by Vidia afterwards which begins, 'Thank you for the lovely and generous note about Pat . . .'

I did not make Vidia go to Hay-on-Wye, though I recall your urging him to go. Vidia was at center stage, speaking his mind. He says and does exactly what his brilliance dictates. It is folly to think that I have any influence over him.

'Having read your African piece,' you say. Again, I do not know what you are talking about. Over the past 30 years I have written a great deal about Africa. Though I understand your intention is to be offensive to my work your entire paragraph is obscure to me.

You obviously intended your message to me to be provocative. You can see that I am not provoked but only fascinated by your tone, your mistaken assumptions and your odd references.

In almost 32 years of friendship with Vidia I have asked for little and have given a great deal, because I admired Vidia's writing. You should not have written to me in those terms. Yet I am still smiling at your mention of my not writing your obituary.

You are newly arrived. You ought to be more careful. Others have been in your position and have felt just as certain and been just as mistaken.

Believe me, should I wish to write your obituary – or anything else – I shall do so, without needing to be asked.

There was no reply. Perhaps this silence was not so strange. In Africa, when an expatriate got married his new wife fired all his servants and discouraged his old friends from coming around. This was a species of that behavior, but without, I was almost certain, Vidia's shadow over it. Vidia was my friend.

In spite of *We'll talk*, and our not meeting, still I knew what he was up to. I saw his recurring photographs, two in Indian magazines that showed him to be greatly changed: darker face, bristly bearded, swollen eyes, frowning mouth, grayer hair – long crazy hair that looked as if it had been nagged at with a jagged implement. As he said, *You carry your life in your face.*

Often, hearing secondhand his eccentric views and outrageous opinions, I laughed, though sometimes uneasily, as when I read that he had told an interviewer, 'French is now of no account, no consequence, a language spoken by some black people and some Arabs' – and of course spoken by the dusky Vidia himself. In a restaurant in San Francisco, he looked at the next table and said to his companion, 'Aren't those the ugliest people you've ever seen? Do you think they were put there to punish us?'

How different we were. Cut off from him, I saw it clearly. I had always known that he dealt with strangers by trying to shock them, while my manner was ingratiating – just listening politely. His views of women ranged from offensive to silly, but also (as eccentricities do) revealed a lot about him: 'My experience is that very few women have experienced true passion.' You had to smile at Vidia, of all people, considering himself a connoisseur of true passion. Much of the time, in these reported comments, he sounded very angry, but I read it as fear. This fear was in his soul. He was a man who, while a student at Oxford, had (as he put it) 'fallen into a gloom' that had lasted twenty-one months.

Long after, he attacked Oxford. He said he 'hated' his college. He had nothing but bad memories, and 'I was far more intelligent than most people there.' He said he had tried to gas himself at Oxford, but failed because 'he ran out of coins to feed the gas meter.' After I had read this disclosure, it was hard to resist the gibe that it was only his parsimony that stood between life and death; had someone else paid, Vidia would probably have succeeded in doing himself in. But in the event, he spent nearly two years in a state of nervous collapse. 'One was terrified of human beings, one didn't wish to show oneself to them.'

To be the guest of honor at a dinner party – that, for Vidia, was bliss, he said. This remark, made to another interviewer, rang true. He said he loved occasions 'when one feels cherished.' To be cherished meant more than flattery and good food and vintage wines; it meant attentive listeners who paid the bill, as I knew. 'He likes paying,' he said of any person who picked up a bill. 'He wants to do it.' And was there any more tangible expression of being cherished than the bestowal of a knighthood? It was the dream of the wily pundit Ganesh Ramsumair, in *The Mystic Masseur*, to be transformed into the unapproachable Sir G. Ramsay Muir. Someone who builds a life on being pleasured by honors and flattery can only have known great rejection and insecurity and a yearning to belong. But then, hadn't Vidia reminded me long ago that in order to understand him I had to know his past as 'a barefoot colonial'?

From my earliest attempts at writing, I had wanted security too. I knew when I had enough. 'Don't wish for too much' was my father's lesson. And he always said, 'Be kind.'

Vidia's temperament was a riddle. There seemed to me nothing lower than being beastly to book-tour escorts and nasty to secretaries, or to any underling who, out of nervousness, made gauche remarks. Did Vidia's compulsion to intimidate such people arise from his having felt rejected himself? He did not make much of his experience of racism, but he acknowledged that he had known it in England. His attitude could have been a case of monumental payback, though it was anyone's guess why his victims were innocent Americans and English flunkies and earnest Hollanders.

Vidia denied being Indian. He saw himself as 'a new man.' But he behaved like an upper-caste Indian. And Vidia often assumed the insufferable do-you-know-who-I-am? posturing of a particular kind of Indian bureaucrat, which is always a sign of inferiority. It had taken me a long time to understand that Vidia was not in any sense English, not even Anglicized, but Indian to his core – caste-conscious, race-conscious, a food fanatic, precious in his fears from worrying about his body being 'tainted.' Because he was an Indian from the West Indies – defensive, feeling his culture was under siege – his attitudes approached the level of self-parody.

He was mistaken about so much. He made confused statements about Africa and seemed to regard the continent as starting in south London and extending to the Caribbean, the whole of it a jungle of jitterbugging 'bush men.' These generalizations appeared to be no more than futile attempts to validate his novel *A Bend in the River*. It represented Vidia's horror of the bush. But in the bush lay Africa's essence, which Vidia never understood was more benign than wild.

In three books, he had changed his mind about India with each one. And he was still wrong. I didn't dispute his views. Challenge him and he was an enemy; treat him handsomely and there was a chance he would be kind. Cherish him and he was yours. Hadn't I cherished him? So we had never quarreled.

'To grow up in a large extended family was to acquire a lasting distaste for family life,' he told an interviewer in 1983. 'It was to give me the desire never to have children of my own.' But he disliked children anyway. There are hardly any children in his books, and no happy ones.

As a father, I was angered that he actively disliked children, because any parent has an animal awareness of that hostility. It made me protective. I also saw that the man who dislikes children and doesn't have any of his own is probably himself childish, and sees other children as a threat. Vidia was the neediest person I have ever known. He fretted incessantly, couldn't cook, never cleaned, wouldn't drive, demanded help, had to be the center of attention.

Now, away from his influence, I saw all this – not that I dared utter it, or think it through as an indictment. I saw him as deeply flawed, and as a friend – our friendship was the consequence of his imperfections, for character flaws seem to inspire the sympathy that lies at the very foundation of friendship. I knew this but kept it to myself, and when I dared to think about it, I inverted it.

To maintain my self-respect and to defend Vidia, I often called him generous when I found him to be mean, and said he was eccentric when I felt he had been cruel. My obituary of Pat was a rosy picture of an adversarial marriage. I did this not to spare Vidia but to spare myself. I was ashamed to say that he treated people badly and that he was casual and presumptuous with me. Had I not repressed this, I would have had to admit that I was weak. But from the beginning I had known that I was a bit afraid of him. It is impossible to see a friend lose his temper with someone and not imagine that same fury turned on you.

I had admired his talent. After a while I admired nothing else. Finally I began to wonder about his talent, seriously to wonder, and doubted it when I found myself skipping pages in his more recent books. In the past I would have said the fault was mine.

I did not want to think about any of this. That was why I

never contemplated writing about him, because writing meant scrutinizing character and giving voice to feelings of disappointment and being truthful. It was much simpler to overlook Vidia's faults. Let someone else be Boswell and write the biography.

But there was that face. Some things I could not overlook, because they loomed too large and were too twisted. His personality dominated his face, which was forever contorted, twisted down in disapproval and misery and suffering, and his nose was thickened with anger. Seeing that face for the first time, Saul Bellow said, 'After one look from him, I could skip Yom Kippur.' The years had given Vidia a fixed and unimpressed mask, scored with the crow's feet of skepticism. He had the blinkless gaze of a raptor. You never wanted to see that face turned against yours.

Once an interviewer mentioned to Vidia that I had said he was compassionate. Vidia rejected the description. He said it was a 'political' word. It is not political at all, of course. But Vidia was right to deflect the word. I had said it in my eagerness to please him.

His books had been part of my education, and were a broader education for showing what was good and what was lame – sometimes on the same page. Some of his books are excellent, even prophetic and wise, and others are unreadable and silly. Critics had used the infantile words 'genius' and 'masterpiece' in connection with Vidia and his work, but I had found his recent books odd and insufficient. He took down the laborious monologues of people, and these lengthy interviews were presented as documentary almost without any intervention by Vidia. Long ago he had impressed me by observing that Columbus never mentioned that it was hot in the New World. In Vidia's *India: A Million Mutinies Now* there is little landscape and hardly any weather. There is no smell, no heat or dust, no sweating men, no lisping saris, no honking traffic, nothing except the sound of yakking Indians. The same is true of the Islam books, which is compounded by his naive grasp of Islam and his ignorance of Arabic, which kept him from understanding the Koran.

He was undeterred. 'I hate the word "novel,"' he told an interviewer. He had always ridiculed the word 'story.' He strongly implied that the novel was dead. I had never in my life heard an intelligent person state this opinion, only academic hacks who knew nothing of fiction. Perhaps his sort of novel was dead. Fair enough, but as always, in generalizing, he spoke for the world. When Vidia changed his mind, you changed yours, or else.

He insisted he was correct: that writing had to be one thing – his thing; that John Updike, who can be very funny and whose elegant sentences give pleasure for their sinuous intelligence – that Updike, whom he singled out, was somehow passé. 'Golden sentences' was Vidia's way of belittling Updike's prose. He felt the same about Nabokov. No shining prose for Vidia, no excursions into the lapidary. 'I don't want [the reader] ever to say, "Oh my goodness, how nicely written this is." That would be a failure.' He commended only a style he termed 'brambly.' He offered the Victorian Richard Jefferies, an obscure Wiltshire naturalist, as a model. Vidia's insistence made me doubt him: I had become wary of his dogmatism.

We write as we can, not as we wish. Updike writes as Updike is able, and I am doing the best I can. I can't choose to be 'brambly' if, say, in describing Yomo's sensuality, I am so sweetened by the mood of reminiscence that I write, 'When she and Julian made love, which was often and always lit by candles, she howled eagerly in the ecstasy of sex like an addict injected, and her eyes rolled up in her skull and she stared, still howling, with big white eyes like a blind zombie that sees everything. Her howls and her thrashing body made the candle flames do a smoky dance. Afterwards, limp and sleepy, stupefied by sex, she draped over Julian like a snake and pleaded for a child.' Let Vidia be brambly. He stopped trying to please the reader. He lost his humor, he blunted his descriptive gift, he denounced universities (as Richard Jefferies had done), he bemoaned readers, he tried to hold a funeral and bury the novel.

He never denied that he was a crank, yet he elevated crankishness as the proof of his artistic temperament, which is irritating for anyone else who has to work for a living. It was a sorry excuse – and from someone who never tolerated excuses for an instant. He admitted being difficult, but instead of seeing this as a weakness, he implied that his difficult nature was a virtue, an aspect of his being special. It is no virtue at all.

I did not mind his contradictions. It is human to be contradictory. He had once claimed that England was second-rate; he spoke of crooked aristocrats and 'bum politicians.' Then he accepted a knighthood. Was he acting logically, by hypocritically joining an establishment renowned for its hypocrisy?

I had found England narrow but far more benign. Vidia had not learned in forty years that the English are not blamers and are not a cruel people – indeed, the traits of passivity, shyness, and modesty predominate. Liking order, the English deplored people who groused – 'whinged' was their wonderful word. 'Mustn't grumble,' they murmured when the going was hard. Vidia was the opposite of phlegmatic: he was an excitable Asiatic – his own word – the more volatile and wounded for his colonial experience, his being slighted by English landladies, and all the postcolonial humiliation a Trinidadian Indian must feel when rejected by blacks on the island.

It made him a blamer. He blamed society, the educational system, people in general. He indulged himself and enjoyed being flattered. He became a regular at dinner parties and powerful American embassies.

This was the fierce-faced friend I saw now, but it was a mute vision. I neither wrote nor spoke about it: Vidia remained a vaguely menacing blur. But the world to me was clearer. Without his response – he didn't answer my letters, he didn't call, I was too far away to provide him any help – I was better able to understand my progress, from being his student to becoming his equal. In my heart, I suspected he was now much weaker and needier than me, which was why he valued my friendship.

Though I did not look into the future, I recalled his saying, 'To all relations, every encounter, there's always a time to call them off. And you call them off.'

After twenty-nine years he had left his publisher, André Deutsch. It is not unusual to change publishers, but it is rare to leave without some sort of farewell. He said nothing to Deutsch, who complained, 'Not even a postcard!' And that was much more than an author–publisher relationship. It was a close collaboration and a friendship. Vidia told me he admired Deutsch for being tough, intelligent, and entrepreneurial, and for having the panache to send suspected dud bottles of wine back in restaurants. After the break with Deutsch, Vidia talked about him very differently.

And speaking of 'you call them off,' what of the mysterious Margaret, who had dropped from view? She and Vidia had met in 1972. I had been introduced to her in 1977, and saw her again in 1979. Vidia had publicly celebrated their love affair and professed his ardor in *The New Yorker* in 1994. Pat had been upset, if not desolated, by Vidia's enthusiastic candor and his telling the world of a sexual relationship that was, after two decades, still crackling away.

Margaret, his shadow wife, had accompanied him on trips while Pat stayed home. 'His lady love,' Pat once said sadly, with a lump in her throat, of Margaret, who went to parties with Vidia. Margaret kept him company on his literary quests. I had not seen her for years, but I heard about her all the time. Because Vidia stayed on the American diplomatic circuit, I was always being told of his appearances. 'Saw your friend Naipaul the other evening,' a diplomat would say. 'We gave a little party for him.' And usually, 'His friend Margaret was with him.'

That was the oddest part. I had heard this talk when he was writing his second Islam book, *Beyond Belief*. Twenty-four years later and he was apparently still passionate, still traveling with Margaret. Then he met Nadira: no more talk about Margaret. I had no idea how that had ended, except that it had to have been swift, and it must have been recent. Pat died. Margaret vanished. Vidia married Nadira. Margaret was in the shadows. An Indian friend of Vidia's, Rahul Singh, wrote in an Indian magazine that Margaret was 'an Argentinian companion' who 'was devastated when he married Nadira.'

To all relations . . . there's always a time to call them off. I took 'all' to be his usual hyperbole for everyone but me. We were still friends. As for his silence, well, he was famous for his silences. All that had happened was that I had received a crazy letter from his excitable new wife. He probably knew nothing about it.

One thing in Nadira's letter puzzled me: her mention of Vidia's forthcoming biography. This as an imminent possibility had never occurred to me. I knew that Vidia had interviewed several prospective biographers but that nothing was settled. The project seemed inauspicious, for who but a masochist would take on the thankless and unrewarding job of being anyone's official biographer? Access to letters had entertainment value – they had, to use a Vidia phrase, 'horror interest.' But that sort of book always verges on hagiography.

The subtext of her letter was: Don't write about him. This offended me. I had become a writer to be a free man, in Vidia's own terms, not to take direction. And yet, when people asked me to write about him, I said no. I had no enthusiasm to write a biography. Until I received Nadira's letter I had not even considered using Vidia as the subject of a book. I would pass my memories and letters to the designated Boswell and let that person do the work. Vidia was my friend. A book about such a friendship was an attractive idea, but it was impossible. Friendship had its rules.

And there was no model: such a portrait had never been done. In literary history no books that I knew about detailed this sort of friendship – say, young Samuel Beckett writing a book about his years with the older James Joyce. The subject of protégés and apprenticeship was one that had fascinated me since my earliest days with Vidia in Uganda. Henry James had written of his friendship with Turgenev in *Partial Portraits,* in the course of which he mentioned Flaubert in a way that brought Vidia to mind.

'But there was something ungenerous in his genius,' James wrote. 'He was cold, and he would have given everything he had to be able to glow . . . Flaubert yearned, with all the accumulations of his vocabulary, to touch the chord of pathos. There were some parts of his mind that did not "give," that did not render a sound. He had had too much of some sorts of experience and not enough of others. And yet this failure of an organ, if I may call it, inspired those who knew him with a kindness. If Flaubert was powerful and limited, there is something human, after all, and even rather august in a strong man who has not been able to express himself.'

Young Gorky, also something of a protégé, wrote about old Tolstoy, saying, 'Although I admire him, I do not like him . . . He is exaggeratedly preoccupied, he sees nothing and knows nothing outside himself.'

So, speaking strictly of writers, such a book had never been done. Anyway, how could one write a book about a friendship in progress? One of Vidia's acquaintances urged me to, saying, 'Not the authorized book, but a shadow biography.' I said no. As friends, our story was incomplete. Vidia himself had said, 'One must write every book as though it is the final work, the summing up.'

'I would never write a book about Vidia,' I said. 'He is my friend. It is impossible to write about him and remain in touch. Vidia himself said that a book must be written from a position of strength. A book celebrates an ending, a finale. When the friend, or the friendship, is dead. It needs a conclusion. It needs a death. I haven't got one.'

20

Sir Vidia's Shadow

Sometimes Vidia, looking like a laughingstock, calling himself V. S. Nipple, strutted in my dreams, tut-tutting, or in those informative early morning episodes of mumming that I saw just as I awoke, he appeared to rehearse my worst fears: black-faced Vidia, scowling West Indian with a walking stick and his funny floppy hat from Rwanda, scolding, sticking me with a restaurant bill I could not pay or giving demoralizing advice. *You must leave her, Paul!* Or, *Problems are good!*

Now and then it was Nadira in my nightmare, wearing the Pakistani national costume, like one of those *burra memsahibs* buying expensive provisions in the Food Hall of Harrods. I was a nervous blushing store clerk in those fantasies, and she was shrieking at me and denouncing my chutney.

I was not dismayed. 'Often miracles happen,' Vidia used to say. He meant in writing, or in the rewards for writing – making the million, becoming 'immensely famous.' So he said. The rest of life was doggedness and uncertainty.

If a person wishes to vanish from your life, there is really no miracle you can work to get him back. In a rational moment you think, Why would I want to see someone who does not want to see me? But urgency makes for confusion. You are stumped. You can't get him to reply to a letter if he has no desire to respond. If you call, the phone simply rings, or else the same answering machine message mocks you in its implacable repetition: *Leave your name after the beep and we'll get back to you.*

Silence is the stern reply, as the English say. Silence is like a darkness. Or was it all a horrible mistake?

I really did not know what to do. Nadira's letter rankled because I was sure she had written it behind Vidia's back. Making a fool of my friend! She sneaked it into the fax machine and then destroyed the original. I had faxed the thing back, and sent it by mail too, but such epistles were easily recognized and intercepted. So the poor little man was still in the dark. She had abused me and forbidden me to write anything about him. As if I wanted to! As if I could! As if I had even dreamed of it!

Suspense is hateful. Hope deferred made my heart sick. I tried to put the matter out of my mind. More important than this, Hong Kong was passing from the hands of Britain into the hands of China, and my new novel, a black comedy taking place at the periphery of the Chinese take-away, was about to be published. I had agreed to a book tour, one week, Sunday to Sunday, in England's reliable spring. April is not the cruelest month; it is the best, my birthday month, full of buds and hope: *Whan that Aprille with her shoures sote*.

It was no ordinary week. The British general election would take place while I was still in London. Great excitement and the premonition of a Labour victory after eighteen years of demoralizing Tory smugness.

I arrived early on a Sunday morning of mist and sun – the sun in April like someone smiling through tears. My hotel was in Kensington, the Royal Garden, with a view east over Kensington Palace and Hyde Park and the rowboats in the Serpentine, the chestnut trees in blossom and the shrouded Albert Memorial.

I was happy being merely a visitor. I had fulfilled my goals: to leave London before I died there, to avoid ever getting a job. I had dreamed of the West Country, but my backup dream was to end up on an sunny island. I was now a man of fifty-five, a resident of Hawaii, a part-time beekeeper. 'Are you the writer?' the immigration officer had asked me that morning. Sometimes such a stranger would also say, 'How is your friend Naipaul?'

Most pleasurable for me was the prospect of seeing one of my children. Around noon, Marcel rang from the lobby and came up to my hotel room. He had just finished writing a novel of his own. He was nervous and proud, but not prouder than I was of him.

'Is there anything wrong, Dad?'

I had been telling myself I was happy, yet he knew there was a shadow.

'Naipaul,' I said.

I told him about Nadira's letter of a month before.

He said, 'No way!'

I told him the rest.

'She sounds stroppy.'

'Vidia would have stopped her if he had known. All that shit about my obituary of Pat.'

'Maybe he does know.'

'Nah. Poor English makes him crazy. The letter was a mess,' I said, and saw that sheet of paper before my eyes, all the printed characters, like a ransom note. 'But I will never know for sure. It's funny. Vidia used to look at someone's essay and say, "Promise you'll give up writing."'

Marcel made an abrupt snoring sound, the signal that he had heard this anecdote many times and was already bored and half asleep.

'I know, I know,' I said. 'But listen. What I want to say is that he used to talk about how relieved the person was when he said it.'

'You've told me that before.'

'How there would be a fracture in a friendship, or a divorce, and he would say, "Problems are good!" "This is good for you." "You are now free." That?'

'All that.'

'Okay, what about lunch?'

'Let's do it.'

That strange transition I always felt in an elevator, holding my breath to offset the pressure in my head from the descent, made me gabble.

I said, 'He doesn't know.'

'You're obsessing, Dad.'

'But I will never know for sure.'

'It doesn't matter. He's the devil. Didn't you say that he never paid for meals?'

'He was generous in other ways.'

Stepping out of the elevator, Marcel said, 'I remember when he came to the house. "And what are you studying, little man?"'

'Was that the last time you saw him?'

'No. You asked me to deliver something to him. A manuscript. A big parcel.'

'*The Enigma of Arrival.*'

'He asked me a lot of questions. He was actually quite nice to me. I was at Westminster, my second year. It was winter. He gave me tea.' We were at the hotel entrance, at the top of a flight of stairs. 'I started that book. It's bollocks. Which way shall we go, left or right?'

Left meant the park and Gloucester Road, right was Kensington High Street and teashops. It had to be left: my first morning in London and left was on one of my ticcy routes, like a circuit printed on my nerves.

'Left,' I said. 'We'll head for Chelsea. The Kings Road is full of places to eat.'

'I think Labour's going to romp,' Marcel said as we stopped at the crosswalk on Kensington Road, waiting for the light to change.

I said, 'If only he would write to me. Then I would know whether he was aware of this whole stupid business. It's amazing. The last time he wrote was after Pat died, over a year ago. This new woman thinks she's Jane Carlyle —'

'Dad!'

'Just listen to me. Don't shush me, I can't stand that. I don't know why this is bothering me.' Maybe it was my being in England again that was bringing it all back and making me short of breath. I had successfully ignored the whole thing in Hawaii. Nothing rang bells there, but London rang bells like mad. 'Maybe she's burning all his bridges, and he'll wake up one morning with no friends.'

As he walked just behind me, I knew that Marcel was gritting his teeth, hating this monologue, but I could not help it. I was grateful I had a listener, even if he was unwilling. I was roused to talk.

'On the other hand, I know he's working on his Islam book, so he is probably closeted with it while she runs his life. It seems so unfair, though. Her letter.'

Down Gloucester Road I was hunched over and ranting, turning from time to time to say, 'Know what I mean? More than thirty years! It's a friendship.'

'You used to say you had no friends.'

'I had a few. What about Jonathan? Vidia was another.'

'You could ring him.'

'Vidia doesn't answer the phone.'

'Write him a letter.'

'I did that. If I do it again I'll look pathetic. If only he –'

We had come to the crooked and perilous part of Gloucester Road where all the accidents happen, the dogleg that makes an almost blind curve where cars hurtle head on into each other, always a sprinkling of broken glass in the gutters. But I was already going numb.

On the word 'he,' Vidia had appeared in that curve, his nigrescent face fixed and stony, walking fast toward me on the sidewalk. He was the scowling, strutting creature from my apprehensive dreams. All my talk had babbled him into being as, in a séance, the murmurs of the medium produce a blob of acceptable ectoplasm that passes for the departed soul or the summoned-up loved one. It was Vidia, looking crazy, which was why I doubted that he could be real, for he was as unlike the man of a year ago as it was possible to be. He was G. Ramsay Muir.

What disconcerted me was that I stopped and he kept walking. He had not seen me. It was one o'clock on a Sunday afternoon, in blazing sunshine. He was thirty feet away.

I said to myself, in a fearful mutter, 'What do we have here?'

Being conscious of the stagy line only made me more nervous, for it was like a line in a play that is spoken in a panicky situation. It does not advance the plot; it focuses and freezes the moment.

Still Vidia did not recognize me, nor see me, evidently. He had to be a vaporous apparition, and yet he seemed solid enough. His face was black, the rest of him looked gray. It was his newly grown beard, salt-and-pepper bristles. He was striding, thrashing the pavement with a walking stick; he wore a fruity little hat, floppy brim and all, a tweed jacket, a turtleneck. He was Ramsay Muir, a little old soldier marching madly north towards Hyde Park. But Marcel and I were on the same stretch of sidewalk. *What the* –?

Seconds had passed. Not even seconds – hundredths of seconds. He glanced in my direction, not at me, and turned from a little English veteran into a little Indian. Into Ganesh Ramsumair.

Small solitary Indians on London streets have a hunted vulnerable look. They know they are the prey of brutes and skinheads. And who will come to their aid should they be thumped? The littlest Indians were picked on and mocked. And so Ganesh did not make eye contact. To a frightened Indian, my son and I were two swaggering Paki-bashers, almost filling the sidewalk, threatening to lamp him.

Vidia! It was he. In a city of seven and a half million, our paths had miraculously crossed. He was fearful, looking at me – more than fearful, something as profound as horror, for he saw a dangerous double, a grim echo. And just a moment before, what had he been thinking? Undoubtedly his Ganesh paranoia had seen all the taunting faces: Drunks and National Fronters and Mosleyites and immigrant-haters and the man who smacked him on the head on this very road at the time he was writing *The Enigma of Arrival* – all the creatures in his personal demonology who threatened his notion of civilization. He had been terrified. Now these wicked twins, bovver boys and Paki-bashers, taking long strides towards him, to boot him up the arse with their Doc Martens.

'Vidia?'

'Paul!' It was a groan coming out of tired and smoke-tortured lungs.

He looked up at Marcel and almost lost his hat from the angle of his head, for Marcel was twice his size.

'And this is your son!'

'Marcel,' my son said, sticking out his hand.

'Where are you going?' I asked.

'I just had my lunch. I'm taking a little walk in the park,' he said in a prissy, nervous voice.

As he spoke he started to move forward again. I had last seen him almost a year before, but he seemed eager to keep going – agitated, anyway.

To detain him I said, 'How is your book going?'

'One more month, one more month,' he said, and took a breath and seemed to strain forward. 'It has been a tremendous labor.'

'I've heard it's good,' I said, inventing a remark, clinging verbally, wanting him to pause so that I could think. I had something to say, but what was it?

'I must go. My walk . . .'

I was hot, I was nerved and trembly, I could hardly breathe. I stammered, saying, 'Vidia, did you get a fax from me?'

'Yes. Now I must –'

'Do we have something to discuss?'

'No.' He had almost broken away. He was moving crabwise, crouching a bit, cramming his hat down.

'What do we do, then?'

He drew his mouth back. His face went darker. His mouth twisted down. It was the look of helpless suffering he wore the very first time I saw him in Uganda. His grip on his cane was sudden and prehensile.

'Take it on the chin and move on.'

The word 'scuttled' came to mind as he moved. He was off, the mimic man personified. He was fearful and he was in a hurry.

He knew. It was over. It never occurred to me to chase him. There would be no more. And I understood the shock of something's being over, like being slapped – hurt as the blood whipped through my body. 'Like being hit by a two-by-four,' my friend had said when Vidia insulted her in Oregon.

Watching Vidia scuttle up the road toward Hyde Park, I noticed something amazing. On this bright day in April, the sun slanting into Gloucester Road, Vidia was very small, and shrinking fast, and it was as if he would vanish before he reached Kensington Road – so tiny, indeed, he cast no shadow. Without a shadow he seemed even smaller than he was, and darker, as though he had no substance. As though he *were* the shadow.

Take it on the chin and move on. It was, as always, challenging advice. But he talked tougher than he looked, because really he looked like Sir Vidia Nye-Powell.

Marcel was saying, 'What a wally!'

I was dazed, because I was liberated at last. I saw how the end of a friendship was the start of an understanding. He had made me his by choosing me; his rejection of me meant I was on my own, out of his shadow. He had freed me, he had opened my eyes, he had given me a subject.

Before we got to Cromwell Road I had begun this book in my head, starting at the beginning. That is everything.

Afterword: Memory and Invention

Not long after *Sir Vidia's Shadow* was sent to the printer I was fossicking among some papers and found an old notebook labelled 'Diary', with a date, and as a sort of title, 'When I was off My Head'. This was an unexpected discovery because, except for some letters, and a detailed one-page dream I had written in a novel-notebook, I had depended on memory alone for my book. Here was a chance to verify my memory.

Thirty-two years ago, in Africa, Naipaul had made me promise never to keep a diary. Such an activity, he said, was an obstacle to the workings of the imagination. Except for the exhaustive notes I made in diaristic travel journals, for the purposes of converting them into a travel book, I had more or less kept my promise. In the year or so it took to write my book about our friendship, I was amazed by how clearly conversations and scenes returned to me. I started each day with a period of meditation, shutting my eyes and pressing my fingers to my temples, like an overacting clairvoyant. By degrees I could hear and see Naipaul. And the activity of writing an episode helped, too, since all writing is itself a memory-jogger.

Another mechanism aided my memory. It was Vidia's very personality: demanding, judgemental, fastidiously attentive; he had kept me alert, not to say self-conscious. Being with him, always just this side of nervous, fearing I would be wrong-footed, I was given something bordering on total recall. In the neurology of memory there had to be something animal, related to survival, in the way anxiety helped one remember sights and sounds. So I was able to write my book, almost without notes.

When I finished, I had two shocks. The first was that the friendship kept unspooling in my mind. I had developed such intense habits of concentration, of remembering and sifting, I found I could not switch off my active memory. In these afterthoughts were snippets of conversation or whole speeches I had not included in the book. I belatedly recalled Vidia's ritually pronouncing, 'I am going to open an account with him,' meaning settle someone's hash; and 'Women of sixty think of nothing but sex;' and how driving with him in Kampala he had once said, 'They call those [road bumps] "sleeping policemen" in Trinidad.'

Some of these memories were whole episodes rather than one-liners. There was a tea party at which a book reviewer Vidia thought I should meet ('He's very civilized, his wife is incredibly rich') played a coarsely comic phonograph record which was loudly lavatorial, causing Vidia to make a frowning face and leave abruptly. And there was a long lunch in London with one of my relatives that did not surface into my consciousness until it was too late to include. That the latter was a fairly disastrous meal a Freudian would put down to repression on my part.

Another vagrant memory concerned Vidia's friend, the writer Colin MacInnes (1914–76), who was a roving journalist in London in the 1950s, as well as a novelist (*City of Spades*, *Absolute Beginners*). Vidia used to say how just a short time with MacInnes socially would draw off all his energy: 'He took away my vitality. He sapped my strength. I was exhausted when he went away.' Vidia frequently had this same effect on me. Many of these after-thoughts were trivial, yet in the detail that makes up a friendship almost everything matters.

Then there was the diary. The many closely written pages in this newly disinterred notebook contained the feverish and wide-ranging garrulity that affects me when I am in a state of funk, as well as the busy sentences of a troubled mind. It was not odd, in my experience, that I had forgotten having kept it. My diary-keeping is rare, and nearly always associated with distress. Far from being an aid to memory, a diary has often been my way of forgetting; the consigning of anxious thoughts to a notebook is akin to dumping them into a barrel – but the obscurity of a trash-barrel rather than the potentially more stimulating cracker-barrel.

The self-mocking suggestion of derangement in the label, 'When I was off My Head' (framed in saner handwriting than the screwball scribble in the notebook), referred to a time of uncertainty in my life that occupied the best part of a year, one of those non-writing periods when I was penetrated to my soul with a sense of being superfluous. I hardly existed, I had nothing to do; I was a wraith, a wisp, a leftover; I did not matter. At such times I have done no work and I have not been reassured when my older son, Marcel, a Russian speaker, has said to me, 'That's not new. It's a recurring theme in nineteenth-century Russian literature. *Lishnii chelovek.* The Superfluous Man, Dad!'

Was that why this diary had a Russian texture and tone, a bleakness composed of cold streets, late nights, littered rooms and dusty answers; and the irrefragable 'What is to be done?' I am smiling as I write this, seeing my disturbed other self as a version of a bulimic Oblomov; but I wasn't smiling then. The irony was that although I had made a solemn promise to V. S. Naipaul not to keep a diary, this notebook was full of accounts I had written of having spent evenings either dining with him or else talking to him on the phone.

If keeping a diary was my technique for forgetting, then I had been successful. Here, in the notebook, described over four pages, was a dinner Naipaul and I had had in Kensington that I had utterly forgotten. The dialogue was good and true. Naipaul sat down and at once told me that he was having problems with his agent.

'I want you to help me with my business problem, and then I'll listen to your sentimental problem.'

His concern was money. He was being undervalued, he felt; sold short. He had a book idea. He was looking for a contract.

'Will you write to someone?' he asked me.

All this was before we even had a menu in our hands. I liked his directness and said I would send a letter, offering the idea – a trip he planned – to my own publisher. Then I told him my dilemma.

His advice was for me to go away – drop everything, leave the country, begin a new life. He was very certain about this – so certain that there was no discussion, he ignored my two-cents' worth and pressed on, talking about his reading. He said (so I saw in this diary) that he was fascinated by Somerset Maugham. He wanted to write something about Proust's essay 'Contre Sainte-Beuve' and Maugham, contrasting the two writers' aesthetics. I said that although I liked Maugham's travel, *The Gentleman in the Parlor* especially, and *Ashenden*, and many stories, I had found much of Maugham unreadable.

Vidia said snappishly, 'I'm not interested in the work, I'm interested in the man.'

In a sudden panicky *non sequitur*, seeking advice, I said I was thinking of seeing a psychiatrist.

Naipaul said, 'No, no, no, no, no.'

'Then what's the solution to my problem?'

'You will never solve it. There is no solution. You will always be divided.'

The next day (and this is the great thing about diaries, the punctilious chronology) he called me in the afternoon and asked whether I had written the letter to my publisher on his behalf. I told him truthfully that I was at that moment writing the letter. He sighed and asked me what he should do about his agent's dereliction. 'This is very bad. He has let me down.'

I said, 'Do nothing.'

This was perversity on my part, just the sort of non-advice he had been giving me. Perhaps he suspected this, because he alluded to my 'sentimental problem' and repeated, 'There is no solution!'

'I'm worried,' I said.

'Don't worry. Enjoy the drama of it.'

Enjoy the drama of going off my head?

A few weeks later, the Nobel Prize was announced. Such announcements, and the weeks of speculation that preceded them, were always hard for Vidia, who was constantly mentioned as a possible candidate. I remembered our discussion, how the Nigerian, Wole Soyinka, had been given the prize; how Vidia had said, 'Has he written anything?', and at last how Vidia had said that the Nobel Prize committee was, as usual, 'pissing on literature ... from a great height'.

But from my diary I saw that the conversation had been longer than I remembered. After denouncing the Nobel Prize committee, Vidia had taken a swing at the writing profession.

'I am losing faith in the profession,' he said. 'I think I have been foolish. It's like suspecting your mistress has been unfaithful to you.'

On a later page of the diary we talked about London bookstores, which in my state of mind were a source of solace to me.

Vidia said they just irritated him. He said, 'I go into bookstores. It's all rubbish! They are like toyshops!'

Was anything lost, I wondered, by these afterthoughts and discoveries being missing from my book?

When I decided to write the book I realized that there was no model for it. Some books existed in which a writer described his or her friendship with another older writer, but these were always glowing accounts in the manner of the scrupulous diarist Boswell writing his *Life of Dr Johnson*, or Johnson himself in one of his earliest efforts, writing about his drunken (and murdering) friend, in *The Life of Mr Richard Savage*, most of it laudatory or riddled with special pleading. *Joseph Conrad, a Personal Remembrance*, by Ford Madox Ford was perhaps the closest of all to what I was attempting, for Ford's account of his friendship with Conrad described a similar age difference, his being young and on the make, as I had been when I first met Naipaul. But even that book was not much use to me, for I was describing the role of a friend not an acolyte; and a friend is often a member of the loyal opposition, trusted most when he is contrary. Much later, I found that what I had attempted somewhat resembled the French oddity, *Rameau's Nephew* (1761), by Denis Diderot.

I knew in advance that some people would misunderstand. Long before publication my book began to appear in gossip columns, for the notion of a literary quarrel – or anything that looks like a quarrel – is like catnip to literary philistines and lazy intellects. In various newspapers journalists used the word 'feud' in connection with my book. But what feud? A thirty-year friendship ended suddenly, without a preamble. A feud is a protracted thing, with endless cut and thrust. The beauty of my book was in the abruptness and simplicity of the denouement. It was in effect a happy ending in which I was liberated to look back upon these three amazing decades, and I saw them as 'desperate, earnest and funny', as Conrad said of his friendship with Ford.

Others, journalists, accused me of 'revisionism'. How Maoist even the language of political correctness had become! Of course, I saw some events differently in my book; but that is what happens with the towering and more truthful vantage point of passing time. The word 'betrayal' was also used – it is the juiciest of journalistic terms. But that is just laughable in this regard, though it is a common observation by non-writers or the literal-minded when they see a piece of work which is a life study. Meditating upon the world and what is most familiar is the preoccupation of writers. Sometimes that includes re-creating our nearest and dearest into subjects. It is in the nature of the profession to make our secrets public, but to give them an imaginative shape and form.

Transforming is what writers do. Only the whole truth helps us to understand the world. The best writers are the most fanatical; so the truest portrait of a writer can never be a study of virtue. The hagiographer is, ultimately, a belittler. Any book that shrinks from suggesting the enchantment of this fanaticism and invites the reader to see its subject as simple and lovable is a confidence trick. And a book has to be new or there is no point pursuing it. I saw that mine had to be a truthful creation, made from memory. All memory is inevitably incomplete, which was why the discovery of the old diary had riveted my attention. But finding that diary proved that I had never needed a diary.

When my book appeared there was no murmur from its subject. Margaret, my former friend's former friend, interviewed in Buenos Aires by the London *Evening Standard*, helpfully said, 'Every word of the book is true.' In that same month of publication – and for the first time ever for Vidia, who used to wince at the very mention of Christmas rituals – the Naipauls sent out Christmas cards.

PENGUIN ONLINE

READ MORE IN PENGUIN

In every corner of the world, on every subject under the sun, Penguin represents quality and variety – the very best in publishing today.

For complete information about books available from Penguin – including Puffins, Penguin Classics and Arkana – and how to order them, write to us at the appropriate address below. Please note that for copyright reasons the selection of books varies from country to country.

In the United Kingdom: Please write to *Dept. EP, Penguin Books Ltd, Bath Road, Harmondsworth, West Drayton, Middlesex UB7 0DA*

In the United States: Please write to *Consumer Sales, Penguin Putnam Inc., P.O. Box 12289 Dept. B, Newark, New Jersey 07101-5289*. VISA and MasterCard holders call 1-800-788-6262 to order Penguin titles

In Canada: Please write to *Penguin Books Canada Ltd, 10 Alcorn Avenue, Suite 300, Toronto, Ontario M4V 3B2*

In Australia: Please write to *Penguin Books Australia Ltd, P.O. Box 257, Ringwood, Victoria 3134*

In New Zealand: Please write to *Penguin Books (NZ) Ltd, Private Bag 102902, North Shore Mail Centre, Auckland 10*

In India: Please write to *Penguin Books India Pvt Ltd, 11 Community Centre, Panchsheel Park, New Delhi 110017*

In the Netherlands: Please write to *Penguin Books Netherlands bv, Postbus 3507, NL-1001 AH Amsterdam*

In Germany: Please write to *Penguin Books Deutschland GmbH, Metzlerstrasse 26, 60594 Frankfurt am Main*

In Spain: Please write to *Penguin Books S. A., Bravo Murillo 19, 1° B, 28015 Madrid*

In Italy: Please write to *Penguin Italia s.r.l., Via Benedetto Croce 2, 20094 Corsico, Milano*

In France: Please write to *Penguin France, Le Carré Wilson, 62 rue Benjamin Baillaud, 31500 Toulouse*

In Japan: Please write to *Penguin Books Japan Ltd, Kaneko Building, 2-3-25 Koraku, Bunkyo-Ku, Tokyo 112*

In South Africa: Please write to *Penguin Books South Africa (Pty) Ltd, Private Bag X14, Parkview, 2122 Johannesburg*

PENGUIN AUDIOBOOKS

A Quality of Writing That Speaks for Itself

Penguin Books has always led the field in quality publishing. Now you can listen at leisure to your favourite books, read to you by familiar voices from radio, stage and screen. Penguin Audiobooks are produced to an excellent standard, and abridgements are always faithful to the original texts. From thrillers to classic literature, biography to humour, with a wealth of titles in between, Penguin Audiobooks offer you quality, entertainment and the chance to rediscover the pleasure of listening.

You can order Penguin Audiobooks through Penguin Direct by telephoning (0181) 899 4036. The lines are open 24 hours every day. Ask for Penguin Direct, quoting your credit card details.

A selection of Penguin Audiobooks, published or forthcoming:

Tales from Watership Down by Richard Adams, read by Nigel Havers

The Brontës: A Life in Letters by Juliet Barker, read by Sian Thomas, Sean Barrett, Susan Jameson and Patience Tomlinson

Cleared for Take-Off by Dirk Bogarde, read by the author

An Ice-Cream War by William Boyd, read by James Wilby

Junky by William Burroughs, read by the author

Oscar and Lucinda by Peter Carey, read by John Turnbull

The Log by Craig Charles, read by the author

Excalibur by Bernard Cornwell, read by Tim Pigott-Smith

The Waste Land by T. S. Eliot, read by Ted Hughes

Ben Elton Live, performed by Ben Elton

10-lb Penalty by Dick Francis, read by Martin Jarvis

The Diary of a Young Girl by Anne Frank, read by Sophie Thompson

Jesus the Son of Man by Kahlil Gibran, read by Eve Matheson and Michael Pennington

My Name Escapes Me by Alec Guinness, read by the author

v. and Other Poems by Tony Harrison, read by the author

PENGUIN AUDIOBOOKS

Thunderpoint by Jack Higgins, read by Roger Moore

Tales from Ovid translated by Ted Hughes, read by Ted Hughes

A Mind to Murder by P. D. James, read by Roy Marsden

Wobegon Boy by Garrison Keillor, read by the author

One Flew over the Cuckoo's Nest by Ken Kesey, read by the author

Rachel's Holiday by Marian Keyes, read by Niamh Cusack

One Past Midnight by Stephen King, read by Willem Dafoe

The Black Album by Hanif Kureishi, read by Zubin Varla

Therapy by David Lodge, read by Warren Clarke

Rebecca by Daphne du Maurier, read by Joanna David

Amongst Women by John McGahern, read by Stephen Rea

How Stella Got Her Groove Back by Terry McMillan, read by the author

And when did you last see your father? by Blake Morrison, read by the author

Felix in the Underworld by John Mortimer, read by Michael Pennington

Into the Heart of Borneo by Redmond O'Hanlon, read by the author

Walking Lines by Tom Paulin, read by the author

The Queen's Man by Sharon Penman, read by Samuel West

The Bell Jar by Sylvia Plath, read by Fiona Shaw

Culloden by John Prebble, read by David Rintoul

A Peaceful Retirement by Miss Read, read by June Whitfield

The Marketmaker by Michael Ridpath, read by Samuel West

Perfume by Patrick Süskind, read by Sean Barratt

Kowloon Tong by Paul Theroux, read by Martin Jarvis

Jane Austen: A Life by Claire Tomalin, read by Joanna David

The Chimney Sweeper's Boy by Barbara Vine, read by Michael Williams

Victoria Wood Live, performed by Victoria Wood

BY THE SAME AUTHOR

My Other Life: A Novel

'A book about doubt and double identity. Its narrator, Paul Theroux, is a man in the middle of a crack-up – a husband who loses his wife; a traveller who goes off the rails; a novelist who stops writing; a self-seeker who can find himself only in aliases ... It's one man's life, but Everyman's crisis. It seems honest. Even if it isn't honest, it's true' *Independent on Sunday*

My Secret History

'Nothing on the shelf has quite prepared the reader for *My Secret History* ... Parent saunters into the book aged fifteen, shouldering a .22 Mossberg rifle as earlier, more innocent American heroes used to tote a fishing pole. In his pocket is a paperback translation of Dante's *Inferno* ... He is a creature of naked and unquenchable ego, greedy for sex, money, experience, *another life* ... Wickedly addictive' *Observer* (Not available in the USA)

The Family Arsenal

Paul Theroux's novel of violence, in the tradition of *Brighton Rock*, is set in the grimy decay of south-east London.

'Brilliant and haunting ... the ingenuities of the plot, the London setting ... the trapped and interwoven people, and the balefully witty observation, have an undistracted force' *Observer*

Picture Palace

For over fifty years Maude Coffin Pratt has levelled her 'third eye' at the beautiful, obscure and obscene, and at the private places and public parts of the famous, from Gertrude Stein to Graham Greene. At her retrospective exhibition her life, measured by camera spools, is rolled out for inspection, except for the frame that really mattered – the exposure that should have been there, but wasn't.

'Maude's voice, harsh, coarse, and yet surprisingly innocent, remains in the ear long after the book has been put down' *The Times*

BY THE SAME AUTHOR

The Mosquito Coast

Allie Fox was going to re-create the world. Abominating the cops, crooks, scavengers and funny-bunnies of the twentieth century, he abandons civilization and takes his family to live in the Honduran jungle. There his tortured, quixotic genius keeps them alive, his hoarse tirades harrying them through a diseased and dirty Eden towards unimaginable darkness and terror.

'An epic of paranoid obsession that swirls the reader headlong to deposit him on a black mudbank of horror' *Guardian*

'An adventure story of the most exemplary kind . . . A work of genuine inspiration, intensely realized' *New York Magazine*

The Black House

A reign of terror begins for Alfred and Emma Munday when they take their failing marriage to the solace of an old country house. There, in the peace and quiet of the Dorset countryside, a strange and beautiful apparition enters their life, disrupts it . . . creates a fatal triangle of fear, fantasy and eroticism.

'Theroux skilfully brings out the strangeness, even menace, lurking beneath the homely and familiar . . . beautifully written' *Sunday Telegraph*

Millroy the Magician

When Jilly Farina walks into the tent at the Barnstable County Fair to see Millroy the Magician her life is transformed. Fixing her with his steely, hypnotic gaze, Millroy performs miracles in front of her spellbound eyes. And when he 'magics' her into his trailer and tells her he will train her to be his assistant, for the first time in her lonely life Jilly feels safe.

'Magical . . . the real success is Millroy himself, who acts unpredictably whenever the reader feels that he has his measure' *Daily Telegraph*

BY THE SAME AUTHOR

Kowloon Tong

'Hong Kong in 1996. Here, as the days tick away towards "the Handover" to China, two last-ditch Brits existing in a fusty time-warp – Betty Mullard from Balham who has been in the colony for almost half a century, and Bunt (short for "Baby Bunting"), her 43-year-old son who still lives with her – become belatedly aware that their time is running out ... Theroux's taut tale about this quivers with resonance, menace and suspense ... The work of one of our most compulsive story-tellers on peak form' *Sunday Times*

The Collected Short Novels

'A brilliant collection of short novels ... the first story here was written in 1966, the last is dated 1998. It's remarkable how well they sit together ... each of the six stories it includes is as tightly self-contained, and as satisfyingly executed, as you could hope for ... a pure pleasure to read' *Observer*

'Intoxicating and indelible ... expertly wrought and disturbing stories that haunt and taunt the reader' *The Times*

The Collected Stories

'Theroux makes and remakes his own world ... throughout this shimmering, kaleidoscopic and very entertaining collection ... The smell, sound, sight of his scenes is always strong, even pungent; and, even more, his dialogue is powerfully but also effortlessly accurate' *Sunday Telegraph*

'A book of many and varied pleasures; to read it is to feel alert, curious, adventurous' *Observer*

On the Edge of the Great Rift
Fong and the Indians • Girls at Play • Jungle Lovers

Three comic and sinister novels set against Africa's vibrant landscape.

Also published

O-Zone (not available in the USA)
Waldo
Saint Jack

BY THE SAME AUTHOR

Non-fiction:

The Kingdom by the Sea

Paul Theroux's round-Britain travelogue is funny, perceptive and, said the *Sunday Times*, 'best avoided by patriots with high blood pressure . . .'

After eleven years living as an American in London, Paul Theroux set out to travel clockwise round the coast and find out what Britain and the British are really like. It was 1982, the summer of the Falklands War and the royal baby, and the ideal time, he found, to surprise the British into talking about themselves. The result is vivid and absolutely riveting reading.

Travelling the World

Paul Theroux has spent a lifetime travelling through Asia, Africa, North and South America, the British Isles, Europe and the Middle East, and his fascinating journeys have become bestselling travel books. Now he has authorized a book of his favourite travel writing, complemented and illuminated by photographs taken by those who have followed in his footsteps.

Riding the Iron Rooster
By Train through China

'[*Riding the Iron Rooster*] finds Theroux chuntering round China for a year, initially with an organized party, later with only a series of semi-official watchdogs for company. His obsessive curiosity brings him into contact with numerous oddities, from the melancholic Mr Fang to the mountaineer Chris Bonington, but we learn most of all about Theroux himself – the armchair traveller's ideal companion' *Sunday Times*
(Not available in the USA)

Also published (not available in the USA)

The Old Patagonian Express
Sunrise with Seamonsters

BY THE SAME AUTHOR

Non-fiction:

The Pillars of Hercules

At the gateway to the Mediterranean lie the two Pillars of Hercules. Beginning his journey in Gibraltar, Paul Theroux travels the long way round – through the ravaged developments of the Costa del Sol, into Corsica and Sicily and beyond – to Morocco's southern pillar.

'This is a terrific book, full of fun as well as anxiety, of vivid characters and curious experiences – perhaps the best of all Theroux's travel books' Jan Morris, *The Times*

The Happy Isles of Oceania

'He voyaged from the Solomons to Fiji, Tonga, Samoa, Tahiti, the Marquesas and Easter Island, stepping stones in an odyssey of courage and toughness ... Not since Jack London has a writer described the Pacific islands so eloquently and informatively' *Observer*

'Panoramically accomplished ... the writing is cool, the reportage industrious and the research rock-solid. Theroux's control of his material is a wonder to behold' *Financial Times*

The Great Railway Bazaar

Fired by a fascination with trains that stemmed from childhood, Paul Theroux set out one day with the intention of boarding every train that chugged into view from Victoria Station in London to Tokyo Central, and to come back again via the Trans-Siberian Express.

'In the fine old tradition of purposeless travel for fun and adventure ... compulsive reading' Graham Greene

The Pillars of Hercules, The Old Patagonian Express, Riding the Iron Rooster, The Kingdom by the Sea and *The Happy Isles of Oceania* read by William Hootkins, and *Kowloon Tong*, read by Martin Jarvis, are all available as Penguin Audiobooks.